Directions in Educational Psychology

Directions in Educational Psychology

Edited by
Diane Shorrocks-Taylor

Whurr Publishers Ltd
London

© 1998 Whurr Publishers Ltd

© Chapter 15 Lucky Duck Publishing

First published 1998
by Whurr Publishers Ltd
19B Compton Terrace,
London N1 2UN,
England

All rights reserved. No part of this publication may be reproduced, stored in a retrieval system, or transmitted in any form or by any means, electronic, mechanical, photocopying, recording or otherwise, without the prior permission of Whurr Publishers Limited.

This publication is sold subject to the conditions that it shall not, by way of trade or otherwise, be lent, resold, hired out, or otherwise circulated without the publisher's prior consent in any form of binding or cover other than that in which it is published and without a similar condition including this condition being imposed upon any subsequent purchaser.

British Library Cataloguing in Publication Data
A catalogue record for this book is available from the British Library.

ISBN 1 86156 046 X

Printed and bound in the UK by Athenaeum Press Ltd, Gateshead, Tyne & Wear

Contents

Dennis Child: an appreciation *Raymond B. Cattell*   ix
Acknowledgements   xiii
Contributors   xv
Introduction *Diane Shorrocks-Taylor*   xvii
Inaugural lecture, 1983 *Dennis Child*   xxi

PART I TEACHING, LEARNING AND LEARNING HOW TO TEACH

Thematic introduction and summary   1
Diane Shorrocks-Taylor

Chapter 1   5

Learning and teaching: current views and perspectives
Charles Desforges

Chapter 2   19

New technologies and learning
Roger Hartley

Chapter 3   39

Diversity in classrooms: effects on educational outcomes
Pam Sammons

Chapter 4   67

Teacher expectations: implications for school improvement
Colin Rogers

Chapter 5 85

Teacher education and psychologies of skill
Peter Tomlinson

Chapter 6 106

Understanding academic performance at university: a research retrospective
Noel J. Entwistle

PART II MEASUREMENT AND ASSESSMENT

Thematic introduction and summary 131
Diane Shorrocks-Taylor

Chapter 7 134

Trends in educational measurement and research methodology
Michael Youngman

Chapter 8 156

Assessing, recording and testing achievement: some issues in accountability, professionalism and education markets
Christopher Pole

Chapter 9 170

Cross purposes: development and change in National Curriculum assessment in England and Wales
Diane Shorrocks-Taylor

Chapter 10 189

Indicator systems for schools: fire fighting it is!
Carol Fitz-Gibbon

PART III SOME ASPECTS OF SPECIAL EDUCATIONAL NEEDS

Thematic introduction and summary 209
Diane Shorrocks-Taylor

Chapter 11 — 212

Helping children with learning difficulties
David Sugden

Chapter 12 — 229

Disruptive classroom behaviour: separating fact from fantasy
Kevin Wheldall and Robyn Beaman

Chapter 13 — 243

Gifted education: education of the highly able
Diane Montgomery

Chapter 14 — 264

Parent–professional partnerships in provision for children with special educational needs
Sally Beveridge

Chapter 15 — 280

The no blame approach to bullying
Barbara Maines and George Robinson

Chapter 16 — 295

Some advances in sign language communication with deaf people
Stewart Simpson

PART IV MOVING INTO THE WORLD OF WORK

Thematic introduction and summary — 309
Diane Shorrocks-Taylor

Chapter 17 — 311

Improving vocational education: NVQs and GNVQs
Alan Smithers

Chapter 18 328

Assessment in the world of work: 'the life of Brian'
Roy Childs

Chapter 19 346

Some technical problems in the use of personality measures in occupational settings illustrated using the 'Big Five'
Dennis Child

Chapter 20 365

Stress in teaching
Cheryl Travers and *Cary Cooper*

Bibliography of Dennis Child's Work 391

Index 395

Dennis Child: an appreciation

Dennis Child OBE

Every profession is likely to find one member who contributes more than many others, and would want to recognize this. Such a one is Dennis Child, Emeritus Professor of Educational Psychology at the University of Leeds.

His first substantial contribution, in 1970, was a book entitled *The Essentials of Factor Analysis*. The great names of the British 'invention' of factor analysis – Spearman, Sir Godfrey Thomson, Burt and others – had just faded into a past generation. Child was not a protégé of any of these, but he had seen, by observation and original thinking, that the most robust future for psychology lay in factor analysis. The bivariate invitation to the physical science method, prescribed by Wundt at the birth of psychology, had not been very productive in this new multi-variate world. Fisher polished the bivariate approach as much as possible, but the numerous little bivariate cognitive studies refused to produce anything of note. On the other hand, factor analysis had been a tremendous help in understanding human abilities. Mainstream psychology seemed unaware of this methodological need and there was scarcely a department in the country that appointed a man to teach in the specialty. Child's account, in part in intelligible geometric terms, laid out an excellent introduction to the field – a classic in its way.

Another of his major concerns was to provide a comprehensive survey in educational psychology, and so he set out to write *Psychology and the Teacher*, first published in 1973. It had a much wider audience and enjoyed a greater publication success than *The Essentials of Factor Analysis*. The Chair of Education at Newcastle upon Tyne in 1976 and in Educational Psychology which the University of Leeds offered to him in 1981, however, demanded attention in other directions. He writes,

> In addition to serving as Chairman of the School of Education in both Universities and being on many university committees, I became engrossed in research and promoting educational psychology in realistic and practical ways.

This included directorship of the Leeds University section of the Assessment of Performance Unit, an adviser for the British Council on teacher education (in countries such as Botswana, Malawi, Mexico and mainland China), adviser on higher educational matters in Portugal, Hong Kong and mainland China, obtaining British Psychological Society recognition for parts of the Leeds MEd degree, and getting qualifications in deaf education (diploma) and a Bachelor's degree in performing arts (dance) recognized by the University of Leeds. He established the Nurse Selection Project which, amongst other things, provided the present standard alternative entry qualification to nurse training (the DC test). For five years he was editor of the *British Journal of Educational Psychology* and general editor for a Blackwell series entitled *Theory and Practice in Education*.

In 1994 he published a noteworthy review of Kline's *Personality: the Psychometric View* (Child, 1994a). He begins with a timely comment on the extraordinary neglect of psychometry in British undergraduate and postgraduate courses, and consequently in psychological experiments. Measurement has been the birth of science – astronomy from astrology, chemistry from alchemy – and it underlies the development of psychology as a science, beyond the intuitions of Freud, McDougall and Murray. He writes

> The strength of the book is that he manages to compress so much information into 150 pages. The weakness is that, in so doing, he is unable to give sufficient technical detail to do justice to the debate....

He refrains from criticizing the light-heartedness which enables Kline to present as equally true the three-, five- and sixteen-factor resolutions of the personality sphere. Many technical issues are ignored. But science has to deal with technicalities. Child, in his review, rightly in my opinion, emphasizes that psychologists are not adequately prepared for the task of understanding the technicalities which sustain their beliefs.

Psychological publication today needs an astringent reviewer like Child, if it is not to deteriorate into old wives' tales that are so voluminous in clinical psychology.

A man needs a rest after a life so full of successful effort as Professor Child's. Twenty years ago, an unsuccessful attempt was made at Cambridge to set up a Society of Multivariate Experimental Psychology, akin to the flourishing American Society. One wonders whether the university departments of Britain could produce 50 or 60 psychometrists to support such a society. One ventures to hope that such a vision may yet appeal to Professor Child, but with reservations on his right to a quiet life.

Raymond B. Cattell

Acknowledgements

I am indebted to Ved Varma for his involvement in the early stages of developing the ideas for this book and for approaching the publishers. His contribution was a most helpful one.

I would also like to thank Dennis Child himself for the helpful advice he has supplied throughout the editing process.

Diane Shorrocks-Taylor

Contributors

Robyn Beaman Manager in Research and Development, Special Education Centre, Macquarie University, Sydney, Australia

Sally Beveridge Senior Lecturer, School of Education, University of Leeds, Leeds LS2 9JT

Raymond B. Cattell Distinguished Research Professor in Psychology, Emeritus, University of Illinois, USA

Dennis Child Professor of Educational Psychology, Emeritus, School of Education, University of Leeds, Leeds LS2 9JT

Roy Childs Director, Team Focus Limited, Maidenhead, Berks SL6 8LR

Cary Cooper Professor of Organisational Psychology, Pro-Vice Chancellor, Manchester School of Management, UMIST, Manchester M60 1QD

Charles Desforges Professor and Director, School of Education, University of Exeter, Exeter EX4 4QJ

Noel J. Entwistle Professor and Director of the Centre for Research on Learning and Instruction, University of Edinburgh, Edinburgh EH8 9JT

Carol Fitz-Gibbon Professor, School of Education, University of Durham, Durham DH1 1TA

Roger Hartley Professor and Director of Computer-Based Learning, School of Education, The University of Leeds, Leeds LS2 9JT

Barbara Maines Educational Psychologist.

Diane Montgomery Professor, Faculty of Social Science and Education, Middlesex University, London N14 4YZ

Christopher Pole Lecturer in Sociology, Centre for Educational Development, Appraisal and Research, University of Warwick, Coventry CV4 7AL

George Robinson Community Action Centre, University of the West of England, Frenchay, Bristol B516 1QY

Colin Rogers Lecturer, Department of Educational Research, University of Lancaster, Lancaster LA1 4YL

Pam Sammons Associate Director, International Effectiveness and Improvement Centre, University of London, London WC1H 0AL

Diane Shorrocks-Taylor Professor of Assessment and Evaluation in Education, School of Education, University of Leeds, Leeds LS2 9JT

Stewart Simpson Chief Executive, CACDP, Pelaw House, University of Durham, Durham DH1 1TA

Alan Smithers Professor and Director, Centre for Education and Employment Research, School of Education, Brunel University, Twickenham TW1 1PT

David Sugden Professor of Special Needs and Chairman of School, School of Education, University of Leeds, Leeds, LS2 9JT

Peter Tomlinson Reader, School of Education, University of Leeds, Leeds LS2 9JT

Cheryl Travers Lecturer, Business School, University of Loughborough, Loughborough LE11 3TU

Kevin Wheldall Professor and Director of the Special Needs Special Education Centre, Macquarie University, Sydney, Australia

Michael Youngman Editor of the *British Journal of Educational Psychology*, and Senior Lecturer, School of Education, University of Nottingham, Nottingham NG7 2RD

Introduction

DIANE SHORROCKS-TAYLOR

In his appreciation, Raymond Cattell has pointed to some of the focal points of Dennis Child's career and achievements. It is not my intention to reiterate here any of his points, only to begin by endorsing them. Instead, I will consider in more detail some of the major strands in Dennis's work over the years and in so doing present the rationale for the organisation and content of this book.

The list of publications given at the end of this book is testimony both to the range and depth of his work and to his contribution to the field of educational psychology. His earliest research was on factors that affect academic performance, beginning while he was still teaching at Bootham School, York and continuing through the first years of his lectureship at the City of Leeds Training College. This early period also saw the foundation stones of *Psychology and the Teacher*, although this did not appear in print until 1973. Also during this period he completed his Master's dissertation, supervised by Ken Lovell, who suggested that he might need to delve into the technique of factor analysis. The result of this delving over a number of years was *Essentials of Factor Analysis* (1970) the book that led to contact with Raymond Cattell and all that followed from that, not least *Motivation and Dynamic Structure* in 1975.

In the late 1960s Dennis had moved to the University of Bradford and in this context, his research interests were extended into the area of undergraduate characteristics and educational attainments while working with Frank Musgrove. Studies of various aspects of undergraduate cohorts resulted in several papers and also in his doctoral thesis.

Several major strands in his research were now established, to be extended in the late 1970s when he was approached by the NHS with a proposition to redesign the alternative entrance test to nurse training. This work did not actually begin until 1983 but it was the request that proved to be the origin of his interest in occupational selection from which came many papers in the 1980s. His work in Leeds after his appointment in 1984 added an interest in a different kind of assessment, that being investigated by the APU Science team already based in the department of education here.

The final theme in his research began in the late 1970s, while he held the Chair at the University of Newcastle upon Tyne. He became involved with the education of the deaf and was a prime mover in establishing courses on communication as well as founding the North of England Conference which ran for 10 years and brought together researchers in deaf education. His own research in the area centred on changes in the use of British Sign Language in schools over a 10-year period.

Given this range and breadth of contribution, the issue of generating a rationale, an organising principle as it were, for a book such as this is not a simple one. One solution would have been to invite papers, in an open-ended kind of way, from colleagues who have worked with Dennis over the years, allowing them implicitly to create a structure and character for the text as a whole. Such an approach was rejected on the grounds that it might miss an important opportunity to evaluate and re-evaluate the changing role of psychology in education, an endeavour that has been obvious in Dennis's work throughout his career.

It therefore seemed appropriate to do two things: first, to delineate the major themes in his work and to use these as the structuring device for sectioning the contributions in the book; and second, to encourage the authors to use this opportunity to summarise work in their field and to suggest ways in which investigation might go in the future. But what were to be the major themes and sections?

In a sense, Dennis himself provided the answer, in the form of the two inaugural lectures he delivered on taking up Chairs in educational psychology in two universities, Newcastle (1976) and Leeds (1981). These two lectures had rather different characters but together they provided key themes and approaches.

In the lecture at the University of Newcastle (Child, 1978) entitled 'Affective influences on academic performance', he summarised research on the question of which personal qualities, apart from intelligence, have a bearing on performance at all levels in the education system. The topic had been the focus of much of his own research in the previous decade and clearly emphasised the role of the affective and social domains in influencing educational achievements and outcomes. Personality factors, motivation, and social contextual influences were centrally implicated in the equation, but the problem (then and now) lies in understanding the influence of each in relation to the others. As he argued:

> The reasons for the lack of useful research findings are not hard to find. Many of the problems which have to be faced by teachers

or researchers in education are as large as life itself; they are multivariate; the hypotheses we generate are cumbersome; our methods are for the most part messy and not elegant or clear-cut. There is little wonder, therefore, that our findings and conclusions are couched in the language of caution and probability. (Child, 1978, p. 5)

He went on to point out that there was a significant gap in our knowledge about the fine grain structure of the learning and teaching process and that this prevented the possibility of giving greater depth to our understanding of the effects of personal or environmental conditions. It is salutary to pose the same question today, almost 20 years later.

A related theme in the lecture was that of 'self-sentiment' (self-image and a sense of self-worth) also affecting educational achievement, particularly for lower attaining children. In this context, he suggested that the influence of the home and of parents was vital:

We underrate the impact of parents and probably overrate that of teachers in the roles which they play in forming a child's view of his or her worth. (p. 19)

thus, in some ways anticipating the moves in the 1980s and 1990s to give parents greater power in the education of their children and the development of research in the area of parental and family influence.

In summary (Child, 1978) he pointed to the major strands for future research, namely:

- the need to look at learning and teaching environments with a view to their reformulation in a way which helps us to monitor student performance
- the need for longitudinal and in-depth studies of the interaction between the academic goals of institutions and the personal goals of students
- the need for a multivariate approach to the investigation of educational achievement
- the need to examine all of these in the contexts of academic value systems of peer groups, parents and teachers
- the need for exploration of ways of discovering and feeding back to students their cognitive competences as a means of enhancing their self-images.

In a sense, his second inaugural lecture (Child, 1984) entitled 'Psychology in the service of education' took some of these summary issues from 1978 and asked the question, where are we now? This lecture is included in full here (pp. xxi–xxxvi) as an important introductory article, so only the key points will be pulled out here. He took the opportunity to review the progress of educational psychology over the century and in so doing to remind us of the importance of an historical perspective both in terms of taking stock and also in learning from our mistakes and blind allies.

His main focus points for the role of psychology were: the increased significance of child development study in relation to understanding more about the learning process, in other words, the child as learner; the increased emphasis on the role of the teacher in the teaching/learning process, including teacher attitudes, classroom behaviours, career expectations, etc.; and the greater focusing on the educational context within which teaching and learning occurs. He placed special significance on the need for more adequate models of instruction, particularly in a situation of ever-expanding technological potential and an increased need for self-sufficiency in learning, by both adults and children. This reading of the runes in 1983 still rewards analysis in the late 1990s.

This tracing of themes in Dennis's work then began to suggest the content and sections for this text: teaching and learning; assessment in its many guises; children and adults with special educational needs; and finally, the application of psychology in occupational settings. Clearly, one of his major emphases has been of the whole field of teaching and learning by both children and adults as well as the teacher training implications of this. Hence the chapters in Part I. Following almost directly from this, is the question of measuring how effective have been teaching and learning, in other words, educational measurement and assessment and the chapters in Part II. Many children and adults experience problems in learning and hence the focus on special educational needs in its many aspects in Part III, following through and extending Dennis's interests and researches with the deaf. And finally, since so much of Dennis's recent work has been in the area of occupational psychology and selection, the focus and chapters in Part IV.

The authors were asked to consider recent work in their field and summarise its significance. This brief, as could be expected with such a wide and illustrious range of authors, has been interpreted in a range of ways, which adds to the interest and richness of the contributions. It has been an ambitious aim, but one that, it is to be hoped, readers will agree has been a worthwhile and informative one.

Psychology in the service of education: a review

Inaugural lecture delivered at the University of Leeds, 1983

DENNIS CHILD

A thorough review in such a rich and varied subject as psychology in education is impossible for a short paper on the subject. All one could hope to do is to take an 'elephantine trot' through the history of the subject, picking up what I see as trends in its development and using these to project into the future. What I have to say relates almost entirely to formal educational settings, although I recognise the important part played by the study of educational influences at home, work or play.

You will also quickly detect that within these formal educational settings my major concern is with the quality and quantity of learning, be it intellectual, social, moral or whatever. The central activity of a formal educational system, in the primary, secondary or tertiary sectors, is the stimulation and advancement of learning especially, but not exclusively, of an intellectual kind. The motives and purposes for which learning is undertaken will vary with place and with time, but each generation of teachers will still be faced with a similar range of fundamental problems of how to expedite and enhance learning in a formal arrangement in such a way as to enable the learner, in time, to be self-sufficient.

This is one of the major concerns of educational psychology. It seeks to discover, by studying the mental, physical, social and emotional behaviour of people, the factors which influence the quality and quantity of learning. Ideally the subject offers to replace trial and error notions and practices with systematic knowledge derived from studies of learners, teachers and the environments in which they operate.

There are, of course, wider issues of concern to other social scientists in education such as the impact of social institutions on individuals or more specific topics such as pupils' family backgrounds, school subcultures, the role of the headteacher and so on. But as far as teachers are concerned these topics become of particular interest when they illuminate the day-to-day problems of learning and teaching.

Historical perspective

Let me first say a little about the origins and growth of the subject. Some form of psychology has been taught throughout the period from the introduction of teacher training colleges in the 1840s. At first, any psychology was embedded in philosophy. Major questions about the mind, consciousness, memory, perception, the senses, etc., were resolved from the security of an armchair. Indeed, in some colleges at first there were no theory papers in education. The examinations were in practical teaching or subjects taken to a more advanced level by the trainees, such as English, mathematics, Latin, Greek, and so forth. The emphasis on raising the academic level of the students seems obvious when you recall that the minimum age of entry to college was 15 and that a student could qualify at 18 for teaching in the equivalent of our junior schools. Many had not gone much further than the junior school curriculum, particularly those who started as pupil-teachers at the age of 12 and then entered college at 15.

During the period up to 1900 at which time the first textbooks in educational psychology began to appear, the curriculum saw the introduction of methods of teaching elementary and class subjects, 'training' the senses and the memory, and devising extraordinary programmes about the order in which the so-called 'faculties' of children developed. The rest dealt with the occasional famous educator (particularly Locke), registers, the Education Code, physical health and notes on lessons. The interesting thing here is that despite the tremendous growth and success in the application of scientific method in the natural sciences, the study of human behaviour by methods of introspection and anecdotal case study persisted and the 'inner states of mind' continued to be described either in terms of the ancient faculty theory or associationism, or both. School subjects were seen as the medium by which intellectual powers could be enhanced. This became known as 'mental' or 'formal' discipline and enshrined the notion that certain subjects provided training in desired mental activities, or 'faculties', and the effects of these mental exercises were general. Latin was said to improve the memory and verbal accuracy; mathematics developed reasoning ability and concentration; science developed powers of observation. Latin declensions and Euclidean theorems were said to exercise the mind like a muscle. Lower down the system where the 3Rs prevailed, the methods of teaching involved group chanting and drill and exercises for the senses. Rote learning would not only stamp in facts, but would provide valuable exercises for the hypothetical structures to do with learning.

The chief beneficiaries of alternative child-oriented perspectives of such educational thinkers as Pestalozzi, Herbart and Froebel were infant or kindergarten children. For the rest, the school subject was the focus of attention.

From the turn of the century to the present time I detect three shifts of emphasis forming a gradual accumulation of concerns in educational psychology. These concerns relate to the roles played in the learning process by, first, the subjects being taught as I have just suggested, second the learner, third the teacher and much more recently the educational context. It is important to emphasise the cumulative nature of these interests. All have been considered over the period mentioned, but with varying degrees of attention.

In a moment I want to say a little more about these changes of interest, but before doing so I want to speculate about the possible reasons for the change of direction at the turn of the century. In the closing decades of the nineteenth century, two immensely important developments took place which completely changed the approach and direction of psychology and consequently its contribution to educational issues. One was Darwin's theory of evolution and the origin of species and the second was the increased significance attached to scientific method especially applied to animal and human behaviour. Pinpointing two developments in this way oversimplifies the complexity of the tides of fashion which washed over the country in the late nineteenth century. But the lasting and wide-ranging effects of these two factors were quite crucial in changing the philosophy of teaching alongside the growing reality of compulsory education for all.

It seems to me that the two major implications of Darwin's work for psychology were the importance which became attached to, firstly, the notion of progression from animal to human and within humans from birth to death, and secondly, the interaction between the animate and the inanimate, that is between animal and environment, in the process of survival.

The first gave substance to the use of animals in experiments as a source of information about human behaviour. The logic was that if humans were one end-product of the progression in the development of the animal kingdom then the study of these less complex, more controllable representatives of the animal kingdom should reveal the basic ingredients of human behaviour – thus animal psychology. Also the study of transitions, both physical and mental, from childhood to adulthood became popular, reversing the Victorian notion of children as homunculi. Darwin himself was deeply interested in this subject and kept careful diaries of children's development – thus child development.

The second influence arising from the notion of compatibility between inherent characteristics and environmental circumstances gave encouragement to three further kinds of development in psychology.

The study of inherent characteristics of 'internal factors' gave birth to instinct and need theories which became fashionable in educational psychology during the first half of this century. Freudian psychoanalysis was also very much influenced by this aspect of Darwin's theory. On the other hand, external or environmental circumstances as sources of systematic study were espoused by the behaviourists from the beginning of this century.

The rapid growth of studies, particularly in child development, animal psychology and behaviourism, was encouraged by the second influence mentioned before, that is the application of scientific method to the study of human behaviour. The scientific study of those attributes which enabled humans to survive, particularly intellectual attributes, inevitably led educational psychologists to search for those qualities which might influence the motivation and academic performance of children. Our predecessors in education became confident that in time, laws of human behaviour would be established and used for the benefit of human interests such as education. So strong was this belief that professors of education were prepared to offer speculations in their inaugural lectures. So things have not changed very much, although I hope mine are a bit nearer the target than the following quotations:

> The last twenty years have witnessed a great development which bids fair to revolutionise our whole educational procedure.... It is not impossible that our children's children [that's us!] will witness the evolution of a body of human sciences not less systematic and comprehensive than the knowledge of physical science which we now possess...

This was from the inaugural lecture of Professor Bompas Smith, Manchester, 1913 (Smith, 1913). To be fair to him, he also said the following, which illustrates one change which came about:

> ... in our work as teachers we must recognise the individual point of view and interests of each boy and girl. All education must be based upon sympathetic insight into the minds of those we teach. We must not treat them simply as units with attributes which for practical purposes are the same. If this principle were always followed we should not find children of four sitting on benches for five hours a day spending most of their time on lessons in reading, writing and arithmetic ... (Smith, 1913)

The functionalist view generated by Darwinism inspired the search for human capacities which correlated with success and gave rise to the mental testing movement. This, coupled with the growth in the study of child development and the first fruits of scientific method applied to human behaviour, brought about a remarkable transformation in teacher training around the turn of the century. The focus was now firmly fixed on the child as learner and the impact of psychological findings on education during the first 50 years of this century was substantial.

One only need compare the curriculum, materials and practices in classrooms at the turn of the century with those prevailing in, say, 1950 to appreciate that those 50 years were golden years for educational psychology in terms of influence. A few examples should suffice to remind you of the contribution.

The design and application of intelligence and school achievement tests is most often associated with the eleven-plus exam. But another, equally significant, development was the school psychological service and the use it made of these and other standardised tests in the detection of learning and behaviour problems. It was the age of norms, when those far above or far below average in academic performance were offered abnormal provision in grammar or special schools. Some account was taken of children's varying levels and rates of performance, by streaming and setting and organizing timetables, so that shorter periods occurred in order to have distributed rather than massed practice. Research on the senses and perception, particularly during the two world wars, had an effect on the use of visual and auditory materials, including improvements in textbook presentation. The growth of teaching aids during this time was impressive, it being done in the belief that all senses should play a part in learning, and so on – there are many more examples.

Although interest in the school subject as the means of training the mind had declined, questions about the appropriateness and presentation of subjects at certain ages, and progression in the level of difficulty of concepts within a subject were still being asked. Graded reading and number books began to appear based largely on the work of researchers in educational psychology. Alternative forms of assessment and evaluation made their appearance, chiefly in America at this time because of the upsurge in multiple-choice techniques and the beginnings of programmed learning.

Thus far, variation in the performance of children was placed squarely on their shoulders. Poor performance was put down to lack of effort or lack of ability on their part. What about the teachers? The fact is that the teacher's role, both in terms of personal qualities and details of the task of teaching was almost ignored up to the 1950s. As Editor of the *British Journal of Educational Psychology*, I commissioned a cumulative index from 1930 to 1980 (Brown, 1982). It is a most instructive document on the changing interests in the subject over that period. Entries relating to teachers occurred six times in the first 25 years (1930–1954) and 27 times in the last 25 years (1955–1980).

These researches include teacher personality, selection, expectations of teaching as a career or of their pupils, their attitude to various aspects of school life and so on. Some of the earliest research looked into the qualities of merit in teachers as seen by pupils. It stretches back to 1896, but it is thinly scattered in the literature (Kratz, 1896; Bell, 1900; Book,

1905). All the findings on this topic to the present come to much the same conclusion – that pupils like teachers to keep order, have a laugh, explain clearly and interestingly, have something to say, be fair and friendly. I'm sure this list won't surprise anyone here.

But there are two things to notice about these research topics. The first is that most of them are isolated from classroom practices. The commonest research techniques involved questionnaires which were completed in the staff room or at home. Little was done until about 10 or so years ago on the actual instructional techniques and their effects on pupil performance. The second thing to notice is that most of the attributes examined are for the most part unchangeable. Personality, attitudes, expectations, sense of humour or friendliness are fairly stable in an individual. These are the reasons, I suspect, why this line of investigation has had next to no impact on educational practices.

The fourth and most recent shift of emphasis casts the net of interest even wider to include the educational context within which teaching occurs. Hargreaves (1977) concludes that:

> ...in the last ten years psychologists, social psychologists and sociologists of education have all converged on the classroom as an important area for educational research. Much of this research... employs a range of well established concepts to analyse classroom life such as attitude, self-image, role expectation, as well as newer concepts such as self-fulfilling prophecy and hidden curriculum...one common theme throughout the literature is what teachers and pupils expect of one another and how they perceive one another.

Other examples of contextual research are those of Bennett (1976) and the ORACLE project at Leicester (Galton, Simon and Croll, 1980). In these one major concern has been the importance of the context generated by the teacher's style. Style in these researches refers largely to the organizational or managerial preferences of teachers in their classrooms which are categorised in various ways such as formal, informal, group instructors, individual monitors, class enquirers and so on. Correlation between these contexts and pupil performance was also explored – and the conflicting and inconclusive results have been a source of enjoyment for those who like to argue the toss between formal and informal arrangements in classrooms.

Again, two things to notice about these contemporary lines of investigation. Firstly, they do occur *in situ* – in the classroom where the learning is actually taking place. It has helped to remind us that the classroom is a unique educational environment with its own particular problems and solutions. Secondly, and unfortunately, I believe, these contextual researches have concentrated on the overtly organizational and affective styles of teachers almost to the exclusion of their instructional and cognitive styles. I am thinking here particularly of the characteristic ways in which teachers unfold areas of knowledge for curriculum planning and execution. Along with a number of other recent researches they are anthropological in the methods used. Of necessity they are descriptive and do not purport to be diagnostic or prescriptive.

Whilst I am amongst the first to accept the worthwhile nature of this line of research in providing more parts for the jigsaw portraying classroom life, I am doubtful as to how much these second- and third-order influences account for differences in the performance of children and to what extent they are, in any case, susceptible to modification. Such stable attributes as teachers' personalities, affective style, or their attitudes to authority or misbehaviour are, I believe, pretty well impervious to adaptation. Like Benjamin Bloom (1976), I think that we have to concentrate on those aspects of life in classrooms which can be manipulated to the benefit of pupils.

The present position

Whatever the reasons, it is clear to me that the contribution of educational psychology research over the last 20 years has been less significant than in the first half of the century. It is interesting to note that those contributions which have made an impact in the last 20 years relate once again to the task of teaching and analysing subjects, and the developing child. Of late this has become an interactive model, particularly in junior school curricula. For example, the norm-referenced aspects of Piaget's work on children's cognitive development and Gagne's hierarchical theory on the organization of subject content and presentation have been extensively plundered and applied by subject specialists to give a highly productive and well-oiled industry in curriculum design. School Council schemes, Nuffield Science and Maths, Science 5–13, Language, Literacy and communications programmes, social and vocational schemes, to mention a few, have sprung into being.

We are very fortunate here at Leeds in having a number of colleagues in the School of Education who have made important contributions to this development. Professor Lovell's work in Piagetian psychology will be well known to many of you. Dr Joan Tough (1977) has a national reputation in the area of fostering communication skills in young children and has produced much useful material for this purpose. Douglas Barnes (1982) wrote about practical curriculum study (and I do not get a cut of royalties for saying so!). Roger Hartley (1980; 1981) has produced programmes for computer-based learning in a variety of topics and he is involved with MEP (Micro-electronics Education Programme) in the evaluation of software.

So far in the development of educational psychology the prevalent models have been static ones. Norm-referenced tests of attainment, intelligence, development, etc., have provided snapshot evidence, one frame in the reel of life if you like, which tells us by how much a child might differ from those of his or her own age, without telling us how the difference comes about. For example, two children with arithmetic ages, say, two years less than their chronological ages as determined by an arithmetic achievement test, or two adolescents with the same low mark in an 'O' level may have very different problems. These problems cannot be determined without a more sophisticated analysis of the specific skills called for by the tests. We have still a long way to go in designing exploratory devices from which diagnoses and corresponding programmes can be formulated. We have theories describing intellectual development, but not theories for assisting intellectual development. Measures from static models identify problems in retrospect. They give few directions for the solution of those problems.

This is a current dilemma for the professional educational psychologists in their work on children's learning difficulties and in giving advice on how to cope. The recent Education Act of 1981 on special educational needs highlights the increasing importance placed on the LEA educational psychologists' role in identification and advice about provision. Education Circular 1/83, which is an advisory document on how the Act might be implemented, makes it very clear that in addition to analysing a child's learning difficulties, there must also be a diagnosis of the special needs for different kinds of approaches, facilities and resources. The burden of responsibility for these provisions has also been placed on teachers in the normal state system. I quote:

> The teacher...is in a key position to observe [a pupil's] response in the classroom, to recognise the child who is experiencing difficulties in learning, and to try out different approaches to help meet the child's needs.

As I have tried to indicate, I am not convinced that we have got the wherewithal to fulfil this latter demand.

This much more dynamic model, placing the teacher in the role of manager of change by progressively adjusting instructional methods to suit each child is, I submit, one obvious growth point in the future and I shall return to it later. It is not a new idea. The second quotation from Bompas Smith hinted at it and Plowden, for another, has said it. But it is not in general a reality in schools. One of the most consistent criticisms contained in the recent HMI reports of primary and secondary education was that brighter children are not stretched enough. Similarly, less able children need more specifically tailored content and method to suit their needs. One reason is that teachers have neither the time nor the opportunity to give the individual attention needed.

Professional educational psychologists are heading in the same direction. The following quotation captures the essence of their views:

> In terms of professional practice the shift in emphasis is quite distinct: the psychologist's appraisal of a child and his difficulties is now much more in terms of the means of achieving change, rather than burrowing into the past or into the psyche in pursuit of causes and explanations...The heart of educational psychology must be the theory and technology of change and this takes the psychologist a long way from being a mere clinician (Gillham, 1978).

The future

The time has come for me to step out on to the plank and make some speculations about the future contribution of psychology to education. In trying to explore new directions in the subject, I soon discovered that two modes of travel were available to me (apart from the plank). Both, of course, are littered with my prejudices about the uses and abuses of the subject. One route (on foot) was to take the existing roads, many scarcely half made up, and build on these in the hope of arriving at some future destinations. The other (by air) involved indulging in speculative flights of fantasy about how the educational world might look in, say, the twenty-first century and guessing about the part which psychology might play in reaching that world.

Earlier I said that we had theories describing learning and intellectual development, but few theories for assisting learning and intellectual development. The reason is that the former are descriptive and therefore much easier to live with than the latter, which are prescriptive. It requires confidence and conviction that we have something positive to say about learning and teaching which will improve levels of performance, and this is the direction in which we shall head. Teaching will become more diagnostic. Learning will become more clearly directed towards greater self-sufficiency in the learner. The history of the learner such as home influences, early schooling, life experiences will be examined more closely for their contribution to later learning. Syllabuses and subjects will be dismantled and scrutinised for improved methods and sequences of presentation and underlying skill processes. More stress will be placed on those aspects of learning and teaching which are alterable and not static. If you agree with even some of these observations, then the next step is inevitable. We will have to develop theories or models of instruction and I want to devote the remaining time to some aspects of these models.

Some people get uptight about the term 'instruction' because it seems to convey a mechanical, dehumanizing, 'do this or else' approach to learning and teaching. That would be a gross distortion of the way it is used by educational psychologists. I believe there are six major features which any theory of instruction must specify and all of them are sensitive to individual differences. I want to give a brief elaboration of these in order to summarise what I see as the main lines of development into the next century.

The six specifications are:

1 the cognitive predispositions of the learner – that is, the knowledge, skills and abilities which a learner brings to a task and which would influence performance
2 the affective dispositions of the learner – that is, the interests, attitudes and self-concept brought to a task
3 how a body of knowledge needs to be structured in order for efficient and effective learning by individuals to take place
4 the sequencing and best methods of presenting that body of knowledge
5 the reinforcement mechanisms necessary to ensure continued interest such as rewards, incentives, feedback
6 evaluation of pupil performance and the system used.

To help in summarizing the advances which might be generated from these specifications, I have cannibalised a diagram from Bloom – of taxonomy fame (1976).

Entry predispositions

The first two represent what are called 'student entry characteristics' or 'predispositions'. In plain language they are about the history of the learner prior to the task in hand, which will be of relevance to that task. Three, four and five, about structuring of knowledge, sequencing of presentation and reinforcement mechanisms, are incorporated into the central part of the diagram under 'instruction'. Learning outcomes are about the effects of learning and must involve evaluation of some kind. Note also that the outcomes become part of the history of the learner and that is why the model is cyclical.

Entry variables such as general intelligence and personality, whilst they give useful background knowledge, are fairly stable and we should concentrate on the other predispositions which can be modified for the benefit of the learner. The numerical, verbal reading, writing, communication skills of the young are inescapable and profoundly affected by child-rearing practices. We have a lot to learn about early home and school influences and of discovering ways of improving these skills by capitalising on this critical early period. Studies in paediatrics and the

Psychology in the service of education: a review

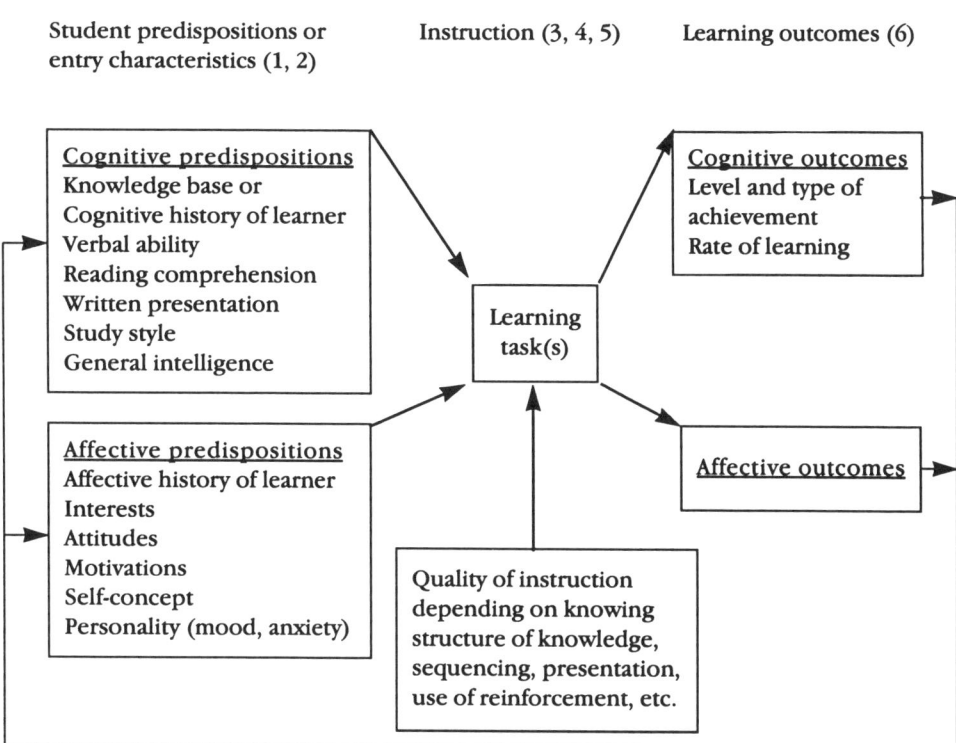

Figure I.1: Adapted from Bloom, B.S., Human Characteristics and School Learning, McGraw-Hill, New York: 1976

physiology of early child development will make significant contributions to educational psychology.

We have only a hazy idea of how a child assimilates and organises knowledge and how this process in turn will affect decision-making and problem-solving. How do previous experiences, and the generalizations formulated from them, impinge upon new experience? One of my colleagues in the School of Education, Dr Driver (1983), is looking at the ways in which children develop specific ideas and concepts in science and how these compete with the accepted generalization in science. Whether we like it or not, children, it seems, formulate their own laws of nature from their experiences and these may be in competition and conflict with those presented by the science teacher. This illustrates very clearly the importance of studying the entry characteristics of pupils from their learning history and of finding ways of unravelling false notions and replacing them with methods for finding more acceptable notions.

Most of us here this evening are teachers. I wonder how many of us are confident that we know, prior to the learning tasks we set, exactly what content and skills will be required for maximum understanding and performance of the learners? My belief is there is a tremendous job to be done in this respect.

I have also listed 'study style' on the diagram. By this I mean the characteristic and unique ways in which an individual tries to cope with the learning process. We each of us have favoured tactics and strategies which we bring to study. How efficient are they? Could they be improved? Is the teaching compatible with our favoured strategies? And so on. Most of the research in this field has been concerned with secondary and higher education (Marton and Säljö, 1976 in Sweden, Biggs, 1978 in Australia, Entwistle and Ramsden, 1983 in the UK). Most of this work gives useful descriptive glimpses of student methods or characteristics. Biggs, for example, gives several amusing thumbnail sketches of methods of study: the 'minimax' method in which the student learns only the bare essentials for a pass, hoping to obtain the maximum mark for a minimum output. There is also the 'opportunist' type who carefully studies the prejudices of a teacher and feeds these back in essays. Unfortunately, the study methods of students in higher education are probably so well ossified that there is little chance of encouraging modifications for improved performance. Yet at the important end of the system, in junior school, we almost completely ignore training in study methods. We wrongly assume that effective methods of study are automatically picked up as children progress through the system. We need detailed researches of how study skills grow and how to teach them to the individual's best advantage.

I need not remind this audience of the central importance of interest and motivation to pupil or student performance. Yet we have a long way to go in trying to comprehend and do something about the credibility gap which exists between pupils, teachers, parents and society as to the place of a formal system of education in the life-chances of an individual. Selling the system gets harder as one reaches the final two years of secondary school life, especially to those with little hope of obtaining 'O' levels or good CSEs. There will have to be a considerable shift in syllabus content and design as changing patterns of work and leisure, individuals' expectations and technological advances bite deeper and deeper into our present way of life. Unfortunately, society inadvertently generates in the young expectations which the educational system can rarely fulfil. Whilst I think there will be progress in the ways I've described, there has also to be an air of reality about what can be achieved with pupils in the first years of life.

Instruction

The central portion of the diagram, Instruction, places great demands on the teacher as a manager of learning. The aspiration of teachers should be to lead learners to a point where they, the pupils, can help themselves. This is becoming increasingly more important as our knowledge base rapidly increases. Information retrieval and self-help are growing in significance. The cheap miniaturization of equipment suitable in educational settings will have a marked effect on educational provision in both the curriculum and teaching arrangements in some subjects. The design of software requires a deep knowledge of the structure of a subject and teachers will need to know more about how to unwrap their areas of knowledge for presentation in a variety of ways. I note in the newspapers recently that the Sinclair home computer is one of the most popular toys this Christmas and educational software is now available for these machines. More parents are becoming more conscious of their role in education.

The simulation of human thinking and action in the form of artificially intelligent systems may have something to offer to teachers. Our inventions are often extensions of ourselves. Telescopes and microscopes are extensions of our eyes, amplifiers our ears, tools and vehicles our limbs. Robotics combines some of these senses and is taking the routine out of some manufacturing industries. Apart from the obvious impact this will have on our work and leisure activities in the future, the study of artificial intelligence must in time have some messages for the analysis and presentation of subject matter, and knowledge about the human being as a learner.

In the next century, self-sufficiency will be the order of the day. This is becoming increasingly apparent in a society where knowledge in discovering 'know-how' is at a premium. There will be a growing and successful pressure for individualization in learning. The research scenario will be one of facilitating those aspects which have to do with the uniqueness of learning for each person. Of course, the convention of classroom methods in which a teacher is with a large group is here for a long time to come, but skills in adapting an ever-increasing range of facilities and opportunities for personalised learning will need to be developed.

Against the trend of thinking in educational psychology at present, I happen to believe that the influence of applied behavioural analysis (the new term for behaviour modification) will become substantial. The principles involved in designing software had their origins in behaviourism. But a second line of development is in the treatment of disruptive children in normal classrooms, and I feel confident that any useful advice on this subject would be gratefully received by the teaching profession. I am told by cognitive psychologists that their chief interest is in how people process internally in acquiring, modifying, manipulating, using or storing knowledge. The focus now is on the inner person for information processing and this is a very important development in recent years. Behaviourists tell me that as behaviour is primarily learned and based on an individual's reactions with his or her environment (including teachers), the important thing is to know how to control that environment to get the desired effects. Their concern is with the external influences on humans. As an eclectic in psychology I find both these propositions and their implications useful in the classroom. The teaching profession would be ill-advised to ignore helpful findings from either cognitivist or behaviourist sources.

To enhance the quality of instruction we shall need to influence the teacher in training. The catch-phrases and methods seeping into the system at present seem to be pointing in the directions I have outlined. A few examples are

- flexi-programmes and adaptive tutoring which are designed to be adjusted to the needs of particular children either by using reproduced materials, video or microprocessor
- courses for students on instructional craft knowledge
- the use of simulation exercises using closed-circuit or recorded TV programmes
- the more extensive use of recorded teaching episodes – sometimes called micro-teaching
- courses in diagnostic techniques and social skills.

In some public sector training institutions which I have visited for the CNAA, some of these innovations are beginning to replace some parts of the conventional psychology and sociology of education syllabuses.

Learning outcomes

In a sense, learning outcomes need to be considered alongside entry predispositions, because one needs to know the destination before being able to choose an appropriate route.

Evaluation is an essential part of the process of learning. Indeed, that's life! The development of skills and tools which enable teachers to make accurate diagnoses and treatment of individual children's problems is crucial and is badly in need of research.

Two particularly interesting growth points, one from the cognitive, the other from affective outcomes, are error analysis and the effects of high and low achievement on future performance – sometimes called attribution theory. In a nutshell, the theory asks – to what do we attribute our success or failure in a given task and what effect does this have on future performance? If we believe that failure is within our control we are more likely to react adversely than if it is beyond our control. If it happens often enough, motivation and self-image of academic achievement decline and performance suffers.

Of more interest to me is error analysis. It has become an important contribution from the researches of the APU (Assessment of Performance Unit) in mathematics, science and English. Trends in the nature and direction of children's incorrect responses to problems are beginning to reveal information which could have much to tell us about the appropriateness of materials, methods of presentation of content, the design of questions, the 'virtuous' errors which children make, and so on.

Each learner has unique characteristics and learning problems. One of the teacher's main tasks is to identify those characteristics and problems (diagnosis) and create appropriate learning conditions (treatments) which will enable that individual to reach required levels of competence.

Clearly, there is ample credible work still to be done by educational psychologists. The more practical and relevant this work can be, the better. All disciplines need a theoretical base and research of this kind is important. But the time is overdue for us to convert more of this theory into practical outcomes. I hope I have left no doubt in anyone's mind this evening that there is plenty of work of this kind to keep us busy for many years to come.

Universities have always aspired to three functions. Two we are very familiar with, that is the creation and transmission of knowledge. But the third tends to be undervalued, that is the application of knowledge. Schools of medicine, dentistry and engineering, for example, have long had this tradition. Schools of education too have this important element of application in their traditions and I am confident that Leeds will continue to be amongst those universities which play a substantial part in applying psychology in the service of education.

References

Barnes, D. (1982) Practical Curriculum Study (London: Routledge and Kegan Paul).
Bell, S. (1900) A study of the teacher's influence. Pedagogy Seminars, 7, 493.
Bennett, S.N. (1976) Teaching Styles and Pupil Progress (London: Open Books).
Biggs, J.B. (1978) Individual and group differences in study processes. British Journal of Educational Psychology, 48, 266-79.
Bloom, B.S. (1976) Human Characteristics and School Learning (New York: McGraw Hill).
Book, F. (1905) The high school teacher from the pupils' point of view. Pedagogy Seminars, 12, 488.
Brown, G. (ed.) (1982) Cumulative Index of Volumes 1-50, 1930-1980. British Journal of Educational Psychology.
Driver, R. (1983) The Pupil as Scientist? (Milton Keynes: Open University).
Education Act (1981) An act to make provision with respect to children with special educational needs. (London: HMSO).
Educational Circular 1/83 (1983) Assessments and Statements of Special Educational Needs (London: HMSO).
Entwistle, N. and Ramsden, P. (1983) Understanding Student Learning (London: Croom Helm).
Galton, M. and Simon B. (Eds) (1980) Progress and performance in the primary school. Report of the ORACLE research at Leicester University.
Galton, M., Simon, B. and Croll, P. (1980) Inside the primary school. Report of the ORACLE research at Leicester University.

Gillham, W. (Ed.). (1978) Reconstructing Educational Psychology (London: Croom Helm).

Hartley, J.R. (1980) Computer assisted learning, in Smith, H.T. and Green, T.R.G. (Eds.), Human Interaction with Computers (London: Academic Press).

Hartley, J.R. (1981) An appraisal of computer assisted learning in the United Kingdom, in Rushby, N. (Ed.) Selected Readings in Computer Based Learning. (London: Kogan Page).

Hargreaves, D.G. (1977)The process of typification in classroom interaction: models and methods. British Journal of Educational Psychology, 47, 274-84.

Kratz, H.E. (1896) Characteristics of the best teacher as recognised by children. Pedagogy Seminars, 3, 413.

Marton, F. and Saljo, R. (1976) Qualitative differences in learning. 1: Outcome as a function of the learning. British Journal of Educational Psychology, 46, 4-11; 46, 115-22.

Smith, Bompas H. (1913) Education as the Training of Personality. Inaugural lecture, Manchester University.

Tough, J. (1976a) The Development of Meaning: A study of children's use of language. (London: Allen and Unwin).

Tough, J. (1976b) Listening to Children Talking. Schools Council Communication Skills in Early Childhood project (London: Ward Lock).

Tough, J. (1977) Language and Learning in Early Childhood (London: Heinemann).

Part I
Teaching, Learning and Learning How to Teach

Thematic introduction and summary

DIANE SHORROCKS TAYLOR

The topic of teaching and learning is clearly of central importance in educational psychology. As several of the authors comment, if the discipline cannot provide analytical frameworks for and explanations of learning and teaching, then it is indeed failing in its role. The six authors of the chapters in this section each take a rather different perspective on the issue, producing different kinds of analyses but thankfully also making some similar points. It is interesting to note that some of the key points many of them make are echoes of those made by Dennis Child in his Leeds inaugural lecture (see pp. xxi–xxxvi).

Chapter 1, by Charles Desforges, sets some broad parameters and locates its central focus on the classroom, the main arena for teaching–learning processes which sets the conditions under which teachers and pupils interact. The explanatory framework he adopts is that of schema theory, involving processes of accretion, tuning and restructuring. These are the stuff of learning and yet, as he points out, teachers seem to have great difficulty putting into practice the insights and lessons these ideas bring. This is an issue also taken up by Peter Tomlinson in Chapter 5, where he presents a detailed analysis of this problem. Desforges goes on to argue that part of the problem in understanding learning and teaching in classrooms is the considerable social and cultural complexity of the situation, added to the fact that research has frequently emphasised the fact that there are many different ways of learning. He finishes with the vital point that what pupils need to learn, perhaps above all, is to learn how to learn, in other words, how to deploy deliberate strategies for coming at knowledge and to adopt appropriate problem-solving strategies, including dealing with anxiety and insecurity.

Although coming from a somewhat different angle, Roger Hartley's contribution (Chapter 2) also gives emphasis to the importance of pupils and students being able to construct their own schematic representations of the task in hand and being able to understand more of their own thinking processes. This is in the context of computer assisted learning, however, which has shown very rapid advance in the last decade or so. New technologies (hardware and software) have become much more widely available in education at all levels and have brought with them not only better grounded approaches to learning but also richer potential for individualising and customising it. Indeed, according to his analysis, it is now possible for students to create their own learning environments, including collaborative learning in small groups, as well as individualised ones. Notwithstanding the enormous potential of the latest innovations in technology in relation to learning, what is still needed is insight as to how best to use these new tools to facilitate higher levels of understanding, metacognitive awareness and creative thought.

Chapter 3, by Pam Sammons, takes us to a very different way of approaching the question of what produces effective learning, in this case, effective schools and teachers. She summarises the changing views about what leads to successful learning, pointing out that it is only recently that we have moved away from seeing the explanations in terms of pupil attributes (IQ, social background factors, motivation) towards acknowledging that schools, individual schools, and what goes on in them does make a difference. Schools and classrooms are highly diverse institutions and places, yet characteristics as varied as time spent in lessons and whole school ethos seem to be of significance in affecting pupil progress. It is also the case that even within the same school, individual teachers and subject departments may produce very different results. Like the other authors, she too emphasises the point that current measures of the 'value' added by a school must be set in context, taking into account the particular circumstances and attributes that characterise it. Without such scene-setting, the analyses are potentially doomed to misinterpretation, with little useful purpose being served for anyone.

One of the characteristics of an effective school and of effective teachers within schools is the displaying of high expectations for the pupils. This is the subject of Chapter 4, by Colin Rogers, in which he moves into the field of social psychology and its application in educational contexts. The issue of teacher expectations and pupil performance has been a seductive one in education ever since the publication of the controversial Rosenthal and Jacobson study in the 1960s. As he points out, however, the problem of definition of 'expectations' is not a straightforward one, since all expectations are relative to a particular school situation: what appear to be high expectations in one school may be comparatively low in the very different circumstances of another school. Neither is it yet clear or agreed precisely what the mechanisms of influence might be.

Rogers distinguishes between probabilistic and prescriptive expectations – the 'is' and the 'ought to be' in the minds and behaviours of teachers. He suggests that both of these have a role to play in school and classroom interactions, but with the emphasis on teachers aiming high and encouraging pupils to share these beliefs and aspirations. What emerges very clearly from this chapter is a real sense of the complexity, not to say subtlety, of the processes of interpersonal perception and judgements that inevitably take place in social organisations such as schools. All of these may have profound influences on motivation, attributions, learning goals and performance.

After these four chapters focusing in the main on pupil learning in school contexts, Chapter 5 by Peter Tomlinson moves on to the question of how teachers learn, in particular how they learn to teach and become skilled facilitators of pupil learning. The framework he uses to try to conceptualise and elucidate the problem is that of skilled behaviour or expertise, since teaching is a complex and open skill, highly strategic and flexible. He presents us with a detailed analysis of the various ways in which the term has been used both in psychological and in more everyday ways, then goes on to show how current views of skill can be applied in teacher preparation situations. As he points out, the present transition in England and Wales to more school-based teacher induction has brought this into even greater focus. Learning the skill, becoming more expert as it were, can be supported and assisted but a significant part of this assistance must come from understanding the processes and issues, and not just be the result of relatively uninformed immersion in classroom teaching. This is perhaps an important way to solve the problem identified by Desforges, that of teachers apparently not being able to translate important insights about teaching and learning into behaviour in the classroom.

Finally, in Chapter 6 Noel Entwistle provides us with yet another perspective on learning and teaching, but this time in higher education contexts. Before summarising the detailed research that has been carried out on factors that make for successful learning in higher education, he outlines a useful history of research methodologies, arguing that although the purpose of educational research has always been to seek to explain significant issues, this has been accomplished in a variety of ways, depending on the *zeitgeist*. Overall, he suggests that the move in research has been away from the development and application of abstract psychological constructs and towards approaches of greater ecological validity. By this he means the detailed empirical investigation of, for instance, student study strategies, levels of application, or involvement in the subject. It also involves an analysis of the way subject matter is delivered in lecture situations or seminars in relation to the learning approaches of the individual students.

The chapters are all rather different in their particular emphases, but at the same time, they seem to converge on some key issues. All the authors acknowledge the great complexity of the teaching–learning process and indirectly point out the limitations of adopting some of the oversimplified explanations of the past. Quantitative analyses must necessarily be multi-layered and multivariate, an emphasis always given by Dennis Child himself, allowing for the complex interplay of explanatory factors: more qualitative analyses must incorporate contextual factors for any full explanation. This is the 'ecological validity' referred to explicitly by Noel Entwistle.

Perhaps a final point of convergence in all the chapters is the recognition of differences in the ways individuals represent knowledge, perceive new information, process it and become more expert. Any explanation of teaching and learning processes and outcomes that does not take account of this vital dimension seems doomed to failure.

Chapter 1
Learning and teaching: current views and perspectives

CHARLES DESFORGES

My remit for this chapter is to describe contemporary perspectives on learning and to consider their implications for teaching, identifying those teaching processes known, on the basis of research, to be most effective at promoting pupils' learning progress.

There is a vast literature on the topic of teaching and an even more extensive body of published work on the matter of learning. Space does not permit even a brief overview of the currently available material. In consequence my treatment here is bound to be selective. I have chosen to focus on classrooms and on the actions and interactions which go on in classrooms in the name of teaching and learning.

Learning and teaching always refer to some content. One always learns something. And although it is common to announce that teachers 'teach pupils', the pupils are always taught something. In regard to the content of teaching and learning, I have focused on large and complex bodies of learning called academic subjects as these are experienced in the classroom.

In the first part of the chapter I describe basic learning processes in terms of contemporary schema theory. Before considering the teaching implications of schema theory I pause to consider classroom culture. Attempts to derive implications for teaching from theories of learning must take into consideration the conditions under which teachers and pupils work together. I review some of the psychological literature on this matter and draw attention, in particular, to the effect of classroom order, classroom work and teachers' assessment processes on pupils' learning progress.

I then focus on teaching pupils to use and apply knowledge as a case study in which to discuss the implications of knowledge of learning for prescriptions for teaching, arguing that teachers need a repertoire of skills if they are to promote learning effectively. Finally, I briefly discuss teachers as learners in classrooms and draw implications for professional development.

Basic processes in acquisition

Learning is both a noun and a verb. As a noun, learning comprises organised previous experience. Little purpose is served by distinguishing learning from memory in this respect.

Students of learning (or of memory) are immediately faced with the problems of adopting a unit of analysis and a way of conceiving of experience – the problem, in short, of adopting a theoretical perspective. Various perspectives on learning have been adopted in the history of psychology and most still have impact on contemporary work. Learning has variously been seen as 'making connections' or as 'problem solving' or as 'information processing' or as 'theory building', (see Brown, 1995 for an introductory overview).

The associationist or connectionist view of learning sees all complex, learned behaviour as built up of basic associations fundamentally resting on innate reflexes (Thorndike, 1931). The single association is the unit of analysis, for example the association of a word with a thing (Skinner, 1957). Associationists have identified the 'laws of association' that is to say, those conditions and circumstances which best support the acquisition of complex behaviour (for example, a facility with advanced mathematics) from basic links (for example, the association of a number name with the appropriate number of objects).

At the other end of the spectrum of models of learning, Rogerian psychologists (Rogers, 1961) have taken the view that the whole person must be considered if learning is to be understood. In this view a person's total life history is brought to bear on new experience in any act of learning.

Perhaps the most prevalent approach in contemporary studies of learning makes use of the somewhat eclectic concept of *schema theory*. In this theory the unit of analysis is the *schema* which represents a person's organised experience as it refers to a specific context or setting. The term denotes the totality of stored knowledge, attitudes and behaviour relevant to a particular subjective experience.

A learner will have a schema, for example, of arithmetic. This schema would comprise all the routines associated with arithmetical problems together with the attitudes or dispositions related to the previous experience of such problems. The routines might be correct or errorful; the attitudes might be conducive to optimistic performance or to dread and fear of failure.

Learning as a verb refers to the processes of schema modification. Learning can be regressive as well as progressive, inhibiting as well as enabling. We can learn, for example, to build bleak images of our self, images which frustrate or even defeat further learning. I have adopted schema theory here as a basis on which to consider classroom teaching and learning.

It is useful to conceive of three basic processes of schema modification (Norman, 1978). These have been termed *accretion, tuning* and *restructuring*. Learning in each of these processes, involves the interaction of experience with what the learner already knows, i. e. with extant schema. Learning modifies extant schema.

Accretion refers to the acquisition of new associations or 'pieces' of knowledge to a schema. It might take the form of the acquisition of a new fact or a new example. A learner might know the names of a range of capital cities. There will be some organised idea, i. e. a schema, regarding 'capital cities', encapsulating what the notion 'capital' means to the learner. Learning the name of a new capital city would be an example of accretion. It would have wide reaching ramifications for the learner in regard to what the new city name now stood for: the name now represents and carries with it the range of implications associated through the schema 'capital'.

Tuning is a process whereby the operation of a schema becomes increasingly automatic. Routines are made more efficient. The basic schema for using a keyboard, for example, may be quickly acquired as an idea. Experience might make the use more fluent. Tuning allows the freeing-up of attention. No new facts are involved. Rather, redundant steps in procedures are eliminated or short cuts are found, often subconsciously.

Restructuring is characterised in schema theory by the creation of new insights. Existing knowledge is re-organised. A new way of looking at past experience is adopted. Once a new pattern has been imposed the new schema informs the further operation of accretion and of tuning. Restructuring is clearly manifest in the child's acquisition of the conservation of discrete quantity. When presented with a row of black discs and a row of white discs in one-to-one correspondence with each other and asked if there are the same number of discs in each row, the non-conserver will say 'yes'. When one row is spread out, the non-conserver judges the longer row to have 'more' in it, presumably on the basis of perceived extension. The conserver judges the quantities to be still the same.

In the transition phase from non-conservation to conservation, it appears that non-conservers operate two conflicting rules. On the one hand an extension judgement says the quantities are different. On the other hand a count suggests they are the same. The contradiction is resolved through the invention of the conservation schema: the rows are the same in quantity because nothing has been added or taken away. Such a schema is proof against all deformations of the appearance of the arrays. The invention of conservation of quantity constitutes a cognitive restructuring of experience.

Although it is convenient for the sake of clarity to describe the processes of schema re-formation (i. e. of learning) separately, the three processes occur together in the course of learning. They are intimately connected. None of the processes is privileged or superior. Restructuring, for example, cannot occur in the absence of an organised body of knowledge. However, at any point in a learner's experience in a domain, one learning process or another might predominate (Norman, 1978.).

From the point of view of schema theory then, there are many different learning processes, each of which plays its part in the acquisition and organisation of schemas. The schema perspective constitutes a simple and powerful model or description of learning. Consider, for example, the very impressive learning by pre-schoolers of their home tongue. By the age of 5, most children have acquired a large, active vocabulary. They can use a range of syntactic structures such as plurals, tenses, moods and voices of verbs and so on. They communicate effectively with a range of audiences.

The learning processes involved in the acquisition of the first language have been revealed through the study of children's errors in language production. For example, most children go through a period of coining odd phrases ('sheeps', for example) or past tenses ('I runned', for example). These errors can be described neatly in terms of schema theory. We might say, for example, that the child learns a string of plurals through associations; dog, dogs; cat, cats. This is accretion at work involving the gradual accumulation of elements. But the child's errors (sheeps, mouses) reveal the construction of a schema for plurals so that new ones can be created. And the child appears to test the theory of plurals against experience. The theoretical creations are repaired as the child gets older, meets correct versions and reconstructs the 'plural schema'.

What implications does schema theory have for the teacher? Before answering this question it is necessary to put it into a broader context.

Theories of learning and the practice of teaching

Many psychologists have been tempted to advise teachers how to teach on the basis of theories of learning (Bain, 1879; Thorndike, 1913; Wertheimer, 1945; Gagné, 1965; Skinner, 1968; Broadbent, 1975). The relevance of learning theory seems obvious. Once we understand learning the role of the teacher should become transparent.

The advice has had very little impact on the practice of teachers (Ausubel and Robinson, 1969; Glaser Pellegrino and Lesgold, 1977; Cockroft, 1982; Eisner, 1983). Ausubel and Robinson (1969) for example, noted that despite favourable responses from teachers on psychology courses, 'the behaviour of these same teachers observed later in the classroom, has typically shown distressingly little influence of the principles and theories which they had presumably learned' (p. iii).

I have discussed elsewhere (Desforges, 1985) possible reasons for the failure of theories of learning to have impact on the practice of teaching. Again, space does not allow a detailed treatment. The main problem, I suggest, is that the theories of learning take no cognisance of the conditions under which teaching takes place, that is to say, the conditions and culture of classroom life. Recently, psychologists studying teaching and learning have turned their attention to this matter and provided a fuller understanding of the context of teaching (see Child's inaugural lecture, pp. xxi–xxxvi). I turn now to this issue as a basis on which to make more productive use of learning theory.

The culture of classrooms

Teaching is not something that teachers 'do' to pupils in classrooms. Pupils are never passive to the actions of their mentors. There are complex interactions between teachers, learners and classroom tasks.

The dynamic culture of classrooms has been well characterised by Jackson (1968). Jackson showed that teachers attend to a large number of different and often conflicting demands. The teacher attends to individual pupils while monitoring the whole class. She must sustain pupils' confidence while at the same time giving corrective feedback. She must give children time to think while keeping up the momentum of classroom lessons and activities.

Teachers organise movement about the classroom and control the flow of events and the distribution of resources. Jackson estimated that teachers take part in 200–300 exchanges every hour of their working day. The teacher's role has been characterised as that of a 'quartermaster' or 'traffic cop'. These analogies serve to convey images of someone working to preserve order on a complex and potentially chaotic situation. The processes of establishing and maintaining order occupy a great deal of teachers' attention and time. Bloom (1976) noted that teachers spend most of their effort in managing learners rather than in managing learning. The focus of pupils and teachers in most classrooms is on the management of classroom work which itself is structured around text books, commercial schemes or other printed materials (see Doyle, 1983 for a review of the main features of classroom work).

Doyle (1986) has argued that all classrooms have key features in common, the features being the central elements of classroom culture. Classrooms are crowded places serving many different needs and purposes. Many events take place, often simultaneously. During discussion a teacher must listen to pupils' comments and answers, watch others for signs of confusion, comprehension or boredom and, at the same time, formulate the next question or point.

There is a rapid pace to classroom life, and disruptions and distractions are frequent. It is impossible to anticipate how an activity will go

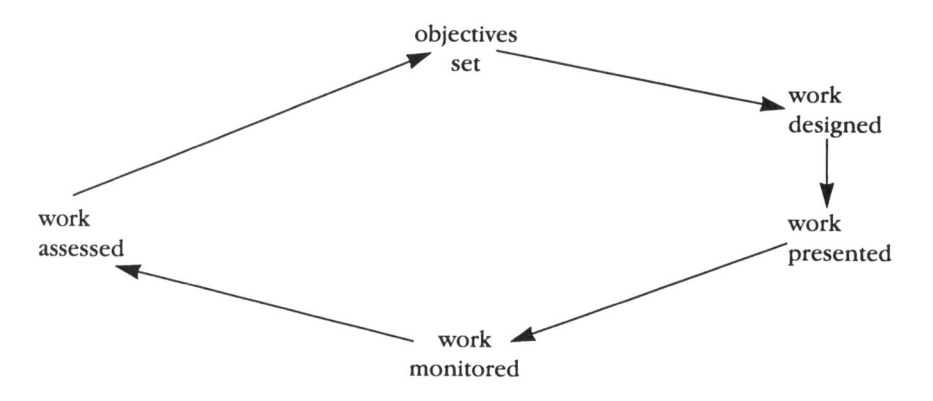

```
            objectives
               set
     ↗                  ↘
                         work
                       designed
   work                    ↓
 assessed                work
     ↖                 presented
               work    ↙
             monitored
```

Figure 1.1: The classroom work cycle

on a particular day with a particular group. The teacher has very little time to think before acting.

Events in the classroom are very public. There is a large number of witnesses to any action, especially to those involving the teacher. If a teacher reprimands one child, a significant portion of the class may learn a sanction. If he or she fails to reprimand a child, the whole class might learn something to their advantage about the teacher's management skills.

Doyle (1986) has usefully characterised the classroom as an information environment. Sources of information include books, displays, work cards and a vast amount of verbal and non-verbal behaviour. But humans can only process a limited amount of information at any one time. In order to adapt to the classroom environment the inhabitants have to learn to make fruitful selections amongst the available information. Some order has to be imposed on the information. Teachers devote a lot of time establishing order and routine as a matter of priority (Yinger, 1980; Clark and Peterson, 1986).

According to Doyle's theory, order is established only in cooperation with the pupils. This is a reciprocal process. Pupils are neither passive nor powerless in this matter. Cooperation is established in the process of classroom work (Jorgensen, 1977). The work set plays a crucial role in the negotiation of order. At the heart of this process is, in Doyle's terms, 'an exchange of performance for grades'. That is to say that teachers set work, pupils carry out the work and teachers provide rewards in the form of good grades and teachers' appreciation. Assessment is a key to this process. Assessment information is particularly salient in establishing order. In Doyle's terms, the work system is driven by the assessment system. If pupils can see clearly what they have to do to get the teacher's appreciation in the form of good grades, they will cooperate in doing the work, that is to say, in the processes of orderly classroom life. Where work is too challenging or where the assessment system is vague, pupils are inclined to withdraw cooperation. Pupils are known to be very resistant to work which has higher level cognitive demands such as problem solving tasks. These present learners with 'risk and ambiguity' in that it is not clear what pupils have to do to earn the rewards or praise or good grades (Davis and McKnight, 1976; Mackay, 1978; Morine-Dershimer, 1983).

Doyle's theory is not an account of how pupils learn. Rather, it emphasises that classroom learning takes place in the work setting established in the classroom. He stresses that the accountability system in the classroom plays a central role in the management of classroom work.

The impact of assessment systems on pupil learning behaviour has been known for a long time (see Desforges, 1992 for further commentary). Assessment focuses pupils' and teachers' attention alike and has tended to narrow curriculum experience to that which can be assessed. More recently, studies of classroom processes (Desforges and Cockburn, 1987; Edwards and Mercer, 1987; Marshall, 1988) have revealed that a great deal of classroom work is precisely that: work. Edwards and Mercer (1987) have documented the processes by which teachers and learners pass mindful learning by in the management of classroom work.

Teachers and children alike adopt the language of the production line to characterise classroom life. Work that is intended to foster learning becomes an end in itself. Pupils, when asked to describe what they are doing respond in terms of 'getting my work done' or 'it's my work' (Desforges and Cockburn, 1987). Teachers also assume that if children are working then they are learning (Marshall, 1988).

Constructive learners in classrooms

I have reviewed research on the basic processes of learning and shown that there are many different ways of learning. All learners have a repertoire of learning skills at their disposal. I have reviewed research on classroom processes and shown that teachers and learners work in a culture which can profitably be characterised as an information environment. Teachers manage learners through the management of work. The work system is driven by the assessment system. Learners apply their constructive learning processes to interpreting the assessment system and shaping the work system in cooperation with their teachers. What has all this got to say for the ways teachers might best promote learning in the classroom culture?

It is worth noting that teachers do not choose the curriculum nor the intended learning outcomes. In Britain, as in most states, the curriculum is determined by Government. Pupils are expected, by law, to cover a wide range of academic subjects. They are expected to learn bodies of knowledge and skills together with attitudes and values appropriate to learning and to being a good citizen. Further, they are expected to acquire various core skills including, for example, numeracy, literacy, communication and problem solving. More fundamentally pupils are expected to learn to use and apply their knowledge and skills in situations outside of school, in their domestic and professional lives, for example.

These different learning outcomes require very different learning processes which in turn would be promoted through different teaching processes as might be expected.

As has been shown, teachers promote learning through managing work. This process can be usefully characterised as shown in Figure 1.1. The work cycle model has promoted several research studies of classroom processes (see for example, Bennett and Desforges, 1984). The research has shown that the cycle is prone to break down in respect of learning.

In the busy classroom teachers' capacity for assessing work is severely stretched. In consequence their assessments are often insufficiently valid for the purposes of work design (Savage and Desforges, 1995). In further consequence, large amounts of work set are either too easy or too difficult for pupils. Bennett and Desforges (1984) for example, found that approximately 50 per cent of the work set to high achievers in primary schools was too easy and 50 per cent of the work set to low achievers was too difficult. The work frequently did not meet the purpose for which it was designed. For example, many tasks intended to give opportunity for practice failed to do so because the work was entirely new to the pupils. Many tasks intended to require cognitive restructuring through problem-solving failed to meet this objective because the pupils were already familiar with the concepts to be discovered.

In the same study, teachers found it very difficult to spot these problems because they were too busy to engage in the detailed monitoring activities necessary to the proper operation of the work cycle. If teaching is to promote learning, an extensive reappraisal of classroom work as a culture is clearly necessitated.

I turn now to an examination of this challenge in the context of teaching children to use and apply knowledge. I have chosen this as, in a sense, a case study, because it encompasses the whole range of teaching and learning processes in a focused way.

Knowledge use and application

Pupils have very great difficulty in using knowledge learned in one situation on problems met in another context (Säljö and Wyndhamn, 1990; Nunes, Schliemann and Carraher, 1993). In one national mathematics survey, for example, it was found that 80 per cent of 12-year-olds could correctly divide 225 by 15. However, only 40 per cent could solve the problem, ' Suppose a gardener had 225 bulbs to place equally in 15 flower beds, how many would be put in each bed?' Most of the failing pupils did not know which number operation to use.

In setting this problem it was assumed that pupils would spot the resemblance between the calculations and apply the core skill of long division. The problems could be said to have a family resemblance. The matter of using and applying knowledge boils down, in this view, to learning to see family resemblances in problems. Despite very great efforts to teach problem-solving based on this perspective, very little success has been achieved (Resnick, 1987).

Some psychologists have called this view of knowledge into question (Brown, Collins and Duguid, 1989). They argue that problems are defined by their context at least as much as by their so-called 'core attributes'. In this view, when we learn something, the context in which we learn it becomes an important part of what we learn. Knowledge may be said to be 'situated'. This means knowledge is an inseparable part of the activity, context and culture in which it is acquired. Specifically, in this view, material taught in classrooms is embedded, perhaps inseparably, in the culture of classroom work. This effect has been well illustrated in a recent study (Desforges and Bristow, 1995). The aim was to explore how young pupils used their knowledge to learn. In maths, science and English, pupils were taken forward in some work until they met, by design, a point of difficulty. They were then given a learning pack to help them move forward. The pack consisted of practical apparatus, work cards and text which explained the way ahead. Although all the children were good readers and readily used the text in science and English, they almost completely ignored it in mathematics. In their view and experience, reading was not relevant to learning in maths. Their view of what counted as applicable knowledge was clearly framed by their classroom experience.

Prawat (1989) has reviewed the evidence on how knowledge application breaks down and has developed a useful framework for understanding what might go wrong. In Prawat's analysis, knowledge application fails when

- the pupils do not possess the knowledge they are required to apply
- the knowledge has been acquired but its relevance is not seen
- the relevance of available knowledge is seen but the pupil lacks an application strategy
- a strategy is available but the learner lacks a 'can-do' attitude necessary to make the effort to succeed.

Each of these points might be seen as a link in a chain. If any link breaks, knowledge application fails. Research on classroom processes shows that many practices bring about weaknesses in the links.

Teachers overwhelmed by curricula overloaded in content use management strategies to ensure speedy coverage. Concepts are taught but there is little time to ensure that they are learned (Desforges and Cockburn, 1987). Practice tasks predominate over problem-solving tasks leaving learners familiar with a routine, but inexperienced in using it non-routinely (Bennett and Desforges, 1984). Most problems set in classrooms are pencil-and-paper challenges well suited to classroom work. They are clean and neat. There will be a solution. They can be solved in a short time span. Most real world problems are messy. They have no solution in a reasonable time span. Pupils' experience is thus limited to the context of classroom work (Brown *et al.*,1989).

Finally, many children lack confidence in themselves as learners and as problem solvers. They feel anxious and develop various strategies to avoid problems (such as withdrawal, disruption or rushed work) rather than developing the persistence necessary to sustain progress.

In order to achieve secure learning and a capacity to apply knowledge, a thorough going attention to each link in the chain is essential through the operation of a wide range of teaching skills.

Teaching knowledge use

Again, Prawat (1989) has provided a useful, research based foundation to indicate the teaching skills found successful in promoting knowledge application. He emphasises that a whole range of skills must be deployed if a successful outcome is to be expected.

The four links need to be strengthened. This requires that teachers establish in their pupils

- an active knowledge base
- strategies of application
- a capacity to deal with authentic, 'real world' problems
- a positive 'can-do' attitude.

An active knowledge base requires that pupils see how ideas and concepts in one domain can interact with those in another domain. This can be achieved through pupils' active participation in concept mapping exercises, brainstorming and compare and contrast exercises. Prawat shows how essential it is for pupils to be articulate about their knowledge, to be aware of what they know. Articulation is most successfully achieved through debating, arguing and through pupils acting as teachers. These activities require pupils to organise what they know in their own minds.

It requires from teachers the capacity to set clear objectives for these activities, to be able to manage group discussions and debates and to prepare pupils for such activities. The principles of managing learning through such methods have recently been set out by Fox (1995).

Teaching knowledge application strategies involves pupils' learning deliberate intellectual processes used to guide work towards a goal.

Essentially, strategies are ways of managing the intellect. Prawat (1989) has shown that pupils are often expected to discover or 'catch' these high level processes indirectly through working on problems. Such an approach has not been successful and Prawat's review shows that strategies are best taught using direct instructional techniques. Essentially this involves the teacher explaining the function of strategies, modelling how to use them and then providing pupils with a great deal of practice with feedback. Kyriacou (1995) has described in detail the research findings on direct instruction and set out the teaching procedures known to be most effective.

An active knowledge base and the skilled application of strategic approaches to problem solving will position pupils well, but if their experience is limited to classroom problems their capacity to manage the mess of real problems will be severely limited. At the same time there are real constraints on how far a classroom can accommodate real world problems. Clearly, time-tables have to be respected and the school has to operate like a school and not like, for example, a factory or a newspaper office. Extensive work has been done on designing work for classrooms which carries at least some of the features of workaday problems (Brown *et al.*, 1989); Newman, Griffin and Cole, 1989).

Finally, and permeating all the above, all the knowledge based teaching will come to nothing if pupils are defeated when faced with a challenge. Pupils need to learn to work through anxiety states if they are to be effective learners. Again, a strategic approach is necessary, this time focusing on how to manage the emotions. Defeatism and dependency are learned reactions to situations. Other reactions can also be learned if carefully taught. In this instance, individual instruction and personal counselling are the appropriate teaching methods. Relevant techniques have been described by Block (1993), Graham and Harris (1993) and Nolen (1995).

Learning teaching

In this chapter I have described basic learning processes in terms of schema theory. I have shown that there are many different learning processes and that each learner has a repertoire of learning skills at their disposal. Before generating implications for teaching from this model, I discussed the culture of the classroom, a culture which sets serious constraints on what can be achieved. In recognition of the constructive power of learners and the constraining culture of classrooms I examined how teachers might promote pupils' capacity for knowledge application through the deployment of a wide range of teaching skills, each appropriate to a particular learning outcome. It has to be recognised, however, that none of this is easy to effect in classrooms, and teachers must cast themselves as learners and devote themselves to professional development if they are to be successful in this endeavour.

I have recently argued (Desforges, 1995) that teachers learn little from experience in classrooms that benefits pupils. Evidence shows that while teachers become more efficient in running off their routine behaviour, they do not appear to promote pupils' learning and understanding any better than novice teachers. Teachers close down on rather than open up to professional restructuring under the conditions of normal classroom culture.

Duffy (1993) has studied teachers' professional development in strategy instruction showing that it takes successful teachers several years to accomplish. The teachers initially exhibited a great deal of resistance to the idea of strategy instruction, many denying that there was a problem.

The teachers then passed through several phases of development before they reaped the benefits in enhanced pupil learning processes. Seashore-Lewis (1993) has shown that individual teachers are unlikely to make progress on their own. Professional learning requires a whole-school commitment from a school to sustain the policies, practises and values necessary to a 'learning organisation'.

Summary

I have suggested that both pupils and teachers have a capacity for constructive learning but that classroom culture is oriented towards production line work which inhibits high quality learning for teachers and pupils alike. Classroom work systems are driven by assessment systems.

Using teaching for knowledge-application as a case study, I have shown that a wide range of task specific teaching skills must be deployed if high level pupil learning outcomes are to be realised.

Finally, I argued that teachers as well as pupils must learn to learn in classrooms.

References

Ausubel, D.P. and Robinson, R.G. (1969) School Learning: An introduction to educational psychology (New York: Holt, Rinehart and Winston).
Bain, A. (1879) Education as a Science (London: Kegan Paul).
Bennett, S.N. and Desforges, C. (1984) The Quality of Pupil Learning Experiences (London: Lawrence Erlbaum).
Block, C.C. (1993) Strategy instruction in a literature based reading programme. The Elementary School Journal, 9(2), 139–52.
Bloom, B.S. (1976) Human Characteristics and School Learning (New York: McGraw Hill).
Broadbent, D.E. (1975) Cognitive psychology and education. British Journal of Educational Psychology, 45, 162–76.
Brown, G. (1995) What is involved in learning? In Desforges C. (Ed.) An Introduction to Teaching (Oxford: Blackwell) pp. 11–33.

Brown, S., Collins, J.A. and Duguid, P. (1989) Situated cognition and the culture of learning. Educational Researcher, 18(1), 32–42.

Clark, C.M. and Peterson, P.L. (1986) Teachers' thought processes. In Wittrock, M. (Ed.) Handbook of Research on Teaching (New York: Macmillan).

Cockcroft, W.H. (1982) Mathematics Counts (London: HMSO).

Davis, R.B. and McKnight, C. (1976) Conceptual, heuristic and s-algorithmic approaches in mathematics teaching. Journal of Children's Mathematical Behaviour, 1, 271–86.

Desforges, C. (1985) Training for the management of learning in the primary school. In Francis, H. (Ed.) Learning to Teach (Lewes: Falmer Press).

Desforges, C (1992) Assessment and Learning. Forum, 34(3), 368–9.

Desforges, C. (1995) How does experience affect theoretical knowledge for teaching. Learning and Instruction, 5, 385–400.

Desforges, C. and Bristow, S. (1995) Reading to learn in mathematics in the primary age range. In Ernest, P. (Ed.) Mathematics Education and Philosophy: On International Perspectives (Vol. 2). (London: Falmer Press).

Desforges, C. and Cockburn, A. (1987) Understanding the Mathematics Teacher (Basingstoke: Falmer Press).

Doyle, W. (1983) Academic Work. Review of Educational Research, 53, 159–200.

Doyle, W. (1986) Classroom organisation and management. In Wittrock, M. (Ed.) Handbook of Research on Teaching (New York: Macmillan).

Duffy, G.G. (1993) Teachers' progress toward becoming expert strategy teachers. The Elementary School Journal, 94(2), 109–20.

Edwards, D. and Mercer, N. (1987) Common Knowledge (London: Methuen).

Eisner, E. (1983) Can educational research inform educational practice? Paper presented to the annual meeting of AERA, Montreal.

Fox, R. (1995) Teaching through discussion. In Desforges, C. (Ed.) An Introduction to Teaching (Oxford: Blackwell) pp. 132–49.

Gagné, R.M. (1965) The Conditions of Learning (New York: Holt, Rinehart and Winston).

Glaser, R., Pellegrino, J.W., and Lesgold, A.M. (1977) Some directions for a cognitive psychology of instruction. In Lesgold, A.M. Pellegrino, J.W., Fokkema, S.D. and Glaser, R. (Eds.) Cognitive Psychology and Instruction (New York: Plenum).

Graham, S. and Harris, K.R. (1993) Self-regulated strategy development: Helping students with learning problems develop as writers. The Elementary School Journal, 94(2), 169–82.

Jackson, P. (1968) Life in Classrooms (New York: Holt).

Jorgensen, G.W. (1977) Relationship of classroom behaviour to the accuracy of the match between material difficulty and student ability. Journal of Educational Psychology, 69(1), 24–32.

Kyriacou, C. (1995) Direct teaching. In Desforges, C. (Ed.) An Introduction to Teaching (Oxford: Blackwell) pp. 115–31.

Mackay, R. (1978) How teachers know: a case of epistemological conflict. Sociology in Education, 51, 177–87.

Marshall, H.H. (1988) Work on learning: implications of classroom metaphors. Educational Researcher, 17(9), 9–16.

Morine-Dershimer, C. (1983) Instructional strategy and the creation of classroom status. American Educational Research Journal, 20, 645–61.

Newman, D., Griffin, P. and Cole, M. (1989) The Construction Zone: Working for Cognitive Change in School (New York: Cambridge University Press).

Nolen, S.B. (1995) Teaching for autonomous learning. In Desforges, C. (Ed.) An Introduction to Teaching (Oxford: Blackwell) pp. 197–215.
Norman, D.A. (1977) Notes towards a complex theory of learning. In Lesgold A.M. Pellegrino, J.W., Fokkema, S.D. and Glaser, R.. (Eds.) Cognitive Psychology and Instruction (New York: Plenum).
Nunes, T., Schliemann, A.D. and Carraher, D.W. (1993) Street Mathematics and School Mathematics (Cambridge: Cambridge University Press).
Prawat, R.S. (1989) Promoting access to knowledge, strategy and disposition in students: A research synthesis. Review of Educational Research, 59(1), 1–41.
Resnick, L.B. (1987) Learning in school and out. Educational Researcher, 16(9), 13–20.
Rogers, C.R. (1961) On Becoming a Person (Boston: Houghton Mifflin).
Säljö, R. and Wyndhamn, J. (1990) Problem solving, academic performance and situated reasoning: a study of joint cognitive activity in the formal setting. British Journal of Educational Psychology, 60(3), 245–54.
Savage, J. and Desforges, C. (1995) The role of informal assessment in teachers' practical action. Educational Studies, 21(3), 433–46.
Seashore-Lewis, K. (1993) The problem of improving knowledge dissemination and utilisation in large urban schools. Paper presented to the International Conference on Dissemination and Utilisation of Research Knowledge. Haifa.
Skinner, B.F. (1957) Verbal Behaviour (New York: Appleton Century Crofts).
Skinner, B.F. (1968) The Technology of Teaching (Englewood Cliffs, N.J.: Prentice Hall).
Thorndike, E.L. (1913) Educational Psychology (New York: Columbia University Press).
Thorndike, E.L. (1931) Human Learning (New York: Century).
Wertheimer, M. (1945) Productive Thinking (New York: Harper).
Yinger, R.J. (1980) A study of teacher planning. Elementary School Journal, 80, 107–27.

Chapter 2
New technologies and learning

ROGER HARTLEY

Although computer based technologies have been used in education for over 30 years, it is only relatively recently that developments in multimedia, interface design and broadband wide-area networking have become affordable and made accessible to non-technical users. These developments, allied to the increasing diversity and demands of education, have prompted greater interest in more open and flexible modes of learning, and have attracted substantial investment at national levels in information technology (IT) and computer assisted learning (CAL). The expectations are not only that the delivery and management of curriculum materials by computer will be more cost effective but that the quality of learning will be improved.

CAL and the authoring of its materials have required the specialised skills of educational and computer technologists. The instructional designs have been strongly influenced by psychologists, notably Skinner with his emphasis on behavioural analysis and reinforcement mechanisms for synthesizing more complex behaviours and, in contrast, Papert who advocated the development of software tools or 'languages' with which learners could express and develop their own knowledge and creative ideas in a principled fashion. However, more recently, the new technologies have enabled stronger commercial interests from the media and publishing to become involved in IT/CAL exploitation with graphically based authoring tools allowing a wider range of participants – including teachers – to engage in the production of CAL materials which can also be developed and delivered worldwide via the Internet.

The rapid development of IT is having a major impact on the workplace, the home and the public services and, in consequence, is placing changing demands on educational curricula and requirements. IT is now seen as an authentic component of the curriculum and also as a tool for improving learning skills. However, assimilating these methods into classroom practices requires a wider range of skills from teachers, and the pace of technological developments is such that education is finding it difficult to determine how they should best be exploited. Recent national initiatives – such as the Teaching and Learning Technology Programme (TLTP) in higher education – have provided a useful impetus, but there are still few evaluation studies available to guide practice. Applications of technology in education are becoming more numerous but they tend to be disparate, pragmatically orientated, and largely descriptive in the accounts they present. In contrast to earlier times when the emphasis was on the exploitation of psychological views of learning, rapid technological developments, the software tools and materials they place in the hands of practising teachers are now creating a rich and wide ranging source of problems and issues which research needs to address. This chapter will try to show how psychology can provide useful frameworks to guide such research and practice.

Learning environments

One of the major influences on learning technologies has been the views of behaviourist psychologists, notably B.F. Skinner. He prescribed learning as stable behavioural changes brought about by the environment through the consequences which follow the actions performed. Hence instruction is a process of designing and implementing a program able to reinforce appropriate responses, through knowledge of results or other tokens, so that the environmental stimulus–response bond is secured. Responses are tuned, shaped and synthesised into more complex behaviours through the management of reinforcement schedules, and it was the practical difficulty of providing and managing such reinforcement in the classroom which led Skinner to propose the use of teaching machines (Skinner, 1954). Since Skinner emphasised the positive reinforcement of 'correct' responses, his instructional schemes were small-step to ensure success and administered linearly through simple mechanical devices or by self-managed programmed books.

Two major difficulties quickly became apparent. Experiments, many administered by computer, showed the informational as well as the reinforcing role of feedback (Anderson, Kulhavy and Andre, 1971). Students learn from their mistakes and a prime purpose of feedback is to locate these errors and provide material to allow them to be corrected. Ideally this requires the teaching machine to be capable of error diagnosis, to retain information about the student (a student model), and apply this knowledge in a range of teaching strategies and tactics which are able to deal with particular types of errors. Instruction has to be adaptive.

A second difficulty is the design of the responsive environment, i.e. providing a reactive representation of the learning domain. The required learned performances can be prescribed as behavioural objectives and analysed into their related task components (Gagné, 1985), but in the Skinnerian model the learning environment becomes funnelled into a linear sequence of tasks to which responses are made and reinforcement given. Student initiatives to question, investigate and suggest have little place in such a pre-stored task curriculum delivered by machine. However, since educational objectives are likely to cover not only the development of concepts and procedures but applications in problem solving (Gagné, Briggs and Wagner, 1992), it is desirable – even necessary – to allow learners to take such initiatives.

During the 1970s the advent of computers in education resulted in several worthwhile and adaptive programs being produced using a curriculum of pre-stored tasks. Particularly noteworthy was the mathematics program of Patrick Suppés at Stanford University where decision rules, based on individual performance data, guided students through strands of the curriculum tasks set at various levels of difficulty. Other developments saw the techniques and formalisms of artificial intelligence (AI) being employed to include knowledge of the subject-domain, student models of performance and understanding, and instructional strategies. Rather than using pre-stored materials, such programs (e.g. the algebra package of Sleeman and Smith, 1981) were able to generate tasks and feedback to suit the instructional aims and the requirements of the student model. However, although effective, these programs required a great deal of technical expertise to design, were time-consuming and expensive to implement, and were restricted to specific and well structured curriculum contexts.

It is during the last decade that the developments of technology in graphical user interfaces (GUI), multimedia and wide-area networking have given a new impetus to the design of learning environments able to take greater account of cognitive psychology and the collaborative nature of classroom learning. These developments go some way towards overcoming the limitations and difficulties outlined previously, but raise their own particular research issues.

A first advantage of GUIs is that students, through mouse-pointing and clicking of icons, labelled buttons and menus, interact directly with the screen display so that it becomes their workdesk. Further, by showing a trace of the student's working the display can stimulate reflection, self-explanation and, since it is open to public view, discussion with other students and the teacher. For example, ALGEBRALAND (Foss, 1987) enables the user to solve algebraic equations by indicating which operators to apply and with a trace of the working shown in schematic form. Backtracking is permitted so that mistakes can be corrected and more efficient solutions sought.

A further advantage is that interfaces can be designed in which students construct schematic representations of the task and, by running these representations as animations or simulation programs, check their understanding. The aim is to design such interfaces so that they release the knowledge of the student and encourage them to develop appropriate mental models which stimulate further reasoning and investigations. The computer thus becomes a learning environment in which the designer's effort is placed not in expensively building 'intelligence' into the instructional system but in providing an interface that releases the intelligence of the user. Nathan, Kintsch and Young (1990) developed such a system, ANIMATE, for solving word algebra problems; and Akpinar and Hartley (1996) have implemented and evaluated a FRACTIONLAB for use with primary schoolchildren.

This latter application placed a variety of 'instruments' – shown visually as icons on the display screen – which children could operate via the mouse to solve or devise problems involving fractions. There was a segmenter which allowed a whole object to be partitioned, under pupil control, and a segment placed in a (labelled) fraction box. Its contents could be copied, portions stuck together and measured (see Figure 2.1). Students had to supply inputs to these operators and regulate their animated procedures – or an output would not be given – so the learning was interactive. Other operators were available for assisting addition and subtraction of fractions and a Lesson Office allowed the teacher to place a curriculum of tasks, with feedback comments, within the program which also kept records of performances. The evaluation study showed substantial gains with children who had learning difficulties with fractions, and indicated that the visual operations of FRACTIONLAB were useful for students to call to mind when solving problems away from the computer.

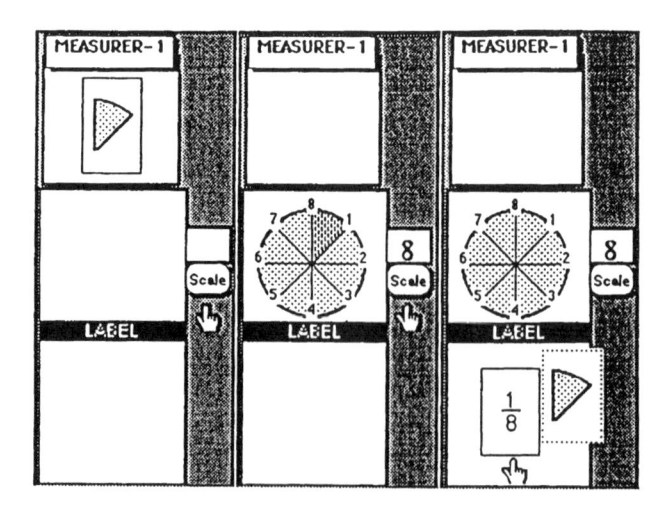

Figure 2.1. The process of measuring

Such responsive learning environments can give more opportunities for students to be investigatory in their methods of working and expand learning objectives from an understanding of concepts to tasks which require reasoning, explanations and problem solving. However, the design principles of interactive interfaces and their effects on various types of learning and problem solving are not well understood. A summary of the relation between cognitive science and human computer interaction (HCI) research is provided by Pollitzer (1996), and Reiman, Young and Howes, (1996), in discussing exploratory learning, note that much of the control of learners' attention and the release of knowledge are dependent on cues supplied by the interface. In the FRACTIONLAB example noted previously, this design principle was followed and operators which were not relevant to particular tasks were faded or not presented to the students. Keeping track of what has been tried and used (as in ALGEBRALAND) is also important.

A more elaborate cognitive model has been suggested by Hutchins, Holland and Norman, (1986). They consider that the interface acts as a type of language by which users make known their intentions to the system, and they define two properties of such languages – semantic directness and articulatory directness. The former is concerned with what is in the user's mind, i.e. intentions or goals, and the capabilities of the language to express these intentions. Articulatory directness applies to the physical form of the expression in relation to that meaning. In brief, the interface should provide a direct link between the task the user has in mind and ways it will be expressed and achieved through the interface. The recommendation is for a 'direct engagement' with the user directly manipulating the objects or icons of interest which are the interactive components of the interface. More experiments are required to test the conditions of learning for which direct engagement is beneficial. Certainly the FRACTIONLAB study (Akpinar and Hartley, 1996) reported significant gains, but Benbasat and Todd (1993), and Eberts and Bittianda (1993), who made comparisons between direct iconic engagement and more indirect command based instructions, are more cautious in their conclusions.

The advent of multimedia, i.e. placing visuals, video, graphics, audio and text under the interactive control of users, has greatly enhanced the illustrative capabilities and educational potential of CBL programs. The retentive properties of visual memory are well documented (Shepard, 1967; Standing, Conezio and Haber, 1970; Mandler and Parker, 1976), and graphics animations and videos can be used as semantic 'anchors' to assist mental organisation. The evaluation study of FRACTIONLAB showed the imaging value of the visual icons and operators when students were solving problems in a later post-test away from the computer. Erdelyi *et al.* (1976) have also shown the hypermnesia properties of imagery, where, in contrast to memory for text, the recall of visual images actually increased on successive post-tests, even though the images were not further displayed.

However, much visual material in current multimedia tutorial programs is illustrative and relatively passive in its demands on the user. Indeed, Botterill and Lock (1993) found that CBL programs on topics in meteorology and weather that were visually based fared less well on post-test performances than more interactive versions based on text. Designing multimedia programs where the visual medium is used to stimulate and organise thinking, and not merely act as a passive illustrative support is a continual challenge. Lee (1996) makes a distinction between multimedia and multimodality where the latter refers to 'the interpretation and regeneration of information presented in different media'. Developing such systems requires interlinking these different representations within a responsive user-system interface design.

Virtual reality (VR) is clearly an example where the user actively works and reasons in a three-dimensional visual world, though the term 'reality' often has to be generously interpreted (Wann and Mon-Williams, 1996). In educational programs where visual metaphors are being exploited, the aim is to make the semantics of the three-dimensional axes and their scales meaningful so that the students' interpretations lead to an adequate understanding of the domain. For example, at Leeds University, the Computer Based Learning Unit, in collaboration with the

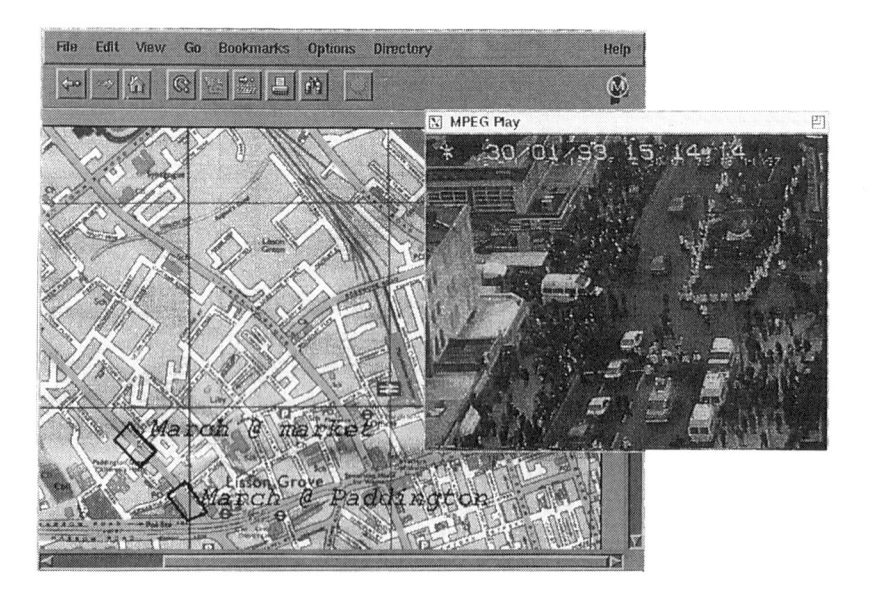

Figure 2.2. The simulation scenario from CACTUS

School of Chemistry, is developing such a three-dimensional system to aid senior students' understanding of reaction kinetics. Specifically the program provides a three-dimensional model of a potential energy surface of a reaction (eg. oxygen–carbon monosulphide) and the display provides a topology of this reaction, contoured and coloured to show differing energy levels. An oxygen atom can be placed on this energy surface with the resulting path indicating if the reaction succeeds and showing the spin/vibration energy properties of the resulting carbon monoxide molecule. Placing the atom at different points on the energy surface and noting the differing consequences provides students with a strong visual/spatial metaphor, but this representation and understanding has to be related to the more formal chemistry of reaction kinetics. It might well be that the use of such metaphors have very different benefits depending on the spatial reasoning ability of students: this is currently under investigation.

Networking can enable learning environments to accommodate several users working concurrently and collaboratively, with the tutor able to monitor this working and provide on-line guidance where necessary. This is often a requirement in the training of complex planning and decision-making skills, for example in the management of large demonstrations and the maintenance of public order. This is a complex task and, if police tactics are maladroit or if incidents are not anticipated and matters get out of hand, the results are not only expensive but damaging to public confidence.

At Leeds, in collaboration with the Metropolitan Police Service, a computer based learning environment, named CACTUS, was designed. It uses a digitised map of Central London displayed on a computer screen to which video sequences can be linked to show typical marches and police tactics in that locality (see Figure 2.2).

The crowd is conceived as a collection of groups of people, each represented by a common icon, that can 'sense' the police presence and tactics, buildings of interest, and the behaviour of surrounding groups. These data probabilistically determine the behaviour to be adopted by a group, and are arranged as a network so that their actions can escalate and subside in a realistic manner. (Typically, these behaviour decisions are made by each group 3–4 times per minute.) The crowd units proceed in real time, tending to follow the groups in front: however, since various types of groups (such as 'activists' or 'hostiles') can form part of the scenario, the crowd may cause a disturbance, or the march may be hijacked, and attempt to breakaway from the original route. The trainees give their instructions (shown on the communications log) to the police units to direct the management and control of the demonstration, and a referee program, after considering the resources involved, decides if these actions are adequate and what are the resulting outcomes. Hence the simulation proceeds in real time, and the figure above (though not shown in colour as it is on the computer screen) displays a typical snapshot of the trainer's screen.

The information given to the trainees can be controlled, e.g. whether the positions and state of the crowd groups are shown as well as the police units and their deployment, and the crowd icons can change colour to indicate their behaviour. Also, to provide further contingency training, the trainer can introduce other groups or reports of incidents as the simulation proceeds. To aid debriefing the simulation is time-line managed so that a scenario can be run in fast time and/or stopped (discussed) and returned to an earlier time point and re-run. These facilities are under the control of the trainer.

In summary, the new technologies are enabling the design of learning environments, capable of stimulating investigatory methods of learning, which are far more ambitious and responsive than the learning programs Skinner had in mind. Yet their designs, if they are to take advantage of these facilities, raise interesting problems which interlink task prescriptions with the cognitive operations being undertaken by users – a research area that Payne (1996) describes as 'cognitive technology'.

Tools for exploratory learning

A second major influence on developments in CBL is the work of Seymour Papert (1980, 1993). In contrast to Skinner, he considered the computer should be used as 'a children's machine' stimulating and encouraging their 'powerful ideas'. Hence the computer was to be a learning rather than a teaching machine, and an agent of change rather than merely supporting the conventional classroom curriculum.

From his background as a developmental psychologist, Papert argued that learning is a constructive process based on experience. What is required therefore is a means (a 'language') for representing and structuring knowledge so that, with computer assistance, students will be stimulated to reflect, experiment with, and develop their experience in a principled fashion. Papert illustrated his views in a practical way by developing a computer language, LOGO, that can take a variety of forms depending on the context in which it is placed – for example in mathematics, English or technology. LOGO allows students to tell or teach the computer how to undertake particular tasks, e.g. draw geometric shapes using command sequences. Hence pupils 'transfer' their own actions as commands to the computer (via the cursor on the display screen or a robotic drawing 'turtle') which the machine tries to execute, delivering feedback through its actions and visual displays which result.

To provide a more abstract framework for developing this procedural knowledge, LOGO uses a computational metaphor and allows command sets to be stored as procedures. Patterns of commands can be demarcated, variables introduced, procedures incorporated as subprocedures within larger programs that can also be recursive. The use of LOGO, therefore, is to be creative and motivating with the students developing their own procedure sets and curriculum of tasks. The resulting displays can stimulate further experimentation and, by diagnosing faults and program 'bugs', the student learns to reason and solve problems. Note that the LOGO system has no knowledge of the curriculum domain (e.g. geometry), it simply responds to the instructions provided by the students, but makes their thinking and actions transparent through the outputs on the display screen and error messages which are given if the procedures are incomplete or inconsistent.

Thus, in contrast to the Skinnerian approach, students develop their own learning environments ('microworlds') through this process of exploration and diagnosis. The curriculum is therefore determined, in Papert's scheme, by the problems and tasks which students set themselves and which develop from procedural knowledge that relates to their experience. Several LOGO-like learning environments have been designed, including construction/design contexts where LEGO kits can be used to build devices (e.g. traffic lights or vehicles) linked to the computer with the student using LOGO procedures to develop and manage their behaviour.

But how should such 'languages' be designed and what are their effects on learning? What are the limitations of the computational metaphor and a system that can only provide feedback via command level displays and syntactic comments on procedures? LOGO has been used widely, particularly in primary education, but the results of several evaluation studies have been equivocal and indeed have led to much discussion on the form such evaluation studies should take. On the one hand should claims about cognitive advancement be tested through carefully controlled experimental studies (Becker, 1987) or, on the other hand, should the creative work of LOGO be appraised through 'work portfolios' and the judgements of experienced educators who observe and comment on their classroom activities (Papert, 1987)?

Papert conceived learning as an individualised process of knowledge construction with students using a LOGO machine to build their own library of procedures stimulated by the curriculum of problem tasks they created and developed. However, in practice, many teachers used LOGO with small groups of children encouraging discussion about their problems and interactions with the computer. There is strong evidence (e.g. Reif 1987; vanLehn, Bull and Kowalski, 1990) that students who self-explain when learning or problem solving perform better in subsequent tests. These benefits also occur from collaborative discussion and when able and less able students work together in experimental or problem solving tasks, both the able and the less-able improve (Brna, 1989). An advantage of LOGO is that it makes the consequences of actions public through the screen displays, which encourage learners in small groups to challenge, question and explain.

Much of learning, for example in science, requires students not only to refine and change their beliefs but to develop new conceptualisations, i.e. to re-represent their knowledge at a more abstract level. Many informal beliefs seem to suit everyday experience, e.g. that heavier objects fall faster than lighter objects, that heavier objects are harder to get moving and stop because of their greater weight pressing on the surface causing greater friction, and that friction is a 'grippiness' between surfaces rather than a force opposing motion. But a way forward is to challenge these notions by developing a 'language' through which students could express and develop qualitative models representing these beliefs and whose output could then be tested against laboratory experiments or Newtonian-based simulations programs. The resulting discussions (with amendments to the models) should assist the required conceptual change.

Such a qualitative modelling system, VARILAB, was developed at Leeds. It enables learners to name objects (e.g. person or boat-motor), give them attributes (such as mass, weight, speed) and associated values (e.g. zero, low, medium, high). Changes to these object-states occur by a 'law of effect' shown by drawing and labelling a causal link (e.g. push) between the icons of the initiating agent (e.g. person) and receiving object (e.g. box). The nature of the change (e.g. increase-forward-speed) has to be stated and also the period when it is active (e.g. by a time interval or when/until a particular object-state is achieved). The system builds up the model in a schematic form on the display screen, and this can be run with the changes being shown as an animation, or as a time-based graph. Note that, like LOGO, the system has no knowledge of the domain; it merely reacts to and shows the consequences of the students' descriptions and instructions.

An evaluation study was carried out with ten pairs of schoolchildren working without the presence of the teacher for four sessions of one-and a-half-hours in four successive weeks (Hartley, 1996a). A Newtonian simulation programme (DM^3) was used in conjunction with VARILAB taking four scenarios:

- a person pushing a box horizontally on a friction surface
- a skater propelled on ice
- a speedboat where the force of the engine could be varied
- a parachutist falling under gravity against air resistance.

The post-test results showed significant improvements but the experiment was not entirely successful and some beliefs were resistant to change. This could occur when students adjusted the model empirically to produce the required output (shown by the simulation program) but did not discuss the causal reasons for these changes and their effects. However, in all cases where such justifications were made, conceptual change was the result. Other difficulties arose when beliefs drew evidence from a variety of contexts, and when reasoning of students was correct but incomplete, e.g. the heavier the object the greater the frictional force so the quicker it will be brought to rest. Students' satisfaction with this reasoning caused them to ignore or to bias their interpretations of speed–time graphs for different masses. Hence there has to be guided discussion, for example, to challenge student cause–effect explanations, to examine conditions and consequences, to pose what-if question and cross-context comparisons, and to assist students in developing more abstract conceptions.

Such discourse can be provided by the teacher, but VARILAB itself was extended and re-designed to be able to take a greater part in these discussions. Posner *et al.* (1982) noted that, for beliefs to be changed, students should have a dissatisfaction with their existing conceptions and be presented with others that are intelligible and plausible in terms of their experience, and which add value to their understanding. Harman (1986) emphasised the ways in which we seek coherence in knowledge by resolving inconsistencies. Hence the redesigned VARILAB is able to present such challenges and critique students' explanations. The system has a view of a physical 'world' of entities and their attributes which can be given values, and where state change effects are brought about by causal agents. Students are able to express their descriptions and explanations using statements that cover classifications, comparisons and contrasts, conditions and consequences, and causes and their effects.

The system has no direct knowledge of Newtonian physics but is able to apply common sense reasoning through, for example, a law of 'effect' – any state change should have an associated causal agent, and more of the agent produces a greater effect and vice versa. The system also has notions of equilibrium and can make inferences about opposing agents from their effects. In this way the system can interpret and reason about student explanations. Additionally, it can examine these explanations for consistency and completeness, noting cause–effect/condition–consequences that are incomplete, challenging inconsistencies and providing suggestions if an impasse is reached. The system is also able to recognise more abstract concepts that do not need to reference a specific entity, and can rewrite explanatory and descriptive statements in these more general terms. In these ways an agreed knowledge base is constructed collaboratively with the student and also expressed as a qualitative model that can be run dynamically. An interface to manage these interactions has been implemented and the system is currently being evaluated.

In summary, providing tools for learning that seek to improve reasoning and problem solving or bring about conceptual change have to allow for a process of knowledge negotiation. How such discourse, whether provided by the system and/or a teacher, can be engineered effectively raises interesting research questions of user-system language design, and the strategies and tactics of argumentation and instructional dialogue.

The teaching–learning community

Until relatively recently much of the research and major developments in CBL were undertaken by specialist units or teams that included psychologists, computer specialists and educational technologists. As noted in previous sections, their work was largely stimulated by psychological views of learning and specialised formalisms and methodologies were developed to allow the materials to be managed interactively by computing systems. These required the use of languages for authoring and associated software tools for which a considerable commitment of time was required to become expert. Hence most practising teachers could only be indirect participants in the instructional designs and developments and, since there was a relative lack of computing equipment for instruction and technical support in schools, CBL failed to make a significant impact on classroom practices, even though national funding was available in the 1980s through the Schools' Microelectronics Education Programme (MEP). Further, few evaluation studies tackled the problems of assimilating these innovations within the curriculum, and in the teaching–learning and assessment procedures of institutions.

During the 1990s, technological developments in multimedia, networking and user-system interface designs have increased the range of educational and administrative applications of computers and made them easier to use by non-specialists. The price of these applications and computing systems is now within the workaday budgets of schools; IT is represented across the curriculum and, in higher education, the major TLTP funded at national level has established well over 100 collaborative projects and developed materials that are being used in teaching, learning and assessment on a regular basis. Multimedia developments have attracted the interest of media specialists with their skills in developing visual materials, publishers with the possibility of electronic distribution of information, and the computing and computing services industry with the prospect of rapidly increasing markets of which education is an increasingly important sector. The difficulty is that education is being faced with these technological developments which it needs to assimilate and exploit, but the speed of change makes their digestion problematic. Hence the research emphasis is shifting from an exploration of psychological views of learning and cognition to issues arising from the application of the technology in educational practice.

The widening of the commercial interest has resulted in software tools that are useful not only in their own domain but also in educational programmes. For example, MATHCAD is capable of solving equations, algebraic and differential, from a wide range of applications. The user has control of many facilities including data visualisation and specialist function sets to which instructional on-line 'books' can be attached. The facilities of the spreadsheet Excel are continually being extended, and it can serve as a base for practical exercises in modelling and elementary statistics that can bring more realism and investigatory methods into learning.

CD-ROM technology has also allowed the compilation of high quality educational material. In physics, for example, ALBERT provides a resource of over 600 simulation experiments which teachers can customise for their own purposes. Gamelike formats – the so-called entertainment programs – should not be discounted, and the Magic Bus geology program, for example, is innovative in its displays and uses authentic educational material that is readily understood and will hold interest. Also, on CD-ROM are electronic interactive atlases that allow users facilities to customise the maps to which a wealth of statistical data is attached. Encyclopaedias, such as those in human or mammalian biology, bring together images, texts, animations and video clips that can be accessed and navigated through key work searches, indexes, thematic icons, and schematic maps.

These high quality resources are being made available at competitive prices and are a rich base for school and home learning. But what are effective models of their use? How do they influence the curriculum and the teaching methods? The Skinner and Papert models firmly placed teachers in the background, not wanting their interference in the user–computer interactions. The resources noted above are designed with no pedagogical theory in mind, indeed they are judged to suit a variety of instructional approaches. Also note that in the Skinner–Papert view the computer was the student's interactive learning desk, whereas the CD-ROM is a type of library resource only available when the student is at the computer, and much of the conventional learning is likely to be paper-based at the student's class-desk or study-room. How are the computer materials to be inter-related to make an educational impact – particularly if access time is limited?

The Internet

Perhaps the technological development arousing most interest is the Internet, specifically the World Wide Web (WWW) which allows materials stored at various locations on server computers to be interlinked so that users can gain access to a large and increasing virtual library. Currently well over a million computing systems world wide form the Internet and, since links can be made between the materials, they hold an extensive network of documents which the user can navigate without needing to know the location of the server computers. Various 'search engines' are available to locate required information which includes institutional and public service data, educational courses, research papers, databases, software products, electronic newspapers, and contributions from numerous special interest groups.

The educational value arises from the types of multimedia documents that can be linked and delivered via the Web, the software tools which allow teachers with relatively little training to become authors of Web documents, and the ways the Web permits collaborative working between teacher-authors and student-users.

The materials can incorporate and link audio, text, still pictures, animations, video sequences and graphics forming a network of document 'nodes'. The links are activated by clicking 'hot words' in the documents, or by initiating keyword searches, or by stating a document address (if known). Bookmarking and backtracking are also provided by the system. Documents can link to simulations (which may reside on another server-computer) and on-line workbooks can thus be developed for students. A further interesting feature is that user-students can add their own comments as annotations to documents, and teacher-authors may canvas opinions or understanding of the materials by incorporating multiple choice questions.

Web documents are 'marked up' using special characters so that their presentation on the screen and active links to other documents can be managed by the computer. These mark-up conventions form a 'language' (HTML). Automatic converters are available to assist the conversion of wordprocessed documents into HTML, so the preparation of elementary WWW documents does not necessarily demand a high level of technical skill. (The CBL Unit at Leeds University developed such a converter, principally for use in Science and Technology: during the first nine months of its release on WWW there were more than 5000 users of the system.) These tools allow teaching staff at different institutions to cooperate in producing a corpus of teaching materials. For example, the Leeds converter was used by a consortium of 24 universities in the USA to produce an on-line undergraduate Computer Science course made available on the Web.

It has to be noted, however, that hypermedia systems have limitations. They usually form an information resource rather than being focused on specific learning objectives, and are restricted in the ways they can respond to the needs of users. Indeed all navigational decisions are under student control, and learners have to decide how to utilise the system to meet differing requirements of browsing, summarising, information gathering and learning. In particular, maintaining a structural sense of the domain and not becoming lost in hyperspace is a well-known problem, though principles of design which take account of attention management, information loading and cognitive organisation have been suggested (e.g. Marshall and Hurley, 1996).

A further limitation is that the computer merely manages the hypermedia materials and does not have a more abstract semantic representation of the visual and textual materials being presented, or relational links. Hence the system cannot interpret, or search, or regenerate information in these different representational forms; nor can it manage user interactions with the hypermedia information sources beyond selection and display. In brief, the system is not multimodal in its knowledge management.

The issue of learner control and what directions and assistance should be given to the student in the management of learning has always been actively debated in CBL. A persuasive proponent has been Merrill (1987) following his experience in the 1970s with the TICCIT system. This showed the value of well-constructed TICCIT material, but also the need for support for a significant proportion of students who were not able to manage their learning effectively. Merrill and Reigeluth have continued this work by producing design principles (i.e. component display theory: Merrill, 1983) for types of content appropriate for particular objectives, such as concept development, procedural learning and the application of principles. They have shown how to incorporate cues and strategy frameworks in which the essence or epitome of topics are introduced then elaborated and synthesised (i.e. elaboration theory; Reigeluth, 1987). Their overall objective is to provide an instructional design framework for open and flexible learning systems which give students tactical support in decision making.

Collaborative learning

Marton (1975) and Entwistle (see his chapter in this book, pp. 106–28) have shown that students in open learning situations adopt different styles of working. Distinctions have been made between *surface* and *deep* learners: the former comprehend textual materials but tend to remain within the bounds of what is written, whereas deeper learning styles probe the author's purposes, self-question explanations and use the material as a basis for their own constructive thinking.

Stimulation towards these deeper methods is best directed by tasks superimposed on the resource materials, by activities that provide interpretive frameworks which are able to give increasing support (and constructive assessment) of student learning. Course outlines, lecture notes, multiple choice questions, related papers and references, can all be placed on-line. Students can also add their own annotations and comments (e.g. the PILS system in pharmacology at Leeds; Ravenscroft, Tait and Hughes, 1996) where evaluation questionnaires of 400 undergraduates rated these facilities as more useful learning aids than traditional lectures). Indeed many universities and colleges, in addition to the Open University, are now making course materials available on-line through distance learning schemes and the modularisation of curricula, and more flexible accreditation pathways are encouraging this trend. However, more adaptive support schemes are needed to guide student learning activities, and this has to be done in a collaborative fashion between the students themselves and with the teacher if it is not to place considerable burdens on tutors at a time when student numbers have increased and staff resources have relatively declined. But, how are such learning collaborations to be engineered and managed effectively, particularly when assessments are typically based on the work of the individual student?

Collaborative methods of working are commonplace in academic communities. There is interchange of information and data on common topics (indeed this was the original objective at CERN in developing the WWW), brainstorming on particular problems, or ensuring relevant viewpoints are covered, critiquing and discussion of papers, and partitioning of tasks to ease the workload. Such collaborations can be made available on-line and through ISDN connections and broadband networking, video conferencing, and the interchange of dynamic visual materials are becoming practical prospects for learning.

The aim then is to allow students to become active participants in this academic community. Bulletin boards and on-line conferencing systems can be useful and give some sense of association, but they are difficult (and time-consuming) to manage in a coherent fashion with student groups. More specialised software, such as Knowledge Tree (Brailsford and Davies, 1995) allows students to interact more directly with course material. For example, using Knowledge Tree, learners can ask questions on-line relating to their reading or the content of lectures. These queries are displayed in a data-forum to which tutor-experts reply. Other students can see these questions and add their own comments or further queries, thus developing argument 'threads'. The course tutor can inspect, prune and structure this material as a knowledge base which cannot be altered by student users. In this collaborative way the course can utilise student contributions and take account of their difficulties and viewpoints.

At Leeds, as part of our participation in the TLTP initiative, a program that simulates a seminar has been developed. Up to 10 students at any time can join an on-line group led by a tutor; its particular purpose being shown on a noticeboard panel on the computer display screen. (The system will accommodate many seminar groups simultaneously.) Students write material on-line following the topic of interest but other seminar members are able to read these documents, adding their annotations and comments, and linking them to particular phrases in the document, paragraph sections or to the document itself. In this way the material becomes a shared resource, shaped by students' perspectives and the regulatory comments of the tutor. Since the system works asynchronously, with seminar members contributing at different times convenient to them, and from different locations using the network, the facility is useful for providing learning support at a distance. It can be used in various collaborative ways, e.g. brainstorming and collecting ideas in solving larger problems, critiquing or reflecting on specific theories or papers which have been covered in a lecture course, debating particular issues, or co-operating in producing a group paper. Though lacking the interactive atmosphere of a live seminar, the slower pace of the on-line system and the open recording of material allows students to be more reflective in their contributions. Again these are stored in a database from which the tutor can produce a more definitive and shaped document (Hartley, 1996b).

Other software that is useful in assisting students to develop and coordinate their ideas in preparation for revision or essay-writing are 'concept-maps' that allow topics or sub-topics to be set out, on-line, as a network of nodes and connecting arcs which can be labelled, elaborated and classified through iconic or colouring schemes. Specialised schemas based, for example, on Toulmin's argument (Toulmin, 1958) structure can help students in assembling and organising material dealing with explanations and hypotheses. Other software being developed allows tutors to attach particular types of comments to word-processed essays which, if made open to other students, can invite their on-line contributions whilst retaining the original student's authorship.

Conclusion

In summary, developments in technology have allowed computer assisted instruction to extend views of learning (whether conceived as the shaping of behaviour or the development of knowledge schema) to a collaborative process of knowledge interchange and negotiation where these interactions stimulate reasoning, evaluation and reflection. The overall aim is to develop students' conceptualisations and skills, with the teacher assisting this process through the design of curriculum tasks and by guiding interactions, so that learners are not merely acquiring knowledge but developing and producing their own explanatory models and viewpoints. To an increasing extent the computer is able to be a participant in this process, allowing the teacher to cater for larger and more varied classes, even at a distance. This is achieved by better communication between user and system via a range of constrained 'languages', graphical interfaces and software tools, by the interactive control of multimedia, and by the use of local and wide-area networking.

The main argument is that these technological developments have enabled teachers, media specialists, information services and commercial interests to greatly expand the range of computer assisted learning and its applications in the classroom. This is not to discount the difficulties of insufficient equipment and resources, the lack of experience and training of teachers, and scepticism about the claims made for computer based methods. However, many of the CBL applications are pragmatic, based on conventional experience and do not bring innovation into the curriculum, or in the learning environments they produce. There are few evaluative studies to guide these developments or practices, which can lead to what John Self (1985) has called the 'institutionalisation of mediocrity'.

The aim of greater self-sufficiency in teaching and learning was anticipated by Dennis Child in his inaugural address which is reproduced in this volume (pp. xxi–xxxvi). It will be interesting to observe if the future bears out his predictions by ensuring that psychology makes a continuing significant contribution to research and developments in the new technologies of learning. The principal aim is to link theories to methodologies and practices in ways which are innovative, demonstrate utility and both inform and convince the teaching community.

References

Akpinar, Y. and Hartley, J.R. (1996) Designing interactive learning environments. Journal of Computer Assisted Learning, 12, 33–46.

Anderson, R.C., Kulhavy, R.W. and Andre, T. (1971) Feedback procedures in programmed instruction. Journal of Educational Psychology, 2, 148–56.

Becker, H.J. (1987) The importance of a methodology that maximises its applicability to research about LOGO. Educational Researcher, July; 11–17.

Benbasat, I. and Todd, P. (1993) An experimental investigation of interface design alternatives: icon v text and direct manipulation v menus. International Journal of Man-Machine Studies, 38, 403–28.

Botterill, J. and Lock, R. (1993) Do students learn more from pictures or from text? School Science Review, 74; 109–12.

Brailsford, T.J. and Davies, P.M.C. (1995) Collaborative learning on networks. University of Nottingham.

Brna, P. (1989) Programmed rockets: an analysis of students' strategies. British Journal of Educational Technology 20(1), 27–40.

Eberts, R.E. and Bittianda, K.P. (1993) Preferred mental models for direct manipulation and command based interfaces. International Journal of Man-Machine Studies, 38, 761–86.

Erdelyi, M.H., Finkelstein, S., Herrill, N., Miller, B. and Thomas, J. (1976) Coding modality v input modality in hypermnesia. Cognition, 4, 311–19.

Foss, C.L. (1987) Learning from errors in ALGEBRALAND. Technical Report IRL-87-0003 Institute for Research on Learning, Palo Alto, CA.

Gagné, R.M. (1985) The Conditions of Learning, 4th edn. (New York: Holt Rinehart and Winston.)

Gagné, R.M., Briggs, L. and Wagner, W. (1992) Principles of Instructional Design, 4th edn. (New York: Harcourt Brace Jovanovich.)

Harman, G. (1986) Change in View: Principles of reasoning. (Boston, MA:MIT Press.)

Hartley, J.R. (1996a) Qualitative reasoning and conceptual change: Computer based support in understanding science. In Winkels, R. and Bredeweg, B. (Eds), Special Issue: Interactive Learning Environments. In press.

Hartley, J.R. (1996b) Managing models of collaborative learning. Computers and Education, 26, 163–70.
Hutchins, E.L., Holland, J.D. and Norman, D.A. (1986) Direct manipulation interfaces. In Norman, D.A. and Draper, S.W (Eds), User Centred System Design, 87–124. (London: Lawrence Erlbaum Associates).
Lee, J. (1996) Roles for intelligence in multimedia: Report on the IMMI-1 Workshop. The Knowledge Engineering Review, 11(1), 69–72.
Mandler, J.M. and Parker, R.E. (1976) Memory for descriptive and spatial information in complex pictures. Journal of Experimental Psychology, Human Learning and Memory, 2, 38–48.
Marshall, A.D. and Hurley, S. (1996) The design, development and evaluation of hypermedia courseware for the World Wide Web. In Furht, B. (Ed.), Multimedia tools and applications, 3(1), 5–32.
Marton, F. (1975) What does it take to learn? In Entwistle, N. and Hounsell, D. (Eds), How Students Learn, pp.125–38. (Lancaster:, UK: University of Lancaster).
Merrill, D.M. (1983) Component display theory. In Reigeluth, C.M. (Ed.), Instructional Design Theories and Models: An overview of their current status. (London: Lawrence Erlbaum Associates).
Merrill, D.M. (1987) A lesson based on the component display theory. In Reigeluth, C.M. (Ed.) Instructional Theories in Action, Chapter 7, pp. 201–44. (London: Lawrence Erlbaum Associates).
Nathan, J.N., Kintsch, W. and Young, E. (1990) A theory of algebra word problem comprehension and its implications for unintelligent tutoring systems. Technical Report 90-02. Institute of Cognitive Science, University of Colorado, Boulder, CO.
Papert, S. (1980) Mindstorms: Children, computers and powerful ideas. (Brighton: Harvester Press).
Papert, S. (1987) Computer criticism versus technocentric thinking. Educational Researcher, April 1987, 22–30.
Papert, S. (1993) The Children's Machine: Rethinking school in the age of the computer. (New York: Basic Books).
Payne, S.J. (1996) Psychology and cognitive technologies. Engineering Psychology, 3, 309–12.
Pollitzer, E. (1996) Editorial: The enduring partnership between cognitive science and HCI. International Journal of Human Computer Studies, 44, 731–42.
Posner, G.J., Strike, K.A., Henson, P.W. and Gertzog, W.A. (1982) Accommodation of a scientific conception: towards a theory of conceptual change. Science Education, 66, 211–27.
Ravenscroft, A., Tait, K. and Hughes, I.E. (1996) Evolving systems for integrated learning support. Technical Report: Computer Based Learning Unit, University of Leeds, UK., LS2 9JT.
Reif, F. (1987) Interpretation of scientific and mathematical concepts: cognitive issues and instructional implications. Cognitive Science; 11(4), 395–416.
Reigeluth, C.M. (1987) Lesson blueprints based on the elaboration theory of instruction. Instructional theories in action, Chapter 8, pp. 245–88. (London: Lawrence Erlbaum Associates).
Reiman, J., Young, R.M. and Howes, A. (1996) A dual space model of iteratively deepening exploratory learning. International Journal of Human-Computer Studies, 44, 743–75.
Self, J.A. (1985) Microcomputers in Education: A critical appraisal of educational software. Chapter 19, pp. 146–55. (Brighton: Harvester Press).

Shepard, R.N. (1967) Recognition memory for words, sentences and pictures. Journal of Verbal Learning and Verbal Behavior; 6, 156–63.

Skinner, B.F. (1954) The science of learning and the art of teaching. Harvard Educational Review, 24, 88–97.

Sleeman, D.H. and Smith, M.J. (1981) Modelling pupils' problem solving. Artificial Intelligence, 16, 171–87.

Standing, L., Conezio, K. and Haber, R.N. (1970) Perception and memory for pictures: single trial learning of 2560 visual stimuli. Psychonomic Science, 19; 73–4.

Toulmin, S. (1958) The Uses of Argument. (Cambridge: Cambridge University Press).

vanLehn, K., Bull, W. and Kowalski, B. (1990) Explanation based learning of correctness: towards a model of the self-explanation effect. Proceedings of the 12th Annual Conference of the Cognitive Science Society, Cambridge, MA. pp. 721–4.(London: Lawrence Erlbaum Associates).

Wann, J. and Mon-Williams, M. (1996) What does virtual reality really need? Human factors issues in the design of three-dimensional computer environments. International Journal of Human Computer Studies, 44, 829–47.

Chapter 3
Diversity in classrooms: effects on educational outcomes

PAM SAMMONS

Classrooms are diverse places, varying in their size and the age and composition of pupils as well as the aims, characteristics and experiences of teachers. Despite the introduction of a National Curriculum (NC) and National Assessment (NA), enormous variety in teaching approaches and pupil experiences is evident. Diversity in practice exists at both primary and secondary level between different classes in the same school as well as in different schools. Do these variations in conditions and practices, and therefore in pupils' experiences of education, matter?

In this chapter evidence concerning more and less effective classroom practices is discussed from the perspective of the growing fields of research into school and teacher effectiveness. A brief background to these fields is given, highlighting concepts such as 'value added' and addressing issues of accountability and the debate over league tables. The main body of the chapter provides a summary of research evidence concerning school processes which appear to be related to greater pupil progress, with a particular focus on effective classroom practices. The question of teaching styles is examined, particularly in relation to recent claims about the supposed benefits of formal 'whole class' approaches. Current models of educational effectiveness which examine school and classroom processes in relation to theories about pupil learning are also explored.

School and teacher effectiveness research

The last two decades have seen increasing academic interest in the study of school and teacher effectiveness in promoting pupils' educational outcomes. This interest arose originally in response to the pessimistic interpretation of findings by researchers in the US (Coleman *et al.*, 1966; Jencks *et al.*, 1972) concerning the potential influence of the school (and by implication, therefore, of teachers and their classroom practice) on attainment. On the basis of such analyses it was argued that whether a pupil attended a particular school (A rather than B) was unimportant. Attainment was seen as primarily determined by such factors as IQ, socio-economic status and race, with schools and teachers making little difference in comparison. It is important to note, however, that Coleman *et al.* and Jencks *et al.'s* research was not intended to imply that schooling and teaching has no influence on learning. One only has to look at literacy rates in countries where access to schooling is limited on the basis of income and gender to demonstrate the positive effects of access to education. Rather, their work concerned the extent to which individual schools, with all their variations in organisation, leadership and curriculum, differ in their diversity in classroom practices and have a differential impact on pupils' learning and development, and thus in terms of pupils' educational outcomes. The studies by Coleman *et al.* and Jencks *et al.* stimulated some researchers to study the nature of any specific school and teacher influences on pupils' educational outcomes in more depth. In other words, they addressed the question of whether variation in the processes of schooling, including what goes on in the classroom, makes some schools or teachers more effective than others.

Undeniably, the sociological and educational research traditions have consistently demonstrated the powerful impact of pupils' background characteristics in relation to both academic attainment (for example in basic skills or public examinations) and also social/affective outcomes such as attendance, behaviour and, to a lesser extent, in areas such as attitudes to school and self esteem. Indeed, school effectiveness studies (see for example the review of such research by Sammons, Thomas *et al.*, 1994) have made an important contribution to the study of educational disadvantage (e.g. Rutter *et al.*, 1979; Mortimore, Sammons and Ecob, 1988; Sammons, Stoll et al, 1988; Tizard *et al.*, 1988; Smith and Tomlinson, 1989). What studies of school and teacher effectiveness have sought to do is to develop ways to identify and separate the influence of the school or teacher from that related to pupils' background characteristics such as term of birth, fluency in English, gender, socio-economic disadvantage (low income and social class) and so on. This is necessary because schools vary enormously in the characteristics of their pupil intakes. It is thus not possible to investigate the possible impact of schooling unless proper account is taken of such differences in intake.

Value-added measures

In particular, the research field has shown that measures of the prior attainments of pupils (ideally measured at entry to school) are vital control measures to include in any study of school or teacher effectiveness and that a longitudinal approach focusing on progress over one or more years is necessary. In this way value-added measures on pupils' relative progress of being taught in a particular school or class can be identified in comparison with progress made by similar pupils in different schools or classes (Gray, Jesson and Slime, 1990; Goldstein *et al.*, 1993; Sammons, Nuttall and Cuttance, 1993; Mortimore, Sammons and Thomas, 1994). Attention is thus given to relative progress rather than absolute attainment levels. This is an important concept, highly relevant to current debates about league tables for the purposes of accountability. In some schools or classes pupils may have made better progress than predicted on the basis of their prior attainment and background characteristics (positive value added) but, because they started at a very low baseline (initial attainment), despite good progress, in absolute terms, they may still be attaining at levels below the national average. This has important implications for the current focus on the use of raw league tables of examination or National Assessment results as measures of school or teacher performance (a topic discussed in more detail below).

Although some school and teacher effectiveness studies have used IQ type ability measures as controls for intake differences between schools or classes, there are arguments against this practice, particularly in studies which do not adopt a longitudinal perspective but seek to measure ability at a time point close to the assessment of pupils' educational outcomes. There is much controversy about the concept of ability (for example, the idea of multiple intelligences may be much more relevant to the consideration of teaching and learning processes than the cruder concept of low or high ability pupils). In addition, the use of IQ type measures ignores the importance of the curriculum and teachers' focus on the development of pupils' skills in different areas. For example, a good measure of prior attainment in reading is a more relevant control measure for studies of pupils' progress in reading than one of IQ. Likewise, a mathematics measure is more relevant for mathematics progress. Also there are arguments about whether it is possible to measure IQ in a culture free way, and whether IQ is primarily an inherited and innate quality or one susceptible to change. For example, Mortimore, Sammons and Ecob (1988) study of junior schools used an assessment of visual/spatial ability (Ravens Progressive Matrices) as well as reading and mathematics measures. They found evidence of school effects on pupils' visual/spatial attainments over a one-year period (Mortimore, Sammons and Ecob, 1988b). In other words, pupils in some classes and schools made relatively more progress and others relatively less, indicating that visual/spatial skills can be enhanced by pupils' educational experience in some schools and classes and therefore should not be seen solely as an innate quality.

League tables and accountability

As discussed above, school and teacher effectiveness research has developed over a period of around 30 years into a major area of academic enquiry involving researchers in many different countries. In recent years it has assumed high profile in the UK owing to the increasing public concern about educational standards and the quality of education provided by schools and the changes following the introduction of an NC and NA. In particular, attempts to apply market forces to schools outlined in *Choice and diversity* (DfE, 1992) were intended to drive up standards via the combination of greater autonomy (under LMS), open enrolment and the publication of examination and NA results. This was explicitly intended to lead to the 'withering away' of so called 'poor' schools (those with low raw results) by parental choice. This 'league table' policy has proved highly controversial. It has been heavily criticised by school effectiveness researchers because of failure to take account of differences between schools in their intakes. As Nuttall (1990) argued,

> natural justice demands that schools are held accountable only for those things that they can influence (for good or ill) and not for all the pre-existing differences between their intakes. The investigation of differential school effectiveness, concentrating on the progress students make while at their school, therefore has a major role to play in the future. (p. 25)

The failure to put results into context has particular consequences for evaluations of the performance of inner city schools and by implication of their teachers. The use of raw results cannot compare like with like and therefore provides a misleading picture of performance. It has the danger of encouraging complacency amongst schools which serve socio-economically advantaged communities and of lowering the morale of teachers working in schools in disadvantaged inner city contexts in particular.

In contrast, value-added approaches which focus on pupil progress can provide more useful performance information which is of relevance to practitioners engaged in school self-evaluation and review or interested in monitoring improvement initiatives. Such research studies can also play a valuable part in improving our understanding of the ways in which schools and teachers influence pupils' educational outcomes and provide information about effective management strategies and guidance concerning effective classroom practices, the main focus of this chapter.

Educational outcomes

The choice of measures of pupil outcomes is a crucial consideration in studies of school and teacher effectiveness. To put it simply, if assessments are used which do not relate to the goals of schools and teachers, they are unlikely to reveal much about the effectiveness of schools and teachers in reaching such goals. For example, if IQ-type measures rather than curriculum related assessments are chosen, the influence of school or teachers would be expected to be smaller. Madaus *et al.* (1979) applied this criticism to the early studies by Coleman *et al.* (1966) and Jencks *et al.* (1972). Measures of pupil performance in skills related to the curriculum (e.g. reading, mathematics, writing at the primary level or examination results at the secondary level) are much more relevant to practitioners' stated goals. However, although academic goals are given a high priority by many teachers and head teachers, and also by parents and pupils, these can only provide indicators of academic effectiveness. Other social and affective outcomes (pupil attendance, attitudes to school and to learning, behaviour, motivation and self-esteem) are also highly regarded.

The use of only one or two outcome measures can only provide a partial picture of school or teacher effectiveness therefore. Early studies of school effectiveness, particularly in the US, have been criticised for a narrow reliance on tests in the basic skills. British research has tended to take a broader approach (Reynolds *et al.*, 1996). For example, studies at the secondary level by Rutter *et al.* (1979) and Reynolds (1982) considered attendance and behaviour as well as examination results. Mortimore, Sammons and Ecob (1988) study of junior education looked at a broad range of academic and non-cognitive outcomes, reading, mathematics, writing, oracy as well as attitudes, attendance, behaviour and self-esteem. The question of consistency in effectiveness in terms of different educational outcomes has received increasing attention from school effectiveness researchers in recent years. For example, even in terms of academic outcomes research reveals the existence of internal (within school) variation in effectiveness in different subjects in many schools and draws attention to the need to examine the departmental level (see, for example, Fitz-Gibbon, 1992 at A-level; Harris *et al.*, 1995; Sammons, Thomas and Mortimore, 1995b; 1997b, Thomas and Mortimore, 1996 at GCSE).

Although attainment is usually fairly highly correlated with social and affective measures such as attendance, behaviour and attitudes at the pupil level, there is rather less evidence about relationships at the school level from effectiveness studies. Studies of secondary schools (e.g. Rutter *et al.*, 1979; Reynolds 1982) tend to show stronger relationships than those of primary schools (e.g. Mortimore *et al.*, 1988; Knuver and Brandsma, 1993).

Studies of primary schools also stress the importance of the class level, in studies of pupil progress over individual school years (e.g. Mortimore *et al.*, 1988; Hill, Rowe and Holmes-Smith, 1995; Luyten, 1995). In other words there can be considerable variation in the educational outcomes of pupils in the same school but taught by different teachers, after control for intake differences. Schools can be viewed as 'loosely coupled' institutions which may vary in their effectiveness at different levels, e.g. department or individual classroom. By using multi-level models of schools which take account of different levels, such as the department and classroom, and a range of outcome measures, a better picture is provided of educational effectiveness than attempts to judge schools' or indeed teachers' performance on the basis of a single indicator (Mortimore *et al.*, 1988; Smith and Tomlinson, 1989; Fitz-Gibbon, 1992; Sammons, Thomas and Mortimore, 1995b).

Such studies suggest that while a few 'outliers' (highly effective or highly ineffective across a range of measures of pupils' educational outcomes) can be identified, for most schools the picture is more complex. Mortimore, Sammons and Ecob, 1988 and Mortimore *et al*'s 1988 study of junior schools identified a few schools which were more effective across a range of outcomes and a few which were broadly ineffective, but found considerable variations in effectiveness for the majority and concluded that school effects on the two domains (affective/social and cognitive) were independent, although at the pupil level there were significant correlations. More recently, Sammons, Thomas and Mortimore's (1995b; 1997b) study of academic effectiveness at GCSE showed that in some cases highly effective and highly ineffective departments co-existed in the same institution. There was also evidence of some variation in effectiveness across time in subject results, demonstrating the need to look at trends in effectiveness over several years. In the light of this they concluded that effectiveness is best seen as both outcome and time specific. Simple distinctions such as 'good' and 'bad' schools ignore the existence of internal variations in effectiveness and are not appropriate for the vast majority of schools (Sammons, 1996).

Key characteristics of effective schools

The school and teacher effectiveness research base has provided consistent evidence of both educationally and statistically significant differences between schools in a variety of measures of pupils' educational outcomes, after controlling for the powerful impact of intakes. This evidence has been found in studies of all phases of education, infant, junior, secondary and post-16 (Reynolds *et al.*, 1996 provides a summary of the contribution of UK research in this area). For example, in terms of overall GCSE results a study of 94 inner London secondary schools revealed differences between the most and least effective schools of 12 GCSE points for pupils of average attainment at age 11, the equivalent to five B rather than five D grades (Sammons, Thomas and Mortimore 1995b). Studies of the primary age group suggest that the effects can be more important (Mortimore, Sammons and Ecob, 1988 and Mortimore 1988) and that they can have a long term impact on pupils' secondary school performance (Goldstein and Sammons, 1997). Given this evidence, the question of why some schools, departments or classes are more effective than others is of considerable practical as well as theoretical importance. Studies of school and classroom processes have attempted to tease out what factors to do with leadership, policy, organisation and practice have a positive impact on measures of pupils' educational outcomes, controlling for intake differences.

A recent review of research into school effectiveness and studies of the effectiveness of teachers and teaching methods was commissioned by the Office for Standards in Education (OFSTED) to inform its revision of the framework for the inspection of schools (Sammons, Hillman and Mortimore, 1995a). This review notes 'the need for caution in interpreting findings concerning "key determinants" of effectiveness' (p. 1), pointing out dangers in attempting to interpret evidence based on correlations in terms of causal relationships. In addition, the authors comment that

> reciprocal relationships may well be important, as may intermediate causal relationships. Thus high expectations may enhance student achievement, which in turn promotes high expectations for succeeding age groups. Improved achievement may benefit behavioural outcomes which in turn foster later achievement. Conversely, lower expectations may become self-fulfilling, poor attendance and poor behaviour may lead to later academic underachievement which exacerbates behavioural and attendance problems (p.1).

Barber and Dann (1996) have drawn attention to the particular problems of the groups they term the disillusioned and the disappeared in the context of schools serving socio-economically disadvantaged inner city areas. By these they refer to pupils who exhibit low levels of engagement or motivation and at the extreme those whose rejection of school manifests itself in persistent truancy.

Acknowledging these caveats, a review of the evidence concerning factors which influence effectiveness is of relevance to practitioners and policy-makers concerned with school improvement and enhancing quality in education. A number of reviewers have drawn attention to the fact that

> There is a core of consistency to be found across a variety of studies conducted here and abroad with a wide range of different methodological strengths and weaknesses. Moreover, there is considerable support for the key findings in related research on organizational behaviour in a variety of work settings and countries.' (Firestone, 1991, p. 9.)

Sammons, Hillman and Mortimore (1995) provide a description of 11 key factors or correlates of effectiveness identified from their literature review (see Table 3.1). They argue that these factors should not be regarded as

Table 3.1. Eleven factors for effective schools

1	Professional leadership	Firm and purposeful
		A participative approach
		The leading professional
2	Shared vision and goals	Unity of purpose
		Consistency of practice
		Collegiality and collaboration
3	A learning environment	An orderly atmosphere
		An attractive working environment
4	Concentration on teaching and learning	Maximisation of learning time
		Academic emphasis
		Focus on achievement
5	Purposeful teaching	Efficient organisation
		Clarity of purpose
		Structured lessons
		Adaptive practice
6	High expectations	High expectations all round
		Communicating expectations
		Providing intellectual challenge
7	Positive reinforcement	Clear and fair discipline
		Feedback
8	Monitoring progress	Monitoring pupil performance
		Evaluating school performance
9	Pupil rights and responsibilities	Raising pupil self-esteem
		Positions of responsibility
		Control of work
10	Home–school partnership	Parental involvement in their children's learning
11	A learning organisation	School-based staff development

independent of each other, and note that the various links between them help to provide a better understanding of possible mechanisms of effectiveness.

Two of these key factors (numbers 4 and 5 in Table 3.1) are directly concerned with the nature of classroom practice and the teaching-learning process. The other factors concern processes (matters such as leadership and management, organisation, goals and expectations) affecting the school as a whole, and which in combination determine the school's culture. They emphasise matters such as the benefits of a safe, orderly working environment, a strong academic emphasis and quality of staff–student relationships. Schools in which there is effective leadership, shared vision and goals fostering consistency of practice and collegiality and collaboration, which have effective methods of monitoring pupil progress (in the classroom, within individual departments/faculties and at the school level) and with a student-centred focus emphasising pupil rights and responsibilities provide a more supportive environment for classroom practitioners and for teaching and learning.

Nonetheless, as Sammons, Hillman and Mortimore note,

> Ultimately, the quality of teaching (expressed most clearly by Factors 4 and 5) and expectations (number 6) have the most significant role to play in fostering pupils' learning and progress and, therefore, in influencing their educational outcomes (1995b: p24).

These three factors, therefore, can be seen to lie at the heart of effective classroom practice as judged by the criterion of positive effects on pupils' educational outcomes.

Concentration on teaching and learning

The primary purposes of schools concern teaching and learning. These would appear to be obvious activities in an effective school, but research suggests that schools differ greatly in the extent to which they concentrate on their primary purpose. Cohen (1983) noted that school effectiveness is clearly dependent upon effective classroom teaching. Similar conclusions about the importance of teaching and learning at the classroom level are evident in reviews by Scheerens (1992), Mortimore (1993) and Creemers (1994). A number of studies have shown correlations between focus on teaching and learning and school and teacher effectiveness. In some cases this focus has been defined by quantifying teachers' and pupils' use of time, and in others it has been defined in terms of other measures of the school's concentration on the actual process of learning and on achievement. It is clearly vital for schools and teachers to focus on the quality as well as the quantity of teaching and learning which takes place. Three features which are found to be important for pupil learning include time, opportunity to learn and quality of teaching.

Maximisation of learning time

Some studies have examined the use of time in schools, and a number of measures of learning time have been shown to have positive correlations with pupil outcomes and behaviour. The measures include:

- proportion of the day devoted to academic subjects (Coleman, Hoffer and Kilgore, 1981), or to particular academic subjects (Bennett, 1978)
- proportion of time in lessons devoted to learning (Brookover *et al.*, 1979; Brookover and Lezotte, 1979; Rutter *et al.*, 1979), or to interaction with pupils in class (Mortimore *et al.*, 1988a; Alexander, 1992)
- proportion of teachers' time spent discussing the content of work with pupils as opposed to routine matters and the maintenance of work activity (Galton and Simon, 1980; Mortimore *et al.*, 1988a; Alexander, 1992)

- teachers' concern with cognitive objectives rather than personal relationships and affective objectives (Evertson, Emmer and Brophy, 1980)
- punctuality of lessons (Rutter *et al.*, 1979; de Jong, 1988)
- freedom from disruption coming from outside the classroom (California State Department of Education, 1980; Hersch *et al.*, 1981).

Collectively, they point to the need for teachers to manage the transition of activities actively and efficiently. Each of these factors has been seen to have a positive relationship with school effectiveness. Researchers who have combined these variables into a single measure of instruction or academic learning time (Rosenshine and Berliner, 1978; Good, 1984; Carroll, 1989) or those who have reviewed this literature as a whole (United States Department of Education, 1987; NREL, 1990; Levine and Lezotte, 1990) have also demonstrated a clear impact of the maximisation of learning time on effectiveness. Of course, measures of time provide only a crude indication of focus on learning. As Carroll (1989) rightly cautioned, 'time as such is not what counts, but what happens during that time' (p. 27), nonetheless, academic learning time and time on task remain powerful predictors of achievement.

In a review of British literature on teaching and learning processes at Key Stage 2, Sammons, Lewis *et al.* (1994) drew attention to findings concerning single subject teaching and the management of teaching and learning time:

> teachers can have great difficulties in successfully managing children's learning in sessions where work on several different curriculum areas is ongoing. In particular, lower levels of work-related teacher-pupil communication and more routine administrative interactions and lower levels of pupil engagement in work activity have been reported in primary school research studies. (p. 52).

Academic emphasis

A number of studies, including some mentioned above, have shown effective schools to be characterised by other aspects of academic emphasis: as judged by teachers and pupils (McDill and Rigsby, 1973); through high levels of pupil industry in the classroom (Weber, 1971; Mortimore *et al.*, 1988); and through regular setting and marking of homework (Ainsworth and Batten, 1974), with checks by senior staff that this had occurred (Rutter *et al.*, 1979). Reviews (Walberg, 1985; United States Department of Education, 1987) have pointed to the importance of both quantity and quality (appropriateness) of homework set as well as the need for good teacher feedback.

Numerous studies of primary schools have also found that unusually effective schools tend to emphasise 'mastery of academic content' as an important aspect of their teaching programmes (Levine and Lezotte, 1990). In Northern Ireland, Caul's (1994) work has drawn attention to the importance of universal entry to GCSE, and an emphasis on academic standards in effective schools. Work by Smith and Tomlinson (1989) has also pointed to examination entry policies as a key feature in secondary school effectiveness. Sammons *et al.* (1995a) reported that academic emphasis (including regular setting and monitoring of homework) and high GCSE entry rates appear to be features of more highly academically effective secondary schools.

An important factor influencing academic emphasis concerns teachers' subject knowledge. For example, Bennett, Summers and Askew (1994) have clearly demonstrated that, at the primary level, teachers' knowledge of subject content is often limited, particularly in areas such as science. Adequate knowledge was seen as a necessary prerequisite (although not in itself a sufficient condition) for effective teaching and learning. In case studies contrasting highly effective and highly ineffective secondary schools, Sammons *et al.* (1995) report that the ineffective schools had experienced high staff turnover and severe staff shortages in specialist subjects which were seen to have acted as barriers to effectiveness.

Curriculum coverage is also important. For example, Bennett (1992) has demonstrated wide variations in curriculum coverage both for pupils within the same class and in different schools. Likewise, Tizard *et al.*'s (1988) work on infant schools pointed to a wide range between schools and classes in what children of the same age were taught which could not be accounted for by intake differences. These researchers emphasised the importance of curriculum coverage: 'it is clear that attainment and progress depend crucially on whether children are given particular learning experiences' (Tizard *et al.*, 1988, p. 172).

One of the perceived benefits (reported by teachers) of the introduction of the National Curriculum, is seen to be greater clarity about the content and experiences to be provided for particular pupil age groups, in particular a reduction in the variation in curriculum coverage for primary pupils. Against this, however, there is some evidence that time for basic subjects (reading and mathematics) has been eroded by pressures to ensure breadth and balance (Campbell and Emery, 1994).

Focus on achievement

Some researchers have examined the extent to which a school concentrates on the achievement of pupils as a measure of academic emphasis. For example, some case studies of American primary schools and reviews have shown emphasis on the acquisition of basic skills or 'achievement orientation' to have a positive influence on school effectiveness (Brookover and Lezotte, 1979; Brookover *et al.*, 1979; Venezky and Winfield, 1979; Glenn, 1981; Edmonds, 1979, 1981; Schweitzer, 1984). The problem with highlighting this type of factor is that outcome measures tend to be at least partly based on tests in these skills for primary schools, or examination achievement for secondary schools, making factors associated with focus on achievement self-fulfilling prophesies. This is particularly true in relation to class-level data, but less of a problem when examining the effect of a shared acceptance of a commitment to a focus on achievement throughout a school.

So, although a focus on teaching and learning is at the heart of an effective school, researchers have approached it from a number of different angles. One interesting attempt to consolidate this work is that of Scheerens (1992) who, drawing on a vast range of international school effectiveness literature, judged effective learning time to be one of only three factors for which there is 'multiple empirical research confirmation'. He considered four aspects to be relevant:

- institutionalised time spent on learning (length of school day/week/year)
- amount of homework
- effective learning time within institutional constraints
- learning time for different subjects.

Although this typology may not entirely capture the essence of 'focus on teaching and learning', it provides a useful framework for pinning down measurable factors that indicate important practical manifestations of this focus.

Purposeful teaching

Practitioners and inspectors seem to be in broad agreement that the quality of teaching is at the heart of effective schooling. Of course, this is partly determined by the quality of the teachers in the school. The recruiting and retention of effective teachers has been suggested as a feature of effective leadership in schools. In some environments (e.g. disadvantaged inner city areas) it may be hard to avoid shortages of experienced and, for some subjects, qualified staff. High levels of staff turnover and absence, can, however, also be seen as much as a symptom as a cause of ineffectiveness in schools. In addition to staff stability, qualifications and experience which impinge on the quality of teaching, factors concerning teachers' planning, classroom management and teaching strategies have been shown to be related to pupil progress. Whereas learning is a covert process that cannot be directly observed, teaching is an overt activity and hence is easier to describe and evaluate

Diversity in classrooms: effects on educational outcomes 51

(Mortimore, 1993), although Levine and Lezotte (1990) have pointed to a number of problems in drawing general conclusions on effective teaching practices. Examining the findings on teaching practices in effective schools research, the outstanding feature that emerges is what we call purposeful teaching. This has a number of elements: efficient organisation, clarity of purpose, structured lessons and adaptive practice.

Efficient organisation

Several studies have shown the importance of teachers being well organised and clear about their objectives. For example, Evertson *et al.* (1980) found positive effects on achievement when teachers felt 'efficacy and an internal locus of control', and where they organised their classrooms and planned proactively on a daily basis.

At the secondary level Rutter *et al.* (1979) drew attention to the beneficial effects of preparing the lesson in advance, and Rutter (1983) later pointed out that the more time that teachers spend organising a lesson after it has begun, the more likely it is that they will lose the attention of the class, with the attendant double risk of loss of opportunity to learn and disruptive behaviour. Various studies and reviews have also stressed the importance of appropriate pacing of lessons to make sure that their original objectives are achieved (Powell, 1980; Brophy and Good, 1986; Levine and Lezotte, 1990).

Clarity of purpose

Syntheses of effective schools research highlight the importance of pupils always being aware of the purpose of the content of lessons (Brophy and Good, 1986; United States Department of Education, 1987; NREL, 1990). In summary, the research shows that effective learning occurs where teachers clearly explain the objectives of the lesson at the outset, and refer to these throughout the lesson to maintain focus. These objectives should be related to previous study and to matters of personal relevance of the pupils. The information of the lesson should be structured such that it begins with an overview and transitions are signalled. The main ideas of the lesson should be reviewed at the end.

Structured lessons

A review by Rosenshine and Stevens (1981) highlighted the importance of structured teaching and purposefulness in promoting pupil progress. The NREL review (1990) drew particular attention to effective questioning techniques where questions are structured so as to focus pupils' attention on the key elements of the lessons. Stallings (1975) pointed to improvements in pupil outcomes through systematic teaching methods with open-ended questions, pupil answers, followed by teacher feedback. Supporting earlier findings by Galton and Simon (1980), Mortimore *et al.* (1988) likewise noted positive effects on progress through teachers spending more time asking questions and on work-related communication in their study of junior education. They also found positive outcomes to be associated with efficient organisation of classroom work with plenty for pupils to do, a limited focus to sessions, and a well-defined framework within which a degree of pupil independence and responsibility for managing their own work could be encouraged. Clearly, for older age groups greater stress on independence and responsibility is appropriate.

A summary of research on effective teachers by Joyce and Showers (1988) concludes that the more effective teachers:

- Teach the classroom as a whole
- present information or skills clearly and animatedly
- keep the teaching sessions task-oriented
- are non-evaluative and keep instruction relaxed
- have high expectations for achievement (give more homework, pace lessons faster, create alertness)
- relate comfortably to the students, with the consequence that they have fewer behaviour problems.

Scheerens (1992) in his analysis of the international body of effective schools research highlights 'structured teaching' as one of three factors which have been convincingly demonstrated to promote effectiveness. His definition of structured teaching is slightly different from that of other researchers but it is worth looking at some of the examples of what he means by it:

- making clear what has to be learnt
- splitting teaching material into manageable units for the pupils and offering these in a well-considered sequence
- much exercise material in which pupils make use of 'hunches' and prompts
- regularly testing for progress with immediate feedback of the results.

Scheerens admits that this exemplification of structured teaching is more applicable to primary schools, in particular in subjects that involve 'reproducible knowledge'. However, he suggests that a modified and less prescriptive form of structured teaching can have a positive effect for the learning of higher cognitive processes and in secondary schools, and he cites a number of studies to confirm this (Doyle, 1985; Brophy and Good, 1986). Gray (1993) is not convinced that this factor is so appropriate beyond the earlier years of schooling, and he suggests that we need to be cautious, given that so much of the early school effectiveness research is focused on disadvantaged schools, thus giving particular weight to the teaching of basic skills. For the promotion of such skills, especially for those with below average levels of attainment, such approaches may be particularly beneficial.

Adaptive practice

Although school effectiveness research shows a number of factors to be consistently correlated with better outcomes, it also shows that application of mandated curriculum materials and teaching procedures does not often bring out gains in achievement. Pupil progress is enhanced when teachers are sensitive to differences in the learning styles of pupils and, where feasible, identify and use appropriate strategies (NREL, 1990). In many cases this requires flexibility on the part of the teachers in modifying and adapting their teaching styles (Armor et al., 1976; Sizemore, Brossard and Harrigan, 1983; Gipps; 1992).

High expectations

Positive expectations of pupil achievement, particularly amongst teachers but also pupils and parents, is one of the most important characteristics of effective schools (United States Department of Education, 1987). However, care is needed in interpreting the relationship between expectations and achievement, since the causal process can run in the reverse direction, with high achievement of past age groups enhancing optimism amongst teachers dealing with succeeding cohorts. However, the weight of the evidence suggests that if teachers set high standards for their pupils, let them know that they are expected to meet them, and provide intellectually challenging lessons to correspond to these expectations, then the impact on achievement can be considerable. In particular, low expectations of certain kinds of student have been identified as an important factor in the under-achievement of students in disadvantaged urban schools (OFSTED, 1993). Mortimore (1993) has commented,

> For a pupil who is regularly taught by a teacher with low expectations the experience can be demoralising and, too often, leads to serious under-achievement (p. 62).

High expectations all round

A large number of studies and review articles in several countries have shown a strong relationship between high expectations and effective learning (Trisman, Waller and Wilder, 1976; Brookover et al., 1979; Edmonds, 1979, 1981; Rutter et al., 1979; California State Department of Education, 1980; Schweitzer, 1984; Stringfield, Teddlie and Suarez, 1986;

United States Department of Education, 1987; Tizard *et al.*, 1988; Mortimore *et al.*, 1988a; Scheerens, 1992; Stoll and Fink, 1992; Caul, 1994; Sammons, Thomas and Mortimore, 1995b). High expectations have also been described as a 'crucial characteristic of virtually all unusually effective schools described in case studies' (Levine and Lezotte, 1990). The important point as far as teachers are concerned is that low expectations go hand in hand with a sense of lack of control over pupils' difficulties and a passive approach to teaching. High expectations correspond to a more active role for teachers in helping pupils to learn (Mortimore, 1994) and a strong sense of efficacy (Armor *et al.*, 1976).

As with most of the factors identified in reviews of school and teacher effectiveness, high expectations alone can do little to raise effectiveness. They are most likely to be operationalised in a context where there is a strong emphasis on academic achievement, where pupils' progress is frequently monitored, and where there is an orderly environment, conducive to learning. In addition, high expectations are more effective when they are part of a general culture which places demands on everyone in the school, so that, for example, the head teacher has high expectations for the performance and commitment of all of the teachers (Murphy, 1989).

Communicating expectations

Expectations do not act directly on pupil performance, but through the attitude of the teacher being communicated to pupils and the consequent effect on their self-esteem (Bandura, 1992). The expectations may be influenced by factors other than the perceived ability or actual attainments of children. For example, Mortimore *et al.* (1988) found that teachers had lower expectations for younger pupils in the class and for those from lower social classes, even when account was taken of children's attainment in areas such as reading and mathematics. But even if teachers do not believe success is possible, conveying conviction that achievement can be raised can have a powerful effect. Teachers may need to monitor either or both their beliefs and behaviour to make sure that this takes place (NREL, 1990). It should also be noted that raising expectations is an incremental process and demonstrated success plays a critical role (Wilson and Corcoran, 1988). Reinforcing this success through appropriate feedback and praise (positive reinforcement) is a key opportunity for communicating high expectations.

Providing intellectual challenge

There seems little doubt that a common cause of underachievement in pupils is a failure to challenge them. The implications of this are that when schools have high expectations of their pupils, individual teachers attempt to provide intellectually challenging lessons for all pupils in their classes. This approach has been shown by several studies to be associated with greater effectiveness.

A piece of British research had some important findings which go some way to explaining the processes through which expectations have an effect. Tizard et al. (1988) in a study of infant schools in inner London found that teachers' expectations of both individual pupils and of classes as a whole had a strong influence on the content of lessons, which to a large extent explained differences in curriculum between classes with similar intakes. These expectations were not just influenced by academic considerations but also by the extent to which a child or a class was 'a pleasure to teach'. The result was that different levels of expectations of pupils were translated into differing requirements for their work and their performance.

Both Galton and Simon (1980) and Mortimore et al.'s (1988) studies of the junior years of primary schools found that in classes where the pupils were stimulated and challenged, progress was greatest. They particularly mentioned the importance of teachers using more higher-order questions and statements which encourage pupils to use their creative imagination and powers of problem-solving. Levine and Stark (1981) also stressed the importance of the development of higher-order cognitive skills in effective primary schools, mentioning in particular reading comprehension and problem solving in mathematics. Levine and Lezotte (1990) and NREL (1990) pointed to a number of other studies with similar findings.

The question of teaching styles

Current publicity about educational standards, particularly in the primary sector, has reopened the debate about the benefits of different teaching styles. This has important implications for teachers concerned with delivering the National Curriculum and meeting the diverse needs of pupils in the average classroom. Recently, following the publication of an international review of science and mathematics teaching conducted for OFSTED (Reynolds and Farrell, 1996) the Chief Inspector argued for a return to so called 'whole class' teaching approaches, citing evidence of higher educational performance in Pacific Rim economies such as Taiwan. In fact Reynolds and Farrell's (1996) review did not test the impact of different teaching approaches but suggested that this was a fruitful area for further study, noting the existence of many cultural differences between Britain and Taiwan, including the value placed on education. They also noted that class teaching approaches in Taiwan could be typified as 'highly interactive' and were not representative of the stereotype of 'formal' teaching, where silent children sitting in rows are passive recipients of knowledge delivered by teachers using a 'chalk and talk' approach.

Certainly some British studies have drawn attention to the benefits of maximising teacher–pupil communication through the use of whole class communication (see Galton and Delafield, 1981; Mortimore et al., 1988;

Alexander, 1992) but have emphasised that this did not imply that a particular style was suited to purposes and situations. Thus, while there is strong evidence concerning the impact of aspects of teacher behaviour and expectations on pupil learning, Sammons, Hillman and Mortimore (1995) argue that school and teacher effectiveness research does 'not support the view that any one particular teaching style is more effective than others'. Mortimore *et al.*'s (1988) study of junior schools is relevant in this context. Their analysis of observational and other data about primary school teachers indicated that teacher behaviour was too complex and varied for the application of simple descriptions of teaching style or approach and that 'teachers could not validly be divided into a number of categories on the basis of differences in teaching style' (p. 81). Similarly, re-analysis of the 'Teaching Styles and Pupil Progress' data (Bennett, 1976) challenged its original study's findings concerning the supposed benefits of 'formal' teaching (Aitkin, Anderson and Hinde, 1981; and Aitken, Bennett and Hesketh, 1981) and point to problems in the use of crude distinctions such as 'formal' or 'informal', 'traditional' versus 'progressive' and attempts to separate and compare groups of teachers operating with distinctive styles. Joyce and Showers (1988) drew attention to the fact that teachers vary in their ways of managing students and learning environments, and in their teaching strategies, which can all affect student learning but did not advocate any specific style(s). Recent primary school reviews highlight the importance of effective management, clarity of objectives, good planning, appropriate and efficient organisation of pupils' time and activities ensuring a high level of industry and engagement, and an emphasis of work communication and intellectually challenging teaching (Gipps, 1992; Sammons, Lewis *et al.*, 1994b).

On the basis of current evidence it can be concluded that flexibility, the ability to adapt teaching approaches for different purposes and groups ensuring a high level of student engagement and maximising teacher–pupil communication is likely to be more beneficial than the adoption of one single teaching style irrespective of context and purpose. As Sammons, Hillman and Mortimore (1995a) note,

> in our view debates about the virtues of one particular style over another are too simplistic and have become sterile. Efficient organisation, fitness for purpose, flexibility of approach and intellectual challengsr are of greater relevance. (p. 25).

Linking teaching and learning

Most accept the view that effective teaching should promote pupil learning and thus pupil progress. Yet, as Mortimore (1993) has observed 'the relationship between teaching and learning is neither straightforward nor obvious' (p. 59) because, while teaching is a behaviour which can be observed, learning is not and can only be inferred from its results (Black, Hall and Martin, 1990). Moreover, the relationship between teaching and learning may well vary for different learners. Some may learn despite unfavourable circumstances, while others may make little progress even with additional instruction. Also, even when pupils share the same teachers and classroom environment, their classroom experiences and thus their opportunities for learning can often differ (due to different curriculum coverage, expectations, pupil grouping methods, etc).

Mortimore (1993) provides a useful account of key aspects of the knowledge and skills which he suggests classroom practitioners need for the complex task of teaching. His conclusions are summarised in Table 3.2.

Table 3.2 Knowledge and skills needed for teaching (after Mortimore, 1993)

Knowledge type	
Curriculum	needs to be sound in principle, detailed in scope and regularly updated
Pedagogical	includes skills of presentation as well as an understanding of how learners learn, and how subject knowledge can be transformed so as to be appropriate for pupils of different age, cognitive skills and experience
Psychological	covers understanding of how young minds operate and awareness of different cultural patterns and family traditions and of how these may help or hinder classroom work
Sociological	the way factors such as race, gender, class or religion may help or hinder successful teaching
School and classroom process	can provide the teacher with ways of planning and monitoring their own work effectively

Specific skills	
Organisation	to sort out materials and sources of information
Analysis	to break down complex bodies of knowledge into coherent components
Synthesis	to build ideas into arguments, propositions and theories
Presentation	to clarify complex information
Assessment	so that pupils' work can be judged and appropriate feedback given
Management	to coordinate the work of individual pupils, groups and the class as a whole
Evaluation	so that teaching itself can be continually improved.

This list, of course, cannot fully encapsulate the full complexity of teaching as Mortimore (1993) observes,

> Gifted teachers bind together these skills and knowledge and, using their imagination creativity and sensitivity, communicate with and inspire their pupils (p. 62).

It does, however, provide a helpful basis for the analysis of classroom practice.

More recently, Harris (1995) has produced a summary of evidence concerning effective teaching (Table 3.3). She draws attention to the ways in which the HMI (1990) conclude that 'good' lessons may be differentiated from 'poor' ones and suggests that this can provide indicators of effective teaching. It should be noted that the HMI list is in accord with many of the findings derived from the school effectiveness fields outlined earlier in this chapter.

Table 3.3 Features of effective teaching (from Harris, 1995 based on HMI, 1990)

Lessons should be purposeful, with high expectations conveyed
Pupils should be given some opportunities to organise their own work
Lessons should elicit and sustain pupils' interest and be perceived by pupils as relevant and challenging
The work should be well matched to pupils' abilities and learning needs
Pupils' language should be developed and extended
A variety of learning activities should be employed
Good order and control should be largely based on skilful management of pupils' involvement in the lesson, and mutual respect

Harris also draws on work by Doyle (1987) which suggests that pupils' learning is enhanced when teachers adopt a fairly structured approach to teaching. Doyle's (1987) work highlights the importance of teacher–pupil interaction (see Table 3.4).

Watkins *et al.* (1996) examine different models of pupil learning and highlight the benefits of active rather than passive approaches which they argue foster high levels of pupil engagement. These authors stress that when planning for effective pupil learning, teachers need to ensure that the tasks and processes promote active learning, collaborative learning, learner responsibility and learning about learning. Watkins *et al.* (1996) further suggest that

> A curriculum which provides coherence for the learner will enhance the ability to make connections in different contexts. Time and guidance for the learner to reflect and make the connections needs to be provided (p. 6).

Table 3.4 Teacher behaviours which promote pupil achievement (from Harris, 1995 after Doyle 1987)

Emphasise academic goals

Make goals explicit and expect pupils to be able to master the curriculum

Organise and sequence the curriculum carefully

Use clear explanations and illustrate what pupils are to learn

Ask direct and specific questions frequently to monitor pupils' progress and check their understanding

Provide pupils with ample opportunities to practise

Give prompts and feedback to ensure success

Correct mistakes and allow pupils to use a skill until it is over-learned and automatic

Review work regularly and hold pupils accountable for their work.

An attempt to link school and teacher effectiveness research with theories about pupil learning is provided by Creemers' (1994) 'comprehensive model of educational effectiveness'. This stresses the three key concepts of quality of instruction and curriculum, time, and opportunity to learn derived from the Carroll (1989) model as important influences on pupils' academic achievement. Creemers (1994) also notes the impact of pupils' background characteristics such as aptitude, social background and motivation which, he argues, influence the extent to which pupils use their learning opportunities and time on task effectively. In addition, Creemers (1994) draws attention to the benefits of consistency in approaches at both the school and the classroom level to ensure that quality, time and opportunity to learn are maximised.

Conclusions

This chapter provides a brief overview of research into school and teacher effectiveness and some of the implications of such studies for practitioners. The findings from effectiveness studies have sometimes been criticised for being just a matter of 'commonsense'. Against this charge, as Rutter *et al.* (1979) pointed out,

> research into practical issues, such as schooling, rarely comes up with findings that are totally unexpected. On the other hand it is

helpful in showing which of the abundance of good ideas available are related to successful outcomes (p. 204).

Reynolds (1995) has thus argued that the field's pupil-achievement focused approach which uses pupil learning as the criterion for measuring educational effectiveness is the 'touchstone' against which we should evaluate different fads and fashions in school and classroom organisation and practices.

The research findings concerning classroom practice discussed here are not intended to be seen as prescriptive, however. They do not provide a 'recipe' or 'blueprint' for effectiveness (Sammons and Reynolds, 1997). As has been argued, teaching and learning and their inter-relationships are complex matters and, given the diversity of teaching situations and contexts, it is unsurprising that simplistic notions concerning the supposed benefits of different teaching styles (contrasting approaches by means of crude dichotomies such as 'formal/informal' or 'traditional/progressive') are not supported by the research base. Nonetheless, evidence that specific kinds of teacher behaviour – such as the use of higher order questions, a prompt start to lessons and planning lessons in advance, high expectations, clear goals, high levels of feedback, positive reinforcement – are related positively to pupil progress is strong.

The reviews of research also suggest that there is much in common in the findings concerning effectiveness for both primary and secondary schools. Despite the broad agreement in findings for both sectors, however, the emphasis or means of expression will often differ. For example, appropriate forms of feedback, praise and rewards and the manner and extent to which pupils are encouraged to manage their learning will vary for different age groups. Ways of focusing on teaching and learning and teaching techniques will also differ for different age groups and those at different stages of development, but careful and appropriate planning and organisation, clarity of objectives, high expectations, intellectually challenging teaching and the maximisation of learning time remain crucial for effective teaching at all stages. Likewise, ways of fostering parental involvement in their children's learning and with the school will also vary markedly between the primary and secondary sectors but are important for success in both.

The reflective practitioner

The school improvement literature lays an emphasis on the teacher as well as the pupil as learner, and teacher development is seen to be at the heart of school improvement efforts. Effective teachers are seen to have a repertoire of skills and are able to apply their knowledge for different purposes in the classroom. The teacher as a reflective practitioner is concerned to extend and add to their repertoire of skills and knowledge and learn from reflecting on their classroom experiences. For example, Mortimore (1993) draws attention to the continuing relevance of questions by the Open University (1981) for teachers to reflect on in relation to the success of specific lessons. The insights thus gained may be used to inform the planning of future lessons to promote pupil learning.

- What did pupils actually do?
- What were they learning?
- What did I do?
- What did I learn?
- What do I intend to do now?

Likewise, Harris (1995) suggests that teachers may benefit from discussing and reflecting on the findings from teacher and school effectiveness research in relation to their current practice and proposes four questions.

- How might you or your school(s) use the findings of research into effective teaching?
- To what extent is active learning time maximised in your classroom/school?
- To what extent do the characteristics of effective teaching feature in your classroom/school?
- What active strategies might you/your school adopt to guarantee more effective teaching?

Of course, the process of self-evaluation and review of teaching and learning practices by individual teachers in relation to their own classroom practice, as well as by the staff as a whole and by the senior management team considering the school as an institution, is not guaranteed to raise effectiveness. Nonetheless, it can be seen as a positive first step in the improvement process which adopts pupil learning and achievement as the criteria for successful teaching and successful schools.

References

Ainsworth, M. and Batten, E. (1974) The Effects of Environmental Factors on Secondary Educational Attainment in Manchester: a Plowden follow-up (London: Macmillan).

Aitkin, M., Anderson, D. and Hinde, J. (1981) Statistical modelling of data on teaching styles. Journal of the Royal Statistical Society, A 144(4), 419–61.

Aitkin, M., Bennett, N. and Hesketh, J. (1981) Teaching styles and pupil progress: a re-analysis. British Journal of Educational Psychology, 51(2), 170–86.

Alexander, R. (1992) Policy and Practice in Primary Education (London: Routledge).

Armor, D., Conry-Oseguera, P., Cox, M., King, N., McDonnell, L., Pascal, A., Pauly, E. and Zellman, G. (1976) Analysis of The Reading Program in Selected Los Angeles Minority Schools (Santa Monica, CA: Rand).

Bandura, A. (1992) Perceived self-efficacy in cognitive development and functioning. Invited address at the annual meeting of the American Education Research Association, San Francisco, April 1992.

Barber, M. and Dann, R. (Eds.) (1996) Raising Educational Standards in the Inner Cities: Practical initiatives in action (London: Cassell).

Bennett, N. (1976) Teaching Styles and Pupil Progress (London: Open Books).

Bennett, N. (1978) Recent research on teaching: a dream, a belief and a model. British Journal of Educational Psychology, 48, 127–47.

Bennett, N. (1992) Managing learning in the primary classrooms, ASPE Paper No 1 (Stoke: Trentham Books).

Bennett, N., Summers, M. and Askew, M. (1994) Knowledge for teaching and teaching performance, in A. Pollard (Ed.) Look Before You Leap? Research evidence for the curriculum at Key Stage 2 (London: Tufnell Press).

Black, H.J., Hall, J. and Martin, S. (1990) Learning, Teaching and Assessment: A theoretical overview (Edinburgh: Scottish Council for Research in Education).

Brookover, W. and Lezotte, L. (1979) Changes in school characteristics coincident with changes in school achievement (East Lansing: Michigan State University).

Brookover, W., Beady, C., Flood, P., Schweitzer, J. and Wisenbaker, J. (1979) School Social Systems and Student Achievement: Schools can make a difference (New York: Praeger).

Brophy, J. and Good, T. (1986) Teacher behavior and student achievement, Ch. 12 in M.C. Wittrock (ed.) Handbook of research on teaching (New York: Macmillan).

California State Department of Education (1980) Report on the special studies of selected ECE schools with increasing and decreasing reading scores (Sacramento, CA: Office of Program Evaluation and Research).

Campbell, J. and Emery, H. (1994) Curriculum policy for Key Stage 2: Possibilities, contradictions and constraints, in Pollard, A (Ed.) Look Before You Leap? Research evidence for the curriculum at Key Stage 2 (London: Tufnell Press).

Carroll, J. (1989) The Carroll model: a 25 year retrospective and prospective view, Educational Researcher, 18, 26–31.

Caul, L. (1994) School effectiveness in Northern Ireland: illustration and practice. Paper for the Standing Commission on Human Rights.

Cohen, M. (1983) Instructional, management and social conditions in effective schools, in Webb, A.O. and Webb, L.D. (Eds.) School Finance and School Improvement: Linkages in the 1980s (Cambridge, MA: Ballinger).

Coleman, J., Hoffer, T. and Kilgore, S. (1981) Public and Private Schools (Chicago, IL: National Opinion Research Center).

Coleman, J.S., Campbell, E., Hobson, C., McPartland, J., Mood, A., Weinfield, F. and York, R. (1966) Equality of Educational Opportunity (Washington, DC: US Government Printing Office).

Creemers, B. (1994) The Effective Classroom (London: Cassell).

DfE (1992) Choice and Diversity: A new framework for schools (London: DfE).

Doyle, W. (1985) Effective secondary classroom practices, in Kyle, M. (Ed.) Reaching for Excellence: An effective schools sourcebook (Washington DC: US Government Printing Office).

Doyle, W. (1987) Research on teaching effects as a resource for improving instruction, in M. Wideen and I. Andrews (Eds.) Staff Development for School Improvement (Basingstoke: Falmer Press).

Edmonds, R. (1979) Effective schools for the urban poor. Educational Leadership, 37(1), 15–27.
Edmonds, R. (1981) Making public schools effective. Social Policy, 12, 56–60.
Evertson, C., Emmer, E. and Brophy, J. (1980) Predictors of effective teaching in junior high mathematics classrooms. Journal for Research in Mathematics Education, 11(3), 167–78.
Firestone, W.A. (1991) Introduction: Chapter 1 in Bliss, J.R., Firestone, W.A. and Richards, C.E. (Eds.) Rethinking Effective Schools: Research and practice (Englewood Cliffs, NJ: Prentice Hall).
Fitz-Gibbon, C. (1992) School effects at A level: Genesis of an information system, in Reynolds, D. and Cuttance, P. (Eds.) School Effectiveness Research, Policy and Practice (London: Cassell).
Galton, M. and Simon, B. (1980) Inside the Primary Classroom (London: Routledge and Kegan Paul).
Galton, M. and Delafield, A. (1981) Expectancy effects in primary classrooms, in Simons, B and Willocks, J (Eds.) Research and Practice in the Primary Classroom (London: Routledge and Kegan Paul).
Gipps, C. (1992) What We Know About Effective Primary Teaching (London: Tufnell Press).
Glenn, B. (1981) What Works? An Examination of Effective Schools for Poor Black Children (Cambridge, MA: Harvard University Center for Law and Education).
Goldstein, H., Rasbash, J., Yang, M., Woodhouse, G., Pan, H., Nuttall, D. and Thomas, S. (1993) A multilevel analysis of school examination results. Oxford Review of Education, 19(4), 425–33.
Goldstein, H. and Sammons, P. (1997) The influence of secondary and junior schools on sixteen year examination performance: a cross-classified multilevel analysis. School Effectiveness and School Improvement, 8(2), 219–30.
Good, T. (1984) Teacher effects, in Making our schools more effective: proceedings of three State Conferences. Kansas City, MO: University of Missouri.
Gray, J. (1993) Review of Scheerens, J. (1992) Effective schooling: research, theory and practice. School Effectiveness and School Improvement, 4(3), 230–5.
Gray, J., Jesson, D. and Sime, N. (1990) Estimating differences in the examination performance of secondary schools in six LEAs: a multilevel approach to school effectiveness. Oxford Review of Education, 16(2), 137–58.
Harris, A. (1995) Effective Teaching. SIN Research Matters, No 3 (London: ISEIC, Institute of Education, University of London).
Harris, A., Jamieson, I. and Russ, J. (1995) A study of 'effective' departments in secondary schools. School Organisation, 15(3), 283–99.
Hersh, R., Carnine, D., Gall, M., Stockard, J., Carmack, M. and Gannon, P. (1981) The Management of Education Professionals in Instructionally Effective Schools: Towards a research agenda. (Eugene, OR: Center for Educational Policy and Management, University of Oregon).
Hill, P., Rowe, K. and Holmes-Smith, P. (1995) Factors affecting students' educational progress: multilevel modelling of educational effectiveness. Paper presented at the ICSEI, Leeuwarden, the Netherlands, January 1995.
HMI (1990) Standards in education 1988–89 (London: DES).
Jencks, C.S., Smith, M., Ackland, H., Bane, M.J., Cohen, D., Gintis, H., Heyns, B. and Micholson, S. (1972) Inequality: A reassessment of the effect of family and schooling in America (New York: Basic Books).
Jong, M. de (1988) Educational climate and achievement in Dutch schools. Paper presented at the International Conference for Effective Schools, London.

Joyce, B. and Showers, B. (1988) Student Achievement Through Staff Development. (New York: Longman).

Knuver, J.W.M. and Brandsma, H.P. (1993) Cognitive and affective outcomes in school effectiveness research. School Effectiveness and School Improvement, 4(3), 189–204.

Levine, D. and Stark, J. (1981) Instructional and Organisational Arrangements and Processes for Improving Academic Achievement at Inner City Elementary Schools. (Kansas City, MO: University of Missouri).

Levine, D.U. and Lezotte, L. W (1990) Unusually Effective Schools: A review and analysis of research and practice. (Madison, WI: National Center for Effective Schools Research and Development).

Luyten, H. (1995) Teacher change and instability across grades. School Effectiveness and School Improvement, 1(1), 67–89.

McDill, E. and Rigsby, L. (1973) Structure and Process in Secondary Schools. (Baltimore, MD: Johns Hopkins University Press).

Madaus, G.F., Kellaghan, T., Rakow, E.A. and King, D. (1979) The sensitivity of measures of school effectiveness. Harvard Educational Review, 49, 207–30.

Mortimore, P. (1993) Managing teaching and learning: The search for a match. Chapter 5 in Busher, M. and Smith, M. (Eds.) Managing educational institutions. (Sheffield Papers In Educational Management, University of Sheffield).

Mortimore, P. (1994) The positive effects of schooling, in Rutter, M. (Ed.) Youth In The Year 2000: Psycho-social issues and interventions (Boston, MA: Cambridge University Press).

Mortimore, P., Sammons, P. and Ecob, R. (1988) Expressing the magnitude of school effects – a reply to Peter Preece, Research Papers in Education, 3(2), 99–101.

Mortimore, P., Sammons, P., Stoll, L., Lewis, D. and Ecob, R. (1988) School Matters: The Junior Years (Wells: Open Books).

Mortimore, P., Sammons, P. and Thomas, S. (1994) School effectiveness and value added. Assessment in Education, 1(3), 315–32.

Murphy, J. (1989) Principal instructional leadership, in Thuston, P. and Lotto, L. (Eds.) Advances in Educational Leadership (Greenwich, CT: JAI Press).

Northwest Regional Educational Laboratory (1990) Onward to excellence: effective schooling practices: a research synthesis. (Portland, OR: Northwest Regional Educational Laboratory).

Nuttall, D. (1990) Differences in Examination Performance, RS 1277/90 (London: Research and Statistics Branch, ILEA).

OFSTED (1993) Access and achievement in urban education (London: HMSO).

Open University (1981) Curriculum in Action (Milton Keynes: Open University).

Powell, M. (1980) The beginning teacher evaluation study: a brief history of a major research project, in Denham, C. and Lieberman, A. (Eds.) Time To Learn (Washington, DC: National Institute of Education).

Powell, M. (1980) The beginning teacher evaluation study: a brief history of a major research project, in Denham, C. and Lieberman, A. (Eds.) Time To Learn (Washington DC: National Institute of Education).

Reynolds, D. (1982) The search for effective schools. School Organisation, 2(3), 215–37.

Reynolds, D. (1995) The Effective Schools: An inaugural lecture, Evaluation and Research in Education, 9(2) 57–73.

Reynolds, D., Sammons, P., Stoll, L., Barber, M. and Hillman, J. (1996) School effectiveness and school improvement in the United Kingdom. School effectiveness and school improvement (special issue of country reports), 7(2), 133–58.

Reynolds, D. and Farrell, S. (1996) Worlds Apart (London: HMSO).
Rosenshine, B. and Berliner, D. (1978) Academic engaged time. British Journal of Teacher Education, 4, 3–16.
Rosenshine, B. and Stevens, R. (1981) Advances in research on teaching. Unpublished manuscript, University of Illinois.
Rutter, M. (1983) School effects on pupil progress – findings and policy implications. Child Development, 54(1), 1–29.
Rutter, M., Maughan, B., Mortimore, P. and Ouston, J. (1979) Fifteen Thousand Hours: Secondary schools and their effects on children. (London: Open Books).
Sammons, P. Complexities in the judgement of school effectiveness. Educational research and evaluation (forthcoming).
Sammons, P. and Reynolds, D. (1997) A Partisan Evaluation–John Elliott on school effectiveness. Cambridge Journal of Education, 27(1) 123–36.
Sammons, P., Nuttall, D. and Cuttance, P. (1993) Differential school effectiveness: results from a reanalysis of the Inner London Education Authority's Junior School Project data. British Educational Research Journal, 19(4), 381–405.
Sammons, P., Thomas, S., Mortimore, P., Owen, C. and Pennell, H. (1994) Assessing School Effectiveness: Developing measures to put school performance in context. (London: Office for Standards in Education [OFSTED]).
Sammons, P., Lewis, A., MacLure, M., Riley, J., Bennett, N. and Pollard, A. (1994) Teaching and learning processes, in Pollard, A. (Ed.) Look Before You Leap? research evidence for the curriculum at Key Stage 2. (London: Tufnell Press).
Sammons, P., Hillman, J. and Mortimore, P. (1995a) Key Characteristics of Effective Schools: A review of school effectiveness research. (London: Office for Standards in Education [OFSTED]).
Sammons, P., Thomas, S. and Mortimore, P. (1995b) Differential school effectiveness: departmental variations in GCSE attainment. ESRC End of Award Report, Project R000 234130.
Sammons, P., Thomas, S. and Mortimore, P. (1997b) Forging Links: Effective schools and effective departments (London: Paul Chapman).
Sammons, P., Thomas, S., Mortimore, P., Cairns, R., Bausor, J. and Walker, A. (1997a) Understanding school and departmental differences in academic effectiveness: Findings from case studies of selected outlier secondary schools in inner London. (School Effectiveness and School Improvement). (forthcoming).
Scheerens, J. (1992) Effective Schooling: Research, theory and practice (London: Cassell).
Schweitzer, J. (1984) Characteristics of effective schools. Paper for American Educational Research Association annual conference.
Sizemore, B. (1987) The effective African American elementary school, in Noblit, G. and Pink, W. (Eds.) Schooling in a social context: qualitative studies (Norwood, NJ: Ablex).
Sizemore, B., Brossard, C. and Harrigan, B. (1983) An Abashing Anomaly: The high achieving predominantly black elementary school (Pittsburgh, PA: University of Pittsburgh).
Smith, D. J and Tomlinson, S. (1989) The School Effect: A study of multi-racial comprehensives (London: Policy Studies Institute).
Stallings, J. (1975) Implementation and child effects of teaching practices in follow through classrooms. Monographs of the Society for Research in Child Development, 40(7–8), Serial No 163.
Stoll, L. and Fink, D. (1992) Effecting school change: the Halton approach. School Effectiveness and School Improvement, 3(1), 19–41.

Stringfield, S., Teddlie, C. and Suarez, S. (1986) Classroom interaction in effective and ineffective schools: preliminary results from Phase III of the Louisiana School Effectiveness Study. Journal of Classroom Interaction, 20(2), 31–7.

Thomas, S., Sammons, P. and Mortimore, P. (1994) Stability and consistency in secondary schools' effects on students' GCSE outcomes: initial results. Paper presented at the annual conference of the British Educational Research Association, 9 September, St Anne's College, University of Oxford.

Thomas, S. and Mortimore, P. (1996) Comparison of value added models for secondary school effectiveness. Research Papers in Education, 11(1), 5–33.

Tizard, B., Blatchford, P., Burke, J., Farquhar, C. and Plewis, I. (1988) Young Children at School in the Inner City (Hove: Lawrence Erlbaum).

Trisman, D., Waller, M. and Wilder, C. (1976) A Descriptive and Analytic Study of Compensatory Reading Programs (Princeton, NJ: Educational Testing Service).

United States Department of Education (1987) What works research about teaching and learning, revised edition (Washington, DC: United States Department of Education).

Venezky, R. and Winfield, L. (1979) Schools That Succeed Beyond Expectations In Teaching Reading (Newark, DE: University of Delaware).

Walberg, H. J (1985) Homework's powerful effects on learning. Educational Leadership, 42(7), 76–9.

Watkins, C., Carnell, E., Lodge, C. and Whalley, C. (1996) Effective learning. SIN Research Matters, No 5, Summer 1996, (London: ISEIC, Institute of Education, University of London).

Weber, G. (1971) Inner-city Children Can Be Taught To Read: Four successful schools (Washington DC: Council for Basic Education).

Wilson, B. and Corcoran, T. (1988) Successful Secondary Schools (Basingstoke: Falmer Press).

Chapter 4
Teacher expectations: implications for school improvement

COLIN ROGERS

For some 30 years the social psychology of education has given a central role to the operation of teacher expectations. The highly influential and equally controversial research of Rosenthal and Jacobson (1968) is still cited as the origin of this work. A steady stream of studies has testified to the enduring interest of researchers in the processes involved together with the complexity and significance of the educational issues concerned. Some of the developments in this field can be traced through reviews and key collections of work including Rosenthal and Rubin (1978), Rogers (1982), Dusek (1985), Miller and Turnbull (1986), Jussim (1989), Goldenberg (1992), and Blanck (1993). A glance through these sources will reveal a variety of models put forward to explain the process of expectation effects with a variety of views expressed concerning what is central.

In recent years this whole enterprise has been given a new emphasis by the search for the key to effective education. The school effectiveness researchers and members of the school improvement movement see expectations as a key to effective schooling. Two recent examples serve to make the point.

Stoll and Fink (1996) set out a detailed review of work into school effectiveness and school improvement. I shall return to explore this in greater detail later in the present chapter. For the moment, let it be noted that the expectations of teachers soon appear in this work as an important component of effective schooling. Drawing on the Halton Effective Schools project, Stoll and Fink indicate three broad categories of factors associated with effective schools. One of these is an 'emphasis on learning'. Amongst other things this includes 'high expectations' held by the school for its students. They also draw on a review by Sammons, Hillman and Mortimore (1995) which concludes with a list of 11 factors for effective schools. Again, one of these is 'high expectations'.

A rather different work also indicates the perceived importance of expectations for effective schooling (National Commission on

Education, 1996). Entitled 'Success against the Odds', this work presents a number of accounts of schools that are judged to be effective even though they operate 'against the odds' in disadvantaged areas. The claimed importance of positive expectations runs consistently through the accounts, each produced by a panel of people external to the school in question. The book's small index contains a number of references to expectations and indeed the indexers thought it necessary to include a separate entry for high expectations, also one of the longest. (Given that this book focuses on successful schools there is no index entry for low expectations.) The report on one of the schools says:

> We have been struck forcibly by how frequently we heard high expectations being expressed of other people in this school. (p 161)

In talking about the staff of another school the team of reporters said

> They subscribe to the view that it is necessary to have high and consistent expectations of all students...(p. 76).

The concluding chapter states that

> The powerful relationship between high expectations and effective learning has long been recognised. (p. 325)

The authors go on to discuss the pivotal role of the school's leadership or management in promoting high expectations and the concomitant success.

This chapter does not intend to offer a review of the school effectiveness literature, nor the recent work on school improvement, nor yet the marriage (of convenience or otherwise) between the two that writers such as Stoll and Fink are keen to promote. Instead, the intention is to offer a consideration of the nature of teacher expectations and their implications for the effectiveness of schools. In so doing I will be touching upon some of the more important and central aspects of the social psychology of education.

One of the magic dozen (or thereabouts) factors

The opening remarks to this chapter indicate the significance of the notion of teacher expectations for effective schooling. This emphasis on the positive goes some way to removing the stigma that has hung over teacher expectations since the publication of *Pygmalion in the Classroom* (Rosenthal and Jacobson, 1968). The teacher expectancy effect literature often portrays expectations and their effects as problematic, in the sense that they cause problems that we, and particularly the students on the receiving end of them, would wish to avoid. However, school effectiveness researchers generally accept value-added notions of effective schooling (see for example Cuttance, 1992). The basic argument here is that effective schools are those which add to whatever a student brings to the school in the first place. This is most readily demonstrated at secondary level where the level of attainment reached by a student at entry is generally known. Further information known to influence secondary school outcomes (parental education levels, parental occupation, income levels and so forth) is then added to the equation allowing predictions of performance at, say, GCSE to be made. Students over-performing against this yardstick are said to have enjoyed a value-added secondary education. Those under-performing have had value taken away by their particular school experience, and the rest are neutral. Effective schools are, of course, those that add value whatever the absolute level of performance might be. Effective schooling is, of course, good schooling. Expectations are a part of effective schooling. Therefore expectations are good. A consideration of what a good expectation is forms the subject of the remains of this chapter. The value-added notion of school effectiveness reminds us that the whole point of schools is to change the young people who attend them. If teacher expectations are a part of this change process, and if the change is in the right direction, then the impact of expectations is to be welcomed and encouraged rather than avoided.

High expectations

How do we describe expectations? The examples from the effective schooling literature generally cite high expectations and then go on to add that these are or ought to be consistent. Is this an entirely adequate basis for a typology of teacher expectations?

Almost certainly not. The high–low dimension is of obvious importance. High expectations refer, for example, to the grades to be achieved at GCSE, the number of days of attendance children will manage over the coming school year or the standards of behaviour to be displayed in the school. These and other examples can all be measured and assessed in some way. As GCSE scores are the simplest to deal with, and form the cornerstone of much of the effective schooling research, let us take them as an instance.

Two teachers express their expectations for the grades students will achieve by the end of compulsory secondary schooling. One indicates a range of Cs to A*s with a definite skew to the top end, the other a range that indicates only a handful of A and B grades with C grades being the best that most of the students are expected to achieve. Who has the high expectations? In one sense the answer is obvious, but also somewhat trivial. High expectations like effective schooling, need to be understood in a value-added manner. If the teacher expressing higher expectations works in a highly selective grammar school then the value-added component of those expectations might be relatively low or even non-existent. In other words, as the student enters the school these high standards are what the regression equations of the school effectiveness researcher would have predicted. The teacher's expectations are a simple reflection of what she or he has experienced in the past and therefore has come to expect for the future. The second teacher, who has the lower absolute expectations, might be expressing greater optimism in that their predictions are higher than might be expected on the basis of student intake characteristics.

Prescriptive and probabilistic expectations

Rogers (1982) drew a distinction between expectations that were prescriptive and those which were probabilistic. Probabilistic expectations represent what we think is most likely to happen. Prescriptive expectations, on the other hand, tend to be expressed by the use of the word 'ought'. People are not just thought likely to perform at a particular level; they ought to. To put it another way, teachers take steps to try to ensure that they will. Prescriptive expectations are more than a passive response to the accumulation of experience; they are more than an individual's own estimate of regression curves. They are an expression of what they think ought to happen, what they want to happen and what they think they might be able to make happen.

Prescriptive expectations are at the centre of the concerns of the school effectiveness researcher. Prescriptive expectations are based on reality. We are discussing expectations here, not fantasies. However, prescriptive expectations can be more than just realistic predictions; they may also represent optimistic views of the future. At the end of the last paragraph I claimed that prescriptive expectations are what people think *ought* to happen, what they would *like* to happen and what they think they can *make* happen. The emphasis in this chapter will be on the third of these three conditions. What are the factors that determine the extent to which people believe themselves to be able to make the desirable happen?

Expectations then vary not only in terms of how high or low they may be, they vary too in terms of the extent to which they are prescriptive or probabilistic.

Individual and shared expectations

Blease (1983) drew a distinction between expectations held by one individual teacher and those shared throughout the school (or a department or any other section of the school that would be meaningful from the point of view of the student). We need therefore to consider ways in which networks of expectations might have different effects from those held by individual teachers. *School* effectiveness implies that effects will take place across the school. In as much as schools make a difference to the progress made by students, and in as much as the expectations held by teachers are part of that effect, then these expectations will be common across the school. School effectiveness researchers have recognised that the school might not always be the most appropriate level of analysis (e.g. Sammons *et al.*, 1994) and that school effectiveness might be a matter of departmental effectiveness. Either way, the recognition of shared expectations requires us to consider a number of further points. Blease (1983) argued that shared expectations would be more powerful in terms of producing self-fulfilling prophecies. Whatever impact the expectations of a single teacher might have will be magnified if repeated from one year to the next, or, in the secondary context, from one lesson to the next. If everybody seems to see us in the same way it must be harder to deny the validity of those perceptions, than if some perceptions are contradicted, or at least not supported by others.

However, there is another issue here that this chapter will wish to address. Models of the teacher expectancy process (e.g. Rogers, 1982) have attended to the ways in which individual teachers build up their initial expectations of individual students. Teachers can draw on a variety of information, and use a variety of processes and sub-processes in the task of generating specific expectations. Shared expectations across a system (school, department, etc.) suggest some commonality of process. There are a variety of ways in which this can take place. For example, the system itself can influence the information available and therefore the formation of expectations. The point to be made here is that system wide expectations, the consistent expectations referred to above, suggest the operation of school culture. The ways in which the culture of the school may influence the expectations held by teachers is another aspect of the process. This will have to be considered in order to achieve a full understanding of the role of expectations in effective schooling.

The functions of expectations

So far, however, we are only beginning to describe expectations in terms of what they might look like, not yet in terms of what they might do. Expectations will also need to be considered in terms of their functions.

Snyder (1992) has considered the functions served by the process of behavioural confirmation (or self-fulfilling prophecies). Although his discussion does not touch directly upon teacher expectations and their effects it does contain some important implications for our present concerns.

Snyder's own analysis concerns the work of social psychologists who have examined behavioural confirmation (and disconfirmation) as a part of the acquaintance process. Such situations, where individuals are beginning a relationship, offer a number of advantages for the social psychologist's research agenda. These situations enable the manipulation of potentially relevant factors in ways that would often be impossible, or unethical, in educational settings. It is important to acknowledge the need for caution in using the ideas emerging from this particular literature here. However, there does seem to be some general applicability to present concerns of the ideas discussed by Snyder.

Teachers will presumably have a concern with the learning of their students and, related to this, the behaviour of their students. The perceptions of students generated by teachers will be rich in terms related to these objectives with students being characterised as fast or slow learners, well or poorly behaved, and so on. A self-fulfilling prophecy occurs when a student who is perceived incorrectly as being of, say, a low level of ability comes to match those assumptions. A functional approach to this process requires us to ask not only how this might happen but also why. Why should a teacher persist with underestimations of a student's potential to the extent of 'forcing' that student to conform to the expectation? Perhaps more tellingly, we also need to ask why students would come to change their behaviour so as to match an expectation that would appear to offer them little. Social psychology, in education and elsewhere, has too often ignored these 'why' questions in favour of 'how' questions. A number of models of the teacher expectancy process exist which set out the various steps involved in the formation, transmission, perception and acceptance of expectations. To the extent that these models are correct they tell us how expectations may be formed, how they may be transmitted, how they may be perceived and how those perceptions may be acted upon. None of this tells us why any of this should happen, in whose interests it might be.

A functional analysis of expectations requires us to think in almost Darwinian terms about the nature of the process. If self-fulfilling prophecies have been taking place in classrooms, often to the disadvantage of students and teachers alike, then we must ask why this has continued. In evolutionary terms forms of behaviour that have no adaptive function would wither and eventually disappear. The converse of this suggests that continuing processes do have some significant purpose that in some way benefits the participants. The challenge of a functional analysis of teacher expectations and their effects is to attempt to say what these benefits might be.

Snyder first draws attention to the function of control. It is useful to conceptualise interpersonal perception as a control system. It is assumed that people construct understandings of others that enable them to predict and control the interactions they have with them (see also Zebrowitz, 1990). The reasons people may have for wanting control over their interactions with others will themselves be varied and will relate to the broad patterns of purposes lying behind the interactional sequence in the first place. The general assumption is that in most instances where we interact with others a sense of control is necessary for us to be able to anticipate a smooth interaction with the other. Social interaction with people we do not know well is always more difficult than with those with whom we are more familiar. We are not likely to be able to anticipate their reactions to our own remarks and moves. When the sensibilities of others are not understood the risk of causing unintentional offence is always greater.

Snyder's second relevant function concerns processes of ego-defence. Behavioural confirmation takes place when one or more of the participants in the relevant interaction are seeking to protect some facet of a self-image that some aspects of the interaction might challenge. As Snyder puts it, some expectations may serve the '...function of protecting people from accepting unpleasant truths about themselves' (p. 95). From the point of view of the teacher, it is not difficult to see how ego-defensive functions might operate. A failing student suggests a failing teacher. Low expectations help to reduce the sense of failure in a number of ways. Failure can be seen as the shortfall between outcome and expectation. Lower initial expectations clearly reduce the probability of failure so defined. (The deliberate lowering of expectations regarding economic well-being is a tried and trusted trick of politicians eager to encourage positive perceptions of themselves by the electorate.) Expectations can also help to direct the apportionment of responsibility (or blame) for failings seen to have occurred. It is clearly helpful to the teacher's ego to 'set things up' so that blame for failure will tend to attach to the student rather than to the teacher. I will return to these functions of control and ego-defence in greater detail later.

The dimensions of expectations

I asserted above that a unidimensional model of expectations was unlikely to provide a sufficient descriptive or analytical framework for the consideration of effective schooling. I have suggested that the degree to which teachers share expectations and the functions served by these expectations also need to be considered. However, this still leaves us with the single dimension of height (are the expectations high or low?). This unidimensional description is still likely to be inadequate to the task of explaining some of the variance between more and less effective schools. It is necessary to add a further dimension of breadth.

A high expectation sets a standard of performance in relation to particular criteria. A low expectation does just the same, simply setting a different standard. I stated above that prescriptive expectations concern the things that people think they will be able to make happen. It is in relation to this aspect that a multidimensional approach is needed.

An example will illustrate the point. A teacher expects low GCSE scores for a particular student. This expectation is currently probabilistic. We are looking at an early stage in the student's secondary school career and the expectation is a prediction based on performance to date. The teacher's prescriptive expectation, however, is higher. This student ought to do better and it ought to be possible to make this happen. How can the prescriptive and the probabilistic expectations be reconciled?

The answer would seem to lie in the breadth of the expectation. In other words we need to consider the other assumptions that a teacher makes alongside an appraisal of where the student will get to if current performance continues. At issue here is the belief system of the teacher regarding the elements seen to determine student success. This will clearly involve assumptions made by the teacher about the levels of ability and motivation characteristic of that student. However, in adding breadth to this we are also going to have to consider the beliefs the teacher has concerning the nature of that ability and motivation. In particular, what does the teacher believe that he or she can do about changing ability and motivational levels? When the teacher sees these characteristics of the student as fixed, or at least not amenable to teacher influence, then a low probabilistic expectation begins to develop into a prescriptive one. However if the teacher sees ability and/or motivation as student characteristics subject to influence by teacher action, then he or she may yet see a low probabilistic expectation take on a higher prescriptive tone.

The discussion so far has drawn attention to a number of claims.

- High expectations are frequently and regularly associated with effective schooling.
- There is an implication following from this that raising expectations will have the effect of enhancing the effectiveness of a school.
- Expectations are not merely actuarial predictions of future performance based on the past, they can contain prescriptive elements relating to what people think ought to happen.
- We need to consider the extent to which teachers might believe themselves capable of changing the outcomes expected on a probabilistic basis to those desired on a prescriptive basis.
- In doing this, teachers are drawing on a multi-dimensional conception of expectations, considering expectations in terms of breadth as well as height.
- Expectations, in common with other aspects of interpersonal perception, are considered to have a functional basis. An understanding of these functions is necessary if any change programmes are likely to be at all effective.
- Effective schools or school departments will presumably have expectations that are common to many if not all of the members of the staff

of that school or department. Shared expectations are likely to be more powerful than idiosyncratic ones in influencing the attainments of students and are therefore likely to be a particularly important aspect of effective schools. However, there is a need to understand the development of school- or department-wide expectations.

In other words, we need to examine the impact of school culture upon teacher expectations, with expectations understood in terms of breadth and height.

The normative basis of expectations

Waterhouse (1991) discusses some of the processes involved when teachers form impressions of students. He makes a number of points including the important observation that the process of building up an impression of a student may well vary from one school to another. However, the main point to draw on here is that teachers will base their perceptions on the idea of the average or 'normal' student. It is, suggests Waterhouse, the normal student who provides the rather indeterminate bedrock upon which teachers build other more idiosyncratic or consociate relationships with other students. In an historical context this has some significance. It presents a different light on the conclusions of other researchers such as Sharp and Green (1975). They have claimed that it is the ideal student who provides the core and with whom teachers form closer more consociate relationships. Students who deviate from this ideal are to some extent rejected and excluded from closer and developing consociate relationships. Waterhouse reports that teachers often find it difficult to say very much about the normal, average student. It is when a student deviates from this average image that the teacher is likely to begin to consider them in relation to the particular needs of each individual.

It seems reasonable to take this argument a step further and suggest that normative variations across schools will have important implications for the setting of expectations. Further, it will often be those who fall below the norm that teachers single out for special attention.

Accounts of expectancy effects have often assumed that teachers form expectations against the yardstick of the ideal student. It would be the ideal that determined what teachers thought ought to be happening. On the assumption that a considerable proportion of the teaching profession shares a view of the ideal, it is possible to suggest that the basis for expectations across the system also have a common foundation. However, if Waterhouse is correct in assuming that it is the normal that determines the basis of perceptions, then expectations will be more likely to vary across schools in line with the prevailing norms. Thus we would expect to find that teachers working in geographical areas with historically low levels of attainment will form lower expectations than those held by teachers working in more favoured areas. Thus the student from such an area might be doubly disadvantaged.

Secondly, Waterhouse's analysis suggests that teachers are likely to form particularly strong and well-formed expectations for those students who deviate from the norm. This may well advantage those who perform significantly above the normal level, but would again serve to disadvantage those whose careers start with below norm performance.

Good intentions, low expectations

The work on teacher expectations of Cooper and his colleagues (Cooper and Good, 1983) provides an example of some of the implications of this. Cooper's work is important for present purposes as it touches upon a number of the aspects of expectations alluded to above. In particular, Cooper's work emphasises the function of expectations and aspects of the breadth of expectations.

Reflecting the concerns of Snyder (1992) Cooper places a considerable emphasis on the control function. He reminds us that we need to consider why teachers would act to apparently disadvantage certain students. Cooper suggests that teachers single out lower attaining students for particular attention as a consequence of teachers' wishes to help their development. The lower attaining student falls into Waterhouse's category of those the teacher perceives in terms both richer and more fully and personally developed than the 'normal' student. These fuller, more consociate perceptions, suggest to the teacher a need for special attention in order to maximise that student's learning. In order to provide this attention the teacher believes that they need to exercise greater control over interactions with these students than with others. This in turn reflects the belief of the teacher that lower attaining (and lower ability) students will gain most benefit from interactions with a teacher where the teacher can direct what happens. Such control is most likely obtained when the interactions take place in relatively private one-to-one settings, and where the teacher is able to initiate the various steps taken. Consequentially, these students find teachers appearing unwilling to accept contributions made to classroom discussions (relatively public settings). Teachers also seem resistant to their contributions even when offered in the private setting of a one-to-one discussion. Cooper completes his analysis by arguing that the impact of this on student attributions is detrimental to the development of positive motivational forms.

This very sketchy outline of Cooper's work serves to illustrate how the road to lowering student motivation and standards of achievement is paved with good teacher intentions. While Cooper's analysis suggests a clear and fairly direct link between teacher expectations and worsening student performance, it is also clear that teachers are seen to be acting with the best of intentions. The problem, of course, is that the action which to the teacher logically follows from these initial expectations has a depressing rather than an elevating effect on the student. The final sting, the core of all self-fulfilling prophecies, is that the subsequent failure on the part of the student to improve, simply serves to confirm the teacher's initial expectations. The damaging cycle of events runs on.

The critical point here is not that the teachers in Cooper's studies held low expectations for their students. When teachers set expectations against a normative background then low expectations are unavoidable for some students. It is the other aspects of the expectations, referred to here as the breadth dimension, that is important. Essentially these further aspects concern the beliefs a teacher has about critical student characteristics, and the consequential beliefs concerning appropriate courses of teacher action.

Models of ability and motivation

The suggestion here is that these teacher beliefs concerning student characteristics will centre upon notions of the nature of ability and motivation. Essentially it is not the teacher's judgement of the level of ability and motivation that it is critical. It is the teacher's view of the nature of these constructs that matters most.

Research in motivation has emphasised the importance of an individual's belief concerning not only the level of their ability but also the nature of that ability. Dweck (1991) presents a particularly clear account of this. Students who perceive themselves as having a low level of ability are clearly likely to experience motivational problems. Life is simply easier in many respects if we see ourselves as being relatively able (in relation to others and to the tasks at hand). However, Dweck argues that low perceived ability does not necessarily lead to poor motivation unless the individual in question also believes that there is little or nothing they can do to improve the situation. Dweck and others (e.g. Nicholls, 1989) have provided evidence to show that people see ability either as a fixed entity or as an incremental facet of a person. As an entity, ability is seen as fixed (perhaps due to genetic factors or the impact of early experience) and as setting a ceiling on the ultimate level of performance possible. Low ability is therefore debilitating because it naturally suggests that one's personal ceiling may be lower than is needed to gain success within the school system or elsewhere. Given this scenario, most of us give up. The incremental view however, holds that ability ought to be understood as a skill, or collection of skills, and is therefore capable of enhancement. Current low levels of ability make life more difficult but do not preclude the possibility of ultimate success. One's focus therefore shifts to ways of enhancing ability, and, in so doing, one maintains motivation. Work by Nicholls (Nicholls and Miller, 1984) has suggested that young children will be unlikely to hold the entity view of ability and are therefore also unlikely to suffer the same motivational difficulties as their older counterparts. More recent work by Dweck (e.g. Cain and Dweck, 1995) suggests that even pre-school children may hold beliefs of an entity kind (although not directed at ability as such) which have a similar debilitating motivational impact.

Other researchers have shown potentially important links between teacher self-efficacy and teacher beliefs. For example, Marshall and Weinstein (1984) show that teachers who see themselves as higher on self-efficacy are more likely to see student ability as incremental. Importantly, of course, these ability beliefs refer to the teachers' views of the students. However, there is no available data concerning the nature of any causal relationships that might be involved here. It is quite possible that a heightened sense of teacher efficacy is a result of the prior belief that student ability is incremental. It is also possible that teacher efficacy beliefs will influence beliefs concerning ability. The nature of these relationships are of obvious importance when considering the implications for school improvement. I will return to the relationship between school culture and teacher efficacy beliefs below. Woolfolk and Hoy (1990) have further demonstrated relationships between general teacher efficacy and a custodial approach to teaching.

While there is some limited evidence to suggest a link between teacher efficacy beliefs and teacher views on the nature of ability, far less is known concerning the nature of the relationship between teacher efficacy beliefs and teacher's attitudes towards student motivation. Indeed, teachers' beliefs concerning the nature of motivation is a sadly neglected area of research. As with ability beliefs, at issue here is not simply the views teachers have about the level of their students' motivation. Of equal, if not greater significance, are the beliefs held by teachers regarding the nature of this motivation.

Rogers (1992) has suggested a number of different models of motivation which could act as guides to teachers' thinking. All of these models have been subjected to extensive research as models of motivation itself. What is unclear is the extent to which they are adopted by teachers and the range of factors that might determine the use that teachers make of them. Each of the models will be reviewed briefly here before their implications are discussed.

The first model owes most to the research and theorising of Atkinson (e.g. Atkinson and Raynor, 1977). Atkinson was concerned to set out the relationship between key aspects of personality and situational variables in the determination of an individual's motivational response to success and failure. The essence of this work, for present purposes, is to see motivation as being essentially a *function of personality*. Although the precise response of a person to any one experience of success or failure is determined by aspects of the situation, it is the relatively stable and enduring characteristics of personality that determines the broad brush of their response. Consistency over time and place is therefore to be expected.

The second model was derived from the work of Weiner (e.g. Weiner, 1986, 1992) who has applied attribution theory to an analysis of motivational dynamics. Weiner's essential claim is that motivational patterns are determined by the patterns of attributions people make for their successes and failures. Attribution theory has assumed that people are concerned to identify credible causes of significant events. Important instances of success and failure therefore, are likely to be understood by reference to what was believed to have made them happen. Weiner has demonstrated that these inferred causes of success and failure can be located on a number of dimensions and that the dimensional characteristics of particular causes determine further consequential beliefs, attitudes and emotions. For example, a cause of success or failure can be seen to be either stable or unstable. Stable causes are not likely to change in terms of how they operate or the level at which they operate, while unstable causes are. Effort is commonly given as an example of an unstable cause of success and failure while ability is frequently cited as a stable cause. (It will be noted that an entity view of ability is being invoked here. If an incremental view was to apply then ability, like effort, would be seen as an unstable cause.) Weiner then goes on to suggest that variations in attribution along the stability dimension will have an impact on future expectations. If events are attributed to stable causes, then more of the same is to be expected. This is essentially a recognition of logic. If the cause of an event continues to operate in a stable manner then it is difficult to resist the idea that the event is likely to be repeated. If the cause is unstable then it must follow that the repetition of the event itself must be less certain. Weiner goes on to develop similar ideas concerning other dimensions such as internal–external and controllable–uncontrollable.

There is a core simplicity to Weiner's ideas that has doubtless helped to develop the substantial level of interest and research effort they have provoked. As always this work has added a number of complicating factors that lie well beyond this present discussion. However, from Weiner's work arises a model of motivation as a *function of information processing*. One interpretation of attribution theory as applied to motivation has it that the rules of cognition which determine the attributions to be made are held in common (at least by those sharing key aspects of a culture) and that individual variation is therefore dependent upon the nature of the information to be processed. In the case of motivation this information will concern the frequency and nature of instances of success and failure. As people begin to develop different histories so their motivational dynamics also begin to diverge.

The third model identified by Rogers draws on subsequent work emphasising the importance of goals and related beliefs. Much of this has been alluded to above and the work of Dweck (Dweck and Leggett, 1988; Dweck, 1991) figures prominently. A goal based approach to motivation emphasises the individual's current goal state and other key beliefs that will determine the nature of their response to the vicissitudes of task engagement. A key distinction is that between learning and ego goals. Under a learning goal an individual focuses on the extent to which they personally have obtained task mastery, their focus is on individual progress. Under ego (or performance) goals the individual is more likely to be concerned with how they might appear to others. Have they presented themselves as capable or incapable? Have they maintained their position relative to other members of the pack? Learning goals also tend to encourage incremental views of the nature of ability. The distinction between the two goal states is most critical for those who are of lower levels of ability because performance goals, and the associated entity views of ability, are particularly debilitating when the task appears to be particularly difficult or when social comparisons tend to be negative. More importantly, it is now clear that changes in the operation of a classroom can have a strong impact on the goals adopted by students (Jagacinski, 1992). Jagacinski's review provides clear evidence for the importance of classroom context in determining the goals adopted by students, but also reveals the clear need for further research in order for the precise impact of the teacher to be laid bare. The third model of motivation then is one conceptualising motivation as a *function of learning goals*.

The three models, stressing the functions of personality, information processing and learning goals, may serve as a potted history of the development of motivation theory itself. However, it is also the case that as theory development has moved from an emphasis on the relatively stable and enduring aspects of personality through to an emphasis on the less stable function of learning goals, there has been an increase in the recognition of the potential for teacher influence. Motivation as personality allows for little in the way of teacher intervention. Teachers subscribing to this view are unlikely to regard personality change as falling within their remit (and the older the students the more likely this is to be the case). The information processing model allows for increased teacher intervention, but again suggests that as time passes, and the weight of the student's history of success and failure grows, the influence of a teacher on student motivation will decrease. However, the information processing model does recognise that information patterns can develop differently across different areas of experience. The student with a history of relative failure in maths, but of success in English, for example, might be expected to have different motivational patterns in these two domains. The most recent goal-based approach offers the greatest role for the impact of the teacher. If learning goals can be influenced by teacher action (the manner of presentation of tasks, the feedback given, the assessment procedures used) then there is always hope that student motivation can be improved. Furthermore, student motivation is increasingly recognised as a joint function of the interactions between teacher and student, rather than as relatively fixed student characteristic.

In relation to teacher expectations and their bearing on the effectiveness of schooling it is the beliefs of teachers rather than researchers that matter. Whatever research evidence might say, if teachers perceive motivation as a stable function of personality then they will make their judgements on that basis. If motivation is seen as fixed, and it is seen as inadequate, then the prognosis is poor. Just as there is limited evidence to show that teachers with greater belief in their own efficacy see student ability as something that can be developed, so it is suggested that higher teacher self-efficacy will also relate to perceptions of motivation as something that teachers can enhance.

School culture

School effectiveness researchers have frequently emphasised the notion of 'school ethos'. Hargreaves (1995) has provided some useful thoughts on the way in which the nebulous concept of ethos can be transformed into a tighter and empirically more useful notion of school culture. However, we still know very little about the precise ways in which school culture can effect teacher expectations and beliefs.

Eden (1990, 1993; Oz and Eden, 1994) has examined the research into the impact of leadership styles in organisations and concludes that leadership can have important implications for organisational culture. In particular, his work has shown how changes in beliefs concerning the nature of ability can have an impact on the behaviour of supervisors responsible for training subordinates. Those who believed that information concerning the ability of trainees related to entity type abilities achieved less in the training than did those who were encouraged to regard initial ability levels as being changeable (the incremental view). The limited nature of the research makes it difficult to build up clear generalisations. However, DeCharms (1976) long ago established the ways in which focused attempts at changing teacher beliefs can lead to changed classroom practice and then into enhanced student motivation. Maehr (1987, Maehr and Fyans, 1989) has also begun the task of analysing school culture with a view to determining its impact upon student motivation and achievement. Maehr and his colleagues also emphasise the importance of leadership functions. They also note that as culture has its impact on individuals through their perceptions of it, then school culture is best understood as a factor relating to individual differences. A number of perceived cultures may exist in the one school (a point that Hargreaves would also accept) and that different cultures may have different effects on various students. This developing emphasis on the ways in which school managers can influence school culture, which in turn impacts student motivation provides confirmation of the early emphasis placed on the importance of the headteacher by the school effectiveness researchers (Mortimore et al., 1988).

Deci and Ryan (1985) and Carl Rogers (1984) have also discussed the ways in which school culture can influence the extent to which teachers are likely to adopt defensive ways of working. In setting out his conditions for a radical reform of education, Rogers suggests that the reform programme must start with administrators and managers. These will then influence teacher behaviour. Teachers, in turn, will influence students. The basis of Rogers' claim is that when teachers experience pressure they will act to preserve their own self-esteem rather than take the risks required to produce effective student learning. Deci and Ryan make similar claims from a different point of origin. A school with a learning focus is not only one that permits students to focus on learning rather than performance. Such a school culture also enables teachers to see learning goals as more important than performance goals. In the pressured school, teacher expectations increasingly take on ego-defensive functions. Low expectations for students serve to protect teachers against the charge of failure. In the learning school, teacher expectations can take on a more productive function encouraging higher (and, for the teacher, potentially riskier) expectations to develop. Several motivation theorists (e.g. Covington, 1992) have discussed the concept of 'intensification'. Governments, keen to improve education, intensify the pressures on teachers, generally through forms of public accountability and contingent funding. Such intensification is likely to have unfortunate effects on teacher expectations.

Conclusion

This chapter has attempted to illustrate ways in which teacher expectancy effect literature continues to have an enduring impact on the broader social psychology of education. In particular it has attempted to show how work on teacher expectations can be seen as central to the interests of the school effectiveness and school improvement movement. Walberg (1981, cited in Maehr and Fyans, 1989) has claimed that student motivation can account for up to 20 per cent of the variation in student attainment. The value added by effective schooling is likely to lie within this 20 per cent. What teachers expect of their students will play an important part in the determination of student motivation. However, it is insufficient to simply regard teacher expectations as ranging from high to low. It is the prescriptive element of teacher expectations that has a special significance for changing student outcomes. This chapter has attempted to show how prescriptive expectations touch upon a range of teacher expectations and beliefs that influence the extent to which they are likely to see desired changes as being possible. Effective schools are 'can do' schools with 'can do' teachers. The challenge for future social psychological research within the classroom is to demonstrate just what a can do school and teacher are and the ways in which these positive elements can be enhanced. Success in this endeavour should increase the proportion of can do students.

References

Atkinson, J. and Raynor, J. (Eds.) (1977) Personality, Motivation and Achievement (Washington, DC: Hemisphere).
Blanck, P.D. (Ed.) (1993) Interpersonal Expectations: Theory, research and applications (Paris: Cambridge University Press).
Blease D. (1983) Teacher expectations and the self-fulfilling prophecy. Educational Studies, 9, 123–30.
Cain, K.M. and Dweck, C.S. (1995) The relation between motivational patterns and achievement cognitions through the elementary-school years. Merrill-Palmer Quarterly, 41(1), 25–52.
Covington, M.V. (1992) Making The Grade: A self-worth perspective on motivation and school reform (Cambridge: Cambridge University Press).
Cooper, H. and Good, T. (1983) Pygmalion Grows Up: Studies in the expectation communication process (New York: Longman).
Cuttance, P. (1992) Evaluating the effectiveness of schools. In Reynolds, D. and Cuttance, P. (Eds.), School Effectiveness: Research, policy and practice (London: Cassell).
DeCharms, R. (1976) Enhancing Motivation: Change in the classroom (New York: Irvington).
Deci, E.L. and Ryan, R.M. (1985) Intrinsic Motivation and Self-determination in Human Behavior (New York: Plenum).
Dusek, J.B. (Ed.) (1985) Teacher Expectancies (London: Lawrence Erlbaum).
Dweck, C.S. (1991) Self-theories and goals: their role in motivation, personality and development. Nebraska Symposium on Motivation, 1990, 38, 199–235.
Dweck, C.S. and Leggett, E.L. (1988) A social-cognitive approach to motivation and personality. Psychological Review, 95, 256–73.
Eden, D. (1990) Pygmalion without interpersonal contrast effects – whole groups gain from raising manager expectations. Journal of Applied Psychology, 75, 394–8.
Eden, D. (1993) Interpersonal expectations in organisations, in Blanck, P.D. (Ed.), Interpersonal Expectations: Theory, research and applications (Paris: Cambridge University Press).
Goldenberg, C. (1992) The limits of expectations: A case for case knowledge about teacher expectancy effects. American Educational Research Journal, 29, 517–44.
Hargreaves, D. (1995) School culture, school effectiveness and school improvement. School Effectiveness and School Improvement, 6, 23–46.
Jagacinski, C.M. (1992) The effects of task involvement and ego involvement on achievement related cognitions and behaviours, in Schunk, D.H. and Meece, J. (Eds.), Student Perceptions In The Classroom (Hillsdale, NJ: LEA).
Jussim, L. (1989) Teacher expectations: Self-fulfilling prophecies, perceptual biases and accuracy. Journal of Personality and Social Psychology, 57, 469–80.
Maehr, M.L. (1987) Managing organisational culture to enhance motivation. In Maehr, M.L. and Kleiber, D.A. (Eds.) Advances in motivation and achievement, Volume 5, Enhancing motivation (Greenwich, CT: JAI Press).

Maehr, M.L. and Fyans, L.J. Jr. (1989) School culture, motivation and achievement. In Maehr, M.L. and Ames, C. (Eds.), Advances In Motivation and Achievement: Motivation enhancing environments, Volume 6 (Greenwich, CT: JAI).

Marshall, H. and Weinstein, R. (1984) Classroom factors affecting students' self-evaluations: an interactional model. Review of Educational Research, 54, 301–25.

Miller, D.T. and Turnbull, W. (1986) Expectancies and interpersonal processes. Annual Review of Psychology, 37, 233–56.

Mortimore, P., Sammons, P., Stoll, L., Lewis, D. and Ecob, R. (1988) School Matters: The Junior Years (Wells: Open Books).

National Commission on Education (1996) Success Against The Odds: Effective schools in disadvantaged areas (London: Routledge).

Nicholls, J.G. (1989) The Competitive Ethos and Democratic Education (London: Harvard University Press).

Nicholls, J.G. and Miller, A.T. (1984) Development and its discontents: the differentiation of the concept of ability, in Nicholls, J.G. (Ed.), Advances in Motivation and Achievement, Volume 3. The Development of Achievement Motivation (London: JAI Press).

Oz, S. and Eden, D. (1994) Restraining the golem – boosting performance by changing the interpretation of low scores. Journal of Applied Psychology, 79, 744–54.

Rogers, C. (1984) Freedom to Learn in the Eighties (Columbus, OH: Merrill).

Rogers, C.G., (1992) The enhancement of motivation: Some core concerns. Conference paper. British Psychological Society, Education Section Conference. November, Berkhamstead.

Rogers, C.G. (1982) A Social Psychology of Schooling (London: RKP).

Rosenthal, R. and Jacobson, L. (1968) Pygmalion in the Classroom (New York: Holt, Rinehart and Winston).

Rosenthal, R. and Rubin, D. (1978) Interpersonal expectancy effects: the first 345 studies. Behavioural and Brain Sciences, 3, 377–86.

Sammons, P., Thomas, S., Mortimore, P., Cairns, R. and Bausor, J. (1994) Understanding the process of school and departmental effectiveness. Conference Paper, BERA, Oxford.

Sammons, P., Hillman, J. and Mortimore, P. (1995) Key Characteristics of Effective Schools: A review of school effectiveness research (London: Office for Standards in Education).

Sharp, R. and Green, A. (1975) Education and Social Control (London: Routledge and Kegan Paul).

Snyder M (1992) Motivational foundations of behavioral confirmation. Advances In Experimental Social Psychology, 25, 67–114.

Stoll, L. and Fink, D. (1996) Changing Our Schools: Linking school effectiveness and school improvement (Buckingham: Open University Press).

Waterhouse, S (1991) Person formulation in the process of schooling. British Journal of Sociology of Education, 12, 45–60.

Weiner, B. (1986) An Attributional Theory of Motivation and Emotion (New York: Springer-Verlag).

Weiner, B. (1992) Human Motivation: Metaphors, theories and research (London: Sage).

Woolfolk, A.E. and Hoy, W.K. (1990) Prospective teachers' sense of efficacy and beliefs about control. Journal of Educational Psychology, 82, 81–91.

Zebrowitz, L. (1990) Social Perception (Milton Keynes, Open University Press).

Chapter 5
Teacher education and psychologies of skill

PETER TOMLINSON

In this chapter I want to argue for the relevance of work on the nature and acquisition of skilful capability for teacher education and in particular to consider some of the factors that may have been and still seem to be hindering its utilisation as a potentially central resource for theoretical illumination and practical effectiveness in this domain. Such a reflective focus seems particularly appropriate by way of a contribution to this *Festschrift* for my former colleague Dennis Child, given our shared concern and parallel efforts as authors to promote the benefits of educational psychology for teachers.

The chapter will start by presenting arguments for the importance in teacher preparation of an understanding of practical competence and its assisted acquisition. I then highlight the basic, traditional notion of skill as purposeful practical capability and suggest how major strands in the modern understanding of skill and skill acquisition are applicable to teaching. But I then also suggest that the topic of practical capability is one in which everyday usage and formal theories within our culture offer a mix of other traditional part-conceptions and terminology that somehow seem to undermine educators' systematic thinking and to close them off from the potential of skill psychology's contribution. Critical awareness of these alternative 'psychologies of skill' therefore seems a prerequisite to any progress in using the well-grounded ones, and that is what the second part of the chapter will deal with. The final section offers a reminder that valid insights from psychology will not necessarily generate simplified quick-fixes. Rather, that as recent research in this area indicates, they may add new impetus to some very old controversies regarding teacher education and training.

Teaching as skill?

The need for conceptual clarity

One of the problems facing anyone who wants to think and communicate clearly about topics as familiar as teaching or skill is that, precisely because of this familiarity, a multitude of existing terms and ideas offer themselves. The flexibility and richness of human language are such that many of these terms can themselves each carry a number of distinct though usually linked senses. Although our intuitive sensitivity to context can often take care of this in everyday talk, this multiplicity of meanings poses a potential for cross-purpose and misunderstanding. Paradoxically, in fact, it is particularly when we try to make headway by thinking such things through explicitly, for example in initial training courses, that progress is threatened by a whole range of conflicting assumptions and thought habits at various levels. To indicate just one form of difficulty, there is, for instance, the tension between our tendency to assume that words must somehow have singular, shared, constant meanings on the one hand, and the evident, but easily forgettable fact, that on the other hand the same word may be used to convey different meanings. Worse, different people can have their own habitual meanings and preferred terms, and still more confusing, the same individual may use the same word differently on different occasions, often quite intuitively, without realising it.

There are many other such tensions. An important general point is that they apply to the word usages brought by both student-teachers and teacher-educators or mentors. Such assumptions and stances therefore need explicit consideration whenever we're thinking about the development of teacher education strategies, at virtually any level. A more specific point is that when it comes to existing understandings of the nature of teaching and teacher preparation, and in particular the nature of skilful capability, then in my experience a fascinating range of ideas tend to be in play.

The need for conceptual clarity may be clear, then, but systematic treatment of the sorts of issue just raised would doubtless require excursions into psycholinguistics, socio-linguistics, philosophical analysis and deconstruction, and so forth (older readers may at this point be muttering that in the good old days we did actually have such a thing as philosophy of education on the UK ITT timetable...). But here we encounter the first of a number of dilemmas, in that there are also various indications that for many people in education, perhaps particularly in this country (cf. Simon, 1988), attempting to conduct such a ground-clearing excursion before 'getting down to the business' is perceived as an unnecessarily academic 'turn-off'. Given the stance I have been taking, the dilemma is rather acute. For not only do I agree with Michael Beveridge (1996) that education needs more, not less, radical reflection, but it seems obvious that failure to confront issues of definition, meaning and value can only perpetuate underlying stances that may actually be getting in the way of teacher education benefiting from otherwise useful intellectual resources, in particular the psychology of skill.

The implication therefore appears to be that a more direct focus on the main ideas may be preferable at this point, letting various qualifications and distinctions emerge in the course of establishing a basic framework. There is of course something of a further dilemma here, in that going straight for the main message may appear prescriptive if the reader doesn't follow up the subsequent argument and discussion. But one has to start somewhere, so let me embark on the more direct approach by explaining what I do and don't mean by the view that teaching involves a typically complex, open kind of human skill.

Teaching as complex, open skill

There are various ways of getting at the common aspects of meaning shared by terms like *skill, capability, competence, expertise* and *art*. We need, however, to distinguish the issue of *definition*, what we mean by a word, from that of *understanding*, how we portray what's involved in what we've just targeted with our definition, though, as we shall see, the two are interlinked.

Defining skill: what are we talking about?

It seems clear that the word *skill* is currently used with a number of possible meanings: It's important to ask whether there is any core concept amongst such meanings which is in any sense more basic than the others. By 'more basic' I mean in the historical sense of being a more firmly established usage of the word and in the linguistic–logical sense that it informs other meanings, which tend to be part-aspects which appear in turn to be derived from it.

Leaving the background arguments for the reader to pursue elsewhere (cf. Griffiths, 1987; Tomlinson, 1995a, 1995b, 1997, in press) and qualifiers for later below, it seems clear that there is indeed such a basic, traditional meaning. If we try to express this in straightforward verbal terms, we get something like:

> being skilled means 'being good at something'.

To be slightly more explicit and systematic, we might want to extend this to:

> A skill is a relatively consistent ability to achieve a particular kind of goal through action in/on relevant kinds of contexts.

Particular skills are thus identified by reference to their content, that is, their goals, action-processes and/or contexts. These can be of very differing sorts, from physical–manual capabilities like carving wood through intellectual–symbolic instances like solving simultaneous equations and translating from one language to another, to social capabilities that are mixtures of other kinds, for instance driving a car in a particular road system. Notice that the above definition does not specify anything about how such purposes are to be achieved, although some writers do like to include *economy* as a characteristic of the actions involved in well-developed skill usage. Nor does it require sure-fire perfection: even the medal-winning Olympic gymnast slips up now and again. Nor, importantly, does it actually specify that the ability must be learned or learnable and still less does it require that it should have been taught, trained or that it be teachable or trainable, let alone by any particular means. What it does focus on is a disposition or capacity to achieve a particular kind of purpose: being 'able to do something' primarily means 'being able to bring about an intended state of affairs'.

From this point of view, though perhaps not from some of the others to be discussed below, teaching surely qualifies as a form of skill. For teaching is a purposeful activity that involves teachers conducting interactions with learners designed to result in the learners acquiring capacities and dispositions they did not have when they started. In other words, teaching is essentially activity seeking to promote learning (cf. Hirst, 1971; Fenstermacher, 1986; Tomlinson, 1995a). It can be done more or less effectively, people can be relatively good or bad at it, generally or at particular forms and in particular content areas, with particular types of learner, age-range, and so forth. So teaching capability is a form of skill, even if in many respects it is an especially problematic form, since to start with even the goals of teaching are difficult to characterise and often highly contested. But to portray the skilful nature of teaching capability and to see how teaching precisely does not correspond to certain other conceptions of skill, it is useful first to consider something of what modern work, particularly from psychology and philosophy, tells us about the typical nature of skilful activity, capability and learning.

Understanding skill: how does it work?

Having targeted what we basically mean when we talk about skill, what characteristics does skill turn out to have when we examine 'how it works'? Although educationists do not seem to have been aware of the fact until very recently indeed (cf. Tomlinson, 1992), the nature of skilled action is something that has been pursued within a number of disciplines and over a considerable period of time. The major area is arguably psychology, where there has been a major cognitive psychological tradition in the study of skill stretching back at least to the Second World War period (cf. Welford, 1968; Gellatly, 1986), recently resurrected in North America under the label of the study of *expertise* (cf. Chi, Glaser and Farr, 1988; Bereiter and Scardamalia, 1993). Philosophy has also been important, with the nature of action a central focus of the philosophy of mind in English-speaking circles (e.g. Ryle, 1949; Polyani, 1956) and of European philosophers such as Martin Heidegger and Maurice Merleau-Ponty (cf. Dreyfus, 1987).

Characteristics of skill

Arguably and for reasons that will become apparent below, the most important aspects of skill to emphasise are those that have just featured in our definition, namely that skill is purposeful and context-sensitive. The purposeful aspect reminds us that skill involves values and motivation. These give point to the activity and are the background that generates a person's goals and drives their action attempts (in combination with their insights into how goals may be achieved and their reading of the situation). Correspondingly, the basic point of the activity of teaching is the promoting of learners' acquisition of capabilities such as knowledge and skill.

It is also important to realise that skills and the activities they generate can vary not only in specific content, but also in general ways. A very important dimension is their openness–closedness, which has consequences for their difficulty, learnability and teachability. The expression was originally coined to refer to the predictability of simple manual task contexts (cf. Poulton, 1957) but seems extendible to what we might call the 'readability' of the task context the performer has to cope with. Thus openness–closedness seems to depend on three qualities:

- the degree of *regularity or irregularity* of features needing to be taken into account: the more regular, the more closed (easier), the more irregular or random the more open (difficult)
- The degree of *clear-cutness or fuzziness* of the feature: the easier to discern, the more closed (easier), the messier and more subtle, the more open (difficult)
- The *simplicity or complexity*: the more such features to be processed, the more open (difficult): juggling five balls at a time, for instance, is more difficult than juggling just two.

In these terms, teaching appears to be a particularly complex, open type of purposeful activity and teaching capability a correspondingly open kind of skill. Its goals are typically complex and messy, so are its contexts: a teacher typically deals with relatively large numbers of other humans at a time, who differ in many relevant ways and who may have their own goals and strategies which may be by no means at one with the teacher's.

Skilled action is also typically characterised by the fluency, economy and ease with which goals are achieved: the expert's performance typically looks fluent, seamless and simple to the observer, and feels relatively effortless and fluent to the performer. This seamlessness actually makes it difficult, especially for novices, to see how the performer is actually 'doing it' and equally difficult for proficient performers to realise how complex their actions are.

This tends to mask another important feature, the strategic nature of skill. Being 'good at' something means having effective ways of doing it, that is, strategies for acting on the relevant contexts in ways that make goal achievement likely. Strategies are particular actions directed towards goal achievement, based on the reading of ongoing events. This not only involves the performer reacting appropriately to what has just happened, but also to what he or she anticipates will happen next, a requirement that is relatively obvious, for instance, in ball games. Indeed, the ways one reads the situation may themselves be counted part of the strategic activity of a skilled performance. Again, as various writers have claimed (cf. Lowyck, 1980; Leinhardt and Greeno, 1986; Tomlinson, 1995a,b) this appears to apply very clearly to teaching, where anticipation is as important as anywhere else: the reactivity as opposed to pro-activeness of student-teachers, for instance, is all too familiar to teacher-educators.

This strategic aspect of the skilfulness of teaching is still more apparent when we recall the open–closed skill dimension. In closed skill situations where things are relatively regular, clear-cut and simple, it is possible to have strategies that are so guaranteed we tend to call them not strategies, but procedures, techniques or, in systems theory, jargon, algorithms. But in more open tasks of the kind teaching exemplifies so well, things are less certain and we can only have heuristic strategies, that is, ways of going about things that have varying degrees of probability of success. Here skill involves much more 'on-line', 'on the hoof' adaptation to less predictable circumstance, drawing appropriately on a repertoire of strategies. Correspondingly, the more open–complex the task, the more strategic ways there may be of achieving it, though even when combined, this is typically insufficient to make success a certainty.

The strategic nature of skill also brings out another of its important features, the fact that it is in various senses knowledge-based. Skilful people 'know how', they have a 'procedural knowledge' of what to do, they carry within them plans of action. But they also have to have some idea of when to do such actions, which must be grounded in some representation of the context and how it works. This is sometimes called 'knowing-that' or 'declarative knowledge', and though often contrasted with 'knowing how', appears in fact to be part of it. Such knowledge also appears to be exceedingly rich and detailed, relatively specific to the relevant action contexts and, importantly, may be deployed at different levels of awareness. These features have also been established in the arena of teachers' practical knowledge (cf. Carter, 1990), where we've heard much in recent years about the intuitive 'craft knowledge' of teaching but also the need for reflectiveness (cf. Schön, 1983, 1987). Variation in the awareness level at which people hold their skilful know-how is linked with two further characteristics: the typical complexity of skilled action and the nature of skill acquisition.

Although skilful action tends to look seamless and simple, close examination typically reveals that it is actually complex and multilayered. Even in its closed, relatively simple forms, skilled action typically involves coordination of sub-actions, the most basic kind being the interplay of the performer's reading of the situation with their actions on it. This is all the more the case to the extent that the goals and contexts are open–complex as described above. Coordination of perception and action must obviously be ongoing in activities that are extended in time, like, say, driving a car, for example. But, as driving also illustrates nicely, skilled activity also tends to be hierarchically embedded: it has actions and sub-actions, skills and sub-skills, embedded within it (e.g. driving includes gear changing, which includes gear lever placement, which includes finding the gear lever, etc.). Moreover, these actions typically require coordinating both within and across levels in ways that are adapted to the situation and its possibilities. Generally speaking, the more embedded the sub-action, the more unconsciously and intuitively it seems to be managed in mature skill. Once again, the features described in this paragraph very much correspond to those that have been pointed out in modern analyses of the demands of teaching (cf. Doyle, 1986) and studies of experienced versus novice teachers (cf. Berliner, 1986).

Acquiring skill

Although in my experience commonsense conceptions are not so precise as to define skill as something that has to be learned, people often take it for granted that this is so. And indeed, the systematic capabilities we are calling skills do typically turn out to be learned through various kinds of action and experience. Mainstream work on skill acquisition (cf. Welford, 1968; Gellatly, 1986; Anderson, 1990; Morrison, 1991; Schmidt, 1991) indicates that it actually involves a number of types of learning, including the acquiring of concepts and forms of awareness, as well as action strategy plans. With suitable experience much of the action and situational awareness deployed in well-developed skill has become automatised and intuitive. Indeed, as driving again shows well, proficient performance in a great many human activities may just not be possible unless much of the component processing has attained this intuitive status. Putting this differently:

automatisation seems to be nature's way of overcoming the severe limitations of our conscious thinking and is thus a major feature of human skill (though not, it needs pointing out, its sole or defining feature).

The mainstream view has been that sooner or later skill acquisition requires a considerable amount of 'learning by doing'. Not just through random bits of behaviour – 'trials' – however, but repeated attempts informed by planning and corrected by relevant and relatable feedback. Although he did not refer to it, this psychological tradition may be linked to aspects of Donald Schön's influential emphasis on reflection-in-and-on-action (Schön, 1983, 1987). The implication is that the acquisition of practical capability requires cycles of plan–attempt–feedback–replan, a process which when done with the same action unit tends to produce a gradual tuning (cf. Norman, 1978) that makes it more accurate, economical and intuitive. Things can often get messy in that different action units may need targeting and breaking down into constituents that are sufficiently manageable for the learner at their current stage. And there then arises the need to reintegrate the part-aspects into an eventual full strategy.

Such acquisition processes can typically take very many forms, different paths and considerable time, but in so far as they're successful, then the traditional view (cf. Fitts and Posner, 1967) has been that skill learners tend to go through three phases:

- a *cognitive phase* in which they're consciously developing plans and awareness of what to do and when; which is experienced as particularly difficult and painstaking
- an *associative phase* in which things start to come together and get more intuitive
- an *autonomous phase*, where the learner is capable of the activity and further learning tends to take the form of unconscious fine tuning and efficiency gains.

Although the classical cognitive psychology view of skill does not make any assumption that skills are necessarily teachable, recent Neo-Vygotskyan work (cf. Wertsch, 1985; Tharp and Gallimore, 1988) has reminded us that humans do tend to need assistance, formally or informally, for their learning by doing. I have suggested in more detail elsewhere (Tomlinson, 1995c) that the basic functions of the skill learning cycle are the obvious indicators of correspondingly basic coaching functions for the assisting of skill development and that this affords a sensible framework for the mentoring of student teachers.

Nevertheless, the suggestion that teaching can be usefully considered as a complex form of open skill is not without its problems. In my experience this idea is resisted by quite a few educationists, though more by teacher-educators than teachers. This seems in some measure due to the somewhat different associations the term skill has taken on within educational culture and so it seems worthwhile to critically examine the various forms of 'skills talk' that have arisen in recent years and, more particularly, the range of conceptions or 'psychologies of skill' they appear to convey. When we do this, I'm afraid we find a situation in which there is a real hindrance to progress, in that the otherwise useful traditional term 'skill' seems to have been hijacked by partial usage and one-sided views (cf. Barrow, 1987). Worse still, other formal theories and everyday usage tend if anything to reinforce the confusion by becoming subtlely tinged with such unfortunate associations.

Alternative 'psychologies of skill'

If one investigates what people understand by the word skill, then in my experience (which has mainly been with teachers taking masters degrees) one typically finds that they either already possess or are quick to recognise the central idea of skill sketched above, i.e. as relatively specific, purposeful capability. But they also evidence a range of other strands, which sometimes appear to take the upper hand when they consider certain sorts of educational issues. Although it is important to go into some detail on these strands, it seems worth pointing out first that many of them spring from a way of thinking that is deeply embedded within Western culture.

This stance is known formally as *mind–body dualism* (cf. Ryle, 1949), so called because it splits the person into two parts, mind and body, which are seen as totally different in nature. Thinking and understanding are mental matters, this view says, they take place in that part of the person known as mind (or sometimes as soul, spirit, psyche and so on), which deals in thoughts, feeling and other mental abstractions. On the other hand, according to this dualism, action and skill have little to do with understanding because they're about doing and doing is different from thinking, it is 'brute action' done by the other part, the physical body. This background splitting of thinking and doing appears to have correspondingly influenced many of the conceptions we find of action capability. Furthermore, this applies not only to everyday conceptions, but also to some influential but limited formal psychological theories, such as behaviourism. This is not perhaps too surprising, since early formal theories in psychology as elsewhere tend to develop originally out of everyday thinking anyway. But the relative clarity of formal models such as behaviourism is such that it can in fact help us discern and counteract both their own shortcomings and those of their more camouflaged versions within the traditional dualist background. So let us examine formal behaviourism first.

Formal behaviourism: the s → r approach

Nowadays in education references to behaviourist psychology tend to be associated with a minority position, the radical approach of B.F. Skinner, and that to some extent with the domain of special educational needs (see the chapter by David Sugden in this volume, pp. 212–28). However, although they seem now to be largely forgotten, for several decades in the earlier part of this century, more developed forms of behaviourism and neo-behaviourism exerted sustained and arguably long-lasting influence. Their influence was particularly on American psychology, but in turn also on educational thinking and in particular the ways educationists' thought about skill.

The paradigm or basic model of behaviourism was known alternatively as the *s → r approach* because essentially it viewed behaviour as *response* (*r*) to a *stimulus* or situation (*s*) impinging on the person (or animal, since the model was designed so as not to have to call on mental notions such as thinking). The stimulus thus caused the response by virtue of connections established by various kinds of associative learning based on reward and/or closeness in time (cf. Tomlinson, 1981).

It is unclear whether in their terms behaviourist psychologists regarded skill as residing in the stimulus–response connection (which would at least fit with the idea of skill as a disposition) or in the actual response (which is how some writers seem to use it and which fits with their emphasis on the observable), though both usages are to be found. But what does seem clear is that we have here a causal-reactive model of behaviour. This is somewhat at odds with the basic traditional conception we saw earlier of skilled action as inherently purposeful and it certainly conflicts with the anticipatory quality that has been seen to be a central feature of skilful performance. So, although neo-behaviourism did eventually develop quite complex notions of 'habit-family hierarchies' and the like (cf. Berlyne, 1965), when it comes to illuminating the nature of skill, the basic *s → r* unit appears to be limited in its application to simple, drill-inculcatable behaviour sequences that could suffice only at best for the kinds of entirely specifiable tasks referred to above as simple–closed.

I suggested earlier that many contemporary educationists are unaware of all this. Paradoxically, however, when it comes to formal ideas about skill, the only contribution many educationists seem to be aware of from psychology is the largely neo-behaviourist work of Robert M. Gagné (cf. Tomlinson and Swift, 1992). Although Gagné shifted during his career from a neo-behaviourist *s → r* outlook to an information-processing position (cf. Gagné, 1965, 1985), his best known contribution was to try to deal with the complexity and hierarchical embeddedness of physical and intellectual skill in terms of the simpler learning processes recognised by the neo-behaviourist approach.

Thus the main skill-related idea available to English-speaking educationists trained since the 1960s has arguably been the Gagnéan/behaviourist view which sees skill as a hierarchy of responses. Correspondingly, in this view, training for skill is seen as first requiring a task analysis, that is, a clarification of the constituent behaviours and sub-behaviours on which they depend, and then as inculcation of this hierarchy from the bottom up, starting with the most specific 'bits'. Thus in the eyes of many educationists, formal Behaviourist psychology has probably pushed the traditional idea of 'skill as integrated capability' towards the dualist 'skills as separate behaviours' view, in spite of Gagné's emphasis on hierarchality. In my view, although the Gagnéan approach does highlight some important features of skill, it clearly also leaves out some other important ones and preserves aspects of the dualist split. In turn, this makes educationists who are aware only of this approach rightly uncomfortable when someone suggests teaching might be considered as a form of skill.

Commonsense behaviourism: skill as doing

These ideas have tended to be relatively explicit and clear in formal behaviourism, but informal everyday thinking about action and skill also tends to harbour behaviourist strands, though more subtly. As is typical of 'commonsense outlooks' (cf. Hargreaves, 1980), for all their richness, they do not tend to be well defined or explicit. This makes them hard to analyse, but probably many of the commonsense elements one currently finds intertwined with other ideas about capability stem not only from our long mind–body dualist tradition, they also appear nowadays to be promoted in turn by the seep-through effect of formal behaviourist psychology, particularly on ideas about training.

The 'action-as-behaviour-separate-from-thinking' side of traditional dualist outlooks tends to view skill in a rigid sort of way, amounting to something like 'being able to do the procedures which guarantee achievement of the goal in question'. Hence we find traditional sayings like 'practice makes perfect', corresponding to a view of skill acquisition by training, which this perspective construes essentially as a matter of showing and telling the trainee 'the right way to do it' and then drilling them in its repetition. This seems the probable basis for the reticence, often strong if also inarticulate, its holders may nevertheless feel about referring to complex, subtle or outstanding capabilities such as musicianship as 'merely skill', with terms such as 'art' being preferred in such cases (cf. Sloboda, Davidson and Howe, 1994).

In the last few decades, moreover, this traditional strand appears to have been extended by the influence of formal behaviourist psychology, as evident in the now widespread adoption in educational and employment circles of behaviourist 'skills talk' (cf. Barrow, 1987). This sort of thing currently seems to be going on, for example, in sports commentators' use of 'skills' to refer to performers' actions as such rather than to their capabilities. Perhaps still more telling is the current popularity of the expression 'transferable skills', apparently to refer to particular behaviours (which as we saw would actually be more properly seen as strategies). In this sort of usage, for example, picking up the telephone and saying something like: 'Hello, this is the School of Education and I'm Pete, a senior lecturer here. How may I help you ?' is nowadays often called a skill. Now it may indeed take some capability to make such an utterance, but it needs to be pointed out amongst other things that this action is not all that's involved in the 'interpersonal skill of telephone reception'. For that skill is basically the capability of getting one's message across effectively to callers, that is, such that they understand the information and feel positive about the interaction.

In this respect, the above utterance is only a strategic action, at best a sub-skill of effective telephone capability: no more, but also no less. No more, in the sense that it may not work in this particular situation at least for some callers (so it would not be 'skilful' to do it in their case), but also no less, in that one has to do some action by way of trying to achieve one's purpose and something like this one might at least seem a plausible strategy to keep in one's repertoire. For, as we saw, skill consists generally in being able and knowing when to deploy actions that make goal achievement likely. As also pointed out, open–complex action of the types that typify human interaction do not tend to admit of the sort of universal, rigid procedures implied by referring to the actual behaviours as the skills, apart from the fact that they're only its expression anyway, since skill is the sort of abstraction we call a capability.

Now while we should not forget that everyday usage is typically full of multiple meanings or that attempts at linguistic purism may have their downsides, the potential dangers within the everyday behaviourist view need particularly to be pointed out in relation to teaching and teacher preparation. There are at least two sorts of problem here, whose familiarity to teacher educators may in turn be seen as evidence for what I'm claiming.

One danger is that insofar as student-teachers harbour anything like this behaviourist conception within their informal intuitions, they will expect sure-fire procedures, 'what to do', to be communicated to them in their courses and to gain skill by practising such actions in the classroom. This is just the sort of 'benign authoritarianism' Perlberg and Theodore (1975) spoke of student-teachers wanting and which was revealed in more detail in a considerable majority of the secondary PGCE student views on the learning of class management capability recently studied in our CLAMP project at Leeds (Tomlinson, Hodgson and Saunders, 1995). A further danger of this is that, as we also confirmed, such students then become likely to seriously downplay or in some cases completely reject the utility of activities designed to generate a better understanding of effective class control strategies, especially when these are at all removed from the practical classroom situation.

In some ways the other negative consequence of commonsense behaviourist assumptions is paradoxically the very opposite and goes together with another traditional strand in everyday thinking about the nature and origins of capability, described in the next sub-section. That is, on the one hand people may possess only a crude behavioural model which applies at best only to closed–proceduralisable skill and its acquisition. Yet they may also have some awareness of the uncertainty, complexity and messiness of what I have called open–complex skill. The result may then be that they may precisely reject the notion that something like teaching should be counted a skill at all. Unfortunately, getting rid of this bathwater may also lose them the baby in that they also get rid of the idea that teaching capability might be learned or promoted in any systematic kind of way. Waiting in the wings then is a well-known traditional alternative, namely the line that 'teachers are born, not made'.

Commonsense nativism: skill as inborn talent

Particularly with respect to capability in performing arts such as the musicianship example cited above, there is a well-established tradition of talking as if capability, especially outstanding capability, were inbuilt at birth. This is perhaps a good example of the way in which the insufficient detail of commonsense models feeds unnecessary polarisations. What seems to happen is that the existence of obvious individual differences in performance capability combines with the inaccessibility of learning processes, or a notion of them as mere repetitive drill, to rule out any role for learning as an origin of such capacities (e.g., outstanding musicianship). It is as though 'if we can not see how you got it, but you clearly have, then you must have had it all the time, i.e. you were born with it'. Rather than 'it has to be learned through some sort of action or experience, but people's aptitudes for such learning seem quite varied, so they acquire it with differing degrees of ease or assistance'.

Musicianship aside, it is hard to tell how prevalent these kinds of nativist tendency may still be with regard to teaching capability and teacher education. The implicitness of such assumptions and a more egalitarian culture are possible reasons why people may distance themselves from such views once they're publicly expressed and overtly analysed. Nevertheless, they may possibly still be lurking implicitly behind notions one still occasionally hears to the effect of 'using school experience to see whether they've got it or not' and the like. Whether this springs directly from innatist assumptions or indirectly from behaviourist thinking, what does seems clear is that neither of these helps us towards optimism, or even, I would contend, realism regarding effective teacher preparation.

Commonsense rationalism: deliberating and deciding

Although I have emphasised the shortcomings of the body–behaviour side of the traditional mind–body dualist view of persons in thinking about skill as thoughtless bits of behaviour, arguably the other, mental side of the split has long been the more powerful in some quarters. The idea has been that human action is intelligently purposeful, which is taken to mean thoughtfully deliberate, since it is the mind that is held to do the thinking and to direct bodily action. This rationalist view was certainly the main target of Gilbert Ryle's analysis in his celebrated 1949 work *The Concept of Mind* and eminent psychologists such as the late Donald Broadbent (Broadbent, Fitzgerald and Broadbent, 1986) have also seen it as the standard commonsense view.

Of course, this sort of view precisely does not tend to go in for talking about professional expertise as skill, doubtless because that term has been associated with the other, non-thinking side of the person. Rather, intelligent action is assumed to be consciously thoughtful. Understandably, then, a rationalist or consciously deliberative, knowledge-based model of action also appears to underlie its notions of professional preparation. On this view, professional preparation should consist in professional education, an induction into relevant forms of explicit understanding and knowledge. As Donald Schön (1983, 1987) has pointed out, historically the professions have indeed tended to move from on-the-job forms of apprenticeship induction to a college-based formal education approach he characterises as based on technical rationality. The idea here is that one first acquires academic knowledge of general principles in a domain, so that one can subsequently apply such insights consciously and deliberatively in practice. Schön himself appears to have been massively influential in arguing that this model does not in fact work, but that it has led to a crisis of professional education and that we therefore require a new epistemology of action, that is, a different understanding of the way that practical knowledge is acquired and deployed within action.

These views are indirectly supported to some extent by proponents of the currently influential cultural psychology–situated cognition view (cf. Lave, 1988) with their studies of the informal and socially assisted acquisition of specialist forms of capability in everyday situations. Paradoxically, however, Schön may actually have also helped perpetuate the rationalist view of skilled action through his emphasis on the term reflection. Having enjoyed guru-status for about a decade, Schön's lack of clarity regarding the nature of reflection (cf. Eraut, 1995) may explain why his constant reference to it could easily perpetuate a common sense rationalist approach to skill, insofar as he may be understood just to be recommending that practitioners really ought to think more closely and consciously about what they're doing. Those keen on the politics and sociology of knowledge might also note that the celebration of Schönian reflectiveness by teacher-educator academics fits suspiciously well with the preservation of a traditional role for them as construed in a dualist, education versus training mode.

The lesson, surely, is that the traditional 'either theory or practice' dichotomy driven by mind–body dualism cannot help us very much and badly needs correcting through the insights of the more integrated cognitive psychology indicated above. A more optimistic view might be that the enthusiastic welcome given to Schön's talk of reflection, particularly 'reflection in action' is precisely an indicator of educators' awareness of the need for such an integrated view, in which the thought does somehow inform the action. In my view, his ideas would benefit from explicit linking with modern cognitive psychological work, as has been done recently in a very elegant framework offered by Michael Eraut (1994, chapter 7).

Mixing the models: the persistence of reductionism

However, even with the availability of the cognitive and other paradigms, the persistence of dualist thinking and behaviourist themes and terminology continue to militate against the effective use of modern insights.

One major way in which this can happen is through the presence of behaviourist elements in viewpoints that are not only independent of behaviourism, but even antipathetic towards it. A paradoxical example is provided by the rising influence of humanistic psychology in education, which occurred originally in the context of careers counselling and then through the pastoral movement of the seventies. This well-developed approach is well represented by the widely known work of Gerard Egan (1990).

I should make clear that I think humanistic psychology in general and this book in particular very useful and relevant sources for teacher education insights (cf. Tomlinson, 1995c). Moreover, the open style and successive revisions over the various editions of Egan's book attest to a truly reflective and committed author. But the positive worth of this contribution is, paradoxically, almost in spite of its behaviourist tendency to view actions as 'skills' instead of as strategies and its failure to reflect much on the nature, in particular the precarious messiness of such action and capability. A paradox arises out of the fact that humanistic psychology was originally founded in America by figures such as Carl Rogers and Abraham Maslow precisely as a 'third force' in psychology, over and against the perceived shortcomings of the then (1940s) dominant paradigms of behaviourism and Freudian psychoanalysis. The traditional ignoring of cognitive skill theory by humanistic proponents perhaps arose because their school was founded before the rise of the experimental cognitive approach to dominant paradigm in academic psychology in the 1950s and 1960s. More generally, educationists often still appear unfamiliar with the experimental, information-processing tradition of cognitive psychology and its current legacy, but rather identify 'cognitive' it with the Piagetian contribution and in particular with conscious, rational thinking – which humanists rightly suspect to be only part of the human story.

Another way in which the dualist–behaviourist tradition can persist is still more subtle, even insidious one might say. Just as Paul Light has remarked that, whatever the actual views of Piaget, his developmental psychology has often been put forward with a decidedly 'maturationist flavour', so even in cognitive psychological treatments of skill, a 'behaviourist flavour' can persist. This may be seen, for instance, in John Sloboda's otherwise excellent chapter in Angus Gellatly's popular and highly recommendable 1986 collection, which has an avowedly cognitive orientation. There the essentially purposeful nature of skill is rather taken for granted, not featuring in the mnemonic offered for remembering its central characteristics. Similarly, the degree of emphasis on routines one finds even in education-oriented pieces also pursuing an explicitly cognitive line (cf. Leinhardt and Greeno, 1986) can easily be taken to imply the sort of sure-fire recipe and drill-inculcation associated traditionally with dualist–behaviourist versions. Still more subtle again is the reductionist-sounding tendency of writers clearly within or appreciative of the cognitive tradition (examples would be Nisbet and Shuksmith, 1986, or Reason, 1990) to reserve the term skill just for the automatised elements of action, rather than for the overall economical ability which I have suggested is the more basic traditional meaning of the term. This is not of course to deny the importance of the highly automatised sub-processes skill typically does include and I grant that this is a rather fine distinction, if nevertheless a basic one.

A third possibility stems from the very complexity of the cognitive psychology of skill. Even the rather bare outline of important general features presented here contains a good number of strands, forgetting one or more of which is easy, but also likely to have its repercussions for understanding real life capability such as that of teaching. Given the human cognitive limitations which the same brand of psychology so clearly illuminates (cf. Boreham, 1994), it is perhaps not too surprising that educational applications of this perspective sometimes do neglect certain aspects or implications.

Such a danger arises, for instance, when educationists use the attractive strategy of studying experts in order to see what characterises their strategic activities, in order in turn to inform professional preparation (cf. Berliner, 1986). In this connection it is perhaps worth commenting that the label expertise also has its problems. On the one hand, 'expertise' may be a desirable alternative to 'skill', in that we've seen the latter appears to have been somewhat hijacked by behaviourism. On the other hand, for some people 'expertise' may have unfortunate connotations of academic–rational perfection. Leaving the terminology aside, however, with goals as contested and complex as those characterising teaching, there is a more substantial difficulty: that of deciding even in principle who actually constitute the 'expert' teachers, let alone identifying them in practice. In this it may be tempting to take the mistaken shortcut of assuming 'experienced' to imply 'expert'. Yet while it may typically take much relevant experience over many months or even years to attain proficiency, let alone 'expertise', experience alone cannot guarantee learning in any skill, particularly complex open ones like teaching. In this connection there is of course a very healthy commonsense dictum, that 'for some people 20 years' experience can amount to one year repeated 20 times' !

Postscript: applications and implications

Although teaching and teacher preparation are surely of such complexity that we need to be open rather than restrictive in what we select for critical appraisal as sources of illumination, it seems to me that modern skill psychology has considerable potential to play a central role, as I have argued here and elsewhere (cf. Tomlinson, 1995c). In particular, I hope the above treatment of the persisting influence of 'alternative psychologies' of skill may go some way towards facilitating an open-minded, if critical, appraisal of this potential by educationists. More modestly, it will perhaps at least alert psychologists to the nature of their task when seeking to share and apply such insights with teacher educator colleagues. I should nevertheless offer some qualifications regarding such application. These will be all too brief, but are important enough to merit at least summary mention.

One cannot simply expect to 'apply' psychological theories unproblematically to educational situations, however well-grounded such theories may be to date. Two amongst the many considerations here are

- the issue of how far such insights 'transfer' from the situations and persons regarding which they were established
- the virtual certainty that educational situations involve more influencing strands than the psychological theory was designed for or is capable of illuminating.

This does not necessarily support the polarised alternative of thinking one has totally to reinvent a pedagogy or applied psychology within the practical situation. But it does mean that when seeking to use any explanatory resource, whether from psychology or elsewhere, one has to be eclectically open to combining it with other insights and experience, as well as critically alert regarding the validity of what is thereby generated.

And while the major point of such endeavours is to illuminate the situation and facilitate effective strategies for achieving goals, nor should one expect this to take the form of simplistic quick-fixes. There are many reasons for thinking, as Edgar Stones rightly persists in pointing out in his *Journal of Education for Teaching* editorials, that teaching is basically complex. If so, any account which validly illuminates teaching and teacher preparation issues is likely to articulate complexities and difficulties, even if this is but the condition for possible development of effective strategies.

This is illustrated in a variety of ways by the case of skill psychology and education, especially if we take the above advice regarding eclecticism and consider a number of currently well-established strands relevant to skill acquisition (not all of them coming from the cognitive tradition or even psychology). A central example is that, generally speaking, the cognitive skill tradition emphasises both planning and the need for considerable feedback-guided practice. The clear implication (cf. Tomlinson, 1995c) is that student-teachers need assistance both to understand teaching in a conscious way and to bring such thoughts into repeated, assisted teaching action.

But current work may also revitalise some very old controversies regarding teacher education and training, even if, hopefully, it also helps us to get to a better-grounded understanding of such issues. We are now getting indications of how powerful a role implicit learning can play in generating action capabilities, with the likely involvement of the sort of parallel distributed processes investigated over the last decade or two (cf. Berry and Dienes, 1993). This may be seen to fit well with the emphasis of writers like Hubert and Stuart Dreyfus (1986) on intuitive processes in the development of expertise, and in turn with cultural psychological studies of ways in which people tend to be informally inducted into everyday skills (cf. Lave, 1988).

All this tends to suggest that 'learning by immersion' may be much more powerful than we thought. Thus, for instance, although a persisting effect of student teachers' past experience as pupils is widely recognised, the strength and specificity of its influence may turn out even more powerful than we tend to assume. But a more crucial, connected issue is also likely to be more contentious. In traditional dualist terms, this is the 'theory versus practice' issue, which in modern guise might be termed 'reflection versus immersion', an issue which has in some respects been sharpened by the transition to school-based teacher preparation in the UK and the ensuing encounter between the somewhat different cultural traditions of teaching and teacher education. The work on implicit learning seems if anything likely to strengthen the 'immersion' position. At any event, this central arena seems to me to be in need of systematic illumination, which it might get to a considerable extent from the sorts of psychological sources focused on here.

References

Anderson, J.A. (1990) Cognitive Psychology and Its Implications, 3rd edn (New York: Freeman).
Barrow, R. (1987) Skill talk. Journal of Philosophy of Education, 21, 187–95.
Bereiter, C. and Scardamalia, M. (1993) Surpassing Ourselves: An inquiry into the nature and implications of expertise (Chicago, IL: Open Court).
Berliner, D.C (1986) In pursuit of the expert pedagogue. Educational Researcher, 15, 5–13.
Berlyne, D.E. (1965) Structure and Direction in Thinking (New York: Wiley).
Berry, C. and Dienes, Z. (1993) Implicit Learning: Theoretical data, empirical issues (Hove, Lawrence Erlbaum).
Beveridge, M. (1996) Address to British Educational Research Association Conference on the Future of Educational Research, Birkbeck College, University of London, 12 July.
Boreham, N.C. (1994) The dangerous practice of thinking. Medical Education, 28, 172–9.
Broadbent, D.E., Fitzgerald, P. and Broadbent, M.H.P. (1986) Implicit and explicit knowledge in the control of complex systems. British Journal of Psychology, 77, 33–50.
Carter, K. (1990) Teachers' knowledge and learning to teach. In Houston, W.R. (Ed.) Handbook of Research on Teacher Education (New York: Macmillan), pp.291–310.
Chi, M, Glaser, R. and Farr, M. (1988) The Nature of Expertise (Hillsdale, NJ: Lawrence Erlbaum).
Doyle, W. (1986) Classroom organization and management, in Wittrock, M.C. (Ed.) Handbook of Research on Teaching, 3rd edn (New York: Macmillan), pp.392–431.
Dreyfus, H.L. and Dreyfus, S.E. (1986) Mind Over Machine: The power of human intuition and expertise in the era of the computer (New York: Macmillan).
Dreyfus, H. (1987) Dialogue with Hubert Dreyfus. In Magee, B. (Ed.) The Great Philosophers: An introduction to western philosophy (London: BBC Books).
Egan, G. (1990) The Skilled Helper: A systematic approach to effective helping, 4th edn (Pacific Grove, CA: Brooks/Cole).
Eraut, M. (1994) Developing Professional Knowledge and Competence (London: Falmer Press).
Eraut, M. (1995) Schön shock: a case for reframing reflection-in-action? Teachers and Teaching: Theory and Practice, 1(1), 9–22.
Fenstermacher, G.D. (1986) Philosophy of research on teaching: three aspects. In Wittrock, M.C. (Ed.) Handbook of Research on Teaching, 3rd edn (New York: Macmillan), pp.37–49.
Fitts, P.M. and Posner, M.I. (1967) Human Performance (Belmont, CA: Brooks/Cole).
Gagné, R. M. (1965) Conditions of Learning (New York: Holt, Rinehart and Winston).
Gagné, R.M. (1985) The Conditions of Learning and the Theory of Instruction (New York: CBS College Publishing).
Gellatly, A. (ed.) (1986) The Skilful Mind: An introduction to cognitive psychology (Milton Keynes: Open University Press).
Griffiths, M., (1987) The teaching of skills and the skills of teaching: a reply to Robin Barrow. Journal of Philosophy of Education, 21, 203–14.
Hargreaves, D. (1980) Common-sense models of action. In Chapman, A.J. and Jones, D.M. (Eds.) Models of Man (Leicester: British Psychological Society), pp.215–25.
Hirst, P.H. (1971) What is teaching? Journal of Curriculum Studies, 3, 1.
Holding, D.H. (Ed.) (1989) Human Skills, 2nd edn (Chichester: Wiley).

Lave, J. (1988) Cognition in Practice: Mind, mathematics and culture in everyday life (Cambridge: Cambridge University Press).
Leinhardt, G. and Greeno, J.G. (1986) The cognitive skill of teaching. Journal of Educational Psychology, 78, 75–95.
Lowyck, J. (1980) Teaching skills and teacher education. Revue ATEE Journal, 3, 173–90.
Morrison, J.E. (Ed.) (1991) Training for Performance: Principles of applied human learning (Chichester: Wiley).
Nisbet, J. and Shuksmith, J. (1986) Learning Strategies (London: Routledge and Kegan Paul).
Norman, D.A. (1978) Notes towards a complex theory of learning. In Lesgold, A.M. Pellegrino, J.W., Fokkema, S.D. and Glaser, R. (Eds.) Cognitive Psychology and Instruction (New York: Plenum).
Perlberg, A. and Theodore, E. (1975) patterns and styles in the supervision of teachers. British Journal of Education for Teaching, 1(2), 203–11.
Polyani, M., (1956) Personal Knowledge: Towards a post-critical philosophy (London, Routledge and Kegan Paul).
Poulton, E.C. (1957) On prediction in skilled movements. Psychological Bulletin, 54, 467–78.
Reason, J. (1990) Human Error (Cambridge: Cambridge University Press).
Ryle, G., (1949) The Concept of Mind (London: Hutchinson).
Schmidt, R.A. (1991) Motor Learning and Performance: From principles to practice (Champaign, IL: Human Kinetics).
Schön, D.A. (1983) The Reflective Practitioner: How professionals think in action (New York: Basic Books).
Schön, D.A. (1987) Educating The Reflective Practitioner: Toward a new design for teaching and learning in the professions (San Francisco, CA: Jossey-Bass).
Simon, B. (1988) Why no pedagogy in England? In Dale, R. Ferguson, R. and Robinson, A. (Eds.) Frameworks for Teaching: Readings for the intending secondary teacher (London: Hodder and Stoughton/Open University), pp. 336–49.
Sloboda, J.A., Davidson, J.W. and Howe, M.J.A. (1994) Is everyone musical? Target paper and peer review. Psychologist, 7(8), 349–64.
Tharp, R.G., and Gallimore, R., (1988) Rousing Minds To Life: Teaching, learning and schooling in social context (Cambridge, Cambridge University Press).
Tomlinson, P.D. (1981) Understanding Teaching: Interactive educational psychology (London: McGraw-Hill).
Tomlinson P.D. (1992) Psychology and education: What went wrong – or did it? Psychologist: Bulletin of the British Psychological Society, 5, 105–9.
Tomlinson, P.D. (1995a) Can competence profiling work for effective teacher education? I General Issues. Oxford Review of Education, 21(2), 179–94.
Tomlinson, P.D. (1995b) Can competence profiling work for effective teacher education? II Pitfalls and Principles. Oxford Review of Education, 21(3), 299–314.
Tomlinson, P.D. (1995c) Understanding Mentoring: Reflective strategies for school-based teacher preparation (Buckingham: Open University Press).
Tomlinson, P.D. (in preparation) Researching Teaching and Learning: Contemporary essays (Sydney: Firebird Press).
Tomlinson, P.D., Hodgson, J. and Saunders, J.P. (1995) The prospects for independent student-teacher learning in the new UK School-based ITT arrangements (or: But the English were always Post-modernists, weren't they?). Paper presented to the EARLI Conference, Nijmegen, The Netherlands, July.

Tomlinson, P.D. and Swift, D.J. (1992) Teacher-educator thinking in the context of radio-assisted practice: More patchwork pedagogy? Teaching and Teacher Education, 8(2), 159–70.

Welford, A.T. (1968) Fundamentals of Skill (London: Methuen).

Wertsch, J.V. (Ed.) (1985) Culture, Communication and Cognition: Vygotskyan perspectives (Cambridge: Cambridge University Press).

Chapter 6
Understanding academic performance at university: a research retrospective

NOEL J. ENTWISTLE

Since the 1960s, there has been a substantial body of research in Britain directed towards explaining the different levels of academic performance among university students. This chapter describes changing trends in this area of research, by tracing developments in a programmatic series of studies carried out by the author and his research collaborators since 1968. The initial section, however, offers a much broader view of the evolution of methods of educational research. It takes up a description of educational psychology, past, present, and future, published by Dennis Child in 1985. However, the historical analysis is presented from a rather different perspective, which is also used to describe more recent research methods and conceptualisations. These general trends then provide a background against which the development of the specific series of research studies on academic performance at university can be set and considered.

The evolution of educational research

Educational research, like all research, is in a continuing process of evolution. That evolution, like evolution in the animal kingdom, does not progress uniformly in a single direction, but by explorations of different forms, the success of which depends on successful adaptation to prevailing circumstances. Educational research evolves by seeking to provide explanations of issues perceived as important at the time, within analytic frameworks which are in tune with the prevailing research *zeitgeist*.

In essence, educational research seeks to describe, and ultimately to understand, the nature of education and the outcomes of learning in educational contexts. It does so partly as a contribution to the general academic enterprise of knowledge creation, but also with the more practical purpose of improving the quality and effectiveness of educational provision. To do so, it has drawn on a variety of disciplines, each of which is itself in the process of evolution. Thus, if we examine the development of educational research, we shall find traces of the influence of a variety of emerging theories and methodologies. Their introduction has, in turn, changed the types of descriptions and explanations of educational phenomena which have been offered.

If we look at education in the broadest terms, we see a system designed to prepare young people for their future vocational and personal lives in society. The theories which account for the form taken by different educational systems draw substantially on ideas from political philosophy, theoretical sociology and history. The research methods adopted in these disciplines are largely interpretative. They are based on the examination of documents and current trends in educational and social policy, often supplemented by interviews with policy makers. The conclusions reached from the analyses are then related to theoretical frameworks drawn from the parent disciplines. Each of the disciplines contributing to the analysis of policy has a lengthy and respected academic tradition, and the methods of analysis are well tried, even though the conclusions reached are necessarily subjective. The acceptance of a particular interpretation depends on how thoroughly and logically relevant evidence has been collected and interpreted, and also on a process of reflective criticism from other researchers which tests the soundness of that interpretation against alternative formulations.

If, in contrast, we look at education with a narrower focus – at the teaching and learning which takes place at school or university – a quite different set of theories and research methods has been used which derives to some extent from empirical sociology, but mainly from psychology. Ideas about psychology developed initially from philosophical enquiry which had used interpretative methods to reflect on human thought and behaviour. Crucially, however, at the turn of the century, psychology adopted the methods of physical science. Physics had developed an extremely efficient set of methods, based on systematic observation and experiment, which allowed hypotheses to be tested in ways which seemed to eliminate subjectivity from the interpretation of the evidence collected. There was also the possibility of setting up a single, crucial experiment to test the validity of a physical law.

Psychology, in its attempt to achieve the status of physical science, abandoned its philosophical roots and relied instead on the objectivity of experimental method. To follow that path, it was necessary to measure and use those measures to predict. An acceptable theory was one which led to accurate prediction. It was relatively straightforward to measure behaviour, and it was soon found that behaviour could be predicted – or, rather, certain behaviours of animals seemed to follow general 'laws of learning'. The success of such predictions led psychologists to extrapolate those laws to human behaviour and to reject the original focus of psychological enquiry – the nature of thought.

In parallel with the experimental tradition, however, an alternative set of methods was being developed which retained the concern with mental processes, but established objective methods of measurement and complex statistical procedures which allowed analyses to be carried out in precise and repeatable ways. With the impetus and resources provided by the need to classify recruits to the armed services in the First World War and subsequently to allocate pupils to different forms of secondary education, tests of intellectual performance were developed, and techniques of multivariate analysis were devised to establish the structure of the intellect. Subsequently, these techniques were extended to identify the structure of the personality and have led, over the years, to five main dimensions being described with a substantial degree of consensus.

Cronbach (1957) pointed out the separation between these two traditions in educational research and also the absurdity of laws of human learning which ignored the known, and marked, individual differences which were known to exist. At that time it could also have been noted that there was another division existing within research on individual differences – between studies focusing on cognitive abilities and those on affective and conative traits (personality and motivation). In relatively few studies did they come together, and where they did, it was by describing intellectual abilities and personality traits as separate variables which could be used in combination to predict academic performance (e.g. Cattell and Butcher, 1968).

Both the experimental tradition of studying learning and the survey methods of investigating individual differences continue to be extensively used in educational research. But they have also been vigorously challenged – not only by theorists from the sociopolitical tradition who are largely unsympathetic to the whole empiricist movement, but also by a new generation of empirical researchers. The challenge has been to the belief that human thought and behaviour can be adequately described through a series of test scores on broadly-based psychological traits, and that general laws of learning and human behaviour are possible.

One line of challenge comes from researchers who have sought to describe behaviour more holistically in social contexts using the methods of social anthropologists – by observing, questioning, and interpreting the meaning of the rituals and traditions underpinning social behaviour (see Parlett and Hamilton, 1972). Looking at classrooms, the parallels with traditional social and cultural practices become striking, and a new tradition of educational research developed using methods adapted from social anthropological research. This approach has concentrated mainly on describing classrooms, often from a sociopolitical perspective. The method describes behaviour patterns, and to some extent motives, but generally shows little concern with the nature of learning or academic performance.

Another line of challenge comes from the idea that humans are goal orientated and adapt readily to different situations in pursuing their own goals. Then, future ideas and behaviour must depend on both the intentions of the individual and the specific situations to which the individual has to adapt. In that way of thinking, simple laws of learning or stable scores on psychological traits cannot be expected to hold true across a wide variety of individuals in differing learning contexts. And yet, everyday experience does suggest that people behave quite consistently. As Bronowski (1965) commented somewhat tartly:

> (If) a (person) does not want to be law-abiding (in the nomothetic sense); very well, then it is time to ask him the rude but searching question, 'Do you want to be lawless?' You refuse to be predictable as an engine is, or an animal; do you aspire to be unpredictable? And if so, are you unpredictable to yourself, the actor, as well as to me, the spectator? Do you base your claim to be a self on the proud assertion that your actions are arbitrary? (No) ... a self must have consistency; its actions tomorrow must be recognisably of a piece with the actions carried out yesterday.(pp. 13–15)

The measurement of such consistencies thus makes sense as *one* way of describing human behaviour. What is still open to question, however, is how those consistencies should be described. To what extent are general psychological traits to be used, or should context-specific variables be introduced?

Recent trends in research on individual differences have, in fact, shown an increasing use of constructs which have demonstrable *ecological validity* – which describe the thought and behaviour of people with broadly similar sets of intentions within a particular context or set of contexts. There have also been attempts to describe broader concepts which combine cognitive and motivational elements into *dispositions*, which also take into account how readily people adjust to different situations (Perkins, Jay and Tishman, 1993; Snow, Corno and Jackson, 1996) The idea of a disposition involves *abilities*, *inclinations* including motives, and *sensitivities* towards context. This definition does not move the whole way towards contextualisation, but the research has sought particular dispositions which are relevant to defined social contexts. It has been argued, for example, that effective learning is related to certain of these triadic dispositions. Bereiter (1990), arguing from a different theoretical pespective, has also suggested the importance of certain 'coherent organisations of cognitive, conative, and affective structures' which link up with particular learning contexts.

Looking at the more recent research on learning, signs of a greater emphasis on ecological validity could be seen in the mid-1970s with the development of an approach to qualitative research which focused on learning in its educational setting. This approach came to be called *phenomenography* (Marton, 1994). It began with naturalistic experiments set up to investigate how university students read academic articles. Marton and his colleagues developed a technique of qualitative analysis of interview transcripts which not only established categories of description, indicating similarities and differences between the students' responses, but also sought to find and interpret relationships between those categories. The first study using this technique led to the description of approaches to learning, with a *deep* approach being directed towards extracting personal meaning and a *surface* approach focusing on memorising and reproducing parts of the text (Marton and Säljö, 1976, 1997).

Marton and his colleagues were at pains to point out that the approach to learning adopted by a student does not represent a stable trait, but is rather the response on a particular occasion to the specific content of the article, under the conditions and context within which the reading has been undertaken. However, Säljö has also described contrasting *conceptions of learning* (see Marton and Säljö, 1997) which show a broader, and possibly more stable, distinction which parallels the deep-surface dichotomy. Asked what they understood by the term 'learning', adults described it in very different ways, ranging from 'the accumulation of discrete pieces of information' to 'the development of personal understanding'. We might, therefore, expect approaches to learning to depend, to some extent at least, on these individual conceptions of learning, developed through previous experience and education.

This outline of trends in educational research has not set out to present any particular approach as being 'right'. Rather, it charts the continuing use of different methods, as well as the evolution of alternative methods and formulations. It also contains an implicit warning against a too ready acceptance of any current orthodoxy. As Hoyle (1972) said when challenging the idea that the 'red shift' in the light from distant galaxies necessarily implied an expanding universe:

> We must be on guard against being the prisoners of the time-order in which information happens to be stored in our brains. (p. 64)

Against this background of general trends in educational research, we can now portray somewhat parallel changes in research into the specific area of academic performance in higher education.

The prediction of academic performance

The attempts in the late 1960s to understand differences in students' academic performance were directed towards its more accurate prediction. The rather weak predictive power of measures of school achievement, such as 'A' level or Highers grades, led to a search for more accurate selection instruments, drawing on the experience of using the Scholastic Aptitude Tests in the USA (Choppin, 1973). But it was realised that other influences on academic performance might also have to be taken into account to achieve substantially higher levels of prediction. In a large scale follow-up study at Lancaster University, a national sample of first-year students was followed through to graduation in an attempt to identify factors related to academic success (Entwistle and Wilson, 1977). Besides using a scholastic aptitude test, additional measures of personality, values, social attitudes, motivation, and study methods were also included in a test battery. These predictive variables from the first year were then compared with levels of degree performance three years later.

Simple correlations confirmed that 'A' level grades correlated with degree performance to only a modest extent (0.29 in pure science down to 0.11 in social science, although higher levels were found in smaller samples of applied scientists and mathematicians). Higher correlations were actually found with scores on an inventory of motivation and study methods (0.33 in pure science and 0.21 in social science). Multivariate analyses of the data were then undertaken. Regression analyses using the whole set of variables in combination to predict degree performance increased the correlations to only a limited extent (0.38 in pure science and 0.25 in social science). Motivation and study methods contributed most to that prediction, along with achievement and intellectual measures.

Factor analysis was then used to make sense of the whole pattern of intercorrelations. One factor was found to distinguish between arts and science, indicating that students in the different subject areas had contrasting sets of characteristics. The other two factors summarised the relationships with academic performance; one factor was defined in terms of high levels of school attainment combined with hard work and an avoidance of social distractions, while motivation and organised study methods were linked to low levels of both anxiety and radicalism in the other factor.

A different form of multivariate analysis was also explored in this study. Cluster analysis brings together individuals whose responses to the tests are similar (as opposed to factor analysis which groups similar variables). In this way, it was possible to identify groups of individuals. Some of the differences reflected contrasting areas of study, but other differences indicated quite different ways of studying. Four of the clusters are of particular interest.

- *Highly motivated, stable scientists* (the most successful group of all). This group contained students with high 'A' level grades who were satisfied with their courses...They were highly motivated and had good study methods. In personality they were emotionally stable and had high scores on theoretical and economic values, linked to a tendency towards tough-minded conservatism. This combination of characteristics suggests a rather cold and ruthless individual, governed by rationality and spurred on by competition to repeated demonstrations of intellectual mastery.
- *Hard-working, syllabus free arts students* (the most successful Arts group). These students did not have outstandingly high 'A' Level grades, although their verbal aptitude scores were well above average. High motivation, good study methods and long hours of study were linked with syllabus-freedom. There were no defining characteristics in terms of personality, but high aesthetic values were associated with radical attitudes.
- *Anxious students who work long hours* (mixed success – scientists doing well). The main defining features (of this group) were high scores on neuroticism and syllabus-boundness, and low scores on both extraversion and (the competitive form of) motivation. They saw themselves as neither likeable nor self-confident. They had no active social life and few aesthetic interests...It is tempting to see these students as being motivated by 'fear of failure'.
- *Students with low motivation and poor study methods* (poor performance). This group contains students who came up to university with below average 'A' level grades, but their...ability appeared to be equivalent to (that of highly successful students)...Their theoretical values were (however) low...(They) showed a marked deterioration in performance after the first year and...had (consistently) low motivation and study method scores...They spent little time on studying and rather more on leisure pursuits. (Many also came) from lower social class backgrounds. (Entwistle and Wilson, 1977, pp. 129–32)

The particular value of these cluster analyses was the way in which they retained full information about links between cognitive, personality and other variables in describing linkages. These links were lost in the factor analyses, through the process of merging and simplification of factor structures. The fuller picture offered by the cluster descriptions provided valuable suggestions about reasons for success and failure.

The link between study methods, motivation, and personality was explored further by John Wilson in a separate study at Aberdeen University (Entwistle and Wilson, 1977, p. 76). Combining scores on motivation and study methods, and examining levels of degree performance for each of four personality 'types', it was clear that consistent relationships came only from extraversion (relationships with neuroticism varied by subject area). It was found that 45 per cent of extroverts had low combined scores on motivation and study methods, compared with 23 per cent of introverts, who also obtained a somewhat higher proportion of 'good' degrees (68 per cent compared with 63 per cent of extroverts). Clearly, personality was related to both study methods and degree performance. However, it was found that the combined scores on motivation and study methods showed a much closer relationship with academic success than had personality (76 per cent of students with high scores had good degrees compared with 50 per cent of those with low scores). Further analyses showed a very similar proportion of extroverts and introverts, who also had high scores on motivation and study methods, obtaining good degrees (extroverts 77 per cent; introverts 75 per cent).

This finding had a substantial influence on the direction of the future direction of the research group at Lancaster. It suggested that variables which directly described behaviour and attitudes within the academic context were likely to be much better predictors than more general psychological variables.

As we saw earlier, regression analyses had indicated that a combination of ability with motivation and study methods made the best combined predictor of academic achievement. Besides this quantitative study, however, an interview study was also carried out which contrasted students with different forms of motivation, and that, combined with the cluster descriptions, led to a realisation that different students perceived their academic environments in very different ways.

> Students of differing personality and motivational types not only tackle their academic work in different ways but, from their descriptions of their university experience, they evidently perceive themselves to be in differing environments. (Entwistle, Thompson and Wilson, 1974, p. 393)

The other outcome of this longitudinal study was a growing conviction that correlational studies did not suggest, in any convincing way, what might be done to improve teaching and learning in higher education. The emphasis on prediction suggested ways of selecting students more accurately in terms of their academic potential, and yet there was so much variance unaccounted for that selection alone was not an appropriate response. We needed to see what could be done to help students study more effectively and to suggest to lecturers better ways of encouraging high quality learning. The advice which Charles Carter, the then Vice-Chancellor of Lancaster University, gave to educational researchers at about that time was forthright. He said:

> The purpose of research into higher education, for most of us, is a practical one. We do not want merely to describe the quaint or

awful things which are going on: we want to make things better... So I hope that...you will...refrain from chasing along familiar paths and surrounding what you find with a spurious erudition; and see if your colleagues can be helped with some of the simple and obvious faults which have persisted in higher education for too long. (Carter, 1972, pp. 1–3)

This injunction struck home. It coincided with our own dissatisfactions with the previous focus of our work and led to a change in direction – an attempt to understand the processes of studying–and not just to describe correlates of different outcomes of learning.

Study strategies and the processes of student learning

The search for concepts having greater ecological validity in describing the processes of student learning did not take long, as the work of Marton and his colleagues was being published as our first survey was being written up (Marton and Säljö, 1976; Svensson, 1977). With the description of the contrasting approaches to learning, we were able to shift our focus to the processes of learning. Initial studies showed that these categories were just as powerful in distinguishing quite different ways of studying in Britain as they had been in Sweden (Entwistle, Hanley and Ratcliffe, 1979). An SSRC research programme was then undertaken which followed both quantitative and qualitative tracks (Entwistle and Ramsden, 1983).

Interviews in the early stages of the qualitative study indicated that besides deep and surface approaches to learning, there was also a strategic approach to studying, depending on well-organised studying and an alertness to assessment criteria. These three categories provided the conceptual underpinning for the quantitative study. The initial interviews had also indicated that there was indeed a certain consistency in the approach, or combination of approaches, to studying adopted by students. It thus made sense to measure typical approaches to studying, at least within a specific course, through an extension of the inventory previously used to measure study methods and motivation. After substantial development work, the *Approaches to Studying Inventory* (ASI) (Entwistle and Ramsden, 1983) was produced. The inventory was given to a national sample of 2208 students from 66 departments drawn from six contrasting subject areas. Factor analyses suggested the existence of four main *study orientations*:

- *meaning* (incorporating the deep approach)
- *reproducing* (surface approach)
- *achieving* (strategic approach)
- *non-academic* (later called *apathetic*, involving disorganised studying and negative attitudes).

Biggs (1976) had independently been developing a *Study Processes Questionnaire*. Factor analyses produced three main dimensions describing study processes which were subsequently seen to cover deep, surface, and achieving approaches to studying (Biggs, 1987). It was particularly interesting to find that both inventories had independently produced three main factors in which a learning process or strategy was associated with a distinctive form of motivation:

- deep/meaning with interest and active engagement with course content (a form of intrinsic motivation)
- surface/reproducing with anxiety about coping with course requirements (fear of failure)
- strategic/achieving with a self-confident and competitive form of motivation (need for achievement) (Entwistle, 1988; Biggs, 1993)

It was also interesting to find a close correspondence between the four orientations and the four clusters described above which came from a quite different set of variables.

The combination of learning process and distinctive motivation within both factors and clusters was readily understandable in both theoretical and experiential terms. Moreover, this combination can now be seen as containing two of the three components of what has since been called a *disposition* (Perkins *et al.*, 1993). In more recent work, the third element of the dispositional triad has also appeared in findings which indicate that students adopting deep or surface approaches also seem to have different sensitivities towards their learning environment (Meyer, Parsons and Dunne, 1990; Entwistle and Tait, 1990; Meyer, 1991). Certainly, students adopting deep approaches are better able to identify, and to appreciate, types of teaching which are designed to support understanding. Approach to studying, as derived from quantitative analyses at least, can thus be seen as a disposition, describing a relatively stable characteristic of the individual student in relation to learning in a specific academic context.

Having data on 66 departments enabled analyses of the ASI also to be carried out with the department as the unit of analysis. These analyses looked at mean scores on approaches to studying in relation to descriptions of departments provided by a *Course Perceptions Questionnaire* developed by Paul Ramsden (Entwistle and Ramsden, 1983). Conclusions from those analyses have recently been summarised in the following way:

> Departments which were perceived to provide good teaching (and particularly help with studying) combined with freedom in learning (offering choice of study method and content) were more likely to have students reporting an orientation towards meaning. Reproducing orientations were more commonly found

in the departments perceived to combine a heavy workload with a lack of choice over content and method...Some departments seem to induce surface approaches in a direct way. Other departments appear to provide contexts within which students find it easier to develop an interest in the subject matter and to use approaches aimed at understanding. The influence is, however, less easy to predict, depending presumably more on individual students...(who) differ markedly in what they want to achieve from their studying. If they *want* to make the academic content personally meaningful, these departments will facilitate such development. (Ramsden, 1997, pp. 213–4)

In subsequent work, the idea of providing an effective learning environment, seen as a coherent, mutually supporting whole, was developed into a conceptual overview of the teaching-learning process in higher education (Entwistle, 1987), which has been developed further as a result of more recent research (for a full description, see Entwistle, in press). The model (see Figure 6.1) indicates how the outcomes of learning depended on an interaction between the characteristics of the individual student, the teaching provided by the lecturer (focusing mainly on lecturing, for simplicity), and the context provided by departmental practices. It focuses on learning strategies and the learning outcomes, and these are placed at the centre of the diagram. Around the outside are the influences on those processes and outcomes. The characteristics of the student are described broadly in terms of variations in approaches to learning – deep/surface – (on the left) and approaches to studying – strategic/apathetic (on the right). The outer set of concepts are narrower in focus and have been shown to be related to these two approaches (Entwistle and Ramsden, 1983) The way students react to the learning environment depends on their perceptions of the teaching and general departmental policies on teaching which they are experiencing – perceptions of the meaning and relevance evoked by the content presented by the lecturer or tutor and of the task requirements which depend on departmental policies on assessment.

Trigwell, Prosser and Taylor (1994) have described three main conceptions of teaching – transmitting information, helping students to acquire the concepts of the discipline, and helping students to develop and change their own conceptions. But underlying these conceptions of teaching are two contrasts. Firstly, there is a distinction between viewing teaching from the perspective of staff and institution, and from that of the student. Then there is a related contrast between seeing teaching as transmitting information and as encouraging learning. These differing conceptions affect the overall way in which the lecturer approaches teaching, from the choice and organisation of course material to the specific teaching methods adopted in class.

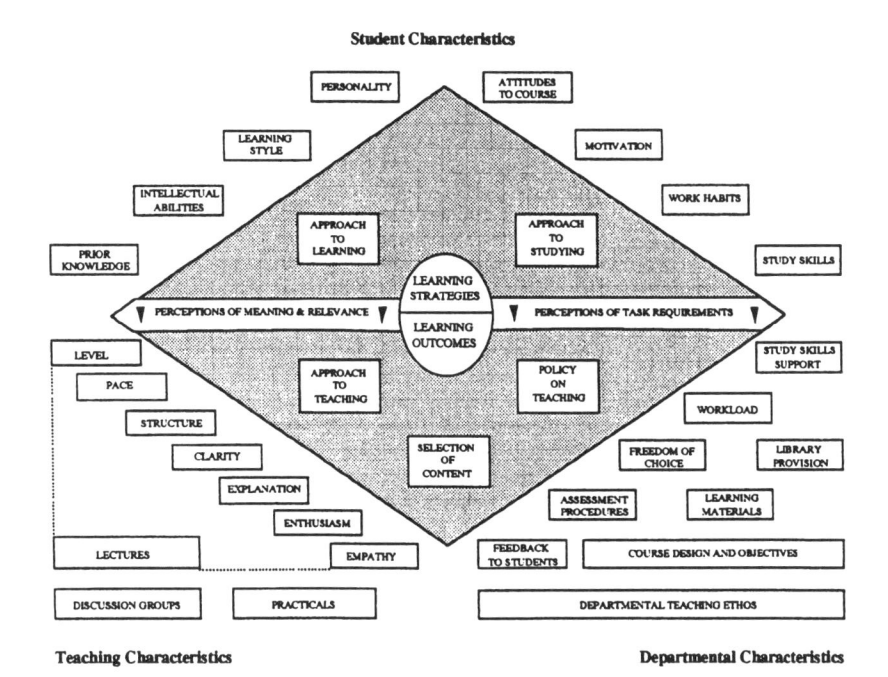

Understanding academic performance at university

Figure 6.1. A conceptual overview of the teaching–learning process.

The approach to teaching can be disaggregated into aspects of 'good teaching' as perceived by students. Taking lecturing as an example, it can be described in terms of the seven components at the bottom left-hand side of the model. These aspects have been identified both in interviews with students (Entwistle and Ramsden, 1983) and from dimensions found to underlie student feedback questionnaires (Marsh, 1987). In the model, the positioning of these elements to some extent parallels equivalent student characteristics linked to the approach to learning (e.g. level at which the lecture is pitched should depend on the prior knowledge of the students; pace depends on intellectual abilities). Other methods of teaching could be disaggregated in a similar way, but there is currently insufficient research evidence to make this convincing.

Finally, other influences on learning outcomes, less directly under the control of the lecturer, are shown in the bottom right of the diagram. Of these, assessment procedures have the most direct and immediate impact on the approach to studying, but it is also influenced by helpful feedback on assignments, freedom in the choice of topics and courses for students, a timetable and workload which is not too demanding, and appropriate support in the development of study skills. These components of departmental provision are backed up by provision of library materials and other learning materials (resource- or technology-based).

These specific aspects are incorporated into an overall course design and stem from the overall departmental teaching ethos (see Entwistle, in press).

The model was designed to illustrate some of the main influences on the quality of learning which need to be borne in mind in designing curricula, and to emphasise the need to provide a learning environment specifically intended to support a deep approach (Entwistle, Thompson and Tait, 1996). But more recently the focus of our research has shifted to look in more detail at that determination to extract meaning and reach a thorough understanding of course material which lies at the heart of the deep approach. Qualitative methods, similar to phenomenography, have been used to explore students' experiences of developing their understandings.

The nature of academic understanding

A recent description of the defining features of the three approaches to learning describe the deep approach as depending on an interplay between an adventurous relating of ideas (holist strategy) and a cautious examination of evidence in relation to conclusions (serialist strategy) (Entwistle, 1995a). This description echoes the earlier idea of the *reasonable adventurer* (Heath, 1964).

> In the pursuit of a problem, (the Reasonable Adventurer) appears to experience an alternation of involvement and detachment. The phase of involvement is an intensive and exciting period characterised by curiosity, a narrowing of attention towards some point of interest...This period of involvement is then followed by a period of detachment, an extensive phase, accompanied by a reduction of tension and a broadening range of perception... Here (the Reasonable Adventurer) settles back to reflect on the meaning of what was discovered during the involved stage. Meaning presumes the existence of a web of thought, a pattern of ideas to which the 'new' element can be related...We see, therefore,...a combination of two mental attitudes: the curious and the critical. They do not occur simultaneously, but in alternation. (pp. 30–1)

The next stage of our research investigated the experiences of students as they actively sought understanding and produced an alternative way of conceptualising the 'web of thought' or 'pattern of ideas' developed by students as they made use of both holist and serialist thinking in preparing for finals.

So far, we have carried out a series of small-scale studies of students mainly from psychology, social history and zoology. Hour-long interviews were transcribed and analysed, not only to identify categories of description, but also to investigate their meaning in relation to previous research findings, and the inter-relationships between them. It became clear early in our analyses of the interviews that, while most students talked about how they were trying to understand their notes, they were describing very different forms of understanding. Those differences we came to describe in terms of breadth, depth and structure. Breadth described the amount of material the student had sought to incorporate in the understanding. Depth indicated the amount of time and effort put in considering what the material meant, while five different ways of structuring the understanding could be seen in the students' responses, varying from no structure at all, through structures which were tied closely to the perceived assessment demands, to structures which represented individual conceptions of the discipline (Entwistle and Entwistle, 1992, 1997).

Although the students differed markedly in the sophistication of the understanding they were seeking, they all tended to describe the experience of reaching understanding in rather similar terms. Repeatedly, they mentioned feelings of connectedness, coherence and confidence in explaining.

> (Understanding?) It's an active process; it's constructive...(It's) the interconnection of lots of disparate things – I think that's probably the best way to describe it – the way it all hangs together, the feeling that you understand how the whole thing is connected up – you can make sense of it internally. You're making lots of connections which then make sense and it's logical...It is as though one's mind has finally 'locked in' to the pattern. Concepts seem to fit together in a meaningful way, when before the connections did not seem clear, or appropriate, or complete...like jigsaw pieces, you know, suddenly connect, and you can see the whole picture...It's (also) the act of being able to construct an argument from scratch. I think if you are able to reconstruct it by yourself, that shows you understood it. (adapted from extracts reported in Entwistle and Entwistle, 1992)

Several students referred specifically to how they were able to visualise – or almost visualise – their understanding through the revision notes they had prepared. They could visualise the pattern they had made to summarise the main topics, but not the words or details. The notes encapsulated students' understanding within a structure which had a mnemonic function for them. Students remembered the structure of their understanding, and they were aware that there was much more detailed knowledge associated with the 'nodes' of that structure which would pull in additional information as they needed it. This can be illustrated by comments from two students.

> I can see that virtually as a picture, and I can review it, and bring in more facts about each part...Looking at a particular part of the diagram sort of triggers off other thoughts. I find schematics, in flow diagrams and the like, very useful because a schematic acts a bit like a syllabus; it tells you what you should know, without actually telling you what it is. I think the facts are stored separately,...and the schematic is like an index, I suppose.
>
> I got on to this process of constructing a kind of mental map... as a quick way of putting down the basics...and making sure I don't leave anything out. ...Then (in the exam) I would just image it again, ...and as I wrote it, (add) my own thoughts on what I had picked up from other reading. That's why I have it, because (it holds things together) whilst you're writing, adding in whatever you're thinking ...and extra detail. (Entwistle and Entwistle, 1991, pp. 219, 220)

The first of these comments came from one of our pilot interviews. It alerted us to the use of visualisation, which became one important focus of the interviews which followed. A re-analysis of the data in collaboration with Ference Marton, using phenomenography more directly, concentrated on how students had experienced their understandings. They repeatedly described a feeling that the material being revised had become so tightly integrated that it was experienced almost as an entity with form and structure. Only its general outline could be actually seen as an image, but additional associated knowledge was felt to be readily 'available', whenever needed.

It was this recurring experience among the students which we came to describe as a *knowledge object*. Its defining features involve an awareness of a tightly integrated body of knowledge, visualisation of structure in a 'quasi-sensory' way, an awareness of unfocused aspects of knowledge (Entwistle and Marton, 1994), and a recognition of how the structure can be used to control explanations during examinations (Entwistle, 1995b). This form of awareness, together with the controlling function, can be seen in the following extract – in which the knowledge object seems to be almost a 'felt presence'.

> Following that logic through, *it* pulls in pictures and facts as it needs them...Each time I describe (a particular topic), it's likely to be different...Well, you start with evolution, say,...and suddenly you know where you're going next. Then, you might have a choice...to go in that direction or that direction...and follow it through various options *it's* offering...Hopefully, you'll make the right choice, and so this goes to this, goes to this – and you've explained it to the level you've got to. Then, *it* says 'Okay, you can go on to talk about further criticisms in the time you've got left.' (Entwistle, 1995b, p. 50)

This extract also draws attention to the idea that the explanation guided by the knowledge object will differ to some extent from occasion to occasion. Other comments suggest that the structure of the knowledge object offers a generic shape to the explanation, but that the particular answer given will depend on the question set and the dynamics of the evolving explanation. Some students were also very aware of how the examination affected the type of explanation they could provide, and of the expectations of the audience for whom they were writing.

> When you're revising...you're trying to convince yourself that you can convince the examiner...You can't use all the information for a particular line of argument, and you don't need to. You only need to use what you think is going to convince the examiner...
>
> The more I have done exams, the more I'd liken them to a performance – like being on a stage...having not so much to present the fact that you know a vast amount, but having to perform well with what you do know...Sort of, playing to the gallery...I was very conscious of being outside what I was writing. (Entwistle and Entwistle, 1991, pp. 220, 221)

In tackling an examination question, then, the best prepared students sought to relate the specific wording of question set to a pre-existing knowledge object, which is then used to guide the emerging logic of the answer and to pull in evidence and examples as required. The student is monitoring the evolving answer in relation to the wording of the question and to a sense of what will persuade the examiners that a deep level of understanding of the topic has been achieved.

Conclusion

The changing research perspective

The investigation of academic performance has been traced through a series of phases during which the methods used and the conceptualisation has changed markedly. The work started with a reliance on psychological constructs to predict academic performance – seen as taken for granted, the examination results. It then changed focus by seeking concepts with a greater ecological validity and offering more insight into the processes of studying which led to those examination results. Research into the distinction between deep and surface approaches showed how learning strategies are affected by perceptions of the various components of aspects of the learning environment, and in particular by the forms of assessment which determine examination results. The recognition of the problematic definition of academic attainment has led to a continuing concern with the nature of academic understanding, and attempts to show how students build up and experience the personal understanding which is the goal of a deep approach.

The difficulty in making predictions about academic performance becomes understandable as we map out the ways in which students with different intellectual and personality characteristics not only study in different ways, but also adjust their approaches according to their perceptions of what is being required of them in a particular course. Students also have their own individual goals in studying, and that again influences their perceptions of study settings (Volet and Renshaw, 1995). Nevertheless, being a successful student does depend on developing a certain expertise, described by Janssen (1996) as *studaxology*. This expertise can be described through research findings and supported within university contexts. Support for learning can be provided in two main ways – indirectly, by teaching, which takes account of what students need in order to develop expertise in that particular discipline (Janssen, 1996), and directly, by helping students to become more aware of their own ways of studying and more active in monitoring their academic progress (Tait and Entwistle, 1996; Vermunt, 1996).

In most of the studies described above, a combination of quantitative and qualitative methods have been used. Over time, both sets of methods have been progressively refined, and yet they rest on fundamentally different assumptions about the way concepts and theories are established. The physical science paradigm, outlined in the first main section above, is dominant in the thinking of most empirical psychologists, to the extent that the value of qualitative studies is often dismissed out of hand. That reaction is understandable, given the academic training of psychologists, and yet it is a barrier towards the imaginative use of complementary methods in educational research.

Of course, it is very difficult to accept, at the same time, the hypothetico-deductive paradigm of the physical scientist, and the inductive, interpretative methods of the phenomenographer; the well-defined statistical analyses of the psychometrician, and the more impressionistic categorisations emerging from interview studies. Psychologists pride themselves on the rigorous ways in which they examine findings, checking each alternative explanation. And yet a similar rigorous and logical process is applied in phenomenography, as the meaning of each emerging category is checked against the instances which delimit it, and in relation to other categories and previous formulations (Marton, 1994). Acceptance of a theory, for most psychologists, is based on the results of replication, using identical, or systematically varied, research designs. Acceptance in qualitative research, as in historical research, depends on a gradual process of critical debate which considers the explanatory range, elegance, and parsimony of concepts (just as Einstein did in his initial thinking about relativity), and the extent to which findings describe a 'recognisable reality' in the perceptions of both researchers and those whose behaviour and situation has been analysed (Parlett and Hamilton, 1972).

It is crucial for empirical educational researchers to realise just how reputable interpretative methods are in other well-established disciplines. Only if the essential validity of both approaches towards describing human behaviour is accepted can we expect the interplay between quantitative and qualitative methods to be used more widely in educational research. And yet it is precisely that interplay which has enabled the studies on academic achievement and student learning to develop as a research area in its own right. Different research methods are quite understandably directed towards differing research goals and derive from alternative theoretical perspectives. The descriptions generally have some validity in describing aspects of their focal concern; yet none adequately describes the complexity of the whole. It is worth remembering Jung's warning:

> We shall probably have to resort to a mixed explanation, for nature does not give a fig for the sanitary neatness of our intellectual categories. (quoted by Jaffe, 1972, p.32)

Supporting student learning

One goal of all this research on study strategies and student learning has been to help students to study more effectively. Even after our first survey, we sought to develop an academic achievement game, which was intended to help students reflect on how they studied and what might influence their success (Entwistle and Wilson, 1977). It was a board game in which students were allocated to different levels of ability and different personality types which affected their ability to deal satisfactorily with a series of events, which were presented as the students progressed round the board by throwing dice. Although the game did help students to reflect on studying, they found the nature of the game too static, while researchers noted the limited use made of research findings in deciding the events and their consequences.

The advent of computer-based adventure games offered another way of presenting research findings in an attractive format (Entwistle, Odor and Anderson, 1988). A story line was developed which took the student through some of the main events of the first year at university. Each series of events was located within a particular scene – for example, choice of courses, attending lectures and taking exams. The students entered the game through 'freshers' week', during which they were asked to fill in a questionnaire – a shortened version of the ASI. Scores on the inventory became a profile, which was updated on the basis of the responses made to subsequent choices. Within each scene, students were faced with choices to make which had consequences dependent, in some cases, on the student's individual profile. If students were unclear how those consequences were arrived at, they could appeal to a chorus (as in classical Greek plays) which explained what had happened. At the end of each scene, a mentor explained the purpose of the whole scene, and related the events and consequences to relevant aspects of the study process. Overall, the game was much more 'principled' than its forerunner, drawing more convincingly on research findings. Yet, the game itself led to over-elaboration and distracted students from its main purpose – advice on studying.

The most recent device to help students with their studying – PASS (Personalised Advice on Study Skills) – again makes use of computers to present principled advice, but in a much more direct way, using hypertext to offer advice at different levels of detail (CRLI, 1995; Tait and Entwistle, 1996). Again, the student starts by filling in a version of the ASI, now supplemented by self-ratings on specific study skills. That information is used to direct the student to advice on areas of reported weakness, although students can also browse freely through the whole range of advice if they prefer. PASS addresses the specific skills areas used in most books or workshops, but presents that advice within a coherent, principled framework derived from research on student learning. Its main aim is to encourage a greater awareness of the purposes in studying and to promote regular and systematic reflection on the skills and strategies being adopted. The materials were developed to work with HyperCard under the Macintosh operating system, but have since been made available on the World Wide Web at http://129.215.172.45/.

Ongoing work has developed the ASI into a questionnaire – ASSIST (Approaches and Study Skills Inventory for Students) – designed to help staff monitor the extent to which their current teaching is encouraging a deep approach to learning. This questionnaire provides indicators of students' reasons for entering higher education, conceptions of learning, approaches to studying, confidence in their current study skills and personal transferable skills, influences on their studying, and preferences for different kinds of teaching (Entwistle, McCune and Tait, in preparation).

One problem in offering study skills advice is that students are often reluctant to spend time accessing it. Only if the advice is presented as a necessary part of the course, and is targeted more specifically on course requirements, are students likely to make use of it. Thus PASS has been directed to staff and departments as well as individual students, and is currently being installed in computer laboratories in several departments. One of the suite of programmes allows staff to display the responses to the inventory of a class as a whole, so as to indicate areas of general concern or weakness. It can also be used as a preliminary to individual advice.

With the rapid expansion of higher education over the last decade, problems associated with under-prepared students and weak learning skills are becoming increasingly troublesome. Universities cannot assume that entering students have already acquired the necessary skills, and will have to provide systematic opportunities for them to be developed in the first year of study (Entwistle and Tait, 1992). PASS is not intended to be the only, or even the main, support for developing effective study skills, but is seen as contributing to an institution's overall policy for supporting student learning.

Thus, the injunction of Charles Carter has been followed. Research into teaching and learning in higher education has been able to provide very direct help both to students and staff. At the same time the studies have evolved, in line with general trends in educational research, to provide much more sophisticated, and ecologically valid, descriptions. The cumulative picture presented from a substantial body of research now shows how academic performance at university depends on a complex interaction between the characteristics and actions of the student, and the learning environment provided by the lecturer and institution.

References

Beaty, E., Gibbs, G. and Morgan, A. (1997) Learning orientations and study contracts, in Marton, F. Hounsell, D.J. and Entwistle, N.J. (Eds.), The Experience of Learning, 2nd edn (Edinburgh: Scottish Academic Press).

Bereiter, C. (1990) Aspects of an educational learning theory. Review of Educational Research, 60, 603–24.

Biggs, J.B. (1976) Dimensions of study behaviour: Another look at ATI. British Journal of Educational Psychology, 46, 68–80.

Biggs, J.B. (1987) Student approaches to learning and studying (Melbourne: Australian Council for Educational Research).

Biggs, J.B. (1993) What do inventories of students' learning processes really measure? A theoretical review and clarification. Educational Psychology, 63, 3–19.

Bronowski, J. (1965) The Identity of Man (London: Heinemann).

Carter, C.F. (1972) Presidential address. Society for Research into Higher Education. Published in Innovation in Higher Education (London: SRHE).

Cattell, R.B. and Butcher, H.J. (1968) The Prediction of Achievement and Creativity (New York: Bobbs-Merrill).

Choppin, B.H.L. (1973) The Prediction of Academic Success (Slough: NFER).

CRLI (1995) PASS: personalised advice on study skills [Computer software and supporting materials] (Edinburgh: University of Edinburgh, Centre for Research on Learning and Instruction).

Cronbach, L.J. (1957) On the two disciplines of scientific psychology. American Psychologist, 12, 671–84.

Dahllof, U. (1991) Towards a new model for the evaluation of teaching, in Dahllof, U. *et al*. (Eds.) Discussions of Education in Higher Education (London: Jessica Kingsley).

Entwistle, N.J. (1987) A model of the teaching–learning process, in Richardson, J.T.E. Eysenck, M.W. and Warren Piper, D. (Eds.) Student Learning: Research in education and cognitive psychology (Milton Keynes: Open University Press/SRHE).

Entwistle, N.J. (1988) Motivational factors in students' approaches to learning, in Schmeck, R.R. (Ed.), Learning Strategies and Learning Styles (New York: Plenum), pp. 21–52.

Entwistle, N.J. (1995a) The nature of academic understanding, in Kaufmann, G. Helstrup, T. and Teigen, K.H. (Eds) Problem Solving and Cognitive Processes (Bergen-Sandviken: Fagbokforlaget).

Entwistle, N.J. (1995b) Frameworks for understanding as experienced in essay writing and in preparing for examinations. Educational Psychologist, 30, 47–54.

Entwistle, N.J. (in press). Improving teaching through research on student learning, in Forest, J.J.F. (Ed.) University Teaching: International perspectives (New York: Garland Press).

Entwistle N.J. and Entwistle, A.C. (1991) Contrasting forms of understanding for degree examinations: the student experience and its implications. Higher Education, 22, 205–27.

Entwistle, A.C., and Entwistle N.J. (1992) Experiences of understanding in revising for degree examinations. Learning and Instruction, 2, 1–22.

Entwistle, N.J. and Entwistle, A.C. (1997) Revision and the experience of understanding, in Marton, F. Hounsell, D.J. and Entwistle, N.J. (Eds), The Experience of Learning, 2nd edn)Edinburgh: Scottish Academic Press).

Entwistle, N. J., and Marton, F. (1994) Knowledge objects: Understandings constituted through intensive academic study. British Journal of Educational Psychology, 64, 161–78.

Entwistle, N.J. and Ramsden, P. (1983) Understanding Student Learning (London: Croom Helm).

Entwistle, N.J. and Tait, H. (1990) Approaches to learning, evaluations of teaching, and preferences for contrasting academic environments. Higher Education, 19, 169–94.

Entwistle, N.J. and Tait, H. (1992) Promoting effective study skills. Module 8, Block A. Effective learning and teaching in higher education (Sheffield Universities' and Colleges' Staff Development Unit).

Entwistle, N.J., and Wilson, J.D. (1977) Degrees of Excellence: The academic achievement game (London: Hodder and Stoughton).

Entwistle, N.J., Hanley, M. and Ratcliffe, G. (1979) Approaches to learning and levels of understanding. British Educational Research Journal, 5, 99–114.

Entwistle, N.J., McCune, V. and Tait, H. (in preparation) ASSIST: evaluating the quality of student learning by questionnaire (Edinburgh: University of Edinburgh, Centre for Research on Learning and Instruction).

Entwistle, N.J., Odor, J.P. and Anderson, C.D.B. (1988) Encouraging reflection on study strategies: the design of a computer-based adventure game, in Ramsden, P. (Ed.) Improving Learning: New perspectives (London: Kogan Page), pp.234–51

Entwistle, N.J., Thompson, J.B. and Wilson, J.D. (1974) Motivation and study habits. Higher Education, 3, 379–96.

Entwistle, N.J., Thompson, S. and Tait, H. (1996) Guidelines for Promoting Effective Learning in Higher Education, 2nd edn (Edinburgh: University of Edinburgh, Centre for Research on Learning and Instruction).

Heath, R. (1964) The Reasonable Adventurer (Pittsburgh, PA: University of Pittsburgh Press).

Hoyle, F. (1972) From Stonehenge to Modern Cosmology (San Francisco, CA: W.H. Freeman).

Jaffé, A. (1972) From the Life and Work of Jung, C.G. (London: Hodder and Stoughton).

Janssen, P.J. (1996) Studaxology: the expertise students need to be effective in higher education. Higher Education, 31, 119–43.

Marsh, H.W. (1987) Students' evaluations of university teaching: research findings, methodological issues, and directions for future research. International Journal of Educational Research, 11(3) (whole issue).

Marton, F. (1994) Phenomenography, in Husen, T. and Postlethwaite, N. (Eds), International Encyclopedia of Education (Oxford: Pergamon), pp. 4424–9.

Marton, F., and Säljö, R. (1976) On qualitative differences in learning. I – outcome and process. British Journal of Educational Psychology, 46, 4–11.

Marton, F., and Säljö, R. (1996) Approaches to learning, in Marton, F. Hounsell, D.J. and Entwistle, N.J. (Eds), The Experience of Learning, 2nd edn (Edinburgh: Scottish Academic Press).

Meyer, J.H.F. (1991) Study orchestration: the manifestation, interpretation and consequences of contextualised approaches to learning. Higher Education, 22, 297–316.

Meyer, J.H.F., Parsons, P. and Dunne, T.R. (1990) Individual study orchestrations and their association with learning outcome. Higher Education, 20, 67–89.

Parlett, M.R. and Hamilton, D. (1972) Evaluation as illumination: a new approach to the study of innovatory programmes. Unpublished report. (Reprinted in Hamilton, D. *et al.* (Eds), Beyond the numbers game (Basingstoke: Macmillan).

Perkins, D.N., Jay, E. and Tishman, S. (1993) Beyond abilities: a dispositional theory of thinking. Merrill-Palmer Quarterly, 39, 1–21.

Ramsden, P. (1997) The context of learning, in Marton, F. Hounsell, D.J. and Entwistle, N.J. (Eds), The Experience of Learning, 2nd edn (Edinburgh: Scottish Academic Press).

Snow, R., Corno, L. and Jackson, D. (1996) Individual differences in affective and conative functions, in Berliner, D. and Calfree, R. (Eds) Handbook of Educational Psychology (New York: Macmillan).

Svensson, L. (1977) On qualitative differences in learning. III – Study skill and learning. British Journal of Educational Psychology, 47, 233–43.

Tait, H. and Entwistle, N.J. (1996) Identifying students at risk through ineffective study strategies. Higher Education, 31, 99–118.

Trigwell, K., Prosser, M. and Taylor, P. (1994) Qualitative differences in approach to teaching first year science. Higher Education, 27, 74–84.

Vermunt, J.D. (1996) Metacognitive, cognitive and affective aspects of learning styles and strategies: a phenomenographic analysis. Higher Education, 31, 25–51.

Volet, S.E., and Renshaw, P.D. (1995) Cross-cultural differences in university students' goals and perceptions of study seeings for achieving their own goals. Higher Education, 30, 407–33.

Part II
MEASUREMENT AND ASSESSMENT

Thematic introduction and summary

DIANE SHORROCKS-TAYLOR

This second section is perhaps the most difficult to introduce, for several reasons. As several of the authors in the first section of this book indicated, in the context of teaching and learning, it is important to acknowledge the vital links between the three sides of this triangle, including assessment. Effective facilitation of learning can only take place if the facilitator (the teacher) has a clear idea of the student's approach to learning, what he or she already knows and can build on this. This, of course, is the role of assessment – ascertaining what is already known and understood and whether other characteristics of the learner might influence his or her approach to the new knowledge, skills or understandings. On a rather different point, it is also evident that issues to do with measurement and assessment enter into parts of the book other than this one, for instance, in the context of ascertaining exceptional need or talent in children, or measuring personality characteristics in the context of selection in the workplace.

In a sense, therefore, other chapters could well have been located under the broad heading of this section and at the same time, the issues addressed here enter into much of the content throughout the book. However, the decision was made to focus here on explicit issues of educational measurement and assessment, especially in the light of the current high profile of testing in Britain and other places in the world.

In Chapter 7, Michael Youngman sets the scene by summarising and evaluating significant issues in educational measurement, some of which were mentioned in Part I. He argues persuasively that the current expansion in information technology has brought quite sophisticated research possibilities within reach of most of us, representing a change in the locus of expertise and a transfer of control. His subsequent summary of current methodologies in educational measurement shows us how important it is to understand and evaluate these in this changed research context.

His summary and evaluation begins with a review of the more traditional methodologies such as Rasch models and generalisability theory. Then, extending the field a little using his preferred term *characterisation*, he presents some key ideas in naturalistic and more qualitative methodologies. The question he poses by the end of the chapter bears more thought. He asks how far have we really moved in educational measurement, notwithstanding all the new possibilities opened up to us by new technologies. The remaining chapters in the section go some way to addressing this question, but the answer is not fully clear. This may well be a point of considerable significance in terms of new directions in educational psychology.

Chapter 8, written by Christopher Pole, brings the focus of the section to the present situation in Britain and in particular to the recent, very radical changes in curriculum and assessment. The analysis he offers is essentially a broad-brush one, charting the socio-political influences in the developments of the national testing system, National Curriculum Assessment. As both he and I (in Chapter 9) argue, the driving principles seem to have been those of 'standards' and accountability and the greater call for more systematic monitoring of pupil progress. Linked to these factors, however, have been teacher appraisal and the emphasis on parental power within the system. One of the central points in his analysis is the eroding of teacher professionalism under the new regime, in the wake of the drive towards centralised control and monitoring. This is in particular contrast to the situation before the advent of the National Curriculum, when records of achievement were gaining ground in schools, representing a more democratic approach to assessment which included both teachers and pupils at the heart of the judgemental process. As Pole suggests, these innovations have been virtually ignored in subsequent developments.

In Chapter 9, I take up some similar points to those made by Christopher Pole, but then move on to look in more detail at the national tests, from the perspective of someone who has been closely involved in the production of some of them. The four key principles of the system (as outlined in 1998) are each taken in turn and used as a vehicle for considering changing theoretical and practical matters. Changes since 1988, as the testing has come on stream for the various age groups, have been from more classroom and teacher-involved assessments, towards more clearcut and 'objective' pencil-and-paper tests. Very different emphases have been given to the requirements of reliability, validity and manageability. It is not clear what will happen to the testing system in the future, except to suggest that it is unlikely to disappear now that it appears to have become a fairly ingrained aspect of work in schools.

Finally, Chapter 10, by Carol Fitz-Gibbon, begins by emphasising the complexity and unpredictability of organisations such as schools and classrooms, and suggesting that we are probably never going to be in the

Thematic introduction and summary

position of fully explaining or modelling this complexity. She argues that the best we can do is to monitor carefully what is going on and watch out for problems – 'fire fighting' as she calls it. As part of this process, it is necessary for teachers to have good information about their effectiveness, in relation both to academic outcomes and broader social and affective factors in their schools and classes.

In one sense, academic outcomes have some quite clear indicators, mostly in this country GCSE and 'A' level results, but she makes an important case for also developing measures of student attitudes and motivation. Work that Fitz-Gibbon and her colleagues have carried out, provides analyses to schools on both of these (academic and social/affective factors), including measures of student career intentions and educational aspirations. The conclusion is that such indicator systems can be used and that they provide useful information that can be used to good effect in the management of schools. School inspections can also provide important formative feedback to schools, especially peer or self-evaluation strategies. However, as she points out, the external school inspection system presently in place in England and Wales has never been subjected to traditional evaluation in terms of reliability, validity and impact. Without this, it is not easy to judge the effectiveness of the inspections nor to justify the very considerable expenditure involved.

The chapters in this section therefore address a wide range of issues in this albeit fairly narrow approach to assessment. All emphasise the need, somehow, to address the complexity involved and to understand the techniques being used to investigate and characterise the system and individuals within it. Assessment outcomes can indeed be of use to teachers and schools, not to mention pupils and parents, but this information needs to be very well grounded, valid and clearly explained if it is to produce the positive effects within the education system that are claimed.

Chapter 7
Trends in educational measurement and research methodology

MICHAEL YOUNGMAN

A general introduction

The systematic study of human situations, typically referred to as research, hinges upon acceptable identification and analysis of relevant evidence. In the field of education, those aspects of humans considered pertinent to the resolution of any problem are likely to be manifold. Futhermore, the research process itself has a variety of influences and consequently its methods are equally diverse. The overall effect is to present a complex enquiry structure that must be appreciated if credible results are to emerge. This chapter seeks to foster that appreciation by introducing a selection of the critical issues involved. Such is the span of issues that only those that seem to be especially influencial can be accommodated in this brief outline.

Even when the important issues have been selected, there remains the difficulty of organising seemingly disparate topics. I have adopted a slightly serendipitous strategy based on an historical accident. It consists of referring back to a major book in this field that appeared two decades ago. By following the themes presented there, I have tried to identify real developments, introducing new techniques where there has been clear innovation. The actual order of presentation is in some ways an embodiment of research itself. There is the accumulation of evidence, more often referred to as data collection. Finally, the evidence is processed – or analysed.

But research should not be construed in such a simple chronology. As I shall try to explain, the interplay between these stages is vital to the validity of the outcomes. Measurement and methodology cannot be separated: the effective researcher will need to appreciate their joint implications. In some ways it is a demanding expectation. My own view is that the effort should be applied to the appreciation of issues, not mastery of techniques. It is no longer necessary for most researchers to learn complex statistical computing procedures (if it ever was!), but it is essential that the application of those tools is understood.

A starting point

Some 20 years ago de Gruijter and van der Kamp's (1976) book *Advances in psychological and educational measurement* appeared. That same year I used a sabbatical term to write my ideas on data analysis into a book, *Analysing social and educational research data* (Youngman, 1979a). Both texts presented contemporary theory and practice on the processing of data generated in educational research. It is noteworthy that in both instances educational research analysis was allied with another human discipline. Since it was virtually impossible at that time to pursue any advanced course in education without studying the disciplines of sociology and psychology, the juxtaposition of education with them in book titles was quite natural. Today the situation is rather different. Any masters course requiring a grounding in psychology would be the exception: any book associating education with sociology would risk rejection.

In developing my thoughts for this chapter, I started by scouring a selection of my past writings. I had reviewed the de Gruijter and van der Kamp book; that review provides a very telling base from which to consider the current state of educational measurement. In my review I suggested that advancing educational measurement needs salesmen, and by that I explained 'it is those who supply the means, usually the computer program writers' (Youngman, 1978a, p.114). It will be interesting to see how far things have changed in those 20 years.

The proliferation of personal computers and information technology

One aspect that certainly has changed is the proliferation of personal computers and the contiguous expansion of information technology in all its guises. In 1976 virtually all data collection was manual and most data analysis was via mainframe computers. Now the personal computer has achieved a combination of power and economy that makes it available as a resource to almost anyone handling human measurement. Such has been the effectiveness of the associated salesmanship that few have ignored the switch to personal control. The design and production of measurement instruments, the recording of data, the statistical analysis of those data, the graphical representation of data summaries, and the preparation of final reports are all likely to be carried out on a personal computer. This transfer of control from experts to individuals is more than just a procedural change. It also implies changes in the nature of human measurement.

National Curriculum Assessment

In England and Wales it is impossible at present to examine current educational measurement without considering the national assessment phenomenon incorporated in the implementation of the National Curriculum. It is an obscure and emotive issue, which fortunately I can leave in the main to Diane Shorrocks-Taylor in her chapter (pp. 170–88). There appear, however, to be two major measurement issues inherent in National Curriculum Assessment. Firstly, such an extensive national operation would be expected to embody current thinking on measurement. Secondly, it might also be expected to generate new thinking, acting as an opportunity to develop, trial and consolidate procedures that would otherwise be too costly for typical research projects.

The education context

The diversity of pertinent attributes

Along with all social inquiry, education usually needs to consider a wide diversity of potentially relevant attributes in pursuing a measurement issue. These attributes vary in level from the individual (classically referred to as the study of individual differences) to the situational or organisational. Because of this variety it is inappropriate to assume a notion of measurement which may convey restricted connotations. Even in the area of human performance, a broadening conception of achievement has led to a questioning of classical test-based assessment. When attributes of schools or curricula or homes are under scrutiny, it is inevitable that alternative characterisations of human involvement are required. Contrasted with many physical studies where a handful of closely related variables may be under investigation, it follows that different strategies may be needed in educational enquiry to ensure that the most pertinent set of attributes has been selected for study.

The identification of criteria

It might appear that the broadening of the range of characteristics to be considered in educational enquiry would inevitably make the identification of those deemed relevant yet more difficult. I suppose the response here has to be yes and no. Yes – more must mean that there is potentially a greater task during the design phase of failing to identify features likely to be worth pursuing empirically. The No response stems from the greater availability of facilities to assist the identification phases of measurement. The plural here is intentional. The development of on-line information searching has made access to previous work a much more prolific and reliable opportunity for most researchers. There is little doubt that, in reality, the traditional book-based review methods were frequently incomplete, arbitrary and painful. They held little guarantee of being able to locate a nucleus of current work in a chosen area. In theory it is now possible for any student with access to relatively common computing facilities to search in a systematic and extensive manner, so that the relevant characteristics within the topic can be identified.

But possibly a more important recent development in the identification of criteria appears in the later stages of research. No longer is the researcher uniquely committed to a limited set of initially identified attributes. With the elaboration of exploratory analytical methods it is now feasible (indeed advisable) to use the power of those methods to curtail the selectivity inherent in earlier thinking. The essence of this stance is not new. Item analysis always commenced with a larger pool of items than could be used in the final test. Factor analysis has regularly been used as a reduction method (Child, 1970; Youngman, 1979a) to identify automatically a smaller set of pertinent variables. This trend has accelerated in recent years with the growth of methods specifically intended to allow data structures to be established, tested, modified and validated. With their availability it becomes worthwhile to begin with a more extensive measurement base (practicalities of testing permitting) and let subsequent analyses exercise some of the empirical discretion. Once this attitude is accepted it is possible to be more adventurous in considering characteristics that might otherwise have been ignored through their assumed low chance of producing significance.

An expansion of methodologies

Alongside the increasing diversity of relevant attributes there has been a similar expansion in the styles of inquiry applied to educational issues. This can be seen readily in any comparison of the contents of texts written in the early 1970s (e.g. Entwistle and Nisbet, 1970) with those produced in the 1990s (such as Bennett, Glatter and Levacic, 1994, or even Robson, 1993). You may feel I have cheated by referring to a text on social research methods, but Robson's title, *Real world research*, reflects precisely the point I make. Education is a potent microcosm of so many social issues that valid study must have access to a suitably broad range of data and methods. Being aware of the possible value of interviews, group discussions, stimulated comment or parental newsletter is as much a part of the inquirer's repertoire as the use of timed tests, attitude inventories, checklists or supermarket till receipts.

Classical measurement

The recognised basis for measurement

Each decade has its repertoire of texts on educational and psychological measurement (for example, Thorndike and Hagen, 1969, or more recently Kline, 1986) and reference to them will tend to show considerable similarity in content. Basic procedures such as the generation of item pools, item analysis, estimation of reliability and validity, and the presentation of tests are embedded within very familiar discussions of the corresponding theory. Variations are offered (Guttman scaling is a notable example) but their actual usage has been infrequent compared with the standard model.

A complementary approach can be seen in the works of Kerlinger (1973) and Nunnally (1967) where a broader perspective is presented. There the issues of behavioural measurement are discussed as part of a complete strategy for using the resultant data. Analysis is deemed an inextricable feature of measurement, and appropriate strategies are developed.

The prevalence of standard attitude models

Probably the most overt indication of accepted practice appears in the area of attitude measurement, if only because it features strongly in published work. Although the attitude model is not entirely parallel to performance assessment, most of the critical stages are common to both. The model remains predominantly a process of item generation, selection and classification. The criteria for selection are essentially reliability maximisation (Youngman, 1979b) and factor analysis has become the accepted answer to the problem of classifying items. Limited validation may be attempted, but cross-validation is rare.

Rasch analysis

It is helpful to mention Rasch analysis within this section, although it is included here more to accentuate the hold of the classical method than to imply that Rasch in any way exemplifies classical procedures. Kline's (1986) discussion of the Rasch method provides an interesting commentary on the progress of the method over the 30 or so years since its emergence. His preliminary presentation (pp. 20–22) gives the main computational details of the method, but he also relates the method to other more familiar approaches (such as Guttman scaling), and draws attention to disagreements over the utility of tests produced by the procedure. Later (pp.199–201) he contends that Rasch should not replace the classical model, suggesting that it could be useful in situations requiring retesting, or in educational testing where an identifiable pool of items exists. If there is to be any single line of development that could replace the classical model, one could see Rasch analysis as a possible contender.

The development base

A framework for detecting trends

When de Gruijter and van der Kamp's (1976) edited work, *Advances in psychological and educational measurement*, appeared the computing revolution was well established. The leading statistical analysis packages such as SPSS and BMD had become widely available, and numerous computer-based analytical innovations were equally in evidence. Amongst them were Veldman's (1967) seminal text *FORTRAN programming for the behavioral sciences* (which presented methods and source text programs) and Wishart's (1969) powerful and versatile cluster analysis package, CLUSTAN. Admittedly the computerisation of behavioural assessment originated much earlier as the work of Cattell and Kaiser amply shows. But the significance of the early 1970s was that these methods became accessible to any educational researcher, either through their own modest programming endeavours (which was how I started), or through the availability of computing resources and expert guidance in the use of those resources.

So de Gruijter and van der Kamp (1976) were able to present methods sufficiently late in their development for potential trends to be suggested. Indeed, in my review of the book (Youngman, 1978a) I appended my views on the likely attractiveness of the main methods to future researchers. The following sections provide brief preparatory outlines of these areas, before examining in detail the current state.

Rasch analysis and item banking

In some respects Rasch analysis might seem a natural phase in the development of tests. Its sample-free features and the potential for item banking appeared to overcome two of the limitations of classical test construction. However, de Gruijter and van der Kamp subsumed Rasch analysis under the more general heading of item banking, although the contributors to that section did foresee substantial advantages from applications of the methodology. Potential usages ranged from individualised testing (rather than group testing as the APU in Britain pursued) to the assessment of progress. Interestingly these suggestions are very similar to those offered by Kline (1986) 10 years later. My comparison of

Rasch analysis and other item analysis procedures (Youngman, 1979b) was less optimistic, failing to detect any benefit in spite of Rasch analysis forcing severe reductions in initial item pools.

The measurement of change

Next to validity in assessment, the measurement of change probably ranks second in terms of attention accorded over the years (Youngman, 1979a). A classic text on the issue is Harris's (1963) edited volume. In de Gruijter and van der Kamp's (1976) book the section on change measurement is by far the longest. It was only when I returned to this book after many years that I realised how portentous it might be; one chapter is by Joreskog and Sorbom, entitled 'Statistical models and methods for test–retest situations'. These two authors are now universally recognised as the compilers of the LISREL package. In my review I wrote

> At the more practical level, the presentation by Joreskog and Sorbom both demonstrates possible solutions, and offers references to available computer programs. (p. 113).

Twenty years later, when 'league tables' and 'value added' are terms that engender such excesses of comment and emotion, one may reasonably be surprised to be revisiting such a perennial problem.

Generalisability theory and Bayesian methodology

The various contributors to de Gruijter and van der Kamp's (1976) survey, writing on Bayesian theory, expressed confident views. They described several current applications and recognised a wide range of potential uses (including generalisability theory and item banking). A general opinion was that whilst classical test theory had shown its value, Bayesian theory offered the possibility of more sophisticated development. Specific applications were rare, but nonetheless available. The generalisability aspect was seen as particularly valuable, allowing problems of reliability, item sampling and test populations to be addressed. As I have already intimated, the classical method had achieved an entrenched status, leaving de Gruijter and van der Kamp to suggest that

> educationalists keep using classical statistical analysis, not because it is good, but because it is familiar...the vast majority went on reporting their KR-20 coefficients as if nothing had happened (p. vii).

Log linear modelling

The logistic linear model is a general method incorporating the Rasch model as a dichotomous case. Its complete form also enables change measurement. A particular strength of the approach is its probabilistic nature, allowing the effects of different interactions to be assessed. It is likely to be better known in its chi-squared variant, usually referred to as log-linear analysis. Although the method only appears incidentally within the main sections of de Gruijter and van der Kamp's text, any evaluation of current trends does need to consider developments involving log-linear methods.

Characterisation

The broader definition of measurement

One noticeable change that has occurred in the past 20 years is a decline in references to measurement in education. Instead, the reader is likely to be confronted with any of a plethora of terms used to describe the process for collecting evidence pertinent to an educational issue. The motives behind this change are not simply fashion. They reflect the broader perception of the context for educational study, a phenomenon I have already outlined. As a consequence of this shift, it is important not to address issues in a manner that might imply limited applicability. Since restricting attention to measurement could introduce such a misconception, my personal preference is to describe data identification processes as *characterisation*. This ensures an inclusive usage which can accommodate traditional quantitative measures alongside the kinds of descriptions emanating from qualitative studies. It also recognises explicitly the possibility of focusing on a wide range of characteristics when establishing the evidential basis of a particular study. In so doing it provides a natural link between the phases in research, a requirement too often forgotten.

Naturalistic and ecological viewpoints

So far I have given relatively little consideration to any theoretical frameworks that might feature in developments in educational characterisation. There are countless theoretical positions from which data collection can proceed. My personal favourite has always been the need to relate research to actuality, and I found fertile support in what used to be called naturalistic inquiry (see for example, Willems and Rausch, 1969). Since then it has been renamed ecological research, mutated into grounded theory, and now seems to be reverting to type as naturalistic research. Regardless of the apparently different stances adopted here, the basic requirement to locate inquiry within events is vital. A successful application does require a close fit to the context, and that is most easily achieved if it is sought from the start.

Measurement in context

Studying the primary school child's understanding of the school as a microscopic society (Buchanan-Barrow and Barrett, 1996) imposes a considerable empirical challenge. The interplay of the very young child's limited understanding and expressive ability, together with the complexity of producing a realistic characterisation of a society, provides an illuminating example of researchers tackling measurement in context. The solution they adopted was multifaceted. It involved devising question and response systems that matched the capabilities of these children. Then it required the employment of two analytical methodologies (log-linear analysis and correspondence analysis, a graphical method akin to multidimensional scaling) that fully accommodated the data structures generated.

Staying with the difficulties of investigating younger children, Smith and Levan's (1995) study of bullying faced the dual problem of working with emotive concepts and eliciting valid data from children. Indeed one aim of this study was to generate a reliable extrapolation of findings from studies researching older children. Their emphasis was on effective instrumentation, developing a range of possibilities before accepting a final version. They did conclude that part of the apparent discrepancy between their findings and those for older children could derive from a 'definitional change hypothesis' (p. 499), highlighting the need for researchers to consider the possibility of covert changes in perceptions as children mature.

Few readers can be unaware of Raymond Cattell's extensive role in the elaboration of measurement methodology. In a collaboration with Dennis Child (Cattell and Child, 1975) he demonstrated the need for a multilayered approach to attitude testing. Emphasising the complex nature of attitude assessment involving, for example, factors of strength, sentiment and drive, they presented 68 principles underpinning motivational measurement (see Kline, 1986, p. 92). Kline felt that the dynamic elements of motivation had yet to be validated, but Boyle and Houndoulesi (1993) have been able to demonstrate the utility of one outcome of Cattell's work in this field, the School Motivation Analysis Test (Krug, Cattell and Sweney, 1976). Adopting an analytical approach, they confirmed the motivational structure proposed by Cattell and Child (1975). In so doing they provide an example of how analysis can effect the link between context and application.

These are three instances (involving data characterisation or analysis or both) that show how human measurement is becoming more context sensitive. In that data and analysis are both implicated, they confirm the artificiality of espousing a compartmentalised notion of measurement. Characterisation does seem to provide a closer conception of the importance of maintaining aspects of context within the overall train of evidence processing.

Qualitative methodologies

I introduce qualitative methods into this account as a recognition of the necessary comparability of different approaches. It is almost a truism that if alternative approaches are not consistent, then at least one is invalid. With the growth of the use of qualitative methods in educational inquiry (indeed, to the point where it is arguable which is now the most prevalent approach) the need to operate comparable criteria becomes increasingly prominent. Characterisation is a clear instance of an operating construct being available across methodologies. It would seem reasonable to hope that other constructs such as reliability and validity would achieve a similar currency.

Processing the data

The broader concept of characterisation implies some degree of analysis. At this point I want to present processing requirements in a more dominant light. Anyone involved with the early developments in classroom behaviour research will immediately recall the analytical problems presented by the mass of resultant data. Flanders interaction matrices were all very acceptable conceptually, but I think it is fair to conclude that no effective analytical procedure emerged in the subsequent computer program boom. They failed at two levels. Firstly they tended to be too onerous to apply, requiring extensive input and output for even the simplest tabulations. More importantly, none of the analytical models matched the conceptual base of the data. Suffice it to say that data processing cannot be separated from characterisations of data.

Meta-analysis

Superordinate to measurement and analysis is the possibility of deriving stronger conclusions from a series of related studies. In some ways, the principle is inherent in traditional methods since sampling and statistical inference do permit some generalisability beyond a single study. Meta-analysis is the term used to describe a range of procedures specifically designed to amalgamate the results of similar studies. Its inception in education is usually attributed to Glass (1976), and Henriksson (1994) summarises its development over the past 20 years. Given the promise implicit in its aims, and the diversity of researches into similar problems in education, it may seem surprising that publications employing the method are still rare. The most likely explanation arises from problems with requirements of the procedures used. A particular difficulty lies in the need for conceptual comparability of measures and samples. Whilst many disciplines in science (including psychology) do operate with a recognised range of variables, education seems repeatedly to want to redefine or modify common constructs. The consequence is that too often researches addressing similar problems fail to employ measures that are directly comparable. The current concerns over international levels of attainments, and class-size research are prominent examples here.

Methodology as measurement

Inter-relatedness of characteristics

Even with the sparsest of research topics (such as those we might pursue in teaching educational inquiry) it quickly becomes essential to examine links between measures. For example, in the area of psychometric testing, Dennis and Evans (1996) contend that

> ...the essential problem is this. When we want a test of cognitive ability we do not want to measure some personality characteristic such as caution or impulsiveness (p. 106).

With the large number of variables featuring in most studies the inevitable consequence is that some multivariate analysis will be required. At one level this requirement is reasonably well covered in measurement facilities. The early development of computerised statistical methods has continued, both in the direction of generalised packages such as SPSS and SYSTAT, and with the provision of specialised techniques of which LISREL is probably the best-known example. Where current support is less effective is in the area of texts. It is still typical for books on social analysis to curtail their coverage at the bivariate level, maybe making passing mention of multivariate methods, or offering repeated use of uivariate methods such as ANOVA. My early attempt to redeem this failure by describing the real-life application of multivariate methods (Youngman, 1979a) has not been followed by a range of obviously successful texts. Certain guides allied to particular packages (eg. Bryman and Cramer, 1990 and SPSS) have become popular, for good reason, but access to procedures able to cope realistically with inter-relatedness remains problematic.

LISREL and structural equation modelling

There can be little doubt about LISREL's (Jöreskog and Sorbom, 1993) prominent role in current research analysis. The acronym LISREL stands for LInear Structural RELationships, but it has almost reached the status of a neologism within social research analysis. As I suggested in my review of de Gruijter and van der Kamp (1976), the fact that Jöreskog and Sorbom (1976) linked their promotion of structural equation models to the provision of an accessible computer package has been critical in this upsurge of interest. Causal path models had been around for some time, but they had not received favour (see Brennan, 1972). The general linear model, GLIM, appeared about the same time, but there the recognised difficulty of employing the routines has probably had the reverse effect in restricting its use.

But it would not be fair to attribute the popularity of LISREL solely to simplicity. Jöreskog and Sorbom's model encapsulates many of the issues I have referred to within this account. It accommodates psychometric properties of the measures, especially unreliability. Clearly it is multivariate in capability, but it is not exclusive as most multivariate methods tend to be. So although it may be possible to tweak methods such as multiple regression to emulate covariance models (Veldman, 1967; Youngman, 1980), LISREL is designed to permit tailored multivariate models to be applied to the target data. Furthermore the revision and retesting of those models is inherent in the system. So the analyses become a natural overlay of the original research questions. This kind of facility has led to a noticeable increase in its popularity.

If anything, the question to ask here may be whether there is a risk of over-use. I understand that at least one American journal has discouraged papers employing the technique. The issue is the perennial multivariate one of serendipity: how far are the findings from one particular application of the method overly dependent on error? Put another way, what confidence can there be that the findings are generalisable? It is perhaps surprising that in spite of the long recognised need for cross-validation in psychometric development (Youngman, 1979a), repetitions are still rare. This is not to imply any failing on the part of Jöreskog and Sorbom, and indeed their procedures do incorporate validation options. The issue is broader, requiring more of a consensual philosophy in measurement generally.

Multilevel modelling

Much of the earlier discussion in this chapter can be subsumed within the modelling aspect of measurement. Structural equation modelling seems to provide an elaboration of the kinds of problem originally tackled by single methods such as factor analysis or multiple regression. They do assume primarily a unitary quality in the sample. Goldstein (1987) offers multilevel modelling as a strategy for addressing the hierarchical features of samples. Multilevel modelling refers to the ability to define different levels within a sample to reflect the true focus of analysis. So, for example, variations within classes can be accommodated fully within analyses without loss of data inherent in class averaging procedures. To an extent this revisits the unit-of-analysis problem. The difference is the presentation of a model that allows the same degree of tailoring with respect to sample constitution as structural equation modelling does to variable interdependence.

The problem has been evident in educational research for some time. Contemporary interest has been stimulated by concerns over differential school performance, both at the consumer level and politically. However in outlining their development of multilevel methods, Paterson and Goldstein (1991) avoid linking the applicability of the methods too closely to one situation. Furthermore, just as Joreskog and Sorbom (1976) recognised the importance of providing accessible opportunities to use recommended procedures, Paterson and Goldstein also present a theoretical structure in association with a computer package, ML^3. Since this particular development is relatively recent, published applications are correspondingly rare (see, for example, Smit and van der Molen, 1996). It will be interesting to see whether future usage confirms the comparable advantages researchers seem to have ascribed to LISREL within its sphere of analysis.

There have been more generalised applications of multilevel modelling, if not with the frequency predicted in 1976. More prevalent have been uses of log-linear analysis to segment effects within tables that might traditionally have been analysed using chi-square. Typical of these is Galloway *et al.*'s (1995) employment of log-linear analysis to isolate effects in three-dimensional tables relating cognitive ability, gender and motivational style in English and mathematics.

Value-added and multiple regression models

Paterson and Goldstein (1991) do refer to multilevel modelling as an extension of the standard multiple regression model. That model has been shown to be extremely versatile, having the potential to tackle a range of measurement situations. One area where multiple regression in general, and multilevel modelling in particular, is currently being applied is in the determination of school effectiveness. What is somewhat disappointing is the slowness with which the educational hierarchy has pursued the problem. My own study of the determinants of pupil progress at primary–secondary transfer (Youngman, 1980) was hardly innovative, implementing a readily available strategy based on Veldman's (1967) programs (Youngman, 1976). The Department of Education and Science was itself using a comparable approach as early as 1979 (DES, *Statistical Bulletin* 15/79). Yet we are still faced with a plethora of so-called 'value-added' models, most of which are little more than crude variants on the covariance analogues developed by the likes of Veldman (1967) and Kerlinger and Pedhazur (1973) over 20 years ago.

Styles and typologies

Another perspective on the seemingly isolationist mentality in educational measurement is detectable in its approach to the categorisation of individuals. Classifying, labelling, typing have been common aims virtually from the beginning of measurement. Indeed it is arguable that human classification preceded measurement. Nowadays we have the identification of styles (cognitive, learning, teaching) as a prime concern, but the objective is the same, grouping on the basis of similarity of characteristics. When Brennan embarked upon his study of numerical classification techniques in the late 1960s (reported in his thesis, Brennan, 1972) he was surprised to discover extensive use of the technique in disciplines such as marketing and botany, but little in education. But even now when Seifert (1995) employs cluster analysis, he is arguing for its use as an innovative approach to counter the tradition of factor analytic study of student goal orientation. In a similar vein, Whitebread's (1996) summary of the outcomes of his use of cluster analysis in a study of children's thinking: 'One of the main aims of the present study was to explore the potential contribution of the new methodology...The results reported suggest the potential is considerable' (p. 17) almost echoes Brennan's thoughts on the future value of clustering.

Brennan's support for clustering was complemented by a rather different implementation of numerical taxonomy in American research. Applications by job analysis researchers (eg. Christal, 1970; Youngman *et al.*, 1978) were closer to botanical taxonomic work, principally through the use of binary data. Their usage reflected the naturalistic stance, involving the recording of large amounts of behavioural data coded in binary (yes/no) form. Numerical classification was used, partly to comply with the naturalistic methodology, but also because existing factor analytic routines could not handle the large data matrices (often exceeding 300 variables).

Following in the wake of these examples, I have regularly found clustering beneficial in overcoming the kinds of non-linear effects Seifert (1995) mentions. A primary–secondary transfer study (Youngman, 1978b) identified a 'disenchanted' group, not detectable by factor analysis. The binary approach has been especially effective in work analysis problems (e.g. with school teachers, Youngman, 1983, or with nurses and technicians, Youngman, Mockett and Baxter, 1988). Most reported applications of classification methods have expressed support for further development of the methodology, yet in education published instances are rare. It is surprising that the quest for styles and typologies has not been more often pursued through cluster analysis. Oddly it is the one substantial methodology that did not feature in de Gruijter and van der Kamp's (1976) survey.

Multidimensional scaling and graphical representations

Visual representation of data has tended to be used as an adjunct to statistical methods, usually to explain concepts (such as scatter plots for correlation), or to summarise in a more accessible form (bar charts, stem and leaf plots). But there comes a point when the graphical presentation supersedes its quantitative origins by substantially enhancing interpretation. Multidimensional scaling can be considered seminal in this respect. It allowed spatial configurations of cases and variables to be generated, extending the outcomes of factor analysis, and consequently the method attracted strong support in the early 1970s (Shepard, Romney and Nerlove, 1972). Subsequent applications in education have not been extensive, with barely a handful of appearances in the *British Journal of Educational Psychology* in recent years. In one example, Buchanan-Barrow and Barrett (1996) use correspondence analysis (Hammond, 1993) to generate a

> pictorial representation of the relationship between categories, and between individuals and groups. It permits a multi-dimensional analysis of categorical data ... (p. 36).

When one considers the wealth of graphical representations demonstrated in Tufte's classic texts (1988 and 1990) it is perhaps surprising that similar developments in educational measurement seem so rare. Elsewhere innovations are in evidence (Totterdell and Briner, 1996, present a time series approach) but it has yet to be seen whether education will embrace these advances.

The elaboration of methods

Even if new methods are not readily apparent, one might expect significant elaboration of existing methods over a 20-year period. There seem to be two aspects here. Firstly the notion of exploratory data analysis has been espoused (Tukey, 1977) as a strategy to escape from assumed limitations of conventional hypothesis testing procedures. Whilst this might not be especially original in itself (in that it extends existing ideas of descriptive data analysis) its main value is in encouraging analysts to be aware of a range of possible approaches to elucidating data structures. That range includes adopting alternative hypotheses or questions: it also suggests using alternative analytical procedures. One possible benefit is the ability to detect patterns that might not otherwise have been evident. There is also the opportunity to corroborate findings through the separate, independent application of different methods. Ultimately, as Seifert (1995) shows, an exploratory approach can lead to the identification of previously undetected features.

The situation regarding procedures is more obvious. LISREL provides elaborations of factor analysis (especially confirmatory factor analysis) that could have important applications in education. Take, for example, the extensive use of published instruments. Regardless of the thoroughness of the original development, there will remain uncertainties about some features. Aspects such as scale structure and reliability (or rather, unreliability) can be investigated through the use of generalisability theory or confirmatory factor analysis. Instances are appearing (Smit, 1996, uses generalisability theory to establish reliability estimates for his scales) but in other contexts (such as the recurrent administrations of the scales of Biggs, 1987) the use of procedural elaborations is less common than might be expected. Nevertheless there are still too many instances of blind pursuance of a method without proper attention to the problem context. It is not at all uncommon to encounter automatic selection of principal components analysis with varimax rotation when it is more likely that the characteristics of the problem are best served by imposing an oblique rotation (Cattell, 1995; see also Child, Chapter 19 on personality in this book, pp. 346-364).

Another major elaboration concerns group differentiation. The identification of differences between groups has always been contentious (Youngman, 1979a), partly through educational researchers' insistence on using t-tests or chi-squared as generalisable methods, even when a particular situation invalidated their application. Nowadays these failings are less common, and the relevant multiple comparisons (Scheffe or Tukey) will usually be applied. But it is less likely that the next stage, a multivariate difference test, will be employed. As has already been stressed, measurement almost invariably involves a large number of interrelated measures. Just as the identification of patterns demands appropriate multivariate procedures, so the confirmation and location of differences will typically require an overall multivariate test followed by suitable analyses of variance and comparisons tests corrected for Type I error.

The availability of methods

It is difficult not to conclude that the availability of methods is probably the main influence on developments in measurement practice. When I first compiled the computer program package PMMD (Youngman, 1976) in 1970 there were so few facilities for non-programmers that PMMD rapidly became popular with educational researchers. Around the same time the commercial development of programs such as SPSS and BMD commenced. As with most aspects of IT, the provision within a small number of popular programs tends to establish usage norms. The dominance of SPSS proceeded apace, to some extent regrettable in view of its onerous learning phase and poorly organised output. I wait with a degree of apprehension to see whether the asquisition of SYSTAT (to my mind a more user-oriented package) results in its demise, or whether SPSS moves closer to the SYSTAT model.

In spite of the increasing power and spread of the major statistical packages there does not appear to be a wholesale improvement in analytical methodology. One positive side to the universal availability of SPSS has been an increase in the use of MANOVA procedures, rather than simple ANOVA. Conversely, factor analytic methodology improves only slowly, and it is unclear why this should be so. One reason may be the glaring deficiencies in some major packages; SYSTAT, for example, offers no oblique factor rotation even though its use is verging on essential (Cattell, 1995, p. 207). Ultimately it may be the extension of LISREL usage that eventually provides the spur to development here with its provision of factor analytic models. Until recently there was an additional impetus to the adoption of structural equation modelling in the form of AMOS (Arbuckle, 1995) a modelling package that started in shareware mode with correspondingly cheap availability. The program moved to commercial distribution in 1995, and it has now been licensed to SPSS. If AMOS is offered in an accessible form within the SPSS structure, there could be a beneficial increase in the use of modelling methodology in educational measurement.

A related phenomenon on the availability front appears in the qualitative domain. The processing of qualitative data has tended to be problematic (for example, students have had difficulty locating workable guidelines and procedures). The program ETHNOGRAPH (Seidel *et al.*, 1988) achieved early popularity in appearing to simplify this problem, but the initial promise did not materialise. Now NUDIST (Richards and Richards, 1990) may be taking on the role of providing a flexible entry facility for qualitative characterisations of data. If availability is as critical as I suggest, the pricing, the platform and the support for the program will be fundamental to its success.

A demonstration: the stress symposium

Many of the issues developed to this point are neatly demonstrated in a symposium on teacher stress published in the *British Journal of Educational Psychology* in 1995 (Boyle *et al.*, 1995: pp. 3–71 and 381–92). The pertinence of measures is addressed by the use of normalised instruments (Pithers and Fogarty, 1995; Chan and Hui, 1995), by the development and validation of new scales (Boyle *et al.*, 1995), or by a combination of both strategies (Hart, Wearing and Conn, 1995). Theoretical concerns are incorporated into the designs by the identification of reference groups, by building upon previous findings, and by structural devices such as identifying moderator variables. The papers are also noteworthy for the diversity of analytical methods they employ to detect effects. Pithers and Fogarty's (1995) main concern is to examine group differences, and a MANOVA model is deemed appropriate. Chan and Hui (1995) needed to establish the utility of an existing measure within their sample before they could pursue the aim of predicting burnout. Consequently their strategy comprised an exploratory factor analysis followed by multiple regression. Boyle *et al.*'s (1995) development of an instrument necessitated a more elaborate confirmation route involving exploratory and confirmatory factor analyses, and the use of large cross-validation samples. They then proceeded to investigate various proposed models linking these measures through the application of LISREL VII's structural equation modelling procedures. Hart *et al.* (1995) also had to demonstrate the acceptability of their adaptations of a range of measures, but their emphasis was on the generation and testing of several different models, again through the use of LISREL VII. As Chan's (1995) subsequent commentary on the studies asserts, the interpretation of the outcomes of the different approaches is by no means uncontentious.

> While there are convergent results, some divergent findings need to be reconciled. Explanations of differences abound, including differences in cultural settings, organisational climates and policies, specifically local teacher stressors, person variables, sample variabilities and differences in operationalising constructs. (p. 384)

So, regardless of the advances in the technology available to the educational measurer, there remains ample opportunity for the individual researcher to consider carefully the actual implementation of those resources.

Trends or trendy?

Conflict between theory and practice

In summarising their hopes, De Gruijter and van der Kamp (1976) wrote:

> Obviously it would be unrealistic to expect a significant change in the common practice of educational testing as a result of a symposium attended by 124 people. However it is to be hoped that this book will be influential in broadening the influence of the symposium. (p. viii).

They do seem to have been unduly optimistic. Regardless of the potential of the theory developed in their book, there is little evidence of substantive development in practice. Their aside about the habituality of educational researchers' reporting of KR-20 (i.e.alpha) is wholly apposite today. Rasch and item banking have all but disappeared from the scene. The only obvious areas where projections from 1976 are manifest are those linked to Jöreskog and Sorbom's LISREL program. So what is the basis of this apparent conflict between theory and practice?

Difficulty or desire?

Anyone who has been involved in teaching measurement and analysis in education will almost certainly have been faced with various shades of reluctance from students. True, the calculating machine approach to teaching statistics adopted by many departments before computers were widely available did make severe mathematical demands. When the machines were replaced by computer programs some tutors continued to impose the calculator philosophy, encapsulated in the dictum 'only when you do the calculations do you really understand the method'. I have never subscribed to that assumption and nowadays there are plenty of texts espousing the understanding and application philosophy of teaching statistics. Nevertheless the general perception of data analysis is that it is difficult. Indeed my personal view is that one potent factor leading to the shift towards qualitative research in the 1970s (coincident with the growth of computer based analysis) was the opportunity it gave to those wanting an escape from statistics.

Personal and political influences

Tracking through the developments described by de Gruijter and van der Kamp (1976), and adding the huge increase in resources available to practitioners and researchers in the past 20 years, it is not possible to attribute a lack of progress to a dearth of facilities. Is the increased attention being given to qualitative procedures an indication of a real desire to abandon traditional measurement? The motivations to pursue studies in education are very different from those operating 20 years ago. Qualifications are student-oriented, with options and self-selected tasks dominant. There is no longer even a hint of core skills in advanced educational study. In that context it is not easy to generate the commitment needed to master a difficult topic in any subject area. And alongside the personal factors there are powerful over-arching political influences. These appear in a variety of arenas, research sponsorship, course support, and National Curriculum testing, for example. But whereas in the 70s and early 80s agents such as the APU or the Schools Council positively encouraged innovation in educational measurement, it is hard to accuse current agencies of similar adventurousness. Just how far is the current disinclination to make best use of earlier advances in educational measurement a trend, or is it education yet again being trendy?

References

Arbuckle, J. (1995) AMOS 3.5: Structural equation modeling and confirmatory factor analysis (Chicago, IL: Small Waters Corporation).

Bennett, N., Glatter, R.and Levacic, R. (1994) Improving Educational Management Through Research and Consultancy (London: Paul Chapman/Open University Press).

Biggs, J.B. (1987) Student Approaches to Learning and Studying (Hawthorn, Victoria; Australian Council for Educational Research).

Boyle, G.J., Borg, M.G., Falzon, J.M. and Baglioni, A.J. (1995) A structural model of the dimensions of teacher stress. British Journal of Educational Psychology, 65, 49–67.

Boyle, G.J. and Houndoulesi, V. (1993) Utility of the School Motivation Analysis Test in predicting second language acquisition. British Journal of Educational Psychology, 63, 500–12.

Brennan, T., (1972) Numerical taxonomy: theory and some applications in educational research. Unpublished PhD Thesis, University of Lancaster.

Bryman, A. and Cramer, D. (1990) Quantitative Data Analysis for Social Scientists (London: Routledge).

Buchanan-Barrow, E. and Barrett, M. (1996) Primary school children's understanding of the school. British Journal of Educational Psychology, 66, 33–46.

Cattell, R.B. (1995) The fallacy of five factors in the personality sphere. The Psychologist, 8, 207–8.

Cattell, R.B. and Child, D. (1975) Motivation and Dynamic Structure (London: Holt, Rinehart and Winston).

Chan, D.W. (1995) Multidimensional assessment and causal modelling in teacher stress research: a commentary. British Journal of Educational Psychology, 65, 381–5.

Chan, D.W. and Hui, E.K.P. (1995) Burnout and coping among Chinese secondary schoolteachers in Hong Kong. British Journal of Educational Psychology, 65, 15–25.

Christal, R.E. (1970) Implications of airforce occupational research for curriculum development. In Smith, B.B. and Moss, J. (Eds.) Process and Techniques of Curriculum Development (Minneapolis, MN: University of Minnesota).

Dennis, I. and Evans, J.St B.T. (1996) The speed-error trade off problem in psychometric testing. British Journal of Psychology, 87, 105–29.

Department of Education and Science (1979) Participation in education by young people in the 16 to 19 age group and its association with socio-economic structure and population density in an area. Statistical Bulletin 15/79. (follow-up: Statistical Bulletin 12/83).

Entwistle, N.J. and Nisbet, J.D. (1970) Educational Research Methods (London: ULP).

Galloway, D., Leo, E.L. Rogers, C. and Armstrong, D. (1995) Motivational styles in English and mathematics among children identified as having special educational needs. British Journal of Educational Psychology, 65, 477–87.

Glass, G.V. (1976) Primary, secondary and meta-analysis of research. Educational Researcher, 5, 3–8.

Goldstein, H. (1987) Multilevel Models in Educational and Social Research (London: Griffin).

de Gruijter, D.N.M.and van der Kamp, L.J.T. (Eds.) (1976) Advances in Psychological and Educational Measurement (New York: Wiley).

Hammond, S. (1993) The descriptive analysis of shared representations, in Breakwell, G. and Canter, D. (Eds.) Empirical Approaches to Social Representations (Oxford: Clarendon Press).

Harris, C.W. (Ed.) (1963) Problems in Measuring Change (Madison, WI: University of Wisconsin Press).

Hart, P.M., Wearing, A.J. and Conn, M. (1995) Conventional wisdom is a poor predictor of the relationship between discipline policy, student misbehaviour and teacher stress. British Journal of Educational Psychology. 65, 274–8.

Henriksson, W. (1994) Meta-analysis as a method for integrating the results of studies about effects of practice and coaching on test scores. British Journal of Educational Psychology, 64, 319–30.

Jöreskog, K.G. and Sorbom, D. (1976) Statistical models and methods for test-retest situations, in de Gruijter, D.N.M. and van der Kamp, L.J.T. (Eds.) Advances in Psychological and Educational Measurement (New York: Wiley), pp. 135–58.

Jöreskog, K.G. and Sorbom, D. (1993) LISREL 8: Structural equation modelling with SIMPLIS command language (Hillsdale, NY: Lawrence Erlbaum).

Kerlinger, F.N. (1973) Foundations of Behavioral Research, 2nd edn (New York: Holt, Rinehart and Winston).

Kerlinger, F.N. and Pedhazur, E.J. (1973) Multiple Regression in Behavioral Research (New York: Holt, Rinehart and Winston).

Kline, P. (1986) A Handbook of Test Construction (London: Methuen).

Krug, S.E., Cattell, R.B. and Sweney, A.B. (1976) Handbook of the School Motivation Analysis Test (SMAT) (Champaign, IL: Institute for Personality and Ability Testing).

Nunnally, J.C. (1967) Psychometric theory (New York: McGraw-Hill).

Paterson, L.and Goldstein, H. (1991) New statistical methods for analysing social structures: an introduction to multilevel models. British Educational Research Journal, 17, 387–93.

Pithers, R.T and Fogarty, G.J. (1995) Occupational stress among vocational teachers. British Journal of Educational Psychology. 65, 3–14.

Richards, T. and Richards, L. (1990) NUDIST 2.0: User's manual. (Melbourne: Replee; later versions, London: Sage).

Robson, C. (1993) Real World Research (Oxford: Blackwell).

Seidel, J.V., Kjolseth, R.and Seymour, E. (1988) The Ethnograph: A user's guide. (Littleton, CO: Qualis Research Associates).

Seifert, T.L. (1995) Characteristics of ego- and task-oriented students: a comparison of two methodologies. British Journal of Educational Psychology. 65, 125–38.

Shepard, R.N., Romney, A.K. and Nerlove, S.B (Eds.) (1972) Multidimensional Scaling: Theory and applications in the behavioral sciences (New York: Seminar Press).

Smit, G.N. and van der Molen, H.T. (1996) Three methods for the assessment of communication skills. British Journal of Educational Psychology, 66, pp. 543–55.

Smith, P.K and Levan, S. (1995) Perceptions and experiences of bullying in younger pupils. British Journal of Educational Psychology, 65, 489–500.

Thorndike, R.L and Hagen, E.P. (1969) Educational and Psychological Measurement, 3rd edn (New York: Wiley).

Totterdell, P.and Briner, R.B. (1996) Fingerprinting time series: dynamic patterns in self-report and performance measures uncovered by a graphical non-linear method. British Journal of Psychology, 87, 43–60.

Tufte, E.R. (1988) The Visual Display of Quantitative Information (Cheshire, CO: Graphics Press).
Tufte, E.R. (1990) Envisioning Information (Cheshire,CO: Graphics Press).
Tukey, J.W. (1977) Exploratory Data Analysis (Reading, MA: Addison Wesley).
Veldman, D.J. (1967) FORTRAN Programming for the Behavioral Sciences (New York: Holt, Rinehart and Winston).
Whitebread, D. (1996) The development of children's strategies on an inductive reasoning task. British Journal of Educational Psychology, 66, 1–22.
Willems, E.P. and Rausch, H.L. (Eds) (1969) Naturalistic Viewpoints in Psychological Research (New York: Holt, Rinehart and Winston).
Wishart, D. (1969) CLUSTAN 1A: User manual (St Andrews: University of St Andrews Computing Laboratory).
Youngman, M.B. (1976) PMMD: Programmed methods for multivariate data. Version 6 (Nottingham University School of Education).
Youngman, M.B. (1978a) Review of de Gruijter, D.N.M. and van der Kamp, L.J.T. (1976), Advances in Psychological and Educational Measurement (New York: Wiley), in British Educational Research Journal, 4, 113–14.
Youngman, M.B. (1978b) Six reactions to school transfer. British Journal of Educational Psychology, 48, 280–9.
Youngman, M.B. (1979a) Analysing Social and Educational Research Data (Maidenhead: McGraw-Hill).
Youngman, M.B. (1979b) A comparison of item-total, biserial correlation and alpha-beater item analysis procedures. Educational Studies, 5, 265–73.
Youngman, M.B. (1980) Some determinants of early secondary school performance. British Journal of Educational Psychology, 50, 43–52.
Youngman, M.B. (1983) Intrinsic roles of secondary school teachers. British Journal of Educational Psychology, 53, 234–46.
Youngman, M.B., Mockett, S. and Baxter, C. (1988) The roles of nurses and technicians in high technology clinical areas. Final report (London: Department of Health and Social Security).
Youngman, M.B., Oxtoby, R., Monk, J.D. and Heywood, J. (1978) Analysing Jobs (Aldershot: Gower Press).

Chapter 8
Assessing, recording and testing achievement: some issues in accountability, professionalism and education markets

CHRISTOPHER POLE

Throughout the late 1980s and the 1990s widescale change which has occurred in primary and secondary education in England and Wales has brought a new and more expansive role for assessment and recording of pupil achievement. The Education Reform Act of 1988 introduced a National Curriculum, claimed to give parents more scope to choose schools for their children, enabled a greater degree of financial autonomy for headteachers and governors and provided the foundations for a national mechanism for testing pupils' progress and achievements.

The implications of the 1988 Education Reform Act have been vast and it is the intention of this chapter to examine some of these in relation to assessment and recording of pupil achievements and progress and to offer a critical commentary on their impact on teachers and pupils.

Assessment and accountability

The rationale for the 1988 Education Reform Act stressed a need for a broad and balanced curriculum, higher standards and parental choice (DES, 1987, 1989) and the methods of assessment which were to accompany the National Curriculum were placed at the heart of the new arrangements for education by providing not only a way of assessing individual children but also of comparing them with their peer group both within and across schools. Moreover, by introducing a system of national assessment the capacity to compare not only pupils but also their schools (Lawton, 1996), on a systematic basis, was introduced. As never before, the proposed arrangements for pupil testing at the ages of

7, 11, 14 and 16, together with the results of public examinations taken at 16 and 18, provided an opportunity for wide-scale detailed comparisons of pupil achievements to be carried out on a national level.

As with the curriculum and funding mechanisms for schools, the 1988 Education Reform Act brought about developments which required fundamental changes from teachers in the way they conducted their work. In addition, the changes in assessment procedures may be seen to embody particular philosophies consistent not only with conservative educational thinking (Simon, 1988) but also with more general economic and social ideology which underpinned much public policy of the time.

In particular, the developments in assessment practices and procedures post-1988 may be seen as an attempt to bring a greater degree of accountability to education (Lello, 1993) by requiring all state funded schools to hold standardized tests based on a centrally determined National Curriculum. The tests which enabled comparisons to be made between schools could, therefore, act as a national benchmark on pupil performance in relation to particular criteria. As a consequence the tests were quickly associated with issues of standards and were seen as a means of improving pupil performance across the board. However, the impact of the tests extends much further than pupil progress and the theme of accountability is an important one in this context.

The post-1988 assessment procedures provided a powerful mechanism not merely for assessing pupil performance but also for checking on the performance of the school as a whole and within the school, as a means of assessing individual teachers. In this sense, the new testing procedures offered an accountability mechanism which operated at a range of different levels.

In the first and most obvious way national tests provide a means of accounting for pupil progress. By linking the tests to Key Stages and targets within the National Curriculum it is possible to argue that testing procedures provide a clear and unambiguous means of assessing pupil progress on a regular basis. The intention or indeed the rhetoric behind this is that the testing procedures act in a formative way allowing a diagnostic approach to be taken by teachers on the basis of test results. The test results then enable teachers to meet the needs of individual children in a more systematic way, based on the existence of hard evidence. By tying the tests into notions of standards, their introduction was seen as a way of raising attainment levels for individual children. The intention was, therefore, that what began or operated as a large scale or macro approach to testing could also operate at the level of the individual pupil. By diagnosing the areas where pupils were underperforming relative to their peer group, the tests could help teachers and pupils to target areas where greater effort was required. In addition, the new testing arrangements meant that pupils would be tested regularly, and their progress from one test to the other could be easily monitored. The assumption here being that learning takes place in a linear fashion, where pupils pass sequentially from one stage to another through a hierarchy of knowledge.

With regard to teachers who would be responsible for operating the tests, the introduction of testing broadly coincided with the development of teacher appraisal. Widescale concern amongst teachers as to what appraisal would entail (Evans and Tomlinson, 1989; Poster and Poster, 1991) and precisely what would be appraised (Wragg, 1987) was fuelled by the obvious capacity to link individual pupil performance in particular subjects to individual teachers. In this respect the tests could act as a means of measuring and monitoring individual teacher performance with regard to their ability to teach the National Curriculum. Fears that teachers would in fact teach to the test (Lawton, 1996) in order to ensure that results were good were expressed in many quarters.

In these respects, therefore, the new testing arrangements introduced levels of accountability to schooling which were not evident prior to 1988. Although the motives were couched in terms of improving standards and formative monitoring of pupils, the side effects of the arrangements allowed for speculation about accountability and control not only in terms of what was taught but also in terms of how it was taught. Moreover, the ideology which underpinned the new forms of testing was one which emphasized a role for monitoring of pupils not just by schools but by a range of other actors whose role in education decision making had been changed by the effects of the 1988 Act. One interpretation of the new assessment and testing mechanisms was that pupil progress in schools had become part of the public domain as more individuals and institutions became party to it. Mrs Thatcher's reflections on educational policy-making in her memoires (Thatcher, 1993) are enlightening in respect of this.

> Alongside the National Curriculum should be a nationally recognised and reliably monitored system of testing at various stages of the child's school career, which would allow parents, teachers, local authorities and central government to know what was going right and wrong and take remedial action if necessary.

The comments are interesting in their combination of monitoring and formative assessment. They serve to reinforce, however, a view of testing and assessment which would increase the degree of accountability not only upon pupils with regard to their performance in the National Curriculum, but also upon teachers and their capacity to deliver the curriculum effectively. The levels of accountability were clearly identified by Mrs Thatcher as parents, local and central government. Such a view of assessment is one which teachers had not previously encountered and for some it proved difficult to accept.

Assessment and the market

Post-1988, testing received a far higher profile (Gipps *et al.*, 1995) in education than ever before. The changes brought not only more tests but new kinds of tests with wide ranging implications. Moreover, a culture of measurement and recording linked to credentialism began to gain importance as schools sought to achieve the best possible results. Time for activities other than those which were to be assessed and tested became scarce. Fears were expressed (Simon, 1988) that the impact of tests would produce a narrowing of the school curriculum for many pupils.

Despite the concerns of some education practitioners and commentators, testing arrangements were presented as a central part of the new package of education which gave choice to parents and provided them with information about school performance upon which to base their choice of school. In this sense test results had the potential to become powerful marketing tools for schools as they sought to attract parents and their pupils. The financial arrangements for school funding introduced by the 1988 Act meant that the more pupils a school could admit, up to its standard number, the more money it would attract. This, coupled with the policy of open enrolment, gave great importance to test results as parents of prospective pupils sought to gather information upon which to base their choice of schools.

For those schools where test results were good, their publication, which was also a requirement of the 1988 Act, offered an opportunity to market the school in a positive way to parents by appealing to notions of academic achievement, high standards and successful teachers. For those with poor results the opposite was the case. Poor test results provided a picture of a poor school where children would fail to achieve. In this sense, the emphasis on reporting test results to parents was an important contributor to the competition for pupils and associated funding in which schools were engaged.

Test results in many ways provided the glue which held the post-1988 model of education together. With open enrolment and parental choice as cornerstones of educational provision, testing, the assessment of pupil performance and the publication of test results provided parents with the information upon which to base their choice of school. Moreover, the National Curriculum, upon which pupils were tested, ensured that parents could compare schools against the same criteria (Brown *et al.*, 1996) on a national basis but perhaps more importantly on a local basis, in order to make their choice. By tying funding directly to pupil numbers, schools were forced to compete in the market for pupils in order to safeguard staffing levels and hence their very capacity to deliver the National Curriculum upon which the tests were based. In all, the 1988 Education Reform Act provided a neat package of education based around issues of competition, the market, choice and standards.

By constructing a system with an emphasis on assessment the role of testing was indeed enhanced beyond recognition in many schools. Prior to the introduction of the new testing arrangements little use was made by schools of what test results there were (Gipps et al., 1995). Annual reports of successes in public examinations at GCSE and 'A' level which appeared in local papers and school prospectuses were perhaps the extent of public use of test results. Testing and assessment were, therefore, essentially summative with little formative use made of results in relation to individual pupil performance or in relation to curriculum design. In this sense, while tests by way of public examinations carried significance for individual pupils, it was essentially a form of low stakes testing for the school. With the enhanced role for testing together with the emphasis on standards, the capacity existed for testing and assessment to play a central role in schools and schooling. The intention was that test results would be used in a variety of different ways which would contribute to overall improvement in standards, methods and outcomes. As such, with the post-1988 requirements, testing became high stakes testing for the school (Lawton, 1996) as the results came to be used as an index of success and hence the basis for parental choice. With regard to the education market, therefore, test results offered a marketing tool which, at face value, operated in the same way for all schools. In practice, however, the tests conveyed nothing other than statistical information about narrowly defined pupil performance. Test results conveyed nothing of the type of school in terms of socio-economic characteristics, staffing levels or the degree to which results may have improved from year to year after starting from a low base. Despite these omissions, the fact that results were publicly available and based on ostensibly objective data made them a powerful aid to marketing of individual schools.

Teachers' professionalism and assessment

The enhanced role for testing and assessment in the overall organization of education necessitated a different role for teachers in testing and assessment procedures and processes. Gipps (1983) in her survey of testing practices found that teachers were generally poorly informed about testing or the uses to which assessment was put. What assessment and testing existed was based largely on standardized reading and mathematics tests which relied on measuring pupil performance against so-called objective criteria. Moreover, there was no compulsion for schools to engage in testing procedures on a regular or scheduled basis. In many local education authorities the demise of the eleven-plus examination meant that there were no national or public tests or assessment prior to GCE and then later GCSE examinations taken at the age of 16.

For many teachers, formal assessment measures and testing did not form a major aspect of their work. The post-1988 requirements, therefore, represented considerable change for many teachers.

The publication of the report of the Task Group on Assessment and Testing (TGAT) (DES, 1988), the group charged with devising the testing procedures to accompany the National Curriculum, made explicit the testing and assessment requirements for teachers. TGAT established that pupils would be assessed by external tests called Standard Assessment Tasks (SATs) which would relate to specific stages of the National Curriculum, and by teacher-focused assessments based on ongoing observations made in the classroom. Results from external tests and teacher assessments were to be drawn together to form a composite picture of the child's progress at the different key stages of the National Curriculum. Where significant differences occurred between external tests and teacher judgements, a process of moderation would bring both sets of data in line. In practice, this process of moderation proved to be too cumbersome (Daugherty, 1995) and eventually the process was abandoned and greater emphasis was placed on test scores than on teacher assessment.

Post-1988 Education Reform Act and TGAT, teachers were, therefore, confronted over a relatively short period of time by a change from a situation of no compulsion in testing to one where testing was at the centre of provision. Beginning in the primary sector the TGAT arrangements were scheduled to pervade all phases of compulsory state education. However, concern over the size of the assessment task relating in particular to the number of classroom assessments and the associated paper work that teachers needed to conduct led to considerable disquiet amongst teachers and an eventual boycott of the tests in 1993. A review of the National Curriculum and testing by a committee chaired by Sir Ron Dearing (Dearing, 1994) led to the upgrading, at least in theory, of teachers' ongoing assessment of pupils. In practice, however, government calls for more objective evidence on pupil performance in relation to the National Curriculum, and the fact that only formal test scores were to be included in published results, led to greater emphasis being placed on the formal written tests, which also became more complex.

The debate surrounding teacher-based tests and more traditional paper and pencil tests is one which goes beyond issues relating to the content and style of the test to incorporate questions about teachers and professionalism. Although the Dearing review placed greater emphasis on the role of teacher-based assessment, it was clear that this was not supported by government officials who preferred a more 'objective' approach to assessment. With paper and pencil tests the role of the teacher was reduced to that of administrator, or, in a more extreme analysis, a technician. The greater emphasis placed on paper and pencil tests, despite the Dearing recommendations (1993, 1994) created a situation in which it seemed that teachers and their judgements were not trusted. An important element of their professional role was, therefore, removed. In effect they could be seen as mere conduits for the knowledge which the National Curriculum embodied.

Underpinning the debate within the education media and academia about the merits and role of teacher assessment was a clear difference of opinion as to its value, which was expressed between the successive Secretaries of State for Education, Kenneth Baker, John MacGregor and Kenneth Clarke and the then Prime Minister, Margaret Thatcher. The differences between the Secretaries of State and the Prime Minister, as Daugherty (1996) shows, were not merely differences relating to the merits or otherwise of teacher assessment. Like many aspects of the 1988 Education Reform Act, they were differences based on political dogma. As Daugherty shows, Messrs Baker, MacGregor and Clarke were prepared to at least pay lip service to the recommendations of the TGAT report, whereas for Margaret Thatcher this was not an option. Daugherty (1996) quotes from the speeches of the four politicians cited above as he shows how teacher assessment gradually moved from the centre to the periphery of testing and assessment methods. He says:

> Superficially it would appear from ministerial statements on the subject that the government's acceptance of the TGAT proposals in June 1988 was followed by a period of nearly three years during which successive Secretaries of State responsible for education reiterated the TGAT case for 'combining' teacher assessment evidence with results from standard tasks and tests. (p. 140)

Daugherty goes on to illustrate the 'lip service' of the Secretaries of State by drawing examples from their various speeches. They show an essentially corporatist view in which both teachers and tests have a voice in providing a comprehensive picture of pupil achievement. The examples are as follows:

> assessment should be a combination of national external tests and assessment by teachers. (Kenneth Baker, speech to the House of Commons accepting the TGAT proposals, June 1988)
>
> [assessment] must both relate to what goes on in the classroom itself and be capable of integration with normal teaching practice. (John MacGregor, speech to the Assistant Masters and Mistresses Association, April 1990)
>
> assessment should combine some of the teachers' own accumulated judgements of pupils' classroom work as well as the results of end key stage tests. (Kenneth Clarke, speech to the Society of Education Officers , January 1991).

Assessing, recording and testing achievement

The statements from the Secretaries of State were clearly at odds with the views of the Prime Minister who in the second volume of her memoires (Thatcher, 1993) makes very clear her mistrust of teachers and modern approaches to teaching. She comments:

> I also believed that too many teachers were less competent and more ideological than their predecessors. I distrusted the new 'child-centred' teaching techniques, the emphasis on imaginative engagement rather than learning facts (p. 590)

This mistrust was evident not least in Mrs Thatcher's view of the role that teachers should take in the testing and assessment of pupils performance within the new National Curriculum. In her view a degree of objectivity in assessment free from teacher bias and trendy educational philosophy was required. Again her memoires are illuminating as she states:

> I had no wish to put good teachers in straight jackets. As for testing I always recognised that no snap shot of a child's classes or a school's performance on a particular day was going to tell the whole truth. But tests did provide an independent outside check on what was happening. (p. 593)

Despite this pluralist view of assessment and testing, the report of the TGAT proved a great disappointment to the Prime Minister as, one suspects, did her Secretary of State who had responsibility for establishing the task group and welcoming its findings and recommendations. Again her memoires provide insight here:

> The fact that it (the TGAT report) was then welcomed by the Labour Party, the National Union of Teachers and the *Times Educational Supplement* was enough to confirm for me that its approach was suspect. It proposed an elaborate and complex system of assessment – teacher-dominated and uncosted. It adopted the diagnostic view of tests, placed the emphasis on teachers doing their own assessment and was written in a impenetrable and educationalist jargon.

The irony of the situation is both amusing and poignant in that what was welcomed by teachers was automatically suspected of being wrong by the Prime Minister who admits to having not read the document. The reflections show that trust and professionalism of teachers had been replaced by a cynical disregard for their capacity to offer well-considered reports on pupil progress which were seen as separate from what was regarded as ideology. Such cynicism casts teachers in the role of bureaucrats who merely administer the tests, rather than professionals who make judgements and take decisions about pupil performance and achievements based on their first-hand interactions with them. The effect was, therefore, to distance the content of the National Curriculum and the pedagogy which teachers used to deliver it from its assessment.

Moreover, the emphasis placed on traditional paper and pencil tests needs to be seen in the wider context and rationale underpinning the 1988 Education Reform Act. Whether one accepts the government concerns with improving standards and widening parental choice or the interpretations of the critics of the Act (e.g. Simon, 1988, 1992) who see it as a crude attempt to apply market forces to education, paper and pencil testing maintains a central role in the new arrangements for education. By removing assessment from the domain of classroom teachers, the effect has been to attempt to objectify the results of the tests and make reports on pupil performance and progress a matter of science and certainty. Where test results are used to provide the basis for school choice by parents, they have a capacity to be used as objective indicators and hence as marketing tools for the school to deploy as they seek to attract more pupils. In this sense, the objectification of assessment is important as parents need to be sure that their choice of school is based on foundations which go beyond what might be seen as the mere opinion of a teacher. In this approach to education where pupil numbers drive finance, it would appear that teachers have been bypassed in the interests of the market. Again this may be seen as further evidence of an attack on their professionalism and as Lawton (1996) points out, means that teachers in England and Wales fall behind their counterparts in other parts of Europe in relation to trust and assessment.

The role of the pupil

Much of the foregoing discussion has identified a role for assessment of pupil performance and progress which is largely prescriptive and narrowly focused in its scope. The emphasis of the tests, whether teacher based or pencil and paper test is upon the measurement and articulation of progress against criteria which are devised externally to the school. As we have seen, the emphasis is upon an objectification of progress and performance in line with national targets which permit the comparison of pupils and schools throughout the country. This standardisation of assessment has meant that pupil performance and progress is now compared with national benchmarks devised centrally by agencies of the government. The effect has been to establish expectations of what pupils should have achieved by particular stages of their education. Such expectations may be based on a notional pupil for whom standard, linear progress is possible. In reality, such a notional pupil may not exist and therefore the extent to which the standard benchmarks for testing prove to be useful may be held open to question.

The creation of standardized benchmarks and a notional pupil serves to distance centralized assessment and testing policies and practice from real pupils, in real schools, with all their attendant social and psychological factors which contribute to progress and achievement which is real, rather than notional.

The centralization of assessment through standardized tests has, in many respects, been achieved in the face of what, prior to the impact of the 1988 Education Reform Act, could be seen as a movement towards a democratization of assessment and reporting of pupil progress. Throughout the 1980s the development and introduction of records of achievement, initially at an individual local education authority level and then later at a national level, by means of the various Pilot Records of Achievement in Schools Evaluation (PRAISE) projects, (PRAISE, 1987, 1988) meant that an emphasis was placed on bringing pupils into the reporting and recording process. Movements towards the democratization of assessment and reporting processes sprang, initially, from a discontent with traditional reporting measures which were seen to be very limited and largely summative with little scope for the formative development of pupils. In addition, there was a concern to encourage greater involvement of pupils in their own learning and its assessment. Rather than assessment and reporting being things that were done to pupils, the emphasis was placed on collaboration between teachers and pupils as the latter were encouraged to take greater responsibility for their own learning.

Alongside a desire for greater pupil involvement were concerns about parents and their role in pupil progress. Again, records of achievement with an emphasis on negotiation and discussion were seen as a way of forging a partnership between pupil, school and home. The partnership was to be a means by which not only achievement could be discussed and celebrated but also future directions identified.

The emphasis which many of the records of achievement schemes placed on pupils identifying their own learning goals and targets, perhaps in consultation with teachers and parents (Hargreaves et al., 1988; Pole, 1993), may be seen as attempts not merely to involve and motivate pupils in the teaching and learning process, but also to give them a stake in defining what should count as progress and achievement. In short, records of achievement offered an opportunity of overcoming an approach to assessment and reporting which had treated the pupil merely as a passive object about whom judgements and reports were made. In theory, though research evidence suggests this was not always the case in practice (Bridges, 1989; James, 1989; Pole, 1993), records of achievement encouraged the active participation of pupils in the reporting and recording process in a way which made assessment formative.

Although the use of records of achievement grew throughout the 1980s in both the primary and secondary sectors, and the Records of Achievement National Steering Committee (RANSC, 1989) recommended that all schools should adopt records of achievement, they were not made mandatory by the Department of Education and Science. As the details of the 1988 Education Reform Act were worked out and in particular the proposals for assessment and testing procedures were made, it became clear that records of achievement would be largely incompatible with a national system of standardized assessment. Although a National Record of Achievement (NRA) was introduced by the Department of Education and Science and schools were encouraged to implement a record of achievement process alongside Key Stage testing and public examinations, the lack of compulsion, coupled with the substantial workload which accompanied the national tests, meant that in many schools the smart burgundy NRA folders were left to gather dust on shelves.

Where records of achievement subscribed to notions of pupil centred assessment and recording of progress, which would mean that no two records of achievement or achievement profiles would be alike, the National Curriculum called for a national system of assessment which facilitated relatively straightforward comparisons of pupils and hence schools, against standard criteria. Once again, the effect has been to distance the pupil from the process of assessment and recording with an approach which gives little attention to individual needs. Moreover, although the different stages at which pupils are tested are designed to provide a formative element to assessment, the nature of the tests and the data which they yield seem more likely to place the emphasis on summative assessment rather than looking for ways in which teachers might enhance pupil progress through support offered in specific areas of weakness identified by the tests.

It would seem, therefore, that the post-1988 arrangements for assessment and recording pupil progress have been introduced with a clear disregard for much of the evidence (Broadfoot, 1982, 1986, 1987; Burgess and Adams, 1985, 1986; Hall, 1989; Munby, 1989) about the benefits to be derived from pupil centred means of recording achievement. Moreover, they have also been introduced with a disregard for the not insignificant amount of government money spent in piloting and evaluating records of achievement throughout much of the 1980s. The market model of education (Bowe, Ball and Gold, 1992) demanded a mechanism for marketing schools to prospective parents and traditional testing methods were seen as the most appropriate means of achieving this. Ironically, however, it was records of achievement that were seen by some (e.g. Stronach, 1989) as the ultimate marketing tool for schools who wished to 'advertise' the achievements of their pupils. However, the unwieldy and personalized nature of the record of achievement was unlikely to facilitate data that could be compared nationally, or easily incorporated into league tables.

Conclusion

This review of assessment and testing arrangements has highlighted a range of issues which are now fundamental to the provision, experience and outcome of compulsory education in England and Wales. Above all, developments in policy and practice since 1988 have brought about a greatly enhanced role for assessment, testing and reporting. Issues of accountability, professionalism, pedagogy, curriculum and choice are all to a greater or lesser extent shaped by the impact of centralized testing.

Attempts at standardization of testing coupled with the publication of test results, league tables and a growing emphasis on credentialism throughout education, may now be leading towards an education system which is driven primarily by a concern for measurable output rather than any notion of process or individual pupil need. Underpinning the new testing arrangements, the market model of education which forces schools to chase pupil numbers in order to protect their level funding, seems likely to ensure that schools continue to work within a system which struggles to find ways of officially recognising and rewarding the wide range of achievements which occur in schools.

Although the changes in assessment have been introduced as part of a package of reform which has sought to improve overall standards in primary and secondary education, as yet there appears to be little independent evidence to suggest that they have succeeded in this. Where there is evidence of improvement, by means of increasing pass rates for GCSE and 'A' level examinations, more than a little scepticism has been voiced by many interested parties. Perhaps a similar amount of scepticism about standardized testing would lead to a re-examination of the arrangements and a recognition that standardized assessment will only ever be valuable when there are standardized pupils.

References

Bowe, R., Ball, S. and Gold, A. (1992) Reforming Education and Changing Schools: Case studies in policy sociology (London: Routledge).
Bridges, D. (1989) Pupil assessment from the perspective of naturalistic research. In Simons, H. and Elliott, J. (Eds.) Rethinking Appraisal and Assessment (Milton Keynes: Open University Press).
Broadfoot, P. (1982) The pros and cons of profiles. Forum 24 (3), 66–9.
Broadfoot, P. (Ed.) (1986) Profiles and Records of Achievement: A review of issues and practice (London: Holt).
Broadfoot, P. (1987) Introducing Profiling: A practical manual (London: Macmillan).

Broadfoot, P. (1996) Education, Assessment and Society (Milton Keynes: Open University Press).

Brown, M., Black, P., Simons, S. and Blondel, E. (1996) Age or stage? research findings relating to assessment framework. In Chawla-Duggan, R. and Pole, C. (Eds.) Reshaping Education in the 1990s: Perspectives on primary schooling (London: Falmer Press).

Burgess, T. and Adams, E. (1985) Records of Achievement at 16 (Slough: NFER-Nelson).

Burgess, T. and Adams, E. (1986) Records for all at 16. In Broadfoot, P. (Ed.) Profiles and Records of Achievement: A review of issues and practice (London: Holt).

Daugherty, R. (1995) National Curriculum Assessment: A review of policy 1987–1994 (London: Falmer Press).

Daugherty, R. (1996) In Search of Teacher Assessment: Its place in the National Curriculum assessment system of England and Wales. Curriculum Journal. 7(2), 137–53.

Dearing, R. (1993) Interim report. The National Curriculum and its Assessment (London: SCAA).

Dearing, R. (1994) Final report. The National Curriculum and its Assessment (London: SCAA).

DES (1987) The National Curriculum 5 – 16: A consultation document (London: HMSO).

DES (1988) National Curriculum: The TGAT report (London: HMSO).

DES (1989) National Curriculum: From policy to practice (London: HMSO).

Evans, A. and Tomlinson, J. (1989) Introduction, in Evans, A. and Tomlinson, J. (Eds.) Teacher Appraisal: A nationwide approach (London: Jessica Kingsley).

Gipps, C. (1983) Monitoring Children: An evaluation of the APU (London: Heinemann).

Gipps, C., Brown, M., McCallum, B. and McAlister, S. (1995) Intuition or Evidence? (Milton Keynes: Open University Press).

Hall, G. (1989) Records of Achievement: Issues and practice (London: Kogan Page).

Hargreaves, A., Baglin, E., Henderson, P., Leeson, P. and Tossell, T. (1988) Personal and Social Education: Choices and challenges (Oxford: Blackwell).

James, M. (1989) Negotiation and dialogue in student assessment and teacher appraisal, in Simons, H. and Elliott, J. (Eds.) Rethinking Appraisal and Assessment (Milton Keynes: Open University Press).

Lawton, D. (1996) Beyond the National Curriculum. Teacher Professionalism and Empowerment (London: Hodder and Stoughton).

Lello, J. (1993) Accountability in Practice (London: Cassell).

Munby, S. (1989) Assessing and Recording Achievement (Oxford: Blackwell).

Pole, C. (1993) Assessing and Recording Achievement: A new approach in school (Milton Keynes: Open University Press).

Poster, C. and Poster, D. (1991) Teacher Appraisal: A guide to training (London: Routledge).

PRAISE (1987) Pilot Records of Achievement in Schools Evaluation – an interim report (London: DES/Welsh Office).

PRAISE (1988) Report of the Pilot Records of Achievement in Schools Evaluation (London: DES/Welsh Office).

RANSC (1989) Records of Achievement. Report of the Records of Achievement National Steering Committee. (London: DES/Welsh Office).

Simon, B. (1988) Bending the Rules. The Baker reform of education (London: Lawrence and Wishart).

Simon, B. (1992) What Future for Education (London: Lawrence and Wishart).

Stronach, I. (1989) A critique of the 'new assessment': from currency to carnival? In Simons, H. and Elliott, J. (Eds) Rethinking Appraisal and Assessment (Milton Keynes: Open University Press).
Thatcher, M. (1993) The Downing Street Years (London: HarperCollins).
Wragg, E. (1987) Teacher Appraisal: A practical guide (Basingstoke: Macmillan).

Chapter 9
Cross purposes: development and change in National Curriculum assessment in England and Wales

DIANE SHORROCKS-TAYLOR

Chapters on assessment are especially appropriate in a book on educational psychology, since this has long been a major focus in the discipline. Indeed, at some points in its history, the two have almost been equated. Assessment is also a field of psychological investigation with which Dennis Child has been associated in a variety of ways over the years. Issues surrounding the measurement of personality characteristics are to the fore in his work (see pp. 391-4 for references to Child, 1964, 1966b,c, 1969c, 1971c,d, 1974a, 1975, 1977a, 1978a), as also in his work on vocational selection procedures (see, for example, his chapter 19 in this book), especially in the context of the nursing profession (1985a, 1988a, 1990a) and the reports to the UKCC (1988–90). However, it must be remembered that for some years he was Director in Leeds of the APU (Science) Project, clearly central in any discussion of assessment in the United Kingdom. This was the first national attempt at monitoring performance across a wide age-phase and only came to an end with the advent of the new National Curriculum. In its own way, it too was controversial, although not on the scale of the new Orders and assessments.

In a sense, this provides a further justification for an emphasis on assessment. Open any newspaper and there will almost certainly be some article on standards of literacy and numeracy (usually falling), examination results, international comparisons of pupil performance, or school league tables and most prominently the National Curriculum and its tests. Assessment is implicated in all these and therefore suggests that we need a much fuller understanding of the nature of the field in order to make appropriate judgements about the information we are given.

The focus of this chapter will be National Curriculum assessment, outlining briefly its origins, considering its major characteristics and charting recent developments and issues in the system.

Some background information: assessment theory meets politics

Most researchers see the origins of the idea of a National Curriculum in the 1970s and in particular in the debate about 'standards' and the role of education in Callaghan's well-known 'Ruskin' speech in 1976. This was in many ways an echo of the controversial Black Papers of the 1960s, a series of highly polemical publications about poor schooling and falling standards emanating from the conservative right-wing, blaming 'progressivism' and 'egalitarianism' for the declining state of education. (Moon, Isaac and Powney, 1990).

In reality, there was precious little evidence either way to indicate, in a reliable way, whether or not educational standards were rising or falling. This point is well argued by Caroline Gipps (1990), who points out that ever since the nineteenth century, the cry was fairly consistently heard that 'standards' were falling in schools. Even with the advent of public examinations it is not possible to make the case either way, since syllabuses have changed in complex and varied ways and in any case such tests are mostly norm-referenced and therefore poor indicators for the comparison of performance over time.

However, it is not necessary to demonstrate falling standards in order to seek to improve teaching and learning in schools and the quality of the performance outcomes. This is an important aim in its own right and one which the National Curriculum (and its assessment system) has ostensibly sought to address.

The origins of the assessment system

The recent moves to centralise control of the curriculum dates back to the 1970s (Daugherty, 1995) and was closely connected with the rise of comprehensive schooling and therefore less selection and monitoring in the school system. At this point, control of the curriculum was mostly in the hands of the Local Education Authorities and the GCE Examining Boards, with monitoring left to Her Majesty's Inspectors. Assessment on a pupil by pupil, school by school basis did not figure large in the debates until the 1980s, in particular with two publications *Better Schools* (DES, 1985) and *The Curriculum from 5 to 16* (HMI, 1985), both of which advocated this rather changed emphasis. It was at this point that 'accountability' and an assessment-led agenda began to emerge in a more formal way in the context of a National Curriculum, which could, of course, easily have been put in place without this formal monitoring dimension.

The issue of evaluation and monitoring on a national scale (and of age groups under the age of 16) had been addressed at an earlier time. In 1974 the Assessment of Performance Unit (APU) was formed, to provide national monitoring of patterns of performance over time in key curriculum areas such as English, mathematics and science. This monitoring was to be achieved through the assessment of national samples of pupils using specially prepared banks of assessment materials and it essentially yielded national evaluation data. However, it did not require all pupils to participate each year and hence the monitoring of the performance of all children and all schools could not be achieved by these means. The APU ceased once the changed political agenda dictated the new National Curriculum assessments.

The Task Group on Assessment and Testing (TGAT), set up in the summer of 1987 was briefed to advise the Secretary of State on the

> practical considerations which should govern all assessment including testing of attainment at age (approximately) 7, 11, 14 and 16 (DES/WO, 1988, Appendix A).

The group, made up largely of 'educational establishment' members, was allowed a fairly free rein (Ball, 1990) until shortly before it was due to report, when it was made clear to them (by the Secretary of State, Kenneth Baker) that the assessment system should serve four key purposes, namely formative, diagnostic, summative and evaluative. This national 'evaluative' purpose was now formally stated for the first time.

It is now rather frowned upon in certain quarters to make reference to these early proposals, but it nevertheless provides not only an important reminder about where it all began, it also acts as a constructive framework within which to discuss current issues. The TGAT Report (DES/WO, 1988) outlined the central principles of the proposed system:

- The assessment results should give direct information about pupil's achievements in relation to objectives: they should be criterion-referenced;
- The results should provide a basis for decisions about pupil's future learning needs: they should be formative;
- The scales or grades should be capable of comparison across classes and schools, if teachers, pupils and parents are to share a common language and common standards: so the assessment should be calibrated or moderated;
- The ways in which criteria and scales are set up and used should relate to expected routes of educational development, giving some continuity to a pupil's assessment at different ages: the assessments should relate to progression.

In four short statements the key characteristics were thus set and in combination they represent both the strength and the weakness of the system. In principle, the recommendations of the report were accepted by officialdom although in practice some aspects were never implemented. Among the most obvious of these were teacher assessment and its role in relation to the Standard Assessment Tasks (SATs) and the purpose of assessment for 7 year olds. The report emphasised the role of the Standard Tasks as moderating teachers' own assessments whereas, in practice, the tests and tasks have consistently taken a higher profile. The report envisaged that for 7 year olds the assessments should have a broadly screening role, but in reality the assessments at this Key Stage (Key Stage 1) have always had a more evaluative dimension to them, involving all children in the cohort.

The TGAT proposals, being broadly accepted, set the framework not only for the assessment system but also for the specifications to the subject working groups, who proceeded to elaborate (for each curriculum subject) the precise content of the curriculum arranged in the complex structure of Programmes of Study, Profile Components (PCs), Attainment Targets (ATs), Levels of Attainment and Statements of Attainment (SoA). Herein lay the seeds of many of the subsequent problems, both in terms of the curriculum specifications and the assessment system fitting alongside them.

In order to address some of these, I will take each of the key characteristics outlined above and analyse some of the most significant tensions that emerged and the solutions put in place to counter them.

Criterion-referenced approaches to assessment

Domain definition and mastery definition

The first use of this term in educational contexts is commonly attributed to Glaser (1963). Criterion-referenced assessment had its origins in the USA, where there has always been an established and widespread tradition of testing in the education system. It became apparent that the widely used norm-referenced assessment methodology and psychometric approaches had little to offer as a teaching and learning tool. On the other hand, criterion-referenced assessment, dealing with an individual's achievements irrespective of the performance of others, was seen as better suited to objectives-based teaching programmes. In the American literature, many different terms are used, namely: *domain-referenced, objectives-referenced, competency-based tests, mastery tests*, etc. In the British literature, the term criterion-referenced is applied to almost any approach that is not overtly norm-referenced. It must be remembered, however, that the two kinds of approach are not fully exclusive.

Strictly speaking, criterion referencing refers to the manner in which a score is interpreted, but in order to map out the parameters on which the score will be based, it is necessary to specify the relevant domains of knowledge, skills, etc. and to set mastery criteria. The more closed and finite the specified domain, the more precise the assessment can be; the more open and broad the domain the more problematic is the assessment of it.

In the context of the National Curriculum a criterion-referenced approach was seen as more educationally viable than others, as indeed it had been introduced into GCSE courses in the mid-1980s (Daugherty, 1995). In practice it would have worked in national curriculum assessments had not the subject working groups been allowed such a free hand to set out detailed and elaborate Programmes of Study and to list vast numbers of Statements of Attainment, in effect, the 'criteria' in the criterion-referenced system, poorly suited to the purposes of assessment.

In a sense, it is history, but it is nevertheless important in charting the evolution of the present curriculum to outline some examples. All the curriculum subject documents stretched to many pages and within, for instance, the 'core' subjects of English, mathematics and science (also Welsh in Wales) many Attainment Targets (the major areas of the curriculum) were delineated each with literally dozens of Statements of Attainment within them spanning the 10 levels of progression in each subject. To give a flavour of these, and the inherent problems they presented as starting points for assessment and domain definitions, the following points are of interest.

- The 1989 version of the curriculum science contained 17 Attainment Targets (ATs) and 393 Statements of Attainment (SoA) over the 10 Levels. The first version of the mathematics curriculum comprised 14 Attainment Targets and 296 SoA across the 10 Levels. In the 1991 versions these were reduced to four (Attainment Targets) in science and five in mathematics. The respective numbers of SoA were 173 (science) and 117 (mathematics). Even with these reduced numbers the task was not eased, not least because some of the reduction in the number of individual SoA was achieved by combining content and thus making their use as starting points for assessment even more difficult.

- In terms of the content of the SoA (technically the assessment criteria), there was enormous variation in the breadth and specificity, not to mention ambiguity, of the 'domains':

    - English, AT3, Level 3a: Pupils should read aloud from familiar stories or poems fluently and with appropriate expression
    - Mathematics, AT3, Level 1a: Pupils should add or subtract, using objects, where the numbers involved are no greater than 10
    - Science, AT1, Level 5: Pupils should identify and manipulate relevant

independent and dependent variables, choosing appropriately between ranges, number and values

These are clearly examples of the age-old problem in specifying assessment criteria (see also Wolf, 1993 in relation to NVQs). A careful path has to be charted between the extremes of vague and ambiguous criteria on the one hand and a proliferation of detailed but trivial objectives on the other. It also partly represents the inherent tension in the curriculum documents between providing teachers (not to mention test development agencies) with a degree of freedom and richness in both curriculum and assessment terms yet being specific enough for reproducible assessments to be carried out. It is a tension that has never been resolved, either in National Curriculum assessment or elsewhere. The end result of such proliferation and ambiguity were assessment outcomes at Key Stage 1 in 1991 (the first full assessments put in place) that were highly problematic in terms of their dependability (Shorrocks *et al.*, 1992).

The problem of domain ambiguity was also compounded by problems of defining mastery criteria for each Attainment Target/Level. It was evident from the questionnaire responses of teachers in the 1991 evaluations that they were confused (despite training) about what constituted mastery and when an SoA could therefore be deemed to have been attained. For instance, in all three core subjects teacher assessments, a significant proportion of the participating teachers took mastery to mean displaying the knowledge on one occasion only, whereas others required children to show evidence on several occasions. Some considered only 'typical' work from pupils whilst others considered only highest achievement or 'best' work (Shorrocks *et al.*, 1992).

The solution has been to abandon the notion of Statements of Attainment (discrete criteria) altogether and to opt instead for global, 'best-fit' Level Descriptions, at least in teacher assessments (see, for example, in mathematics DfEE, 1995a). It has yet to be seen how such a system will work and it is not easy to estimate the dependability of the outcomes. To illustrate this point, teachers may not find it any easier to assess against the following Level description in a reliable way, as opposed to the former SoA at the same Level and AT.

- Number, Level 3 (level description): Pupils have extended their understanding of place value to numbers up to 1000 and approximate these numbers to the nearest 10 or 100. They have begun to use decimals and negative numbers in contexts such as money, temperature and calculator displays. Pupils use mental recall of addition and subtraction facts to 20 in solving problems. Pupils use mental recall of the 2, 5 and 10 multiplication tables and others up to 5 x 5 in solving whole number problems involving multiplication and division including those that give rise to remainders. They are beginning to develop other mental strategies of their own and use them to find methods for adding and subtracting two-digit numbers. They use calculator methods where appropriate. Pupils also solve problems involving multiplication or division of money by whole numbers. (DfEE, 1995)

- Number, Level 3 (Statements of Attainment)

    (a) Read, write and order numbers up to 1000.
    (b) Demonstrate that they know and can use multiplication tables.
    (c) Solve problems using multiplication or division.
    (d) Make estimates based on familiar units of measurement, checking results.
    (e) Interpret a range of numbers in the context of measurement or money.
    (DES/WO, 1991)

The problem of aggregation

A second major problem in this kind of approach to assessment is that of combining the results of the attainment of individual elements (criteria) into a single, meaningful score, bearing in mind that at each aggregation point, important information is lost. In the case of the early versions of the National Curriculum the situation was highly complex. The curriculum subjects were mostly broken down into (first) the broad areas in the subject (the Profile Components) which in turn were broken down into Attainment Targets (smaller but definable areas of knowledge and skills). Each Attainment Target was, in turn, divided into the 10 Levels of Attainment, and within each of these Levels were located the Statements of Attainment, the first points for the recording of attainment.

In the early days of the development of the Standard Assessment Tasks, rules of aggregation obviously needed to be set out for combining scores at these various points in the hierarchy. Given a variable number of SoA at each Level and across subjects (varying from one SoA at a Level to more than 10) mastery criteria for the Level were needed as well as aggregation rules for then combining the scores from each AT into Profile Components and finally into a whole subject score. Looking back it seems amazing that a system of such byzantine complexity was allowed to develop, particularly as it had, in theory, to be applied not only in the SATs, but also by teachers in their own record-keeping and assessments.

The solution arrived at was basically a combination of a minimal assignable grade plus a partial tolerance approach. In other words, where there were only one or two SoA at a Level, they both had to be attained for the Level to be awarded (i.e. the 'n rule'). Where there were three or more SoA at a Level, then the partial tolerance, 'n minus 1' rule applied, where one less than the total number was required for the awarding of the Level. The effect of this, only noted afterwards (Shorrocks *et al*.

1992), was that the attainment of a Level became increasingly more demanding as the number of SoA increased beyond three.

The content domain for Levels where there were one or two SoA could be considered to be relatively small in relation to those where there were three or more. As the number of SoA assessed exceeded two, the application of the 'n minus 1' rule became demonstrably inequitable in terms of comparative attainment. As the number of 'criteria' at a Level increased, not only were pupils required to perform successfully over a much greater content domain, they had to attain more in proportional terms. It must also be stressed that the actual content domains of the SoA were very different in the demands they made, so that the picture painted so far is even further complicated: at certain Levels, even though there were many SoA, the comparative easiness of some of them affected the ease or difficulty of attaining the Level.

There was yet a further complication in this aggregation system. Given the large number of ATs in mathematics and science, it was clear that a Standard Assessment Task could not cover all of them. Teachers were required to provide a summative assessment score in each AT for each pupil and in the final aggregations, these Teacher Assessment scores had to be used to fill in the 'gaps' so the total subject score could be reached. However, for ATs where a SAT score was available, this was automatically entered as the definitive score, with moderation procedures in place for cases of disagreement. In the first year of the implementation of the assessments at Key Stage 1, the SAT outcomes were frequently higher than those awarded by the teachers (again evidence of teacher uncertainty about the criteria and mastery levels implied). The SAT therefore had the effect of raising the final scores in all three core subjects, although its precise effects varied from subject to subject. In the second year of implementation, teachers learned very rapidly, and the scores overall were higher (Shorrocks, 1995)

With the first major revision of the curriculum in the core subjects in the early 1990s this complexity of aggregation procedures was eased, and with many fewer ATs in mathematics and science the majority could be addressed in the SAT. The implication of this for the status of Teacher Assessment judgements, however, was of great significance, a point that will be addressed again in a later section of this chapter.

At this point, however, other forces were at work to modify the number and complexity of the SoA at the various levels, not least the agitation from teachers about the complexity of record-keeping it imposed. Tick-lists and portfolios of 'evidence' for each pupil abounded, making final summative judgements awkward and diverting teachers from detailed and relevant planning and using the assessments in a genuinely formative way. Teachers at Key Stage 1 had soldiered on with both the curriculum and the assessments for several years, but it was only when Key Stage 3 assessments came on stream in the summer of

1993 that the discontent became focused and yet more changes were instigated (Dearing Report, 1993).

The effects of this were to lose the notion of Statements of Attainment altogether, in favour of shorter Programmes of Study and the use of Level Descriptions as 'best-fit' guides (for each Attainment Target) for teachers in their own assessments. The problems of such an approach have been mentioned earlier (p. 175–6) but one further point should be made. If the National Curriculum has had any merit and effect on the quality of teaching and learning in schools (and many have argued that it has) it has probably arisen as a result of teachers addressing the detail of what was to be taught and planning in more systematic ways.

If the assessment system has had any effect on this quality and on standards attained (and this is much more open to question) then it is probably because of a new focus not only on what has been taught, but on exactly what has been learned. Almost by its nature, the National Curriculum demands a detailed consideration of pupil learning in all its facets. Viewing pupils in this more differentiated way seems less likely to lead to generalised and perhaps partial judgements about individual pupils: it seems to hold the possibility of overcoming 'halo effects' and negative expectations and hence improving achievement. The apparently regressive step backwards towards more global judgements is disappointing in this context.

The implications of the latest round of changes in the curriculum specifications for the test development agencies were also wide-ranging. In any case, at Key Stages 2 and 3, the advent of pencil-and-paper tests (as of 1993), less recognisable content 'criteria' within the tests and a marks-based approach to scoring had already indicated a move away from direct criterion-referencing. From here on, the term used in official circles was 'criterion-related assessment'. The message being carried was that all questions in the various test papers are derived from the specification of the curriculum appropriate to each Key Stage, but that once generated and packaged into a test paper, the questions become vehicles for collecting a total score of marks which are not assigned to particular Attainment Targets or 'criteria'. Instead, threshold scores (cut-scores) are set, using a range of different kinds of judgements, which determine the Level awarded on any paper or total test.

For example, in setting the Key Stage 2 mathematics tests in summer 1996 (addressing Levels 3–5), several methods were used in order to decide appropriate cut scores.

- The application of a 'criterion-related algorithm', whereby appropriate proportions of the number of marks attributed to each of the three Levels of questions were calculated and cut scores arrived at.
- Statistical equating with the scores of the previous year was carried out.
- Angoff procedures were applied (Angoff, 1971).

A judicious combination of information from these sources was used to set the final thresholds. Of these three, the Angoff procedure is perhaps the least well-known but it is a technique used quite widely in the current setting of National Curriculum thresholds. A panel of expert judges (in this case experienced Year 6 teachers of mathematics) considers each item in the final versions of the tests and decides whether minimally competent pupils at Level 3, Level 4 and Level 5 would be able to answer the question correctly, of course noting the requirements of the mark schemes. This is done independently at first and the scores recorded. At the next stage, the panel as a whole must agree on these decisions and it is a combination of the various probabilities generated by these judgements that can then be used to arrive at the decision about the appropriate cut-scores for Level 3, Level 4 and Level 5. As a technique, it is not without its weaknesses, but as part of a decision-making process it is useful. It is also being developed and extended in its usage in the context of the National Curriculum, both in England and Wales and in Northern Ireland (Morrison, Busch and D' Arcy, 1993).

Reliability and validity issues

The notions of validity and reliability are central to any discussion of assessment: assessment needs to be fit for its purpose and to produce results that can be relied upon. The question to be addressed here is the extent to which existing definitions of validity and reliability are appropriate in the context of National Curriculum assessment.

Validity is conventionally defined (Anastasi, 1990) as , '*what* a test measures and *how well* it does so'. However, other definitions have proliferated, emphasising, for instance, content (the extent to which the assessment is relevant to the content domain being addressed), prediction (the extent to which a test is capable of predicting future performance) and the extent to which the inferences being made in any assessment is warranted (more recent definitions of construct validity).

As Wiliam (1993) argues, what many writers have not taken into account is the social context in which the assessment takes place, clearly a much broader definition of the term. Messick (1980) tried to remedy this by including the complex relationship between 'basis' and 'function' in assessment. In other words, a recognition that assessment is based on evidence, has consequences, and produces results that have to be interpreted and used. The framework he suggests is given in Figure 9.1. By interrelating these variables, emphasis is given to the fact that the uses of assessment outcomes are a significant consideration in the validation process. National Curriculum assessment is high-stakes assessment, where not only are individuals being judged, but also teachers, schools and in effect the whole system. In these circumstances it is even more important to take this broader notion of validity and to recognise that

		Function	
		Result interpretation	Result use
Basis	Evidential basis	Construct validity	Construct validity and relevance/utility
	Consequential basis	Value implications	Social consequences

Figure 9.1. Messick's framework for the validation of assessments.

there may be a significant tension between the evidence and consequences of testing.

Just as the notion of validity demands some rethinking in the context of the National Curriculum, so does reliability. Traditional measures are not appropriate, based as they are on norm-referenced approaches to testing. Criterion-referenced tests (as classically conceived) are not designed to emphasise differences among individuals and hence the range of scoring outcomes can be lower. In fact, after an 'ideal' teaching programme and effective learning on the part of the pupils, it should be possible for all candidates to obtain high scores. The more limited variability of criterion-referenced tests mean, however, that traditional estimates of reliability are likely to generate misleading results.

It is more appropriate, therefore, to use the term *dependability* (Brennan and Kane, 1977) for criterion-referenced tests so as not to create confusion. In National Curriculum assessment, the outcomes, arrived at by the kinds of means outlined earlier, are expressed in terms of levels for each subject. The main question therefore becomes, how dependable are the outcomes in terms of accurately placing individuals in the appropriate 'category' (level). It is basically a matter of drawing accurate lines between 'masters' and 'non-masters' at each level, a situation that Figure 9.2 depicts in its most simplified form, taking the example of probably the best known assessment situation of this kind, the driving test.

		Domain score classification.	
		Non-master	Master
Test score classification	Fails test. Non-master	True-negative decision	False-negative decision
	Passes test. Master	False-positive decision.	True-positive decision

Figure 9.2. Agreement between domain and test score mastery

The 'domain score classification' implies the 'true' skill situation which any test only ever samples. On the basis of this sampling (the test score classification) there are two kinds of correct decision (the 'true-positive' and 'true-negative' cells) and two kinds of incorrect decision (the 'false-positive' and 'false-negative'). Above all, this kind of test (the driving test in this example) must aim to maximise correct decisions and minimise incorrect ones. The assessment instrument (the test) should be designed to achieve this, but it should be borne in mind that the two kinds of incorrect decisions have different consequences. From the point of view of road safety, false-positive decisions are important since they imply incompetent drivers on the road. False-negative decisions imply re-testing with all its resource implications. To minimise the false-positives, a stricter criterion could be applied but this could increase the proportion of false-negatives.

By analogy, in the context of National Curriculum assessment, the aim must also be to minimise incorrect decisions and correctly assign pupils to Levels, using probability calculations. However, as we have seen with the example of the driving test, the precise ways in which the thresholds are drawn (the cut scores between masters and non-masters) depends to some extent on the nature and purpose of the test. The driving test is vital in terms of road safety and implies as strict a mastery criterion as is reasonable and appropriate. In National Curriculum tests, there is also a question of consequences, as the argument about validity emphasised. The aim should be to set thresholds that minimise incorrect placements but consideration should be given to the implications of misplacements.

This testing is indeed high-stakes testing: schools are judged and ranked in terms of the outcomes, and individual pupils are assigned Levels which may have considerable consequences for them. The results may be used for selection (streaming, perhaps) or for grouping decisions within a class, particularly in primary schools. Both these kinds of decisions may influence the kinds of opportunities and learning experiences provided for the child and well as feelings of self-esteem and worth. These are not low stakes in relation to longer term life chances.

Formative assessment within the system

The Report from the Task Group on Assessment and Testing (TGAT) suggested as one of its cornerstone principles that the assessment system should contain both formative and summative aspects (see p. 172). The traditional argument against this is that any test instrument is devised for a particular purpose and that different purposes demand rather different kinds of test questions and 'package' characteristics. The TGAT group were clearly convinced that this was not entirely the case, and of course to some extent it is true. None of these distinctions is totally hard and fast, particularly if the domains (the curriculum) being addressed are manageable and the test instrument specifications are wide-ranging and flexible. The problem of National Curriculum assessment, however, is that in reality neither of these conditions came to be.

On the other hand, in emphasising the formative dimension, the direct link was made to the teaching–learning process and to planning strategies on the part of teachers, which many would see as vital to the process of improving the quality of what goes on in schools and to the raising of standards of performance.

From the beginning in the TGAT Report (DES/WO 1988), the formal emphasis was on the central role of Teacher Assessment, in both its formative and summative guises, as the cornerstone of the system. In formative terms, moderated Teacher Assessment was to provide the engine for improved classroom practice and in summative terms it was to become an important aspect of reporting, alongside Standard Test outcomes. In reality, given the political imperatives of the dominance of the national test scores, this has never come to pass and therefore teachers (not to mention others in the system) have never been clear exactly what it is for.

The only time when its 'poor relation' character was minimised was in the very early Standard Test administrations at Key Stages 1 and 3, when the proliferation of Attainment Targets in the core subjects of mathematics and science required that TA scores be incorporated into the overall aggregation profile. The slimming down of the number of ATs in the core subjects has meant that all are now potentially addressable by the Standard Tests, so Teacher Assessment is no longer necessary for these calculations. Instead, as a result of the Dearing Review (1993), Teacher Assessment is accorded a separate status from the tests and is reported alongside the test scores.

What it has meant, however, is that teachers have had to develop new recording systems, a process that has had particular impact at Key Stage 1, not only because it was the first Key Stage to implement the curriculum and assessments, but also because of the comparative lack of experience of such detailed measuring of outcomes. Check lists, tick boxes, 'can-do' lists and portfolios of evidence sprouted in primary schools throughout England and Wales and studies of exactly how the recordings were carried out revealed some interesting information. An HMI Report of 1992 showed that few teachers were recording in a directly 'criterion-referenced' way according to Statements of Attainment. Instead, many used less detailed listings or worked with implicit notions of 'levelness' in judging children's work and performance overall. The work of the research group led by Gipps and Brown (e.g. McCallum *et al.*, 1993) has identified a range of models of teacher response at Key Stage 1, which vary along the dimensions of the degree of systematicity in approach, the extent of integration with teaching, and ideological underpinning.

One final point should be made about formative assessment approaches in the context of the national tests and tasks. Some of the most recent developments from the Schools Curriculum and Assessment Authority have included initiatives to carry out evaluations of children's responses and error analyses in the test scripts. This resulted in a publication for teachers, sent to all schools (SCAA, 1996) outlining the main findings and thus potentially giving teachers more insight into how the test scripts can be used to learn more about children's skills and understandings in order to inform planning and teaching. In so far as this is appreciated and taken up, then the formative aspects of what appear to be fairly arid test results can be exploited to the advantage of the system.

Moderation procedures and the system

In a sense, the matter of moderation has partly been addressed at earlier points in this chapter. From the beginning, it was seen as a vital aspect of the proposed assessments, relying as they did on the interpretation and application of varied 'criteria' of performance.

In the early days of assessment experience at Key Stage 1 (the first to come on stream in 1991) moderation had a significant role. It was, however, locally devised and administered, with no overt procedures for more nationally-based systems to be put in place. In the national evaluation of the first year of the Key Stage 1 round, emphasis was drawn to this (Shorrocks *et al.*, 1992). The 'local' administration was by Local Education Authorities, which varied enormously in size. At the extremes, one LEA in the national sample contained only 26 primary/first schools and 850 children in the relevant age-group, whilst the largest contained 375 primary/first schools and over 11 000 children in the relevant age-group. Wide variation also existed in the ratio of trainers to teachers, implying training cascades of very different levels of steepness. However, the aspect of training that received consistent praise was attending agreement trials within and between schools, which was seen as helpful in assessment terms but also important in terms of wider professional development for teachers.

By the time the Key Stage 3 Standard Tests came along (in 1993), it was clear that a different notion of the nature of the tests was emerging from government; they were to be basically comparatively short, written tests to be administered as efficiently as possible, particularly with this older age cohort of pupils. In this revised situation, moderation seemed to be viewed essentially as an administrative issue with quality assurance dimensions (Daugherty, 1995).

At all Key Stages, the move towards pencil-and-paper tests (even to a large extent with 7 year olds at Key Stage 1) has changed the need for moderation, as has the move toward the external marking of test papers. In a sense, the dependability of the outcomes now rests on the effectiveness of the threshold-setting procedures along with the accuracy of the marking. For all subjects, the marking and responsibility for the training of markers is in the hands of a single, 'lead' agency which at least begins to ensure some national agreement and consistency. At the moment, however, little direct evidence is available in the context of National Curriculum about the application of exactly similar marking criteria or about error rates in marking. It is interesting, however, that a similar problem should have been noted by Child (1989) in the context of error rates in scoring in the DC test for nurses.

Progression and the assessment system

The TGAT originally suggested that the subject working groups should define up to 10 levels of attainment in each area of the curriculum, covering the age range 5–16 years.

> We shall use the word level to define one of a sequence of points on a scale to be used in describing the progress of attainment in the Profile Component. The sequence of levels represents the stages of progression. (DES/WO, 1988, para. 100)

'Progression' thus became central to the system. In some ways this was a positive step, in that it provided a cohering device for the curriculum and its assessment across the different phases of education (primary/first, middle, secondary). It should in theory facilitate planning and communication among teachers in the same phase and also across phases and Key Stages. Even thus far on in the implementation, however, there are still apocryphal tales about schools ignoring the information provided by (in particular) other Key Stages, some even preferring to administer standardised attainment tests or broader verbal reasoning tests of ability and to use these results as the basis for grouping, etc. Recently recognising and addressing this problem, SCAA have published a document suggesting ways of improving cross-Key Stage communication and progression (School Curriculum and Assessment Authority, 1996).

But where did the idea of a single 10-level scale come from in the first place? According to reports, it emerged from experience of graded assessments, which were becoming increasingly popular in the mid-1980s. However, from the beginning, questions were posed as to whether this was entirely appropriate, even in principle, for such a wide age and phase range. The argument was that the results would be too course-grained to be helpful either to teachers, parents or central government or to yield meaningful data about progression. Additionally, there emerged the problem of the different demands of the different levels in the different subjects, all of which served to emphasise the issue. The strains indeed began to show, and have been addressed by attempts to introduce tests that break down 'level' scores into within-level gradings, say A, B, C D and E.

The Dearing review clearly saw this as one of the most problematic aspects of the whole system (Dearing, 1993) since it devotes many pages to a consideration of the present situation and possible alternatives, namely independent graded outcomes at the end of each Key Stage. The jury is still out and it is obviously an issue to be considered further. Also, we as yet have little published evidence on the progress of the first Key Stage 1 age cohort (aged 7 in summer 1991 and 1992) who have since taken the Key Stage 2 tests at age 11. This will no doubt provide evidence to inform the debate, and will, of course, be closely related to notions of school effectiveness and 'value-added'. If this is done it is vital that it is done appropriately in statistical terms in order to avoid the trap of using crude and invalid measures in such a high-stakes context.

Discussion and conclusions: purposes, cross-purposes and experience.

It is a long established principle in assessment circles that the first question to ask about any proposed assessment is 'What is it for?' The answer to this question strongly influences the nature of the questions asked, the delivery and response modes chosen and the kinds of analyses and interpretations that can be put upon the outcomes. In the case of National Curriculum assessment, it was the contention that the range of purposes suggested by the TGAT Report could all be addressed within the one system. In a sense, the difficult experience of the 1990s has been the proof that this was not possible.

This chapter has unashamedly returned to this starting point, namely the recommendations of the TGAT group, since no full analysis of issues and changes could have been made without this. At the time, the proposals were seen as liberal and enlightened by educationists and those in the field of assessment; they appeared to subscribe to some of the better approaches available and to be located directly in a context of improving teaching and learning in schools. With the benefit of hindsight, it becomes more evident that the enterprise as a whole was too ambitious, trying to serve too many masters and too many purposes.

In fairness, it does represent a brave attempt (possibly the only one so far in any country) to put in place a curriculum-based, criterion-referenced assessment system across three very different age phases but within a single framework. In many ways it has provided useful information, though not perhaps of the kind predicted. Notwithstanding the backtracking and all the changes, other countries are learning from our mistakes (for example Hong Kong and South Africa) as are we ourselves. There has also been a considerable contribution to assessment theory, not all of which is yet published.

The system might have worked better if a tighter rein had been kept on the subject working groups, especially those in the core subjects which were to be the first focus of implementation. Less proliferation of curriculum specification and less variability across subjects would have made a better starting point, as would a fuller brief about the nature of the documentation as starting points for assessment.

On the other hand, it is rather like the tale of the traveller who, on asking for directions to a particular place, was told not to start from here! It could be that we have arrived at something like the position we should have started from, given the now evident agendas. In particular, the following are of significance: a more streamlined curriculum specification; clearer understanding among teachers in all age phases about the relationship between teaching, learning and assessing; teachers better prepared for the endeavour; and tests more fully worked through with their characteristics and purposes clearer. Different agendas would, of course, dictate different approaches.

It is interesting to speculate why 7 year olds at the end of their Key Stage 1 experience should have been chosen for the first programme of implementation. It is the shortest Key Stage and hence one where the assessments would follow on fairly fast from the start if implementation. But in many ways it was the most awkward place to begin, not least because there was little experience of assessment in infant schools and the assessment of such young children requires very particular approaches.

The early SATs for this Key Stage made a creditable attempt to marry up the central issues of valid assessment activities that produced dependable results and which were at the same time manageable in the classroom, when 30 or more children had to be included. Herculean efforts were made by infant teachers in the first few years, notwithstanding certain changes and honing. But an outcry did predictably follow, leading almost inevitably to more tightly constrained and 'formalised' assessments, with a more pencil-and-paper character. This shift represents a changing balance between the three key aspects – validity, dependability and manageability. The earliest SATs emphasised validity with perhaps slightly less emphasis on dependability and manageability, no doubt the result of the influence of the early childhood education lobby. The kinds of SATs that followed emphasised manageability and dependability at the expense of validity.

The position is now more consolidated, with the tests at all key stages beginning to be accepted if not loved. There is, however, still an uncertain relationship between the competing demands and purposes. It seems that a single assessment system may be able to serve more than one purpose but only at a price and only if it is properly primed and resourced. It is precisely the cross-purposes involved and competing agendas, most particularly in time-scales and training or preparation, that have caused much of the trouble. Even now there is little sense of shared purposes by all participants and interested parties: teachers, pupils, parents; the wider community; and central government. Until there is, the unease will probably continue.

References

Anastasi, A. (1990) Psychological Testing, 6th edn (New York: Macmillan).

Angoff, W.H. (1971) Scales, norms and equivalent scores, in Thorndike, R.L. (Ed.) Educational and Psychological Measurement (Washington, DC: American Council on Education).

Ball, S. (1990) Politics and Policy Making in Education (London: Routledge).

Brennan, R.L. and Kane, M.T. (1977) An index of dependability for mastery tests. Journal of Educational Measurement, 14, 277–89.

Daugherty, R. (1995) National Curriculum Assessment: A review of policy 1988–1994 (London:Falmer Press).

Dearing, R. (1993) The National Curriculum and its Assessment: Final report (London: School Curriculum and Assessment Authority).

Department of Education and Science/Welsh Office (1985) Better Schools (London: HMSO).

Department of Education and Science/Welsh Office (1988) National Curriculum Task Group on Assessment and Testing: A Report (London:DES/WO).

Department of Education and Science/Welsh Office (1991) Mathematics in the National Curriculum (London: DES/WO).

Department for Education and Employment/Welsh Office (1995) Mathematics in the National Curriculum (London: DfEE/WO).

Gipps, C. (1990) The debate over standards and the uses of tests. In Moon, B., Isaac, J. and Powney, J. Judging Standards and Effectiveness in Education (London: Hodder and Stoughton).

Glaser, R. (1963) Instructional technology and the measurement of learning outcomes. American Psychologist, 18, 519–21.

HMI (1985) The Curriculum from 5 to 16 (London: HMSO).

HMI (1992) Assessment, Recording and Reporting: A report by HMI on the second year, 1992–93 (London: HMSO).

McCallum, B. McAlister, S., Brown, M.L. and Gipps, C. (1993) Teacher assessment at Key Stage 1, in Research Papers in Education, 8, No. 8.

Moon, B., Isaac, J. and Powney, J. (1990) Judging Standards and Effectiveness in Education (London: Hodder and Stoughton).

Messick, S. (1980) Test validity and the ethics of assessment. American Psychologist, 35 (11), 1012–27.

Morrison, H., Busch, J.C. and D'Arcy, J. (1993) Reconciling end-of-Key Stage test scores and classroom-based assessment: a role for the Angoff procedure in British assessment. Paper presented to SCAA Conference, London.

School Curriculum and Assessment Authority (1996) Promoting Continuity Between Key Stage 2 and Key Stage 3 (London: School Curriculum and Assessment Authority).

Shorrocks, D., Daniels, S., Frobisher, L., Nelson, N., Waterson, A. and Bell, J. (1992) The Evaluation of National Curriculum Assessment at Key Stage 1: Final report of the ENCA 1 project (London: Schools Examination and Assessment Council), p. 295.

Shorrocks, D. (1995) Evaluating National Curriculum Assessment at Key Stage 1: Retrospect and prospect. In Broadhead, P., Research in early years education (Clevedon, Multilingual Matters).

Wolf, A. (1993) Assessment Issues and Problems in a Criterion-Based System (London: Further Education Unit).

Wiliam, D. (1993) Reconceptualising validity, dependability and reliability for National Curriculum Assessment. Paper presented at Symposium on The Reliability of National Curriculum Assessment, BERA.

Chapter 10
Indicator systems for schools: fire-fighting it is!

CAROL FITZ-GIBBON

Dennis Child's inaugural lecture at the University of Newcastle upon Tyne was delivered with all the elegant good humour which consistently marks his demeanour, whether discussing psychology or grandchildren. It was entitled 'Affective influences on academic performance'. In rereading it I was struck by his report of Cattell's view that intelligence is not a better predictor of achievement than motivation or personality. 'His psychometric inventories accounted for some 75 per cent of the variation in school achievement marks in equal proportions – 25 per cent each.' (p. 6, referring to Cattell, Sealy and Sweney, 1966 and Cattell and Butcher, 1968). Doubtful of these claims, Professor Child reported a replication (Glendenning, 1974) in which 70 per cent of the variance was explained in which intelligence and personality accounted for about the same proportions and motivation half as much.

These themes have not disappeared from educational research. A recent representative of these correlational studies, for example, used a small sample of students of education (370 female, 153 male) in order to study interrelationships between motivation and achievement (Mitchell, 1992). Motivation was measured by questionnaires with Likert-type items to create scales and by direct self-report. Intrinsic and extrinsic motivation were measured as separate scales and 'although intrinsic motivation seems to come closest to what motivation means in the minds of these students and perhaps of people in general, it is extrinsic motivation that is the stronger (though negative) predictor of GPA.' The typical college-student sample and the widespread use of GPA (grade point average as given in universities) in some US research is unfortunate. GPA consists of teacher-given grades and the standards will almost certainly vary from subject to subject and from one instructor to another. Mitchell

---

This is a revision of a paper presented at the annual meeting of CREATE in Gatlinburg, Tennessee, in July 1994.

concludes with reasonable warning about the use of motivational variables for predicting college achievement, noting that 'the price in time' must be considered as must the 'relative fakeability' of the items. The purpose behind these efforts at prediction was not made explicit. Perhaps the implicit purpose was 'understanding', that elusive, chimerical but energising goal.

Pragmatic and practical approaches tend to throw up different questions. In his inaugural lecture at the University of Newcastle upon Tyne, Professor Child was concerned with a need to 'monitor student performance':

> We need longitudinal and depth studies of the interaction between the academic goals of institutions and the personal development of students...We must explore ways of discovering and feeding back to students their cognitive competences as a means of enhancing their self-images. (p. 20)

Dennis Child believes in research, in the use of validated methods to address practical questions. He negotiated a lectureship in Research Methods out of a demonstrator post when he arrived to take up the Chair at Newcastle upon Tyne. Such posts were unusual in the UK and, occurring some years before the Research Assessment Exercises began, it was not entirely appreciated in what was then a teaching-focused department. The post provided the chance to develop a strong group of research-trained students and research-based activities. These led to performance monitoring projects such as ALIS (A-level Information System) presaging the widespread adoption of what came to be called 'value-added' approaches.

Professor Child ended his inaugural with the following sentence from *The Prediction of Academic Achievement* by Lavin (1965):

> Academic achievement is determined by complex interactions of predictor variables: therefore, we need models that attempt to approximate this *complexity*. [emphasis added]

Interestingly, complexity is now the name of the game in physics, economics and many more disciplines as it becomes a recognisable state of nature (Waldrop, 1992). In 'Policy for the unpredictable', published in 1979, Gene Glass suggested that widely applicable research findings may never be found in social science. The most we can hope to do is to watch out for problems: 'fire fighting'.

Perhaps 'understanding' in social science is not going to mean the enumeration of time-constant laws of the kind that give one a feeling of knowing what will happen next. Whether dealing with organisms or organisations, we are dealing, it now seems, with complex and unpredictable events. The central concepts are those of *feedback*...the flow of multi-faceted information and consequences from the environment... and *local organisation* as opposed to central control. Complex systems manage to develop effectiveness...as measured by survival and success...not by being told what to do but by getting regular feedback and being able to adapt flexibly.

Schools as complex systems

Of course, analogies prove nothing. However, they often underpin scientific intuition and lead to advances. Since education is nothing if not a complex system, with multiple networks and feedback loops, it would be strange indeed if some of the findings from the new, computer-driven models of complex systems did not apply to it (Tymms, 1990; Fitz-Gibbon, 1993, 1996; Tymms, 1994). However, regardless of the acceptability or otherwise of analogies with developments in science, there is probably widespread agreement on the need for schools and teachers to have good information on their effectiveness (and also efficiency). The 'understanding' that must be sought in the complex world of evolving systems is principally of how to provide accurate and useful feedback, a process that can be thought of as distributed research, analagous to distributed computing. It is to some major features of parts of the resulting data that this chapter now turns.

ALIS has been in operation since 1983 (Fitz-Gibbon, 1985, 1991, 1992). Another project is YELLIS (Year 11 Information System) which we felt ready to make available nationally in 1993. Both are considered in this paper.

Both ALIS and YELLIS rest on (a) tests and questionnaires administered in schools and (b) the system of curriculum-embedded, high stakes, authentic testing which the UK has always known as 'exams'. Arguably, these provide better measures of 'achievement' than the ubiquitous Grade Point Average. The external examination system is a fundamental support, enabling schooling to be fair and effective. It enhances teacher–student relationships, supports delivery standards and underpins quality assurance procedures, in particular by the provision of feedback to the units of responsibility. Without it neither equity nor effectiveness can be adequately assessed on an on-going basis. We will consider first the cognitive outcomes of education and then other important outcomes.

The major features are summarised in Table 10.1 and some of these features are discussed below under the headings 'Cognitive outcomes' and 'Affective and social outcomes', both themes of Professor Child's inaugural lecture.

Table 10.1. Indicator systems for schooling effects on 16 and 18 year olds.

Outcomes	Indicator System for Students' Progress Between the Ages of	
	14–18 years (the YELLIS project)	16–18 years (the ALIS project)
Cognitive outcomes	• Students' achievement in external examinations at age 16 (GCSE)[a]	• Students' achievement in external examinations age 18 ('A' levels)[a]
Affective outcomes	• Students' attitudes to main subjects: English, maths and science • Students' attitudes to their school or college • Students' response to school processes • Students' feelings of being over-or under-challenged in the major subjects	• Students' attitudes to each subject studied for the examinations at age 18 • Students' attitudes to their school or college ('customer satisfaction')
Social outcomes	• Students' aspirations • Students' freedom from fear (bullying, insults, safety)	• Students' aspirations • Students' participation in extra mural activities (as a 'quality of life' indicator)
Behavioural /life chance outcomes	• Continuing in education after the period of compulsory schooling • Jobs achieved	• Earnings • Perceived quality of life • Retrospective satisfaction • Residual effects of effective schooling on achievement in higher education

[a] The externally set and marked examinations would be described in the US as 'authentic' (essays are written, problems are worked out, maps are read, data is analysed), high stakes (certificates are issued which influence admissions to further educational opportunities and job prospects) and curriculum embedded (the examinations test what has been taught, which has followed a published syllabus).

Cognitive outcomes

Whereas feedback to teachers on student behaviour in the classroom is immediate and unambiguous – with the consequence that most teachers rapidly learn classroom control – feedback about their instructional effectiveness is harder to come by. How can teachers learn about the effectiveness of their teaching? How can they know the answer to the crucial question: are other teachers getting better results in this subject although working with similar students? The only way to provide an answer to this question is on the basis of student-by-student, subject-by-subject data in the framework of a large scale monitoring system, covering many institutions in which other teachers are teaching the same subjects to similar students. This requires, of course, some agreement on curricula in order to have curriculum-embedded testing. Walker and Schaffarzick (1974) warned adequately against trying to compare outcomes from different curricula.

The likelihood is that the UK examinations, providing authentic, curriculum-embedded assessments, are sensitive to instructional effects and can therefore be used to provide feedback to teachers about the effectiveness of the instruction they provide.

Given that we have a nationwide system of external examinations taken at age 16 and age 18 we have there a framework in which the relative progress of students can be measured. The average grade from all the subjects taken at age 16 (the Grade Point Average at GCSE) is the best single predictor for any subject at age 18 (Advanced Level or 'A' level). By matching the input GPAs with the output 'A' level grade a scattergram can be plotted and a regression line calculated.

Representative actual data are shown in Figures 10.1–10.4 for physics, with regressions drawn separately for sex, examination board, and school departments. It can be seen that it is departments which show the greatest range of results. It is departments – a proxy for what goes on in the classroom – which account for the most variation in outcomes. This finding is consistent with a recent attempt to summarise the literature on experimental tests of 'school effects': the meta analysis of Wang, Haertel and Walberg, (1993) which supports just this point about proximal classroom variables as opposed to distal variables:

> Distal variables, like state, district, and school level policy and demographics, have little influence on school learning (Wang *et al.*, 1993, p. 276).

The authors commented that this finding was

> inconsistent with current conventional wisdom which argues for policy-driven solutions, like school re-structuring, school-site management, and tougher teacher credential requirements and evaluation.

However, we can see here the potential for interactions. School site management without good outcome measures and feedback may be ineffective. Equally, feedback can hardly be effective if given in a situation in which there are few options for action, e.g. without the conjunction of site management.

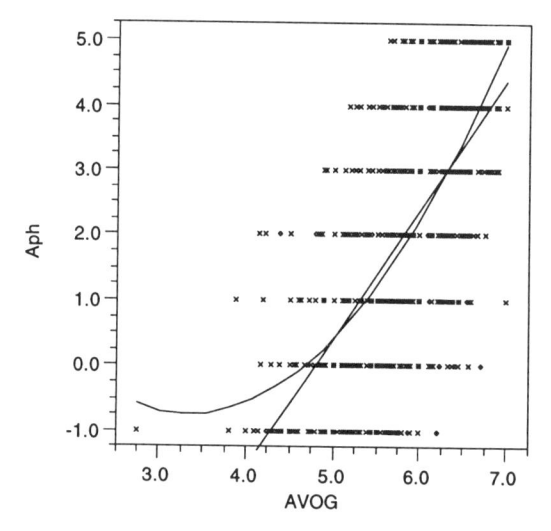

Figure 10.1. Regression of 'A' level physics grades on average examination grades at age 16. The vertical axis represents grades on a single subject taken at age 18, in this case physics. The horizontal axis represents the average grade obtained on all examinations taken at age 16 (usually about 8 subjects). For 'Aph', i.e. the 'A' level grade in physics, 5 = A, 4 = B, etc. For 'AVOG', i.e. average grade at age 16, 7 = A, 6 = B, etc. These particular scales are used for historical reasons. A linear and a quadratic equation have been fitted, giving the line and the curve.

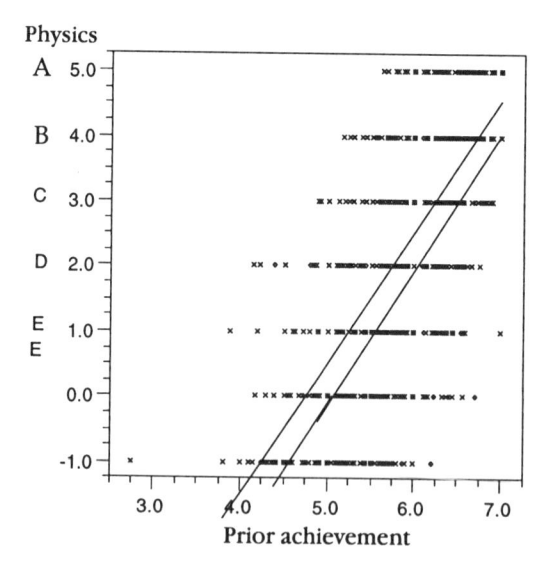

	Sex = 1 (male)	Sex = 2 (female)
Rsquare	0.47	0.49
Root Mean Square Error	1.43	1.32
Mean of Response	2.06	1.85
N	693	189

Figure 10.2. Regression of 'A' level physics grades on average examination grades at age 16, with separate regression lines by sex.

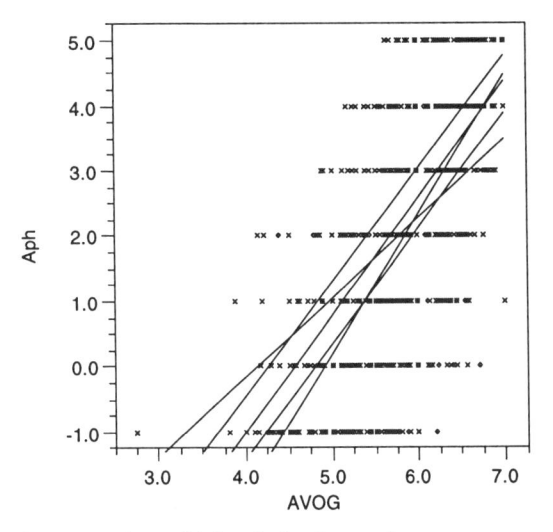

Indicator systems for schools: fire-fighting it is! 195

Figure 10.3. Regression of A-level physics grades on average examination grades at age 16 by examination board.

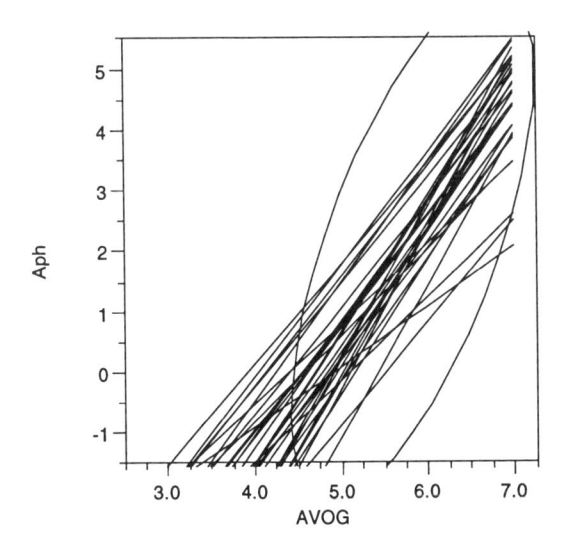

Variable	Mean	Std Dev	Correlation	Signif. Prob	N
AVOG	5.83	0.661	0.67	0.0000	665
Aph	2.09	1.950			

Figure 10.4. Regression of A-level physics grades on average examination grades at age 16 by school department.

The finding by Haertel *et al.* that the type of school is not an important factor in measures of student progress ('value added') was well illustrated by a study of independent (private) schools that were in receipt of special funds to take students out of state schools and educate them in the independent sector (Tymms, 1992b). He found that state comprehensive schools, the selected independent schools, colleges (somewhat like the US community colleges) and religious schools in the sample of 93 institutions showed few consistent differences in terms of value added. With larger datasets in subsequent years, it is increasingly clear that the type of institution is only weakly and inconsistently related to effectiveness.

Given all the data in the monitoring system for the particular subject, a predicted grade can be produced for each student based on the overall, pupil-level, simple regression line. If many students in a particular class actually achieved higher grades than predicted (positive residuals), this might be due to effective teaching. Thus the average residual for a class is about as fair an 'indicator' as can be produced. It is the best available because the average GCSE score (the GPA at age 16) is reasonably strongly correlated with subsequent achievement at age 18 (correlations from about 0.5 to 0.7 are common, varying from subject to subject).

Reservations regarding the use of multilevel modelling for a first-generation indicator system have been expressed elsewhere (Fitz-Gibbon, 1991). Here let it briefly be noted that the average residuals differ little if sample sizes are over 30, the multilevel modelling is less well accepted and understood than simple regression and the shrinkage can seem unfair if 100% data is used. These complete data can be seen as a population that simply needs to be described, not treated as a sample for inferential statistics. Recent work on the Value Added National Project has further substantiated the position that simple ordinary least squares measures are entirely adequate (Trower and Vincent, 1995; Tymms and Henderson, 1995).

The average residuals can be expected to vary from year to year and indeed they do. The question then arises as to how large an average residual has to be to merit praise (if the average residual is positive) or concern (if the average residual is negative.) The answer to this is that schools will know before the monitoring teams or statisticians will know. We can test for statistical significance and indicate the expected amount of variation from year to year due simply to sampling, but it will be those closest to the data who will arrive at a working knowledge of the substantive significance of the indicators.

One way to display the data is by using the format developed by W.A. Shewhart and adopted by W. Edwards Deming as a Statistical Process Control graph. (Figure 10.5) The indicator (in this case the average residual) is plotted from year to year, from left to right. There are symmetrical lines above and below the indicator which are the upper

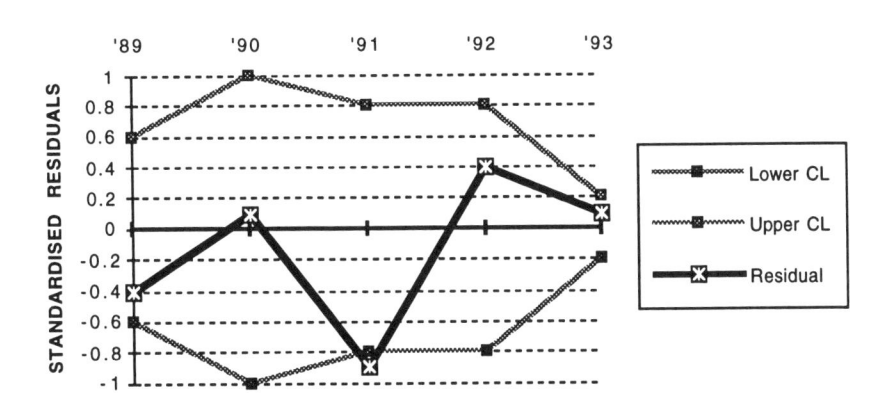

Indicator systems for schools: fire-fighting it is! 197

Statistical Control Chart: CHEMISTRY 1989–1993

[Chart showing standardised residuals from '89 to '93 with Lower CL, Upper CL, and Residual lines]

Figure 10.5. Shewart-style graph for monitoring school effectiveness.

and lower confidence limits. A residual is likely to vary between these limits, from year to year, simply due to the various samples of students who show up in the class each year. How wide these confidence limits are is determined by three factors:

- the variability of the individual results in the class (the more variation in the class the more the average can be expected to vary and therefore the wider the limits)
- how many students are in the class (the more students the less the averages will vary and therefore the narrower the limits)
- the level of 'confidence' chosen, arbitrarily.

This latter may seem unsatisfactory but that is the nature of statistics (see Carver, 1978). As already mentioned, practitioners will know before researchers what is substantively important. If, for example, the year 1991 in Figure 10.5 had been a year in which a teacher had been ill, a poorly qualified supply teacher had taken over and students had been very dissatisfied and did worse in chemistry than in their other subjects, then you may well feel that the limits were well chosen. In a year for which there was corroborating evidence of problems, the indicator had moved beyond the limits. If on another occasion you saw such an out-of-limit result even though you were not aware there had been anything wrong, you might want to investigate. Had the syllabus not been covered? Were the students not taking an important complementary subject? Had the teacher or textbook changed?

This kind of retrospective diagnosis is an important way of learning from experience and developing hypotheses grounded in the data. To assist this process at the level of the individual student we provide, each year, a list of the students showing for each their prior achievement measure, predicted grade, actual grade and residual. Teachers and heads of departments study these lists and generate hypotheses as to what might explain them. Increasingly these data are provided on computer discs, in spreadsheets to facilitate further analyses.

The past and future of value-added systems

It should be noted that although the examination system has been in place in the UK for decades, and new examinations are being introduced for students of 7, 11 and 14 years, the growth of value-added systems has been largely a grass roots growth, led by schools and researchers more than imposed by local or the central government (Gray, 1981; Goldstein, 1984; Reynolds, 1985; Aitkin and Longford, 1986; McPherson and Willms 1987; Mortimore, Sammons and Ecob, 1988; Nuttall et al., 1989)

The interest in value added certainly increased when the government insisted on the publication of school performance tables (generally referred to as 'league tables') which show the percentages of students obtaining various examinations results (such as passes with grades A, B or C in 5 or more subjects). The revision of the inspection routines have also increased schools' interest in data. However, from the interactions with teachers and administrators at conferences, the rapid growth of the ALIS and, recently, YELLIS projects appears to be based also on a concern for every student as a vital part of professional motivation.

How can a national system meet this grass-roots need for a consideration of the progress made by every student, without being impractical and expensive? One possibility would be a sampling strategy followed by the provision of software that enabled the residuals to be calculated in the school. Each school could develop expertise in data management and exploration and would be able to track progress taking account of the national data. The access to national data is essential since only with an adequate sample can the different difficulties of various subjects be taken into account each year (Fitz-Gibbon and Vincent, 1994) and fair comparisons made.

Another way forward for a national system could be the inclusion of prior attainment measures with applications for the next stage of testing. The calculation of the regression lines could then take place as part of the examination feedback. Value-added measures would be delivered with examination results.

One benefit that might accrue from the provision of regular feedback on value added could be that such a system might attract and retain the kind of teachers who are motivated by achieving recognisable results and by feedback which reinforces intrinsic motivation. Teachers who attend to measured outcomes may be particularly effective – it is at least a hypothesis worth testing. Is this a personality variable that has been overlooked?

However, an important reservation must be that cognitive achievement must not be seen as the single criterion for good schooling. Other outcomes matter. We do not want to set up systems so fraught with anxiety and competition that these destroy the quality of life of teachers and students. We need, therefore, to include other indicators of the quality of schooling.

Affective and social outcomes of schooling

If we care about quality of life, we must measure it. Indicator systems give strong messages about what is considered worth the effort of measuring and this means that we should not restrict any indicator system solely to cognitive outcomes. We must also measure affective and social outcomes. How do we do this?

Unlike the achievement data, which will be available to the school, data on students' attitudes are not readily available. Whilst we may eventually move towards optical mark read systems and sampling as for cognitive outcomes, we are at present working directly with over 1000 schools to measure their students' attitudes. The simplest way is to use a questionnaire to students. Not, however, a mailed out or handed out questionnaire, but one specially administered in school with the aim of getting 100 per cent response rate. The conditions of administration must be such that students know that anonymity is guaranteed and are encouraged to take the questionnaire seriously. We have used various approaches to obtain good quality data. In the early years of the project the questionnaire was administered by the author using an audio tape to ensure the same instructions and explanations were used in each school. Then 'data collectors' were trained to take over and a network developed around the country. Examination conditions were set up with desks well separated and staff requested not to stay in the room or, if they did, not to go near the students. A letter was given to students in advance of the data collection to make it clear that their opinion was being seriously requested.

In recent years many schools and colleges have chosen to give the questionnaire themselves and in this case other precautions have to be introduced. A data collector from the university is informed of the timing of the administration and may drop in to monitor; students are provided with plastic envelopes in which to seal their completed questionnaires. These cannot be opened without destroying them. Finally, students are asked at the end of the questionnaire whether or not the conditions of administration were in accordance with the requirements as listed on the audio tape, such as having no staff near desks. We also give a phone number for students to contact us should they have any complaints or queries.

Having gone to some lengths to ensure quality in the data, how do we measure attitudes? With a variety of summated items for each of which there is a 5-point response scale. One set of six items measures response to each subject (e.g. 'I look forward to lessons in this subject') Another scale is composed of six items measuring attitude to the school (e.g. 'I would recommend others to take their A-levels here'). There is also a simple count of a number of extramural activities (sports, music, travel) to obtain a measure of participation in a variety of experiences, one aspect of 'quality of life' perhaps. In addition to these numerical indicators, students' responses to open-ended questionnaire items are typed up and mailed to head teachers (principals) without, of course, any reference to which students made the comments. These comments have sometimes had an impact more powerful than the numerical indicators.

Table 10.2. Correlations

	A-level physics grade	Average Ach .@16	SEX	Attitude to School	Attitude to physics	Residual physics
A-level physics grade	1.00	0.67	−0.05	0.15	0.33	0.74
Average Ach .@16	0.67	1.00	0.12	0.11	0.18	0.02
SEX	−0.05	0.12	1.00	0.06	−0.06	−0.17
Attitude to school	0.15	0.11	0.06	1.00	0.32	0.09
Attitude to physics	0.33	0.18	−0.06	0.32	1.00	0.28
Residual physics	0.74	0.02	−0.17	0.09	0.28	1.00

An important affective outcome is students' intentions regarding further study, a measure of academic aspirations. The summated scale measuring their 'likelihood of staying in education' is regressed against prior achievement so that under-aspiring groups can be identified.

All these measures and more are tabulated or graphed and then fed back to schools in individual booklets for each department. This provision of department-based feedback enables the school management to allow the system to be confidential in the early years of participation – for indicator systems can appear very threatening until people discover that datasets are not nearly so dramatic nor so stark as rumours. The confidentiality of schools is maintained by the use of code names chosen by each school. All schools see all the data. Each school knows only its own codename.

Alternatives or supplements to indicator systems

Quantitative monitoring is a *sine qua non* but it is not sufficient. Compliance monitoring, unannounced visits, checks on the validity of the data collection procedures, should also be implemented. To pick up unanticipated effects requires that independent observers visit schools.

Indicator systems for schools: fire-fighting it is!

How often, at what cost and whether or not they are called 'inspectors' are difficult questions. In short, a variety of procedures need to be adopted to maintain quality and provide feedback. Their acceptability will depend upon the use to which the information is put.

There are some methods which are already popular, which is not to say that they are effective. Let us consider three such methods: mutual inspections, expert inspections, and market forces.

Mutual inspections

Can schools 'inspect' or 'evaluate' each other? A team of 'inspectors' can be created with representatives from several schools for the inspection of a particular school. Then new teams can be formed for the inspection of schools of the erstwhile 'inspectors'. Private schools seem to favour mutual evaluation. It sounds good – evaluation by those actually doing the job, by those who understand. Alas, there are problems with such arrangements. Here is what one participant in a mutual inspection/accreditation visit had to say:

> Experience over six years of serving on (an accreditation scheme) has demonstrated that the process lacks the rigour necessary to provide schools with constructive criticism. There are no objective criteria in the...process, and its value is vitiated by the reluctance of peers to expose themselves to reprisal. (Mitchell, 1990)

The accreditation visitors suffer both from fear of reprisals and from the fact that they are simply pulled away from a demanding job. To fail a school would be to create considerable amounts of work for themselves, on appeals and recommendations.

> Perhaps the most damning feature of peer teams is that they visit each others' schools. Horse-trading is a constant hidden agenda. You find, after the fact, that punches were pulled at this or that school because the principal is to visit the team chair's school next year. At a particularly poor school, a superintendent refused to go along with my desire to withdraw accreditation because she said: 'I'm not here to deal with the problems of this district.' (Mitchell, 1990, p. 78)

Inspections by experts

In the UK we have recently had visited upon us a very expensive system of inspections commissioned from the newly created Office for Standards in Education (OFSTED). An inspection involves pre-announced visits lasting about a week. Inspectors sit in lessons, interview, examine documents and then write a report. Some of the reports have designated schools as 'Failing' without any adequate numerical data on effectiveness. There has been no evidence provided by the inspectorate of its own reliability, validity or impact, let alone value for money. An inspection is not qualitative research – it is too intrusive, disturbing, short term, unsophisticated and amateurish. Inspection as represented by OFSTED may be simply an anachronistic remnant of old English power structures. A more democratic and sophisticated approach has been adopted by the agency which inspects colleges. The Further Education Funding Council (for colleges) has published a slim volume about its approaches (FEFC, 1993) with many references to a developing system, a dialogue between assessors and assessed, an encouragement to have quantitative performance indicators and the intention to have a member of staff from the college with the inspectors at all times.

Market forces

The Conservative government in the UK (1979–97) believed in the value of privatisation – of schools as well as other necessities of life such as water, health care, and electricity. This led to some policies which have been widely welcomed: the 'local management of schools' legislation required school districts to devolve more than 80 per cent of their budgets to schools, according to a public formula which is driven largely by student numbers. This policy has introduced considerable competition between schools for students. The intensity of the competition depends upon accidents of bus routes and distances. In some areas it is alleged that the competition lies not in parents choosing schools but in schools choosing parents and their offspring. Studies of the impact of these competitive policies are in progress and the outcomes must be awaited (Woods, 1992; Black 1994).

Future developments

The Value Added National Project

Given the UK commitment to testing at least three curriculum areas (English, mathematics and science) at the ages 7,11, and 14, along with the curriculum-embedded, authentic examinations at ages 16 and 18, there will be a framework of data on which to build value-added systems. We have the contract to undertake the statistical trialling and conduct a pilot for a national value added system. As of July 1997, schools were being consulted and a national system should soon be in place. In particular we are charged with creating something which is both statistically valid and readily understandable by parents, school governors and the general public. Given correlations of 0.9 between residuals based on multilevel models and ordinary least squares (OLS) regression, it seems likely that the simple 'readily understandable' OLS methods can be used for initial feedback. A second stage of exploratory data analysis before anything is published would seem to be desirable.

Conclusions

Is it possible to evaluate schools? Yes, to a degree. If you are willing to attribute to schools some degree of responsibility for their residuals (measures of relative pupil progress) then numerical measures can be developed within a framework of fair, curriculum-embedded examinations.

Should the motivational and personality measures that have figured so prominently in educational psychology play a role? It is difficult to say. The data we are seeing in monitoring systems is dominated by system-effects: prior achievement explains about 50 per cent of the outcome variation at the pupil level. Other variables add little to the prediction of cognitive outcomes and the time constraints and 'fakeablity' to which Mitchell (1992) alluded are important in working systems that must make the data collection procedures in schools as painless as possible.

The issues that dominate indicator systems are affected by both the data and by political agenda. For example, there will be pressure to produce whole-school indicators although the evidence is that the major source of variation is what happens in departments or classrooms, not the organisational or structural features of schools. Given this situation, whole school indicators are not useful.

The rich, longitudinal data that Professor Child called for in his inaugural address will begin to come on stream as the monitoring projects bed down and are extended. Meanwhile Gene Glass's conclusion that the best way forward may simply be 'fire-fighting' may be well supported.

References

Aitkin, M. and Longford, N. (1986) Statistical modelling issues in school effectiveness studies. Journal of the Royal Statistical Society. Series A, 149(1), 1–43.

Black, P.J. (1994) Performance assessment and accountability: the experience in England and Wales. Educational Evaluation and Policy Analysis, 16(2), 191–203.

Carver, R.P. (1978) The case against statistical significance testing. Harvard Educational Review, 48(3), 378–99.

Cattell, R.B. and Butcher, H.J. (1968) The Prediction of Achievement and Creativity (Indianapolis: Bobbs-Merrill).

Cattell, R.B., Sealy, A.P., and Sweney, A.B. (1966) What can personality and motivation source trait measurement add to the prediction of school achievement? British Journal of Educational Psychology, 36, 280–95.

Fitz-Gibbon, C.T. (1985) A-level results in comprehensive schools: The Combse project, year 1. Oxford Review of Education, 11(1), 43–58

Fitz-Gibbon, C.T. (1991) Multilevel modelling in an indicator system, in Raudenbush, S. and Willms, J.D. (Eds), Schools, Pupils and Classrooms: International studies of schooling from a multilevel perspective (London: Academic Press), pp. 67–83.

Fitz-Gibbon, C.T. (1992) School effects at A-level: genesis of an information system, in Reynolds, D. and Cuttance, P. (Eds), School Effectiveness, Evaluation and Improvement (London: Cassell), pp. 96–120.

Fitz-Gibbon, C.T. (1993) Monitoring school effectiveness: simplicity and complexity. Paper presented at ESRC Seminar Series in School Effectiveness and School Improvement, Sheffield.

Fitz-Gibbon, C.T. (1996) Monitoring Education: Indicators, quality and effectiveness (Cassell: London).

Fitz-Gibbon, C.T. and Vincent, L. (1994) Candidates' Performance in Science and Mathematics at A-level (School Curriculum and Assessment Authority).

Further Education Funding Council (1993) Assessing achievement. Circular 93/28 (Coventry:FEFC).

Glass, G.V. (1979) Policy for the unpredictable (uncertainty research and policy). Educational Researcher, 8(9), 12–14.

Glendenning, A. (1974) Personality, motivation and ability measures as predictors of achievement. MSc thesis, University of Bradford.

Goldstein, H. (1984) The methodology of school comparisons. Oxford Review of Education, 10(1), 69–74.

Gray, J. (1981). School effectiveness research: key issues. Educational Research, 24(1), 49–54.

Gray, J., Jessan, D., Jones, B. (1986) The search for a fairer way of comparing schools' examination results. Research Papers in Education 1(2) pp 91–122.

Lavin, D.E. (1965) The Prediction of Academic Performance (Wiley: New York).

McPherson, A.F. and Willms, J.D.(1987) Equalisation and improvement: Some effects of comprehensive reorganisation in Scotland. Sociology, 21, 509–39.

Mitchell, J.V.J. (1992) Interrelationships and predictive efficacy for indices of intrinsic, extrinsic and self-assessed motivation for learning. Journal of Research and Development in Education, 25(3), 149–55.

Mitchell, R. (1990) Site visits in the accreditation process of the Western Association of Schools and Colleges (WASC). Evaluation and Research in Education, 4(2), 75–80.

Mortimore, P., Sammons, P. and Ecob, R.(1988) The effects of school membership on pupils' educational outcomes. Research Papers in Education, 3 (1), 3–26.

Nuttall, D.L., Goldstein, M., Prosser, R. and Rasbash, J. (1989) Differential school effectiveness international. Journal of Educational Research, 13(7), 769–76.

Reynolds, D. (1985) Studying School Effectiveness (Lewes: Falmer Press).

Trower, P. and Vincent, L. (1995). Secondary Technical Report: Value Added National Project London: SCAA.

Tymms, P.B. (1990) Can indicator systems improve the effectiveness of science and mathematics education? the case of the UK. Evaluation and Research in Education 4(2), 61–70.

Tymms, P.B. (1992a) Accountability – can it be fair? Oxford Review of Education, 19(3), 291–9.

Tymms, P.B. (1992b)The relative success of post 16 institutions in England (including assisted places schools). British Educational Research Journal, 18(2), 175–92.

Tymms, P.B. (1994) Theories, models and simulation: School effectiveness at an impasse. Paper presented to the ESRC School Effectiveness and School Improvement seminar: London.

Tymms, P.B. and Henderson, B. (1995) Primary Technical Report: Value Added National Project London: SCAA.

Waldrop, M.M. (1992) Complexity: The emerging science at the edge of order and chaos (London: Viking).

Walker, D.F. and Schaffarzick, J. (1974) Comparing curricula. Review of Educational Research, 44(1), 83–112.

Wang, M.C., Haertel, G.D. and Walberg, H.J. (1993) Toward a knowledge base for school learning, Review of Educational Research, 63(3), 249–94.

Woods, P. (1992) Responding to the Consumer. International Congress for School Effectiveness and Improvement, Victoria, Canada.

Part III
Some Aspects of Special Educational Needs

Thematic introduction and summary

DIANE SHORROCKS-TAYLOR

In the introduction to this book, it was emphasised that Dennis Child had close involvement with the deaf community and courses for teachers of the deaf. His work has therefore demonstrated some emphasis on children and adults with special needs in the context of education. One of the chapters in this section (by Stuart Simpson) deals explicitly with current issues in the education of the deaf, but it was felt that a wider perspective needed to be taken on special educational needs, not least since it is important to contextualise initiatives in one area against a background of more wide-ranging analyses. Given the importance of this whole topic of special needs in education, contributions were invited from specialists in several areas, most of which are of considerable current interest.

Chapter 11, by David Sugden, provides a general introduction to the topic of learning difficulties. He stresses the need for clarity about the precise nature and definition of any 'difficulty', (a task that is not always easy, given the subtlety of some of the problems), and the intervention implications of this. One of the most telling points in the chapter concerns generality versus specificity in deciding on an appropriate teaching intervention strategy. A wider consideration of teaching approaches and methods for a whole class or group may, of itself, bring about improvements in learning for those with special needs. This said, however, more specific teaching strategies may be called for with individual children.

He goes on to discuss in more detail the major approaches to teaching children with special needs, some of which have met with mixed success. This includes behavioural approaches, perhaps most strongly associated with Kevin Wheldall, one of the authors of Chapter 12. However, while acknowledging the positive contribution of behavioural approaches, Sugden emphasises more cognitively-based methods and perspectives in teaching. Echoing some of the work of Dennis Child, he suggests that three elements need to be considered in deciding upon a strategy: the task to be learned; the characteristics and experience the child brings to the situation; and the context in which the learning takes place. Interestingly, these are points that emerge (albeit in somewhat different guises) from several of the chapters in this sections, as well as other sections too.

Wheldall and Beaman's work has mostly been in applied behavioural approaches to classroom teaching, but Chapter 12 does not focus specifically on this theoretical framework. Instead, they consider more broadly the question of discipline in schools, against the current (international) interest and the suggestion made by the media that schools are close to anarchy and that discipline is breaking down. They rightly stress the need for informed debate on the matter as an antidote to the wilder statements often heard from outside. Classrooms are places where a wide range of individual experiences, understandings and needs are brought together, giving enormous scope for children (especially boys, according to the research) being uninvolved and off-task and therefore potentially disruptive. The perspective they finally present is that a proportion of pupils in classrooms may indeed be troublesome, but this disruptiveness seldom takes the form of extreme violence or rudeness. Instead, it is frequently about talking out of turn in class or non-concentration on work. This could undoubtedly influence the quality of the learning that takes place, but it is a far cry from the total disorder sometimes portrayed in the media.

Chapter 13, by Diane Montgomery, reminds us that the needs of pupils in schools must be considered in very broad terms, to include children with special abilities and talents that also need acknowledging and developing. The chapter begins with the issue of defining 'giftedness' (or the preferred term, 'high ability') and stressing the complex relationship between high ability (or specific talent) and achievement in educational terms. This reiterates the kinds of arguments made by Dennis Child about the influence of factors other than academic ability in educational achievement. She also addresses important issues in the assessment of high ability or talent, again relating to the content of the last section in this book.

Her conclusion is that we need to move beyond oversimplified testing and towards other approaches to the identification of special abilities that may have more educational validity. Her final section of analysis, covering possible strategies for educational provision for these pupils, bears considerable similarity to issues raised by David Sugden. This provides significant reassurance that the principles are similar even though the children being considered may be very different.

Sally Beveridge in Chapter 14 also requires us to take a broader-than-the-classroom perspective, focusing as it does on parents and their involvement in the education of their children. Her arguments are applicable to mainstream schooling as well as to parental involvement

Thematic introduction and summary

when children have special educational needs. She rightly points out that there have been political as well as educational imperatives in the present emphasis on parental involvement, but whatever the origins, the outcome is to be welcomed given the strong evidence that children's progress is enhanced when parents and teachers work together. One of the major sections of the chapter deals with the ways in which parents are included in the new Code of Practice (1994) procedures, alongside children who have their own role and rights in the process. She finishes with an eye to the future and suggests that the focus should be on helping parents to participate in a better-informed way in their dealings with schools and the other agencies involved.

Another topic that is at the forefront of public interest is that of bullying, both at school and at work. The focus of Chapter 15 by Barbara Maines and George Robinson is on bullying in school, which includes an outline of their own approach to intervention as well as outlining others. At the beginning of the analysis, they point out that it is only recently that educational psychologists have emerged from being users of tests and assessments to being more fully involved in trying to solve some wider problems arising in schools, such as bullying. They begin by explaining bullying as sustained acts of aggression over time, involving a complex relationship between the bully, the victim and the 'onlookers'. The 'onlookers' are significant in the process since they have the choice to either intervene or, in effect, collude in the aggression being directed towards the victim.

Many schools and LEAs have begun to take the problem very seriously, seeking and implementing whole-school policies in an attempt to remedy the situation. Most of these initiatives emphasise understanding the complex processes involved and avoiding 'labelling' of those involved. Their own 'no blame' approach deals with bullying through teacher discussion with both bully and victim, as well as wider group (pupil) discussion, with the final responsibility for a solution handed over to the pupils themselves. They also stress the importance of the involvement of parents in the process.

Finally, Chapter 16, by Stuart Simpson, brings us full circle to the direct research and teaching interests of Dennis Child, presenting as it does an overview of current issues in the education of the deaf. It is salutary to be reminded that there are over 50 000 sign-language users in Britain and 8.4 million of us with hearing problems of some kind. He provides us with an historical account of the controversy in deaf education between those advocating 'oralism' (the learning of speech and lip-reading) on the grounds of better integration of the deaf into the wider community and those advocating 'total communication' (i.e. using a wide range of communication, including sign language and sign-supported English) since this is seen as the more natural form of communication for the deaf.

It is also interesting to note that current advances in technology (hearing aids, for example) have made it increasingly possible to exploit even small amounts of residual hearing for those who have it, and that the possibility of earlier diagnosis of deafness in young infants helps in their overall development process and education. The process of integrating hearing-impaired pupils into mainstream classrooms or linked units has advanced well in recent years and a focus of future development is on training yet more users of sign-language (a full and distinct language in its own right) so that even wider integration may become possible.

In conclusion, the chapters in this section by no means address all aspects of special educational needs, nor indeed many of the most significant problem and issues. What they do, however, is give a general set of frameworks in some key areas that in many ways complement some of the themes evident in Dennis Child's work.

Chapter 11
Helping children with learning difficulties

DAVID SUGDEN

Many children in our schools evidence some form of learning difficulty. This difficulty may be of a temporary nature, due to some unforeseen circumstance in the child's life, or it may be more pervasive, with long term consequences. If a difficulty is identified, it usually goes beyond the type of difficulty experienced by all children, such as they cannot work out a particular maths problem, they cannot read some difficult word, they cannot understand a particular exercise, etc. The difficulty is more serious than these short term problems, and the range of difficulties is usually presented as mild, moderate, severe or profound and multiple. As one would expect with labels of this kind, the boundaries between them are less than clear, and variations will exist between organisations such as schools and local education authorities. Indeed this variation also extends to differences within and between professionals such as teachers and educational psychologists.

When a child has been identified as having a learning difficulty, what is the exact nature of that difficulty? Is the difficulty of not learning 'enough' in that he or she does not retain information? Is it that the child does not learn fast enough and requires a longer time in which to acquire information? Is it that the child does not reach the appropriate level or standard in a particular area? It could be that the child's difficulties are more subtle in nature in that he or she can learn specific skills and pieces of information but is totally lost when asked to use this newly acquired skill or information in a new situation. These are the characteristics of some children which teachers and parents see every day. Again, many individuals have difficulties with generalisation or transfer, but when it becomes a regular feature of a child's functioning, then the child can be said to have a learning difficulty.

Another dimension to the learning difficulty concept is the general or specific nature of the problem. When a child shows a pervasive difficulty in a particular area, is this difficulty expected, and in line with other attributes of the child, or is it unexpected and appears out of line with the child's potential? For example, a child may be fine when using language, giving verbal answers to verbal questions, or be quite socially adept. But when literacy is involved, such as reading or placing ideas on paper, some children have tremendous problems. When this occurs and the child's literacy difficulties do not tally with other abilities, he or she is said to have a specific learning difficulty. If the child also shows certain idiosyncratic ways of processing and producing information in the literacy area, this specific learning difficulty is often called *dyslexia*.

Our approaches to intervention provide similar questions and dilemmas. Many decisions involve whether it is better to concentrate on individual pupils making specific plans for their individual needs, or whether an approach which improves all teaching across the full range of children without singling out any particular group is the way forward. The traditional approach is the former; the latter is part of the ideology of some proponents of inclusive education with ideas which are stimulating and provocative. Inclusive education goes beyond integration in that integration is catering in mainstream schools for children who were previously in special schools; inclusive education however, starts from first principles, one of which is that all children are included and the school is designed around this full ability range. Inclusive education overlaps with effective schooling and while providing a goal to aim for, has unclear boundaries and presents paradoxes in both theoretical and practical perspectives. (Clark, Dyson and Millward, 1995; Sugden, 1996).

For the moment, it does appear that individual approaches are more commonplace and particularly with recent legislation and the introduction of the Code of Practice (DfE, 1994a), they are what teachers will address. Individual approaches do not mean that children are taught individually; it simply means that plans and strategies for their curriculum and teaching are developed for the individual, and implemented normally in a mainstream classroom setting which may include support at various times. The first step in any plan is to identify accurately and assess the child's difficulties as early as possible (Chazan, Laing and Davies, 1991) to lead smoothly into the intervention process.

Identification and assessment

When we consider the process of identification and assessment we are faced with a number of issues, which cover legal, ideological, psychological and educational fields. The legal aspects involve the details of various education acts which have a direct bearing on the identification of learning difficulties (Education Act, 1981; 1988; 1993). Following the Warnock Report (DES, 1978), the Education Act of 1981 abolished categories of 'handicap' and replaced them with the concept of special educational need (SEN), which exists if a child has *learning difficulty* which calls for special education provision to be made. A learning difficulty is then defined in terms of:

(a) a significantly greater difficulty in learning than the majority of children of their age, or
(b) a disability which either prevents or hinders them from making use of educational facilities of the kind generally provided in schools within the area of the local education authority concerned, for children of their age, or
(c) a child under 5 years of age who is or would be, if special educational provision were not made for him or her, likely to fall within points (a) or (b) when over that age.

Thus children are described not in terms of their handicap or what they cannot do but in terms of their educational need. Special educational needs is a continuum of need which is serviced by a continuum of provision. An important estimation by Warnock (DES, 1978), and one which has had great influence, is that one child in six at one time, and one child in five at some time during schooling, would require special educational provision. This has had important implications for the concept of integration as special schools catered for children with particular difficulties but only around 2 per cent of children were educated in these schools. Thus if around 20 per cent of children required some form of special schooling, 18 per cent of these would be in mainstream schools.

The focus in this chapter is not the full range of children with special educational needs who technically could all be classed as having learning difficulties, but those children who have learning difficulties in the traditional sense that involves cognitive limitations or impairments, or lack of experience and these have a direct effect upon their learning. It does not include those children who have a learning difficulty because of a sensory impairment (blind or deaf), because of a physical disability, or because they have emotional or behavioural difficulties.

The 1988 Education Reform Act had important implications for children with learning difficulties, which were indirect in the form of local management of schools and the National Curriculum. Local management of schools had, and continues to have, importance for who are admitted to which schools. Couple this with the entitlement of all children to the National Curriculum, the advent of school 'league tables' and it is easy to see how the ethos and nature of a school can be affected. Of more direct influence was the 1993 Act which restated the 1981 definition of learning difficulties, and from this Act came the Code of Practice which all schools now are asked to follow. The Code of Practice and the associated DfE (1994b) Circular (6/94) places particular emphasis on the role of the SEN co-ordinator and on school issues which need to be addressed to provide effective whole school approaches to meeting special educational needs in mainstream school. The Code of Practice identifies a number of fundamental features and principles:

- it requires pupils to be identified and assessed through cooperation between schools, agencies and parents
- it recognizes that there is a continuum of special educational need which is reflected in a continuum of provision
- children with special educational needs require a broad and balanced curriculum including the National Curriculum
- parents' wishes are of the highest importance
- pre-school children may have special educational needs which require the intervention of LEAs and Health Services.

A major part of the Code of Practice is concerned with assessment and identification which is conducted through five stages, of which the first three are school based. At stages 4 and 5 the LEA share responsibility with the school.

School-based stages are seen as a continuous and systematic cycle of planning, action and review which the school puts into operation to cater for the child's needs. It is a gradual extension of good practice, systematically introducing expertise when required.

- *Stage 1.* involves examining the child's work in the normal school environment, and the class or subject teacher providing additional help, such as differentiated materials in the classroom.
- *Stage 2.* A decision to intervene at stage 2 level is made after a stage 1 review or if parents, teacher or other professionals feel intensive action is necessary. The lead role for stage 2 is taken by the school's special needs coordinator who gathers all the available information from the school, parents and other agencies such as health service professionals. This information is then used to draw up an *Individual Educational Plan (IEP)* for the child. This plan is a formal document which builds upon the existing curriculum and should make use of the materials, resources already available to the teachers so that it can be implemented in the normal classroom. As at all levels, the pupil is reviewed.
- *Stage 3.* At stage 3, the SEN coordinator again takes the lead role. At this stage expert advice or help from outside agencies is brought in to give specialist input to the IEP (educational psychologists, speech, physio- and occupational therapists). Targets for the plan are set and the SEN coordinator convenes a review and if the child's progress is not satisfactory then the child should be considered for *statutory assessments.*
- *Stage 4.* The needs of most children will be met under the three school-based stages but for a small minority of children the LEA will need to make a statutory assessment of special educational need. The statutory assessment procedure involves professionals from a variety

of disciplines assessing the child and providing information. The LEA uses the above information to decide whether a *statement* (*see Stage 5*) of special educational need will be made.
- *Stage 5.* The statement is Stage 5 of the five stages of assessment and provision as laid down by the Code of Practice. It is usually the culmination of attempts at other stages to manage the child's difficulties and needs. Previously the statement was the only formal way for a child to obtain specialist help for his or her needs.

All of these stages are seen as progressive in nature and interact with the teaching approaches being employed. They are seen as a framework from which teachers and other professionals can draw upon to link identification, assessment and teaching methods. It is a system involving a gradual addition of help and expertise starting with minor modifications to teaching and organisation in classrooms through to major changes occasionally involving specialist techniques. From stage two onwards individual educational plans are made for the children and bodies of literature have emerged in the last two years which are aimed at supporting teachers to make and carry out these IEPs.

Teaching children with learning difficulties

Over the past 30–40 years a number of individual approaches have been proposed as panaceas for children's learning difficulties. Many of them have their backgrounds firmly based in psychology while others are more eclectic in nature drawing upon a number of disciplines and classroom practice. It is possible to compile lists of such approaches, but a more useful and appropriate method is to examine them in groups by relating these broad groups to a series of questions:

- Where did the methods come from?
- What is their rationale?
- What do the programmes emphasise?
- What do the programmes look like?
- How effective are they?

I will outline four such 'approaches' while recognising that hybrids and alternatives are available. Three of the four stem from the discipline of psychology – those from the psychometric, behaviourist and cognitive camps. The fourth is strictly eclectic and is driven by practices in the classroom.

Ability training

Historically, the first approach has been called *ability training* (Ysseldyke, 1973; Ainscow and Tweddle, 1979) or *diagnostic–prescriptive* and was popular in the 1960s and early 1970s. It is based on the principle derived from factor analytic studies that there are a number of 'abilities' present in children and these abilities indicate a predisposition to perform a number of tasks. Thus from statistical analysis of reading, abilities may include visual discrimination, visual memory, perceptual motor tracking and so on. Activities representing these abilities would then be taught to the children with the hope that this would improve reading. Abilities are seen as the underlying components of a given set of tasks so that if these abilities are acquired they will improve a wide range of tasks thus enabling the child to transfer or generalise, activities which are thought to be particularly problematic for children with learning difficulties. Early behaviourists in this country were particularly critical of this approach with authors such Ainscow and Tweddle (1979) dismissing it with words such as:

> there is no theoretical or experimental justification for including objectives which are intended to train supposed psychological abilities (pp. 129–30).

Ainscow and Tweddle at that time were promoting behaviourist approaches to intervention and it is interesting to note that Ainscow is now dismissing all individual approaches as being less than productive (Ainscow, 1993).

The evidence we have from meta-analysis is pretty ambivalent. Kavale and Forness (1985) report on investigations into perceptual motor programmes which represent a wide assortment of techniques aimed at improving abilities necessary for both perceptual-motor functioning and academic achievement. They examined 180 experiments representing 13 000 subjects and 637 effect sizes. Overall the mean effect size was 0.082, which represents virtually no effect, and as 48 per cent of the effect sizes were negative, the probability of obtaining any positive response as a result of training was only slightly better than chance. In short, there is nothing to indicate effective intervention. With psycholinguistic training, better results have been obtained with an examination of 240 studies yielding an overall effect size of 0.39 from an average of 50 hours of psycholinguistic training. Put another way, the average subject receiving such a programme would move to the 65th percentile while the ones who did not receive the training would remain at the 50th percentile. Although some success was obtained, these methods are now rarely used as approaches to intervention, because they are difficult to use with the National Curriculum, and are at odds with the more competency-based world. Some of the activities that they involve are employed in so-called reading readiness schemes. As in many areas of education, special education tends to flow from one extreme to the other and approaches based on individual behavioural methods began to take over in the 1980s and are still currently prominent in many curriculum areas.

Behavioural approach

Behavioural approaches became hugely popular and successful giving rise to a number of specific intervention techniques as well as general approaches, and a whole issue of the monograph series of the *British Journal of Educational Psychology* was devoted to its influence (Fontana, 1984). For a contemporary view of this topic, see the chapter in this book by Wheldall and Beaman (pp. 230–43). There is, however, still some confusion as to what actually constitutes the essence of behavioural approaches and this confusion is heightened by the discrepancy between theoretical concepts and practical applications. In their purest forms, principles upon which approaches are based include

- a concern with the observable
- behaviour is learned
- learning is a change in behaviour
- learning is governed by the antecedents and consequences of the behaviour. (Wheldall and Merrett,1984)

During the late 1970s and throughout the 1980s behavioural approaches provided a structure and optimism that were of immense benefit to teachers. The methods derived from these principles included the use of behavioural objectives, a specific form of task analysis, precision teaching, direct instruction and an analysis of the context in which learning takes place. Most of these involve a great deal of prescription, thereby placing the teacher in a position to structure and organise the learning of the children. It is an optimistic approach placing the emphasis clearly in the teacher's hands; no longer was it justifiable to note that the child could not read because he or she had undifferentiated brain damage; the child could not read because he or she did not have the prerequisites for reading, and to acquire these the task is to be broken down in a linear fashion, and the child taken forward in small steps. The use of objectives was the cornerstone of the approach; objectives are concerned with prescribed outcomes for the learner as opposed to what the teacher intends to teach. A typical objective would note 'following a period of instruction the child will...to a certain standard...under certain conditions'. The learner is then moved towards these outcomes in a series of small observable and measurable steps. In one sense all curriculum sequence involves identifying elements in the teaching process, but in behavioural approaches it uses behavioural definitions of the learning outcome as the elements (Norwich,1990).

Task analysis using behavioural objectives involved simplifying the task by slicing it up into smaller related component parts. Often this was done in a sequential manner such as in forward and backward chaining, fading, shaping and error discriminant analysis (Ainscow and Tweddle, 1984). At other times it was simply sliced into more manageable parts with no particular order inherent in the process. Precision teaching became a further development in this ideological stance (Raybould,1984). Precision teaching was in fact a misnomer as it was a method of recording rather than a method of teaching. It involved the child being assessed usually in criterion-referenced terms followed by a series of short term objectives which specified pupil performance in observable measurable terms. These objectives were tested daily by the use of 'probes' and progress was recorded and charted in a detailed and methodical manner. The teaching arrangements were recorded in relation to the pupil's performance. Progress was sequential and the child was more globally assessed at regular intervals; the programme was evaluated and changes made if deemed necessary. A final out come of behavioural approaches came in the form of direct instruction (Engleman and Carnine, 1982). This was a total teaching method involving setting of objectives, task analysis, direct teaching of these objectives, strategies for teaching, strategies for reducing and correcting errors and has resulted in a number of teaching packages aimed at reading and mathematics. It has also been the subject of in-depth evaluations in which favourable outcomes have been recorded when compared to other approaches to teaching children with difficulties, although it should be noted that the variance within a particular method or approach to teaching often exceeded the variance between methods (Abt Associates, 1977). All of these approaches have come from the original behaviourist principles, and in many cases they have been extremely successful in a number of school situations.

Although approaches based upon behavioural psychology have proved popular and influential, they are not without criticism. Sugden (1989) criticised this approach, noting that it is reductionist in nature, breaking down complex and subtle skills and information into rather crude observable approximations. In addition, it does not take into account the cognitive processes of the child and it views the child as a passive recipient of environmental information rather than an active seeker of the same. He also notes the difficulty in promoting generalisation using this approach. Norwich (1990) reports much antagonism towards behavioural approaches as emanating from the perception of it being overly mechanistic and prescriptive, with the teacher being viewed as a technician rather than as a skilled flexible professional able to respond to the varied demands of individual children. This prescription also restricts the skills of teachers, as many of the packages on offer leave little for the creativity of the teacher (Engelman and Carnine,1982).

Norwich(1990) also reports that there have always been variations in the way that objectives have been used by various proponents. For example, Ainscow and Tweddle (1979) did not refer to behavioural psychology but for psychologists like Wheldall and Merrett (1984) and Solity and Bull (1987) this was a cornerstone of their work. In addition Ainscow and Tweddle changed in 1988 by recognising the limitations of the objectives noting their tendency to narrow the curriculum, isolating children, making teachers feel insecure about children achieving the objectives. As Norwich (1990) reports, Ainscow and Tweddle (1988) still kept objectives and yet used the same criticisms of objectives made by process professionals. As I shall elaborate later, an interesting twist is that now Ainscow believes that all individual approaches are less than effective in dealing with children's learning difficulties. Other supporters of behaviourist approaches have also modified their stance, although still within a behaviourist framework, calling their current position 'behavioural interactionist' (Wheldall and Glynn, 1989). The original behaviourists are changing and moving closer to involving the cognitive processes, learning styles and aptitudes of children, which possibly another revision of their stance will bring. If and when this happens the term behaviourist may be a misnomer.

Cognitive approach

Another approach to dealing with children's difficulties has been loosely called the cognitive approach. I say loosely because it is not like the behavioural approach in that a precise set of definitive characteristics can be identified, yet it does have a number of underlying characteristics. If behavioural objectives are the set programmed software of the education field, the cognitive approach is the fuzzy logic. In the cognitive approach there is an emphasis on means, not necessarily ends, with a constructivist view about knowledge and how it is attained; any sequencing comes as a result of the interplay of the child's resources and the nature of the task and not simply the latter. The child is seen as an active seeker of information and this activity is channeled into the appropriate curriculum material.

In a cognitive framework, an understanding of learning difficulties is best understood from an analysis of three interacting variables: the resources the child brings to the situation; the task to be performed; and the nature of the environment in which the learning takes place (Keogh and Sugden,1985; Dockrell and McShane, 1993; Beveridge,1996)(Figure 11.1).

From these interacting variables it is possible to analyse how the learning difficulty has come about and make preparations for some kind of intervention. I stress the interaction of these variables because they do substantially overlap and it is difficult to view them in isolation. Dockrell

                          Task to be learned

Resources of ←——————————————————→ Context in which
the child   learning takes place

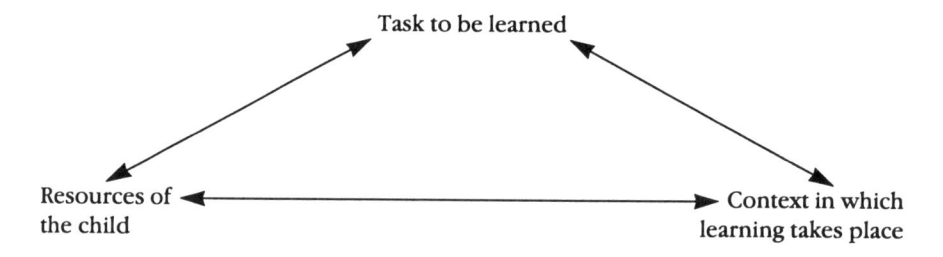

Figure 11.1. Interactive variables in the cognitive framework

and McShane (1993) describe an example of a child who comes to school and is unable to write her name. The possible reasons for this are multiple. First, the child may lack the experience with this kind of task; her experience at pre-school level did not provide her with the appropriate skills for the task. This of course blends into the resources of the child; at the present time she does not have the background to complete the task, but she may have the potential to do so given appropriate instruction, experience and modification of the task. Any assessment therefore examines the child's experiences and how she has been taught, and modifies the task accordingly. The popular way to do this is by task analysis, a method which is used by all professionals no matter what their underlying principles may be. However, a major difference between cognitive and behavioural approaches is that in the latter the task is analysed according to its structure and the child fits in at the appropriate level. In a more cognitive approach, I believe the term 'learning context analysis' is more appropriate as this emphasises the interactive nature of the process and it is not simply learning a task. Certainly, however, the simplification of the task to match the total resources of the child is an essential part of facilitating learning in children with learning difficulties. So the task can be simplified by breaking down into steps which are sequentially organised, by presenting the task in different ways, by asking a series of 'enabling/assisting questions' or by giving and fading out various means of support. This is much more in keeping with what teachers would call differentiation. In effect we are altering both the nature of the task and how the environment is structured. In this case the environment is the immediate teaching method such as options in presentation and in response to the pupil. Together with the modification of the task, it can be seen how the teacher is in direct control of two parts of the learning outcome cycle with an indirect influence on the third. The teacher now can modify the task according to the total resources of the child, not just level of learning; the learning context can be adjusted for the same, allowing the child access to that particular task, and this in turn increases the resources of the child. Then the cycle of this interactive teaching can start again.

Other approaches

A number of approaches have emerged from the general cognitive perspective, some from a pure information processing approach (Annett, 1989; Ashman and Conway, 1989) while others using more social interaction methods. The latter is usually attributed to the work of Vygotsky, and, using these theoretical underpinnings. Gallimore, Tharp and Rueda (1989) have proposed that through collaboration with more competent others, individuals with moderate learning difficulties can have their performance enhanced. Vygotsky argued that at certain stages in a child's development there is a need for assistance from a more capable other. As the child advances through this stage, the amount of assistance declines. This stage is the zone of proximal development and describes the difference of what a child can do with the help of a more capable other. Unassisted performance reflects the current level of development while assisted performance reflects the next stage to come. Gallimore *et al.* (1989) discuss these principles from their Kamehameha Early Education Project (Gallimore *et al.*,1982) which had as its goals the development of a reading programme that was effective, required few changes in normal school practices, and was in sympathy with the culture and language of native Hawaiian children. The programme involved a number of key features such as the teacher asking 'enabling' questions; the focus of instruction was an emphasis on comprehension for two thirds of a daily 2 hour language arts programme; the teacher's questions are not pre-planned but responsive to the children's contributions; the teachers are guided in their questioning by an explicit strategy which teaches children to weave together old and new information; and the sessions are fast paced. This was a difficult learning process for most teachers, and although in-service training was helpful, it took video recording of the sessions together with instruction in order for the skills to be learned. When the teachers were proficient in the approach, the results were very encouraging.

Other projects have used cognitive principles as the basis for their work. The Process Based Instruction classroom model (Ashman and Conway, 1989) is one such project and is based upon information processing models and utilising sophisticated problem solving strategies. Another is Instrumental Enrichment (Feuerstein, 1980) which is one of the original programmes and has probably inspired more offshoots than any other. Although these projects and programmes differ in kind, they are linked by fundamental principles which involve taking account of the cognitive processes of the child and are not merely programmes developed in isolation and driven by curriculum ideology.

If this model was expanded it would easily fit into a total ecological model of intervention originally proposed by Bronfenbrenner (1979), and contains a central microsystem which consists of school and classroom based approaches but moving outwards to an environment which contains family (see the chapter by Beveridge, pp. 264–79), friend and cultural expectations, support and influences. Once the child is in the classroom the teacher is faced with the situation as to how to structure the teaching (i.e. the context of learning) taking into account the nature of the task and the resources the child brings to the learning context. The detailed theoretical underpinnings from a cognitive approach have been ably described elsewhere (Ashman and Conway, 1989; Sugden, 1989; Dockrell and McShane;1993).

If we examine practical programmes from the three approaches it is not always easy to make direct comparisons because the overall goals are often different. For example, many behavioural programmes are specifically aimed at teaching specific skills and do not deviate from these aims, whereas both cognitive and ability training may have wider aims with generalisation being a major one. If we take comprehension of a story read out loud followed by answering questions as an activity that occurs in most pre- and primary schools, and we set as our goal the improvement of such skills, how would the approaches look in their purest forms? The ability approach would be to examine the underlying abilities and improve them, involving listening skills, discrimination of words, retention of words and phrases which could involve a certain amount of memory training; the hopeful effect of this would be to transfer to the story telling session those abilities which are thought necessary for story telling. A behavioural approach would involve lots of repetition of the story and of the questions with the story broken down into a number of sequential parts and each part taken as an entity until it was learned and then placed back into the overall story. A cognitive approach could involve a series of 'assisting' questions based on Vygotskian principles in which each subsequent question was based upon the answer given to the previous one. Most teachers would argue that they use all of these techniques, and that they are used flexibly according to the needs of the child. However, the efficacy of these individual approaches has been the source of some debate within professional communities (Vygotsky, 1978).

The three approaches I have briefly outlined, while differing in emphasis and principles leading to a variety of practices, do have some elements in common. First they are all discipline-based from theories in psychology. Secondly, they are all based on the premise that specific programmes aimed at individuals are the appropriate and most efficient methods of helping children with learning difficulties. However, there has been a recent change of direction emanating from unexpected sources, with the individual approach being questioned and all but ruled out in favour of an approach which works towards effective school for all. Ainscow (1993) who, as we have seen, has a long history of promoting individual approaches, has made the assertion

I have to say that during my career I have spent considerable time and energy attempting to find ways of teaching that will help special children to learn successfully...my conclusion is that the search for such specialised approaches tends to be a distraction... [and] framing our responses in this way tends to distract attention away from much more important questions relating to how schooling can be improved in order to help all children learn effectively (1993, p. 5).

Ainscow's premise is that an individualised perspective could work to the disadvantage of the pupils it is intended to help. He notes that the individualised approach heightens the impact of labels and could limit the expectations we have of certain children. Secondly, and related to the first, is the influence such approaches has in dividing schools into 'types' of children, and framing our response in this way tends to distract away from the main aim of providing effective education for all children. Thirdly, segregated forms of education which often accompany individualized approaches often have a narrow and restricted curriculum, and even a support teacher in a classroom can be seen as a barrier between the child being supported and the rest of the classroom. The resource issue is a further complication with difficulties in children being linked to resources and often an increase in difficulties identified and children being classified in order to obtain additional resources. Finally, individualised programmes maintain the status quo whereby the problem lies within the child and works against global school improvement initiatives. Ainscow maintains that by framing our responses to children with difficulties in this way leads to a situation where children are divided into types, the wider political, social and environmental contexts are not addressed and deflects attention from examining how schools can improve the learning capability of all pupils.

His answer to this is to take on this wider perspective and aim for effective schools for all by employing a curriculum perspective which defines educational difficulties not in terms of the child but in terms of the tasks, activities and classroom conditions. Shared experiences in the classroom such as considering the difficulties faced by some children in the class as a means of improving the learning situation for all children. This will lead to cyclic interactive process culminating in an ever-increasingly efficient provision for all children.

The overall school policy is the key to improvement for all and Ainscow lists the key conditions as including teachers sharing ideas and plans and helping one another in the classroom. It involves providing leadership and giving responsibility for this to a greater number of staff. It involves including students in the change process. Of great importance is the vision of the school by the head and senior colleagues of what the school should look like and how each colleague fits into this vision. Finally, Ainscow wishes to see more celebration of success with staff positively reinforcing each other's work and bringing some collective credit to the school.

These arguments, although persuasive, do not leave me totally convinced of the alternative proposals. It is true that labels still exist but it is impractical to see how provision for individual needs can be done without identifying some group. It is not the identification of the group that is the problem, it is how this identification is viewed. An analogy can be made with competition: it is not that competition is undesirable, but how the results of competition are evaluated. If losing is bad and winning is good, then competition by definition can do harm to more people than it can do good. Similarly with identifying individuals. If individual differences are accepted as the stuff of life without the qualitative evaluations placed upon them, then provision for individual needs should not have negative connotations. In addition it appears to be impractical and ideologically unsound to make a distinction between effective schools for all and individualised approaches. As Norwich (1993) notes in his response to Ainscow, improving schooling for all could depend upon improving schooling for some individuals as part of the overall plan for an effective school. I also believe that by portraying individual methods as placing the problem firmly in the child's camp, Ainscow is setting up straw men. A cognitive approach has long identified the difficulty as a transaction or dynamic interaction between relevant variables and these can include teaching method, the curriculum tasks, activities, the teachers helping each other and the larger organisational perspective (Sameroff and Chandler, 1975). One of our main aims is to take away the negative connotations associated with special/individualised programmes and provide children with the appropriate educational support whether that be at the individual, institutional or societal level. The effective schooling for all linking with appropriate individual programmes are not mutually exclusive approaches.

Concluding comments

Issues in special education tend to reflect those in general education, only heightened by the lack of time, resources, skill and expertise and the problems children with special educational needs bring to the school context. Therefore approaches to helping children with learning difficulties focus attention on issues which apply to education in general and which have been picked up as areas of particular interest.

A first issue is how direct the teaching needs to be in order to facilitate learning in children. This is particularly important for children who do not spontaneously generalise but is also of importance for all children. The wisdom we are receiving from special education is that the methodology depends greatly on the outcomes that are desired for the children. The more specific the outcomes the more direct the teaching appears to be a crude simplification of the situation, but it is not without foundation. If generalisation is not required then problem solving, process oriented teaching would not appear to be useful. A simple sight vocabulary of, say, 50 functional words might be best learned by direct teaching using behavioural methods involving objective, task analysis and daily monitoring. If however, an outcome involves investigation and learning how to learn, then direct forms of instruction would seem to be inappropriate. Carefully constructed assisted questioning or scaffolding of the kind advocated by the Vygotskian camp could be part of the solution.

Class versus group or individual instruction is linked with the direct/indirect issue and also with the issue of inclusion. It attacks the heart of what we mean by special educational needs. It could be asked what is special about special education and many would answer that it specifically addresses the needs of individuals by assessing accurately and providing teaching which is geared to these needs. It is has often been noted that it is not special needs we should be addressing but individual needs, and therefore all children should be educated according to these principles, not just a select group who we deem to be special. This could articulate with the saying that teaching in special education is an extension of good practice and not something which is distinct, different and highly technical. Of course it is true that some children, because of their needs, will require specialist techniques – conductive education, British Sign Language, sensory integration therapy – but for the vast majority of children with special needs an extension of good practice which might include more detailed assessment, differentiated materials, different modes of responding, instructions and demonstrations given more clearly, succinctly and possibly repeated, etc. is possibly what is required. The list goes on, but there is little in this list which should not be an expectation from teachers who are indulging in 'good practice'. So why is this not accepted and we reject totally the notion of special needs or indeed learning difficulties? In answering this the paradoxes start to appear. If we move towards more class teaching as the media and politicians encourage then the time required for this type of good teaching is lost. If we move towards individual programmes with extra resources in terms of time and personnel for some children we may be helping the children, but by tacitly separating these children and giving them extra resources, we are drifting away from a pure inclusive setting.

A personal view is one of graded responses to meet the needs of all children. I see no reason why all children, whatever their learning needs, should not be on the same school site. Once on this site children should be included as a right in all activities as far as possible. The ethos of the school is vital, with all understanding that differences are to be celebrated and value judgments about the person as a whole are not made on the ability to learn. The knowledge and principles we have from research on effective schools could be our starting point. Collaboration between appropriate professionals, parents and children is a reasonable expectation. Children with learning difficulties should be supported according to their needs; some will be able to be taught in mainstream classes as a group for much of the time; in this mainstream class they will receive help when required but should also be encouraged to work independently and with the rest of the class on group activities. The extra help they require may be of a non-specialist kind. As the learning needs of the child increase so support may need to be more often employed together with a greater degree of specialism, often resulting in the specialist psychologically derived programmes I have described. With some children much of their week may be with specialist help in a separate class, but the school ethos is that they are an integral part of the school, and should be working, mixing, learning, playing with their peers as much as possible. We are often presented with inclusion and integration issues as all-or-none affairs together with polarised teaching approaches when graded responses would be more appropriate.

References

Abt Associates (1977) Education as Experimentation: A planned variation model. Reports to the US Office of Education (Cambridge MA: Abt Associates).
Ainscow, M. (1993) Towards Effective Schools For All. Seminar Paper 2 Special educational needs policy options group (Stafford:NASEN).
Ainscow, M. and Tweddle, D. (1979) Preventing Classroom Failure (Chichester: Wiley).
Ainscow, M.and Tweddle, D. (1984) Early Learning Skills Analysis (Chichester: Wiley).
Ainscow, M. and Tweddle, D. (1988) Encouraging Classroom Success (London: David Fulton).
Annett, J. (1989) Training in Transferable Skills (Sheffield: The Training Agency).
Ashman, A.F. and Conway, R.N.F. (1989) Cognitive Strategies for Special Education (London: Routledge).
Beveridge, S.E. (1996) Spotlight on Special Educational Needs: Learning difficulties (Tamworth:NASEN).
Bronfenbrenner, U. (1979) The Ecology of Human Development: Experiments by nature and design (Cambridge, MA: Harvard University Press).
Chazan, M., Laing, A.F. and Davies, D.L. (1991) Helping 5 to 8-year-olds with Special Educational Needs. Theory and Practice in Education series, Child, D. (Ed.) (Oxford: Blackwell).
Clark, C., Dyson, A. and Millward, A. (1995) Towards Inclusive Schools? (London: David Fulton).
Department for Education (1994a) Code of Practice on the Identification and Assessment of Special Educational Needs (London: HMSO)
Department for Education (1994b) Circular Number 6/94: The organisation of special educational provision (London: DfE).

Department of Education and Science (1978) Special Educational Needs: The Warnock Report (London:HMSO).
Dockrell, J. and McShane, J. (1993). Children's Learning Difficulties (Oxford: Blackwell).
Education Act (1981) (London: HMSO).
Education Act (1988) (London: HMSO).
Education Act (1993) (London: HMSO).
Engleman, S. and Carnine, D.W. (1982) Theory of Instruction: Principles and practice (New York: Irvington).
Fontana, D (Ed.)(1984) Behaviourism and learning theory in education. Monograph Series No. 1, British Journal of Educational Psychology.
Feurstein, R. (1980) Instrumental Enrichment: An intervention programmes for cognitive modifiability (Baltimore, MD: University Park Press).
Gallimore, R., Tharp, R. and Rueda, R. (1989) The Social Context of Cognitive Functioning in the Lives of Mildly Handicapped Persons (Basingstoke: Falmer Press).
Gallimore, R., Tharp, R.G., Loat, K., Klein, T. and Troy, M.E. (1982) Analysis of reading achievement test results for the Kamehameha Early Education Project: 1972–1979, Technical Report No. 102 (Honolulu: Kamehameha Schools, Bishop Estate, Center for Development of Early Education).
Kavale, K.A. and Forness, S.R. (1985) The Science of Learning Disabilities (Windsor: NFER).
Keogh, J.F. and Sugden, D.A. (1985) Movement Skill Development (New York: Macmillan).
Norwich, B. (1990) Reappraising Special Needs Education (London: Cassell).
Norwich, B. (1993) Towards Effective Schools For All: A response. Seminar Paper 2. Special educational needs policy options group (Stafford: NASEN).
Raybould, T. (1984) Precision teaching, in Fontana, D. (Ed.) Behaviourism and learning theory in education, Monograph Series No. 1, British Journal of Educational Psychology, 43–75.
Sameroff, A.J. and Chandler, M.J. (1975) Reproductive risk and the continuum of caretaking casualty, in Horowitz, F.D. (Ed.) Review of Child Development Research, Vol 4 (Chicago, IL: University of Chicago Press).
Solity, J. and Bull, S. (1987) Special Needs: Bridging the curriculum gap (Milton Keynes: Open University Press).
Sugden, D.A. (1989) Special education and the learning process, in Sugden, D.A. (Ed.) Cognitive Approaches in Special Education (Basingstoke: Falmer).
Sugden, D.A. (1996) Moving towards inclusion in the United Kingdom? Thalamus. 15(2) pp. 4–22.
Vygotsky, L.S. (1978) Mind in society: the development of higher psychological processes, Cole, M. John-Steiner, V. Scribner, S. and Souberman, E. (Eds and trans.) (Cambridge, MA: Harvard University Press).
Wheldall, J. and Merrett, F. (1984) The behavioural approach to classroom management, in Fontana, D. (Ed.) Behaviourism and learning theory in education, Monograph Series No. 1, British Journal of Educational Psychology, 15–43.
Wheldall, K. and Glynn, E (1989) Effective Classroom Learning: A behavioural interactionist approach. (Oxford: Blackwell).
Ysseldyke, J.E. (1973) Diagnostic–prescriptive teaching: the search for aptitude treatment interactions, in Mann, L. and Sabatino, D.A. (Eds.) The First Review of Special Education (Philadelphia, PA: JSE Press).

Chapter 12
Disruptive classroom behaviour: separating fact from fantasy

KEVIN WHELDALL AND ROBYN BEAMAN

Preamble

Dennis Child, in his inaugural address on taking up his chair of educational psychology at the University of Leeds in 1981, commented:

> Against the trend of thinking in educational psychology at present, I happen to believe that the influence of Applied Behavioural Analysis (the new term for behaviour modification) will become substantial. The principles involved in designing software had their origins in behaviourism. But a second line of development is the treatment of disruptive children in normal classrooms, and I feel confident that any useful advice on this subject would be gratefully received by the teaching profession (Child, 1984).

Fifteen years on, one can see that Dennis's wise words were, indeed, prophetic, for not even those of us intimately involved in the behavioural movement in British education in those early days could have imagined the successes that were to follow. Dennis was, moreover, true to his convictions, featuring as time went on, in subsequent editions of his classic text, *Psychology and the Teacher*, coverage of behaviourally based research on effective classroom behaviour management including, for example, reference to Wheldall and Merrett's work on the Positive Teaching Project conducted from the Centre for Child Study at the University of Birmingham during the 1980s. It is, then, with particular affection and respect that we contribute this chapter on managing problem behaviours in the classroom to this volume honouring Dennis on his retirement and his substantial contributions to British educational psychology.

In this chapter we have chosen not to focus on behaviour management but instead to explore the issue of problematic classroom behaviour *per se*, drawing on an up to date review of the literature and our own extensive researches in this area, since the status of discipline in our schools is a topic frequently vented in public.

The debate about whether school discipline is breaking down, or worse, has already broken down, rages in the media with monotonous regularity. There are probably good reasons (apart from academic or pedagogic concerns) why this topic stimulates such public interest. First, when it comes to education and schooling, it seems that everyone is an expert since everyone has been to school and many may also have their children's school experience to draw on as well. The criterion for entering the public debate on discipline in school, then, is very easily satisfied. One only has to listen to talkback radio to have this view confirmed. As radio pundits frequently comment when discipline in schools is being discussed, 'the switchboard is running hot on this one ... it seems everyone has got an opinion'.

Moreover, discipline in schools seems to be one of those topics that regularly attracts the attention of politicians, particularly at election time. Somehow, aspiring education ministers are wont to argue, the perceived lack of effective discipline in schools is symptomatic of some greater, deeper social malaise; the existence of Western civilisation as we know it being under siege, as evidenced by the problems faced by teachers in classrooms. This is, of course, primarily portrayed as being the exclusive fault of the government of the day, regardless of their ideological orientation.

In interesting contradistinction to this very public debate about discipline in the classroom is the fact that classroom teaching has been described as 'the second most private act'. What takes place in classrooms is, by and large, the 'secret' of only those present. While everyone is an expert on discipline in schools, very few people can draw upon anything other than their own, subjective, experience. But in an area that captures public attention, our attitudes should be influenced by the realities of the situation, not by biased, selective or exaggerated reporting. Attitudes, whether ill informed or not, are powerful societal forces. Attitudes influence the voting preferences of electors. They determine who shall govern. It is of great importance then, that we as researchers attempt to inform the debate about matters such as school and classroom discipline with data with findings derived from objective empirical educational research. We have a responsibility to provide the evidence whereby rhetoric can be challenged or confirmed. Our aim here is, simply, to separate fact from fantasy and to attempt to determine the real state of affairs as regards the prevalence and forms of disruptive classroom behaviour typically experienced by teachers.

The need to manage classroom behaviour

It is now commonly agreed that effective teacher management of classroom behaviour is an essential prerequisite for effective classroom teaching and learning (Rosenshine, 1971; Brophy, 1985; Wheldall and Glynn, 1989). It is a necessary, but not, of course, sufficient condition for effective teaching and learning to take place. If the teacher is prevented from teaching, or students are prevented from getting on with their academic work, as a result of either their own inappropriate behaviour or that of others, then clearly little of educational value is likely to be achieved.

This is particularly true in inclusive classrooms where teachers are attempting to meet the diverse educational needs of students ranging widely in ability, including those with manifest disabilities and special needs. Teachers will struggle to provide effective instruction to such students if they are continually distracted from their central instructional function by the need to deal with the disruptive or inappropriate behaviour of other students. Moreover, those students who are particularly behaviourally troublesome or disruptive may be considered as having special education needs in their own right, since their own academic progress will be particularly seriously affected as well as that of their peers. The child whose behaviour is continually disruptive, or who is even quietly, but regularly, 'off-task' is seriously educationally disadvantaged, since academic engaged time is one of the most important correlates of academic progress.

Consequently, it is not surprising that the study of troublesome classroom behaviour has long been evident in the educational literature. From an historical perspective, enquiries into the behavioural profile of children in classrooms may be seen to have been largely focused on behaviour not problematic to the child, but problematic to the teacher. Wickman (1928a), for example, in his seminal study carried out in the United States, emphasised the distinction between problematic behaviours within the child *per se*, as against problematic behaviours within the classroom. Wickman asserted that the general pervading characteristic in the problems enumerated by the teachers in his study was that they represent 'disturbances' (Wickman, 1928a, p15).

> Behaviour problems, in the teachers' estimations, thus appear to be active disturbances that attack the standards of morality, obedience, orderliness, and agreeable social conduct. In the teachers' list there is a conspicuous paucity of items describing child problems which are indicative of social and emotional maladjustment but which are not directly disturbing to school routine (Wickman, 1928a, p. 15).

Wickman extended his work to a much larger sample and found once again that teachers' reactions to behaviour problems of children were determined in direct relation to the immediate effect on the teachers themselves (Wickman, 1928b, p. 37). While much of Wickman's terminology is now out of date and value laden, and his methodology may be open to question, his findings have been largely corroborated by subsequent research.

Ziv (1970), building on Wickman's earlier work, investigated the views of psychologists, teachers and children regarding troublesome classroom behaviour in Israeli schools. He found that children's views were largely in line with teachers' (rather than psychologists') views on what constitutes troublesome behaviour. Children's and teachers' rankings of behaviours from a 30 point list (based on Wickman's 50 item list) were highly correlated, in contrast to children's and psychologists' rankings (Ziv, 1970, p. 43). While Ziv found similarities between teachers and psychologists rankings (unlike the earlier findings of Wickman), he also noted some differences between the two groups when looking at the ten most serious problems selected. He hypothesised that while teachers 'consider what disturbs them within the classroom framework (pupil behaviour), the psychologists consider the "whole"' (Ziv, p. 45). This finding supports Wickman's earlier claim, perhaps rightly, that teachers are concerned by disturbances directly affecting them in the classroom. Walker *et al.* (1988) confirm such a view, stating that teachers as a rule are more likely to refer students (for behavioural assessment and intervention) who exhibit 'externalising behavior disorders' (such as aggressive behaviour, noncompliance, out of seat behaviour) (p. 9), while they under-refer (or do not refer) students with 'internalising behavior disorders' (such as shyness, timidity, withdrawn behaviour) (p. 9).

Our central concern here is precisely with these same aspects of student behaviour: teachers' perceptions of behaviour which they deem to be problematic or troublesome within the regular classroom. Consequently we will focus in turn on teachers' perceptions of the prevalence of troublesome students in their classes, the extent to which these perceptions of misbehaviour are mediated by student gender, and finally the types of behaviour teachers consider to be particularly troublesome. This will, we believe, help to inform classroom practice on managing student behaviour on a day-to-day basis, since we need to know the precise nature of the problems before we can attempt to offer solutions.

Prevalence of behaviourally troublesome students

Chazan and Jackson (1971, 1974) assessed the degree of behaviour problems of a large sample of children from a variety of socio-economic areas in England and Wales at the point of school entry, and again two years later. They suggest that 12–15% of young children exhibit behaviour difficulties in their first years of schooling (Chazan and Jackson, 1974, p. 35). Whitmore and Bax (1984), however, found that only 6% of students from inner city primary schools in London had 'disturbed' behaviour at school entry, rising to 7% by age 7–8 (p. 33). In contrast, McGee, Silva and Williams (1984) found in their study of 7 year olds in New Zealand, that about 30% of the sample of 951 children were identified by parent or teacher ratings as having a high level of reported problem behaviour, although a much smaller number of the children (5%) were identified by both the parent and the teacher as having problems (p. 257). Using an alternative definition, the authors considered that '12% of the sample (111 children of the sample of 951) had a significant behaviour problem in that it was long-term, having dated at least from school entry, and/or both parent and teacher agreed that the child showed problem behaviour' (p. 258). They refer to a range of findings from previous studies citing prevalence rates between 6 and 25%, arguing that, despite the variation, it would appear that a 'significant proportion of children suffer from behaviour problems during their early schooling' (McGee et al., 1984, p. 251–2).

Our own research has also addressed this issue. In a random sample of 198 primary teachers from within one representative local education authority in the UK, Wheldall and Merrett (1988) found that, on average, teachers perceived 16% of the students in their classes as being behaviourally troublesome (p. 17). Similar findings were reported in a study by Wheldall and Beaman (1994) which surveyed a representative sample of 161 teachers of primary aged students in New South Wales, Australia (p. 74). Teachers typically reported that they found 15% of students in their classes to be behaviourally troublesome.

Houghton, Wheldall and Merrett (1988) similarly reported the perceptions of a random sample of 251 British secondary teachers, finding that a higher average figure of 20% of students in the class were considered as behaviourally troublesome (p. 308); the same figure (20%) being found by Wheldall and Beaman (1994) when they asked the same question of 145 Australian secondary school teachers (p. 79). An unpublished study of 86 secondary teachers in Western Australia (Nicholls, Houghton and Bain, 1991) found that teachers, on average, indicated 13% of the class to be behaviourally troublesome; a somewhat lower figure. But, in a study of five high schools in a densely populated inner suburban area of Sydney, Australia carried out by Wheldall and Crawford (see Wheldall and Beaman, 1994), teachers reported that they considered, on average, that 31% of the class was troublesome.

Clearly, there is a range of conflicting data available concerning the prevalence of student behaviour problems in schools. McGee *et al.* (1984) make the valuable point that the variation in prevalence rates probably 'reflects differences in the ages of the children, differences in geographical location of the populations and varying techniques for identifying children with problems' (p. 251). Suffice it to say, the average classroom teacher could typically expect to find 2-9 students with some level of behaviour problem in a class of 30 students at any one time.

Gender differences

Chazan and Jackson (1971, 1974) found that boys in their sample presented more behaviour problems than girls, particularly in relation to 'restlessness' and 'aggression' (p. 46). This finding was supported by Hartley's (1979) study of sex differences in the classroom behaviour of infant class children which found that the classroom behaviour of boys was considered less favourably than that of girls by teachers and students alike (Hartley, p. 192). Confirming these findings, McGee et al. (1984) found that more boys than girls were identified at age 7 years as having a behaviour problem. As the authors confirm, this finding 'agrees with many other reports in the literature' (McGee et al., p. 257). Similarly, Stevenson, Richman and Graham (1985) found from a representative sample of 535 subjects that at age 8 there were significantly more boys with behavioural deviance than girls (p. 228).

The classroom behaviour literature also certainly supports such a finding, again including our own research in this area. Wheldall and Merrett (1984) indicated that boys were generally regarded as being more troublesome and disruptive than girls (p. 90) by their sample of British junior school teachers. In a further study of British primary school teachers, Wheldall and Merrett (1988) found that boys were regarded as the most troublesome, and the next most troublesome student in the class by three-quarters of primary teachers (p. 13). Similarly, Houghton et al.(1988) found that boys were selected 71% of the time by their British high school teachers as being the most behaviourally troublesome student in the class (p. 309). Wheldall and Crawford (see Wheldall and Beaman, 1994) found in their study of secondary teachers from inner suburban schools in Sydney, that a boy was cited as being the most troublesome student in the class in 84% of classes. For their broader Australian samples, which included both metropolitan and country teachers, Wheldall and Beaman (1994) found that 91% of primary teachers (p. 71) and 88% (p. 77) of secondary teachers selected a boy as the most troublesome student in the class.

Nichols et al. (1991) also found that 90% of Western Australian high school teachers considered a boy to be the most troublesome student in the class and when Fields (1986) requested 30 Australian primary teachers to select the most difficult student in the class for inclusion in his study on preventative management of behaviour problems, teachers selected a boy without exception (Fields, p. 55). Similarly, in another large study on discipline in South Australian primary schools, Johnson, Oswald and Adey (1993) reported that 80% of teachers considered that only a small minority of students were 'difficult to deal with...[but]... students identified as difficult to manage were usually males' (Johnson *et al.*, p. 301). Interestingly, Stuart (1994), in an Australian replication of Wickman's early research, found no gender differences in the data, noting, however, that 'it was still a fact that more boys than girls are referred to classes for the emotionally disturbed' (p. 227).

On this issue at least, then, the evidence is unequivocal: boys are consistently perceived as more behaviourally troublesome than girls, at both primary and secondary levels.

Types of classroom misbehaviours, their severity, and their frequency

Our own research also explored teachers' perceptions of the time they spent managing the behaviour of students in their classes, Merrett and Wheldall (1984) finding that 62% of their sample of 119 junior class teachers in the West Midlands in the UK considered that they spent 'more time than they ought' on matters of order and control (p. 89). In the same vein, Wheldall and Merrett (1988), from a random sample of 198 primary teachers, found that 51% of primary school teachers considered that they too spent more time on matters of order and control than they ought (p. 18). Wheldall and Beaman's (1994) Australian sample of 161 primary teachers confirmed the views expressed by their British colleagues, with 48% reporting that they too spend more time than they ought on managing classroom behaviour (p. 71).

The results of our research into *secondary* teachers' views on time spent on managing disruptive behaviour largely mirrors the primary teachers responses. Houghton et al. (1988) found that 55% of secondary teachers' considered that they spent more time than they ought on matters of order and control (p. 303). A very similar response (53%) is reported by Wheldall and Beaman (1994) for their Australian sample of 145 secondary school teachers (p. 75). Moreover, in a study of five high schools in a densely populated inner suburban area of Sydney, Australia carried out by Wheldall and Crawford in 1991 (see Wheldall and Beaman, 1994), a high 76% of the 212 teachers included in the study reported that they spent more time on matters of classroom order than they ought.

In contrast to the amount of time spent on managing classroom behaviour, Merrett and Wheldall (1984) found a consensus of opinion among teachers that the most common and the most troublesome classroom behaviours were relatively trivial (p. 90), a finding which was subsequently to be consistently replicated. These findings contrasted sharply with the information presented by the National Association of

Schoolmasters/ Union of Women Teachers in the UK in their pamphlet entitled *Pupil violence and serious disorder in schools*, which claimed on the basis of a sample of 3910 teachers that, 'more than four out of five respondents said the problems of pupil violence and serious disruption had grown worse over the last decade' (NAS/UWT, 1986, p. 3). (It should be noted, however, that their questionnaire return rate was less than 5% and was thus likely to be a somewhat biased sample.) Interestingly, Lawrence and Steed (1986) found that of 53 head teachers surveyed in their study, 60% believed that the onset of disruptive behaviour had changed significantly over the previous 10-year period, and was occurring earlier (62%), although media impact on teachers' attitudes over this time period should be taken into account when considering such findings.

Rather, in the Merrett and Wheldall study (1984) teachers identified 'talking out of turn'(TOOT), 'disturbing others' and 'non-attending and disobedi-ence' as the 'chief irritants' (Merrett and Wheldall, 1984, p. 90). Similarly, Wheldall and Merrett (1988), from a random sample of 198 primary teachers (93% response rate), confirmed that 'talking out of turn' (reported by 47% of teachers) and 'hindering other children' (reported by 25% of teachers) were considered as the most troublesome behaviours in their classrooms (p. 13). Very similar findings were obtained for the most frequent troublesome behaviour and even for the most troublesome behaviours of the most troublesome individual student in the class (Wheldall and Merrett, 1988, p. 13).

In a similar study of a random sample of 251 secondary teachers in the UK, Houghton *et al.* (1988) found that 'talking out of turn' was once again the most troublesome (50%) and the most frequent (49%) misbehaviour of the class as a whole, and of the most difficult individual student in the class (48%) (pp. 297, 305–7). McNamara (1985, 1987) also addressed the problem of inappropriate and disruptive behaviours as perceived by 200 British secondary school teachers using a variant of the original questionnaire employed by Merrett and Wheldall (1984). 'Inappropriate talking' was rated as the most disruptive behaviour by most teachers, followed by 'orienting behaviours' and then by 'non-attending and disobeying'. Motor behaviours such as 'out of seat' and 'aggression' were rarely selected.

Johnson *et al.* (1993), in their large sample of 777 South Australian primary teachers, found that teachers ranked the most difficult student behaviours as 'talking out of turn', 'idleness' and 'hindering others' (p. 296). Moreover, again in Australia, in a sample of New South Wales high schools, Conway, Tierney and Schofield (1990) also found that the majority of behaviour problems faced by teachers were minor, such as 'distracting others', 'talking to others' and 'inattentiveness' (p. 6). Even where classroom discipline is rarely a problem, 'talking out of turn' is the behaviour that teachers consider as being the most troublesome to them.

Jones, Charlton and Wilkin (1995) report that only 28% of teachers of first and middle school classes on the small Atlantic island of St Helena consider they spend more time than they ought on matters of order and control. But 43% of teachers still nominated 'talking out of turn' as being the most troublesome behaviour of the class as a whole, this same behaviour being the most disruptive and the most frequently occurring behaviour of particularly troublesome children in this study (Jones et al., p. 139).

Continuing the work carried out in the UK, Wheldall and Beaman found very similar behaviours were considered troublesome in the Australian context. Wheldall and Beaman (1994) found that 'talking out of turn' was reported by 49% of their sample of 161 New South Wales primary teachers as being the most troublesome behaviour of the class as a whole, followed by 'hindering other children' (16%). When asked what was the most frequent troublesome behaviour of the class, teachers once again nominated 'talking out of turn' (57%) and 'hindering other children' (14%). Likewise, the most troublesome behaviour of the most troublesome student was 'talking out of turn' (reported by 39% of teachers), followed by 'hindering other children' (18%). These results replicate the findings of Merrett and Wheldall (1984) and Wheldall and Merrett (1988) referred to earlier.

In a parallel study involving Australian secondary teachers, Wheldall and Beaman (1994) found that, like their primary school counterparts, 'talking out of turn' was considered by 40% of teachers to be the most troublesome behaviour, and by 47% to be the most frequent troublesome behaviour, of the class as a whole. The second most troublesome behaviour (22%) (and also the most frequent misbehaviour, 21%) was reported to be 'idleness/slowness', a result which varies from both the primary teachers' response in the Australian data and the study of British secondary teachers (Houghton et al., 1988). As in the UK study, however, Wheldall and Beaman found that the most troublesome behaviour of the most troublesome individual student was again 'talking out of turn' (41%), followed by 'hindering other children' (18%). Even in Wheldall and Crawford's study of inner suburban Sydney schools (see Wheldall and Beaman, 1994), where 76% of teachers reported that they spent more time on matters of order and control than they ought (perhaps suggesting more entrenched behaviour problems in these classes), 'talking out of turn' was still reported by 47% of teachers as the most troublesome behaviour of the class as a whole, followed equally by 'disobedience', 'making unnecessary noise' and 'hindering other children', all scoring 11% of teacher responses. Once again the most *frequent* misbehaviour was 'talking out of turn' accounting for 60% of teacher responses, followed by disobedience (9%). In line with most other findings, the most troublesome behaviour of the most troublesome individual student was again 'talking out of turn' (46%), followed by 'hindering other children' (14%).

The results of these recent Australian studies provide strong evidence that the nature of problematic behaviours in the classroom does not appear to be bound by particular cultural contexts or expectations. The replications of the British findings, while being somewhat tedious to report (and, no doubt, to read!) in the light of their similarity, may be useful when attempting to determine both effective and generic behavioural strategies for the management of classroom behaviour. If teachers, by and large, find the same behaviours problematic, the task of addressing the difficulties faced by them every day becomes easier to address.

Not all the data, however, point to 'talking out of turn' as the main behavioural bugbear of teachers. In contrast, Borg and Falzon (1989, 1990) found that stealing, followed by cruelty/bullying and rudeness/impertinence were perceived as being the most serious behaviour problems faced by their sample of 844 primary teachers in Malta. Stuart (1994) found similar findings (i.e. stealing followed by cruelty/bullying as the most troublesome behaviours) in a study of 105 New South Wales secondary teachers which replicated Wickman's earlier work. Kyriacou and Roe (1988) found that the perceptions of their sample of British teachers were dominated by 'disruptive' behaviours, describing aggressive and antagonistic personality traits as being the behaviour problems teachers find most difficult to manage. This difference in the data may be explained by Fields' (1986) useful distinction between classroom behaviour problems and behaviour occurring outside the classroom. The more severe forms of misbehaviour, such as theft, vandalism, aggressive and defiant behaviours, are more likely to occur in corridors or lunch rooms and outside school buildings rather than within the classroom (Fields, p. 54).

To recap the story so far, it is clear from the literature reviewed above that while the evidence concerning estimates of the prevalence rates of behaviourally troublesome students is equivocal, to say the least, there is consistent evidence to show that teachers perceive boys as more behaviourally troublesome than girls. There is also convincing and mounting evidence to suggest that the classroom misbehaviours that teachers find most troublesome are relatively innocuous but occur so frequently as to be a recurrent cause for concern.

Prior to the completion of these studies, it was widely believed by the media, and some sections of the community, that classroom violence and serious disorder and disruption were commonplace in schools and that these were the major problems facing teachers. But even when pressed to focus on the most troublesome behaviours of the most troublesome student in their classes, the category 'physical aggression' was cited by less than 1% of primary teachers, in our recent Australian study (Wheldall and Beaman, 1994). At the secondary level, physical aggression and verbal abuse were, again, very rarely cited. These findings are particularly interesting as it is often claimed that the problems facing secondary teachers are different from, and more serious than, those facing primary teachers. But it appears safe to assume that the classroom behaviour problems experienced by most primary and secondary teachers are similar and are relatively innocuous. This is not to say that serious incidents do not occur occasionally in some schools but they are certainly not as frequent as the media would have us believe. Physical violence appears to be a problem encountered (thankfully) by relatively few teachers but many, if not most, teachers have their job made more difficult by the frequent occurrence of the relatively minor misbehaviours which we have identified above.

We have referred, on several occasions, to the separate study completed by Wheldall and Crawford (reported by Wheldall and Beaman, 1994) of a sample of 212 Australian high school teachers from schools in an inner suburban area of Sydney, commonly regarded as quite a tough area. In this study, we specifically asked the inner suburban teachers if they had ever been verbally abused (86% responded affirmatively) and also whether they had been verbally abused in the last year (50%). This most often took the form of swearing or name calling. When we asked comparable questions about physical abuse, 25% claimed to have been abused at some time during their teaching career and only 8% during the previous year. Such abuse mainly took the form of being pushed or handled by a student rather than being hit. Consequently, it is not surprising that so very few of these teachers nominated either physical or verbal abuse as particularly troublesome since neither occurs very frequently and they are usually not terribly serious when they do.

In the Elton report on discipline in schools (DES, 1989; see also Wheldall, 1992), the official report of a formal public enquiry completed in the UK, in part prompted by the claims of the NAS/UWT document referred to earlier, no evidence was found for increased incidence of serious disruption. As the deputy chair of the investigating committee made clear: 'There simply does not exist the kind of historical database which would enable comparisons to be drawn with any confidence' (Bennett, 1992, p. 1). Rather the Committee was impressed by the weight of research evidence that most teachers were concerned with 'relatively trivial but persistent misbehaviour' that was causing disruption to their lessons (DES, 1989, p. 11).

Our earlier classroom behaviour focused studies, completed in the UK, were (at least) among the first to show that the major behaviour problems facing both primary and secondary school teachers were relatively minor misbehaviours which occurred with very high frequency. The Elton Report subsequently confirmed, by commissioned independent research inspired by the evidence formally presented to the Committee of Enquiry by Wheldall and Merrett, that 'talking out of turn' is by far the most pressing discipline problem facing teachers rather than classroom violence or serious disruption. Consequently, they were forced to conclude in the Elton Report (Department of Education and Science, 1989; Wheldall, 1992) that reports of indiscipline and violence in schools in the UK had been greatly exaggerated and that most teachers were concerned with relatively innocuous but frequent and irritating, trivial misbehaviours. This conclusion was, however, in some ways anticipated by Mills (1976) who, in an unpublished large-scale survey of all secondary schools in a large education authority in the UK, assessed the incidence of seriously disruptive behaviour of older (13-plus) secondary students:

> '... contrary to the picture given in the popular press of the main problems in the schools, day to day, being of physical assault on teachers by pupils, or bullying, or vandalism or the use of gangs and older members of the family to exert pressure on the school, in order to break down its authority, it is seen that these are comparatively exceptional occurrences...' (p. 303)

What then can we conclude from these findings? In short, we believe that teachers are right when they complain about the 'bad press' and 'sensationalism' surrounding media accusations of violence in schools. Such reports have grossly overstated the case and are not supported by the research evidence, as we have shown. It should be emphasised that the most frequent and the most troublesome student misbehaviours of concern are remarkably similar for all samples of teachers questioned and are relatively innocuous. 'Talking out of turn' alone accounts for almost half of the first choices of teachers in all samples, followed by, for example, hindering other students or idleness and slowness. These are hardly major crimes but they are the sorts of behaviour that teachers find themselves commenting upon frequently. Most teachers would agree that 'talking out of turn' and 'hindering other students' are not particularly serious misbehaviours but when occurring at a great frequency they can be, at the very least, irritating and time-wasting, and over time ultimately exhausting and stressful. The good news is that these sorts of classroom behaviours have been shown to be particularly amenable to resolution by 'positive teaching' methods at both primary and secondary levels (see Merrett and Wheldall, 1990; Wheldall and Glynn, 1989; Wheldall and Merrett, 1984, 1989).

References

Bennett, R. (1992) Discipline in Schools: The report of the committee of enquiry chaired by Lord Elton, in Wheldall, K. (Ed.). Discipline in Schools: Psychological perspectives on the Elton Report (London: Routledge), pp. 1–9.

Borg, M. and Falzon, J. (1989) Primary school teachers' perception of pupils' undesirable behaviours. Educational Studies, 15, 251–60.

Borg, M. and Falzon, J. (1990) Primary school teachers' perceptions of pupils' undesirable behaviours: The effects of teaching experience, pupils' age, sex and ability stream. British Journal of Educational Psychology, 60, 220–6.

Brophy, J. (1985) Classroom organisation and management. Phi Delta Kappa, 5, 2–17.

Chazan, M. and Jackson, S. (1971) Behaviour problems in the infant school. Journal of Child Psychology and Psychiatry, 12, 191–210.

Chazan, M. and Jackson, S. (1974) Behaviour problems in the infant school: changes over two years. Journal of Child Psychology and Psychiatry, 15, 33–46.

Child, D. (1984) Educational psychology: Past, present and Future. In Entwistle, N. (Ed.) New Directions in Educational Psychology. Vol. 1: Learning and teaching. (Lewes: Falmer Press).

Conway, R., Tierney, J., and Schofield, N. (1990) Coping with behaviour problems in NSW high schools. Conference paper presented at the National Australian Conference on Behaviour Problems, July 1990.

Department of Education and Science (1989) Discipline in Schools (The Elton Report) (London: HMSO).

Fields, B. (1986) The nature and incidence of classroom behaviour problems and their remediation through preventative management. Behaviour Change, 3, 53–7.

Hartley, D. (1979) Sex differences in classroom behaviour in infants schools: The views of teachers and pupils, British Journal of Educational Psychology, 49, 188–93.

Houghton, S., Wheldall, K. and Merrett, F. (1988) Classroom behaviour problems which secondary school teachers say they find most troublesome. British Educational Research Journal, 14, 297–312.

Johnson, B., Oswald, M. and Adey, K. (1993) Discipline in South Australian primary schools. Educational Studies, 19, 289–305.

Jones, K., Charlton, T. and Wilkin, J. (1995) Classroom behaviours which first and middle school teachers in St Helena find troublesome. Educational Studies, 21, 139–53.

Kyriacou, C. and Roe, H. (1988) Teachers' perceptions of pupils' behaviour at a comprehensive school. British Educational Research Journal, 14, 167–73.

Lawrence, J. and Steed, D. (1986) Primary school perception of disruptive behaviour. Educational Studies, 12, 147–57.

McGee, R., Sylva, P. and Williams, S. (1984) Behaviour problems in a population of seven year old children: Prevalence, stability and types of disorder: a research report. Journal of Child Psychiatry, 25, 251–9.

McNamara, E. (1985) Are the techniques of behaviour modification relevant to problems of concern to teachers in secondary schools? Behavioural Approaches with Children, 9, 34–45.

McNamara, E. (1987) Behavioural approaches in the secondary school, in Wheldall, K. (Ed.) The Behaviourist in the Classroom (London: Allen and Unwin), pp 50–68.

Merrett, F. and Wheldall, K. (1984) Classroom behaviour problems which junior primary school teachers find most troublesome. Educational Studies, 10, 87–92.

Merrett, F. and Wheldall, K. (1990) Positive Teaching in The Primary School (London: Paul Chapman).

Mills, W.P.C. (1976) The serious disruptive behaviour of pupils in secondary schools in one local authority. Unpublished M.Ed thesis, University of Birmingham.

NAS/UWT. (1986) Pupil Violence and Serious Disorder in Schools (Rednal: National Association of Schoolmasters and Union of Women Teachers).

Nicholls, D., Houghton, S. and Bain, A. (1991) Teacher reports of troublesome behaviour in West Australian high schools. Unpublished manuscript, Department of Education, University of Western Australia.

Rosenshine, B. (1971) Teaching Behaviours and Student Achievement (New York: Prentice Hall).

Stevenson, J., Richman, N. and Graham, P. (1985) Behaviour problems and language abilities at three years and behavioural deviance at eight years. Journal of Child Psychology and Psychiatry, 26, 215–30.

Stuart, H. (1994) Teacher perceptions of student behaviours: A study of NSW secondary teachers' attitudes. Educational Psychology, 14, 217–30.

Walker, H., Severs, H., Stiller, B., Williams, G., Haring, N., Shin, M. and Todis, B. (1988) Systematic screening of pupils in the elementary age range at risk for behavior disorders: Development and trial of a multiple gating model. Remedial and Special Education, 9(3), 8–14.

Wheldall, K. (Ed.) (1992) Discipline in Schools: Psychological perspectives on the Elton Report (London: Routledge).

Wheldall, K., and Beaman, R. (1994) An evaluation of the WINS (Working Ideas for Need Satisfaction) training package. Report submitted to the New South Wales Department of School Education, 1993. Special Education Centre, Macquarie University.Collected Original Resources in Education, 18(1), fiche 4 E01.

Wheldall, K., and Glynn, T. (1989) Effective Classroom Learning: A behavioural interactionist approach to teaching (London: Basil Blackwell).

Wheldall, K., and Merrett, F. (1984) Positive Teaching: The behavioural approach (London: Allen and Unwin).

Wheldall, K., and Merrett, F. (1988) Which classroom behaviours do primary school teachers say they find most troublesome? Educational Review, 40, 13–27.

Wheldall, K., and Merrett, F. (1989) Positive Teaching in the Secondary School (London: Paul Chapman).

Wickman, E.K. (1928a) Teachers' list of undesirable forms of behaviour, in Williams, P. (Ed.) (1974) Behaviour problems in school pp. 6–15 (London: University of London Press). Reprinted from Children's behaviour and teachers' attitudes (New York: Commonwealth Fund).

Wickman, E.K. (1928b) Teachers' reactions to behaviour problems of children, in Williams, P. (Ed.) (1974) Behaviour problems in school pp. 16–38 (London: University of London Press). Reprinted from Children's behaviour and teachers' attitudes (New York: Commonwealth Fund).

Whitmore, K., and Bax, M. (1984) Who to treat, who to refer? Association for Child Psychology Newsletter, 6 (2), 33–4.

Ziv, A. (1970) Children's behaviour problems as viewed by teachers, psychologists and children. Child Development, 41, 871–9.

Chapter 13
Gifted education: education of the highly able

DIANE MONTGOMERY

In the fifth and most recent edition of the textbook *Psychology and the Teacher*, Child (1993) outlines giftedness with reference to Gardner's (1990) theory of multiple intelligences and Sternberg's (1986) triarchic theory and sets this information within the chapter on intelligence. It is in this framework for most of the century that a consideration of giftedness has been made, on the basis that items on most such tests measure a 'g' factor of general intelligence and thus a person in the top 10 per cent on one test (words, numbers or graphics) will seldom be below average on another (Brand 1996). In the education field it is considered that an IQ of 140 or above denotes a form of giftedness now called 'high ability' and an IQ of 160 represents 'exceptionally high ability'. Those with IQs over 140 make up about 1% of the population although in practice slightly more than this can be expected to be identified (DES, 1974). The numbers in a school's age cohort defined in this way can thus be very small and so some teachers have been known to say that they have never met a gifted child. However, it has long been clear that an intelligence test does not always tap high ability nor is high measured IQ the only indication of giftedness and even the highest of IQ may lead to mediocre performance and average achievement.

Some key issues

The concept of giftedness, the nature of giftedness and talent and the methods of identification have been in a continuous state of development and change for over 100 years. It is a complex area, and giftedness in practice appears in many forms such as mathematical and literary gifts, chess, artistic and musical ability, managerial and leadership skills, social and physical skills and so on. The extent to which these are separate intelligences (Gardner, 1993) is debatable. The term 'giftedness' itself has been given up for 'high ability' so that the notion of 'gift' as some pseudomagical property, rare and precious, can be circumvented and replaced by this more neutral term. People can agree more easily on its use and more readily recognise it without having to specify a particular level or in the case of giftedness the highest level. The level of ability needed to achieve has also been the subject of research.

Some researchers link high ability and talent and use the terms synonymously; others regard them as separate types of high ability with talent linked to performance in a skills orientated area such as music, art and sport.

High ability does not necessarily lead to a high level of achievement. Low achievement may, of course, also point to an unrealised potential. The extent to which potential can in fact be assessed is also at issue. Associated with unrealised potential is an area of increasing concern defined as underfunctioning (Butler-Por, 1987). Why individuals appear to underfunction is another important set of issues some of them linked to personality, emotionality and the social context, others to disability, gender, culture and ethnicity.

Vestiges of giftedness can tend only to be seen in retrospect when the high ability has led to some extraordinary productivity in a particular field. Many may seem highly able, even equally able to the 'gifted', but have been unable to direct their abilities in a sustained way to effect the highest achievement. Other factors come into play here, such as motivation, practice, expertise and even chance. Studies of infant prodigies, who seem without prior experience to produce mature work of a significant nature recognised for its merits by experts in the field, have shown that not all grow up to be gifted adults and that massive amounts of practice may have been overlooked. Conversely, many eminent persons did not reveal their abilities until maturity. Early identification of a gifted elite has been pursued energetically in many countries. Governments seem to be particularly keen to find this elite and give them special provision even though research has shown that early selection and segregation may be misguided.

Changes have also occurred in the assessment area, which it will be important to note in particular, there has been a move away from IQ testing towards assessment through provision and performance.

Most recently Cropley (1994) has put forward the notion that there is no 'true' giftedness without creativity and this extraordinarily difficult quality to define and quantify is experiencing a renewal of research interest after a period of relative quiescence.

Measurement and assessment

Assessment of ability has been intimately related to intelligence testing until recently. The term 'measurement' implies that there is an accuracy and a scale which is agreed that can be used to define levels of ability and high ability itself. An IQ test does not give such a definitive score and different tests can yield different results. However, individually administered tests were found in the Terman (1925, 1937) studies to be more reliable than group tests for identifying high ability. The test in most widespread use in the high ability field is the Wechsler Intelligence Scale for Children (WISC-R) which has been translated into many languages. It is useful because it offers an assessment of verbal and performance abilities. Thus wider abilities are tapped, offering the inclusion of both right and left hemisphere functions. There is, however, growing awareness that the paper-and-pencil tests used by schools to select pupils for ability 'do not measure what has been learnt in schools in any way that is useful in the social arena' (Ediger, 1994, p 172). Equally, Standard Attainment Tasks seen in objective tests emphasise lower order rote learning, harm the educative process and do not reveal the potential of the highly able (Feller, 1994).

Over time a number of levels of IQ have been identified as cut-off points denoting high ability. In certain Local Education Authorities in the UK a cut off point of 145 was used because so few children would be screened in for special provision, under 1 per cent, that it would cost very little to make it available. The ceiling of around 135 on some group tests could also mean that no children at all were identified! In the Terman studies a threshold for inclusion was an IQ of 140 on the Stanford–Binet test which is now regarded as verbally biased favouring children of higher socio-economic background. His subjects were also referred for testing by the teachers whose judgment of high ability was relied upon to put pupils forward. Teachers, however, are not always capable of recognising high ability unless they receive some training (Painter, 1982; Denton and Postlethwaite, 1985).

Ogilvie (1973) in his UK survey took a threshold of 130 IQ which enabled the inclusion of approximately 16 per cent of the school population and Callow (1983) set a level of 115. The thresholds became set progressively lower because at each level it was found that many highly able children were still being left out. Thus it was that in the Learning Difficulties Research Project (Montgomery, 1985, 1991) that after the initial pilot studies all the children were included in the special enrichment work and a beneficial effect was found across all levels of ability.

Although IQ tests are still extensively used in most countries where convergent thought and the selection of a gifted élite and 'mental Olympics' are valued there has been a move away from reliance upon such techniques in relation to education provision, particularly in North America where investment in high ability research has been in the order of billions of dollars. It is as the conception of the nature of high ability and talent has developed that the methods of identification have been seen to need to change to keep pace.

The nature of high ability and talent

The earliest method of identifying the able was to look at publicly acknowledged achievement and then undertake retrospective analyses as in Galton's (1869) study of hereditary genius and Cox's (1926) biographical studies of 300 eminent men. Whereas the general public like to regard high ability as unidimensional and narrow, often akin to madness, high intellectual ability by its nature is general and versatile as Cox's studies showed. She found that the most highly able subjects showed more than average abilities across several areas. Leonardo da Vinci is perhaps the most famous representative of her science/art cluster. Others had high ability and talent across clusters such as Charles Dodson/Lewis Carroll and a number of leading politicians today are gifted linguists or novelists. Cox estimated the IQs from her data, and thus the extent to which high IQ was predictive of high ability remained an open question.

With the introduction of psychometric testing at the beginning of the century the potential of the intelligence test to identify ability at an early age and thus predict to later achievement was anticipated. Terman's (1925) longitudinal studies which were to have a major influence upon the area as they were followed through for more than five decades, showed eventually that an intelligence test alone could not predict high achievement. When 300 highest achievers and 300 lowest achievers in his sample – matched for IQ – were followed up, it was found that what distinguished the two groups was the emotional stability and persistence of the high achievers. Thus personal characteristics were found to be of major significance in realising any potential. Terman's subjects' achievements were substantial 25 years later but he was of the opinion that perhaps one might achieve national status but would not be heard of in 100 years, despite the fact that his sample had a mean IQ of 154.

Hollingworth (1926) in a long term study of ten individuals with IQs of 180 identified 'special' talents, areas of outstanding potential or performance, which she said were independent of general intelligence. It was de Haan and Havighurst (1957) who drew together the strands emerging from a number of such studies and successfully broadened the concepts then in use. They identified domains of excellence:

- intellectual ability – demonstrated in high school achievement or academic aptitude
- creative thinking
- scientific thinking
- social leadership
- mechanical skill or ingenuity
- talent in fine arts areas.

Their work was inspired by Guilford's (1959) three dimensional model of intellect in which he identified 120 different 'cells' or types of intellectual functioning:

- Five *operations*: evaluation, convergence, divergence, memory, cognition
- Six *products*: units, classes, relations, systems, transformations, implications
- Four *contents*: figural, symbolic, semantic, behavioural.

Of particular significance were the notions of convergent and divergent thinking processes, and criticisms were levelled at IQ tests for requiring only convergent thought whereas divergent thinking was necessary for high levels of achievement. Getzels and Jackson (1962) researching the relationship between intelligence and creativity came to the conclusion that a threshold of about 120 IQ was necessary for any significant level of creative productivity. The debate led to an interest and research in the nature and measurement of creativity particularly by Torrance (1966) who produced the first 'tests' of creativity measuring fluency, flexibility, originality and elaboration. These last two seemed to correlate best with later achievement but were the two aspects most difficult to design and assess. The study of creativity expanded in the, 1970s (de Bono, 1970, 1976; Covington *et al.*, 1972; Noller, Parnes and Bondi, 1976) and as a result there was a broadening of attributes to include curiosity, openness to ideas of others, toleration in dealing with ambiguity and complexity, risk-taking, imagination and the use of fantasy, humour, finding essences and construing relations. After a period of quiescence there has recently been a resurgence of research in the subject, new test instruments have been developed (Urban and Jellen, 1986), and Cropley's (1994) proposal that there can be no 'true' giftedness without creativity is of particular significance. It was Renzulli's strong defence of his 'three-ring' concept of giftedness that set the modern trend in the gifted education field. He defined giftedness as the capacity for, or demonstration of, high levels of performance in any potentially valuable area of human endeavour (Renzulli, 1977). (Figure 13.1). This much broader definition of giftedness encompassed Terman's and Torrance's findings and showed that there was a much larger group who could be considered to be potentially gifted.

More recently, according to Tannenbaum (1993), giftedness and talent have been used synonymously to:

> encompass publicly valued abilities possessed by no more than one or two per cent of the people at each developmental stage. Creativity is regarded as representing one or two aspects of giftedness (or talent) namely innovation or invention that deserves

Gifted education: education of the highly able 249

critical acclaim in contrast to the other aspect of giftedness (or talent) which refers to highly developed proficiency in highly demanding tasks. Genius is the most advanced extension of giftedness (or talent) or creativity, denoting Olympian level accomplishments by the rarest of adults' (Tannenbaum, 1993, p. 3)

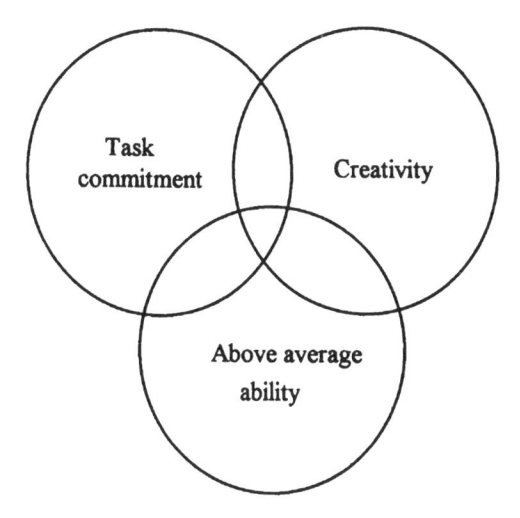

Figure 13.1. Renzulli's three-ring model.

Feldhusen (1992) refers to it as superior aptitude or ability in any worthwhile area of human development, regarding it as a developmental phenomena emerging out of general aptitude into specific career orientated abilities. Giftedness and talent are, however, not always thought to be synonymous. Giftedness has been regarded as high ability generally of the kind needed in IQ tests ('g') whereas talent has been connected with specific ability ('s') including creativity in an area of performance such as music or art.

Freeman (1991) concluded from her longitudinal case studies that we cannot identify with any certainty those babies who might grow up to give consistently superior performance on any one measure or in any field of endeavour.

> But we do have information about the kinds of early home preparation which encourages gifted potential to flower, which centres around a stimulating home environment and lively minded, concerned mentors, parents and teachers. (Freeman, 1991, p. 33)

She concluded that such influences were particularly important for children with high potential who were able to extract more from such experiences than their less able peers and siblings. The characteristics identified in her research were infants who pay close attention; are attracted by novelty; enjoy challenge; and make concerted efforts to achieve whatever goal is set. She identified advanced language as one of the earliest signs (p. 34) as well as the ability to delay gratification.

Talent

Talent is usually defined as a domain or specific gift or ability such as seen in art, music, science, ballet, chess or mathematics. The characteristic form is that the individual appears to have a high ability or precocious talent in the presence quite often of seemingly modest abilities in other areas. For example, Peggy Somerville was a talented painter with a mature style at the age of 3 years. Mozart at 7 composed and played significantly well. It does not mean, however, that talent development is automatic, it requires the complex interaction of opportunity, diligence, interest and motivation, belief in oneself, and models and mentors who facilitate the vision and crystallize the experience (Elshout, 1990). Of course some people are multitalented and have very high measured IQs as well. Many children may never be exposed to such facilitating experiences and environments and their talents will never be uncovered.

Creativity

Creativity can be regarded as a form of talent as well as a set of fundamental attributes underlying a number of performance areas (Feldhusen, 1992). It refers to an innovative, ingenious and productive response to ordinary problems. This is often characterised by a flexible approach to thinking, the capacity for induction and use of analogies and models in new and productive ways. According to Simonton (1988) the creative person is particularly good at producing associations and then recognising the significance of the new configuration which has occurred. There is hence a need for inclusion of flexibility and creativity training and experience in education (Feldhusen, 1990) if the country is to maintain its economic position after the millennium.

Incorporating creativity opportunities into the National Curriculum is particularly problematic despite Dearing's (1994) attempt to cut down the content. Opportunities to play with materials and ideas are characteristic of creative thinkers and producers but takes time and has little place in our current systems of education.

Multiple intelligences and multidimensional concepts of ability

It is a short step from de Haan and Havighurst's (1957) proposal broadening the concept of ability to the theory of Gardner (1983, 1993) of 'multiple intelligences' in the following areas: linguistic, musical, logico-mathematical, spatial, interpersonal and intrapersonal. His data is however, somewhat limited and anecdotal (Mönks and Mason,1993) and it is Sternberg's (1986) triarchic model which has gained wider acceptance and upon which it is proposed that curriculum provision is based.

Sternberg proposed three sub-theories in his model of ability.

- Sub-theory 1 (*componential*) has three parts.
    - Metacomponents: executive processes needed for planning, monitoring and decision-making in a problem-solving situation.
    - Performance components: processes needed for executing the task
    - Knowledge acquisition components: used in the selective encoding, combination and comparison operations.
- Sub-theory 2 (*experiential*): the ability to deal with novelty and to automate or habituate information processing.
- Sub-theory 3 (*contextual*): selecting, shaping and adapting to real world environments.

As can be seen, this theory is very much about the control and executive processes which we can identify as higher-order thinking processes. It is these with which education for all students should be involved (Resnick, 1989; Paul, 1990) and it is greatly to the disadvantage of the able when it is not. The more creative the able pupil, the more frustrating and mundane a didactic curriculum can become.

The identification of ability

There are three main methods used in addition to IQ and attainment tests already discussed.

Checklists and trait rating in identification

During the last two decades many secondary schools in the UK have not used a selection system and have taken pupils in to mixed ability classes giving them a year to settle and for the subject specialist to assess ability based upon attainment in academic subjects and literacy tests. The pupils may then be 'set' for ability in the core subjects such as English and mathematics. Some schools 'set' in a wider range of subjects. Even within these 'sets' it had been noted that highly able children were being missed just as they had been with IQ tests, and checklists or traits for the identification of able children were a feature of developments and training for teachers in the 1980s (Kerry, 1983; Wallace, 1983; Montgomery, 1985; Denton and Postlethwaite, 1985) for example:

- a wide range of hobbies and interests
- curiosity and investigativeness in approach

- keen powers of observation
- a facility for hypothesising and dealing with abstract ideas
- originality of ideas, unusual imaginative powers
- may have learned to read and write at 2–3 years without direct teaching
- superior reasoning powers and also powers of induction
- superior development of verbal skills and vocabulary knowledge
- follows complex directions easily
- very good memory span for age
- powerful attention and concentration span
- a good sense of humour
- detailed interest and extensive knowledge at an early age in the origins of the universe, God and the solar system (Montgomery, 1996).

Teachers do need some training in the development and use of such checklists and would find that the possession of six or seven of these attributes would be likely to denote an able pupil. However, it is also possible that a child who possesses a detailed interest and knowledge of football teams or motor bikes but no other signs of any of the above has a concealed and latent ability which may go undetected as the focus of the interest is not valued. There is now the tendency in this field to include within the able group any individual with a single area of high achievement or ability.

Shore (1991) identified seven characteristics in which highly able children differed from others as follows:-

- *Memory and knowledge-* they knew more, they knew what they knew better and could use it better
- *Self regulation* - they expertly guided and monitored their own thinking on task
- *Speed of thought processes*: they spent longer on planning but arrived at answers more quickly as experts do
- *Problem presentation and categorisation*: they extended ideas beyond the information given, identified missing data, excluded irrelevancies and grasped essentials more quickly
- *Procedural knowledge*: they used organised and systematic approaches to problem solving and engaged in flexible switching amongst strategies
- *Flexibility*: they had an ability to see alternative configurations and adopt alternative strategies
- *Preference for complexity*: they increased the complexity of games and tasks in play situations to increase interest.

These characteristics are reminiscent of those found in adult experts by Nickerson and Perkins and Smith (1985)

Gifted education: education of the highly able 253

> Experts not only know more, they know they know more, they know better how to use what they know. What they know is better organised and more readily accessible and they know better how to know more still. (p. 101)

However, it is now recognised that there are many highly able individuals who do not learn to behave like experts and this is blamed upon a form of education which is regarded as unsuitable for the development of 'higher order skills'; it is known *as didactics* (Glaser, 1985; Resnick, 1989; Paul, 1990).

Process analyses in identification

There are a number of different forms and strategies currently in use such as process analysis of performance on tests including IQ tests and the learning potential assessment device (LPAD) (Feuerstein, 1980, 1993, 1995); assessment of learning potential based upon Vygotsky's zone of proximal development (ZPD); and adaptive assessment which integrates assessment and instruction (Birenbaum, 1994).

Curriculum based assessment

Curriculum based assessment was originally described by Shore and Tsiamis (1986) as performance based assessment (PBA). In PBA any children displaying high achievement in any area are deemed gifted and then given special provision. Although this may seem to be an open system there are many groups known to underfunction or be disadvantaged and so their performance remains unexceptional (Butler-Por, 1987; Yewchuk and Lupart, 1993; Montgomery, 1997). It is for these reasons that CBA has been reinterpreted and revised (Montgomery, 1996) to describe a method in which the ordinary school curriculum can be made 'special' and offer cognitive challenge to all children and in particular the highly able. The main methods by which this can be achieved are outlined below.

Educational provision for able pupils

High quality schooling which will stimulate the highly able and improve the achievements of the disadvantaged has apparently escaped the wit of educators, legislators and researchers alike according to Passow (1990) in his review of 25 years of research and practice in gifted education. Nevertheless in the last 10 years some progress has been made. In the UK differentiation of the curriculum to meet the needs of pupils has been made a statutory requirement and several methods were outlined in the HMI (1992) report on able children.

Didactic methods (lecture methods) are particularly unsuited to groups with a wide range of ability and literacy skills, but it is possible to teach mixed ability classes when appropriate methods are used. Nevertheless, if provision were more flexible and not locked into age cohort progression and teacher-directed study it would be possible to plan for wider differences in learner's needs, particularly at secondary level. It ought to be possible for any pupil in school to follow distance and self-directed programmes of study. The organisation of rooms, resources and tutelage also needs to be better integrated, with programmes of study negotiated between teachers and learners rather than being teacher-directed and curriculum led. Provision needs to be closely related to the defined needs of the able and differentiation needs to be incorporated within it.

Forms of differentiation

It seems to me that differentiation can be organised under two main headings: structural or systems approaches and integral approaches in which the basic curriculum is individualised and forms a whole life-style approach. The structural approach deals mainly with groups, and in this system it is less certain that the same basic curriculum is available to all.(Figure 13.2)

Structural		Integral
Acceleration		Differentiation
Compacting		Enrichment
Streaming		Mentoring
Setting	Flexibility	Learner managed Learning
Vertical groups		Layering
Grade skipping		Assessment
Enrichment		Developmental Differentiation
Segregation		
Product Based		**Process Based**

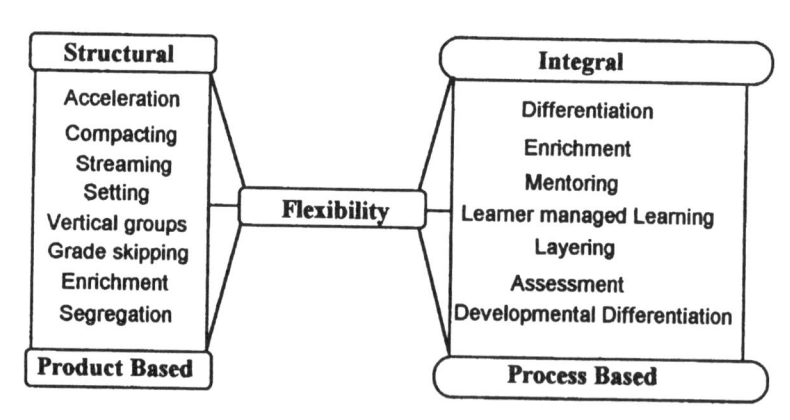

Figure 13.2. A model of different types of educational provision.

The structural methods all involve accelerating the learner through curriculum contents in various ways. Even some enrichment materials merely teach what the learner could expect to learn in another phase of education, for example, primary pupils might be given sections of the secondary school or even university curriculum in the periods allocated to 'enrichment'. This form of provision is 'bolted on' to the normal classroom activities, whereas a more sophisticated form which is integral to the normal curriculum is what is required. If differentiation is integral or built in to the mainstream work all children can have an opportunity to profit from it. Most structural approaches tend to be product or content based whereas integral approaches have to be concerned with process, in particular cognitive processes in which there is both content and method.

Criteria for the design of curriculum materials for the able

According to Poorthuis, Kok and Van Dijk (1990) one of the central problems in the education of the gifted was still the lack of proper curriculum materials. They argued that enrichment materials 'for the gifted' should meet the following criteria:

- They should be beneficial to the development and use of higher order thinking abilities.
- They ought to provide the possibility to explore continually new knowledge and new information.
- They should learn and encourage students to select and use sources of information.
- The content should aim at a complex, enriching and in-depth study of important ideas, problems and subjects, and at integrating knowledge between and within subject areas.
- They should offer the opportunity to increasingly engage in autonomous learning activities.

These researchers have produced a curriculum analysis tool for evaluating curriculum materials for these attributes. What is of interest is their definition of what 'good' curriculum materials for the able should consist. It is consistent with a trend world wide which recognises that there must be a move in curriculum development for the able to develop their higher order cognitive abilities and in particular their metacognitive skills (Span, 1993, Renzulli, 1995).

> Metacognition – a person's awareness of his or her own cognitive machinery is a vital component of intelligence. (Flavell, 1979, p. 907)

Structural forms of differentiation offer strategies for more and more content acquisition rather than the development of metacognition. How cognitive goals can be achieved will be exemplified by focusing upon three models of integral differentiation.

Integral differentiation

- *Layering*: setting of different tasks at different levels of difficulty suitable for different levels of achievement, differentiation by inputs.

- *Enrichment*: provision of special materials and packages for individual and small group independent study to broaden or deepen understanding in an area.
- *Developmental differentiation*: setting of common tasks to which all can contribute their own inputs and so progress from surface to deep learning and thus be enabled to achieve more advanced learning outcomes.

Of the first perhaps the best that can be said is that it offers more than the formal or didactic methods of teaching to the middle, but there are inbuilt disadvantages. In differentiation by inputs teachers provide some core work in which all pupils may participate but after that they provide different work within the same context at different levels – simpler conceptual and practice work for the slower learners and more complex problem-solving extension work for the able groups. What has to be appreciated is that in this system the students doing the easier work can begin to feel lower in value. This can in the long run prove academically handicapping, for these students come to expect that they can never achieve a high standard in any sphere of activity and cease to try so that they compound their difficulties and begin to fall further behind. An underfunctioning, learning disabled or disadvantaged pupil can frequently be assigned inappropriately to a slow learning group and emotional and behavioural difficulties are frequently the result (Montgomery, 1997) for it is the teacher who has to select who will do the advanced or less advanced work. There are in fact a number of studies which have shown that teachers need training to do this successfully (Denton and Postlethwaite, 1985).

Differentiation by outcome, another form of layering, is where all students can participate in the same lesson but different assessment tasks are set at which they progressively fail. Differences in the outcomes achieved may not reflect the different levels of ability, for when able students are set the same task as all the rest it may appear so mundane that they give a low-level formatted response and can regularly underfunction.

These forms of differentiation are no more than a within-class selective education system which supports a didactic method with all the potential for social and political division which is witnessed in structural systems.

However, it is a mistake to think that putting together a class of highly able pupils means that differentiation becomes unnecessary. In fact these children will be found to be as widely different in abilities, knowledge, skills and interests as a 'mixed' ability class and can prove to be far more demanding to teach by any method. Didactics dampens able students' learning and damages motivation and achievement in the less able.

Gifted education: education of the highly able

Enrichment is widely recommended in the gifted education field and there is a developing industry in the preparation of study packages. The term came into fashion in the 1930s when Hollingworth and others found that it was better to keep the able with their age group rather than accelerate or segregate them (Gowan and Demos, 1964, p. 14; Ziehl, 1962; Arends and Ford, 1964) and it is recommended by the National Association for Able Children in Education (NACE) in the UK. Passow (1982), former president of the World Council for Gifted Children, recommended four guidelines for the development of enrichment programmes :

- modification of the curriculum to provide additional breadth or depth
- modification of the pace of presentation – speeding up the rate to suit individual needs
- modification of the nature of the material to take account of needs and interests
- development of process skills such as those of creative and critical thinking, heuristics and problem solving, and affective and interpersonal communication and skills.

Once again one can see the convergence upon those aspects of education which centre upon the learning of higher order thinking skills. Any enrichment package should be carefully examined to ensure that it is not merely content acceleration and that it really does meet Passow's criteria. A rough guide to this can be to ascertain whether the activities and questions require operations at the three upper levels of Bloom's (1956) taxonomy of educational objectives - analysis, synthesis and evaluation. The Motorway Project, Townscapes and the Village of Edensfield, written by the Maidenhead Group of teachers, are very good examples from which to learn.

Enrichment as currently conceived remains essentially a bolt-on provision but the methods and materials could be redeveloped to become integral to the core curriculum (Montgomery, 1991) and so benefit a wider range of pupils. The strategies outlined in the next section can be found in some enrichment materials.

Developmental differentiation is a form of enrichment which is built into the curriculum so that all children may benefit. It can take account of the range of individual differences and assumes that even in so-called homogeneous groups the range of differences in thinking abilities, knowledge, language and literacy skills, social , emotional and perceptual development will vary considerably as does the experience and learning history which each brings to the curriculum task.

The key features of developmental differentiation are:

- an identification through provision strategy
- the national curriculum as the subject content
- the use of cognitive process teaching and learning methods
- assessments which are both formative and diagnostic.

These can be converted into objectives and fulfilled by incorporating teaching and learning methods into class teaching which to promote cognitive functioning and metacognition as defined by Sternberg (1986).

Cognitive process teaching methods

Cognitive methods are the core of developmental differentiation and enable it to be achieved. They are based in critical thinking theory (Resnick, 1989; Paul, 1990) and are the means by which higher order thinking and metacognitive skills can be developed through the ordinary curriculum (Montgomery, 1995,1996). Six cognitive process pedagogies are outlined below.

Games and simulations

Simulation games contain the elements of real situations and groups interact with and can become part of the reality. Role playing is often an important part of the game, for example, in working with a class of children on the problems of bullying or stealing it is often useful to organise small-group role play so that individuals can practice expressing their own and other's feeling as well as analysing the issues and suggesting solutions or resolutions to the problems. Characteristic of all games is that they must be followed by a discussion and debriefing session about what transpired so that educational and metacognitive objectives can be achieved. In this case it can also have therapeutic outcomes.

Similar curriculum games on deciding where a hospital/castle/ monastery/ housing estate can be built can be used to introduce these subjects in historical, social and geographical studies. Each group gives a brief presentation of the attributes of the site and their resolution of the arguments for and against. The teacher can then use the experiences to help the class reflect upon which features make the best site; they can also look at real sites and use their knowledge to learn more about them. The method brings them to a deeper realization of the conflicts of interest, the needs and purposes of users, owners, builders and land use, both modern and historical, than a question and answer introduction might have done. At the same time the children can contribute their own knowledge, develop discussion and negotiation skills, communication and presentation skills, and have fun.

Cognitive study skills

Study skills are a form of self-directed learning and frequently involve active work on verbal, pictorial or textual material. Although reading skills are taught in primary school it is not usual to teach higher order reading and cognitive skills such as these in any sector of education although they are considered to be essential to the educated person and a requirement for success in higher education.
The following can be applied across the curriculum:

- locating the main and subordinate points
- flow charting
- completion and prediction activities
- sequencing
- comparing and contrasting
- drafting and editing
- marking and assessing work using external and internal criteria
- organising: tabulating, classifying, ordering, diagramming, categorising
- drawing inferences, abstractions and analogies
- recognising intent, bias and propaganda
- planning and monitoring one's own learning
- micro teaching
- managing one's own learning and keeping it on schedule.

Study skills like these are different from skills involving lower-order activities such as using a dictionary or an index and finding one's way about a book and what its main contents are, or recovering factual information from text and making notes for projects and essays.

Real problem solving and investigative learning

Human nature is such that if you present a person with an open-ended situation in which the answer is not given, the mind automatically tries to solve and make closure. This notion of the human as scientific problem solver and investigator from birth was put forward by Kelly (1955). Although not everything can be converted into a problem, there is considerable scope for doing so across the curriculum.

Characteristic of the approach is that there needs to be plenty of content material for research to help develop ideas and strategies or verify solutions. Because the activities start from the children's own ideas and knowledge, each is building up their own cognitive structures and knowledge hierarchies and thus can interrogate the various sources. The teacher in this setting is not the only interactive resource but also the manager and facilitator of learning.

Experiential learning

Kolb (1984) defined the experiential learning cycle in which it was important that practical experience had to be reflected upon in order to achieve higher order learning. However, a learning spiral might be a more accurate interpretation of the process (Montgomery, 1993) for at each turn, the talking about the experience and then the reflecting upon the learning process adds to the sum of knowledge and skills changing the process and the understanding in an additive way. At each point mediation – judicious questioning – by the teacher (Feuerstein, 1993) can facilitate the process. Experiential learning is essentially action learning, and it is surprising how much children can remain passive in classroom learning.

Although learners may learn without direct experience by observing and modelling others, and able learners are particularly adept at this, it does not mean that direct experience is not useful. The experience does however have to be cognitively challenging.

Collaborative learning

Collaboration means that children work with each other towards the framing and design of problems as well as in their resolution or solution. Frequently what is meant to be cooperative group work is no more than pupils sitting together in groups doing individual work. Studies showed that interactions within the groups were mainly between children of the same sex and not related to the task in hand (Galton, Simon and Croll, 1980; Bennett, 1986). Pupils in groups on average spent two thirds of their time on individual work interacting with no one. The 5 per cent of time actually spent talking about the task was most likely to be requests for information. It was the exception rather than the rule to find a group working as one.

Bennett (1986), using a computer programme to provide decision-making tasks, observed triads in homogeneous and heterogeneous groups and found that the the high ability children understood the decisions and attained 95 per cent success whichever type of group they worked in. Thus working with average and low attainers did not damage their capacity for achievement, a concern which has frequently been raised.

One of the most useful sources on practical collaborative learning activities is by Bowers and Wells (1985). Circle time, conflict management and many other creative and problem solving activities are described in it or can be applied to real world problems. The strategies can also be incorporated into content areas as well as the resolution process:

- definition
- expressing feelings

- creating options
- goal setting
- actioning one 'best fit' option
- verifying, evaluating and modifying a solution.

Brainstorming, role play and a wide range of action learning strategies are illustrated and have been well tried and tested in schools and colleges. The other pedagogies already described all profit from having pupils work together in co-operative pairs and groups.

Language experience methods

Language experience methods were first described in relation to the teaching of language and literacy in children with reading difficulties. Where these pupils were having difficulties acquiring basic literacy skills, their own words and stories were used as the texts for them to learn to read. Frequently the word processor is used instead of a scribe to assist pairs in story writing (Peters and Smith, 1986). The edit, spell check and print facilities are particularly encouraging to the young writer. The material can be made into story books with pictures, which have a motivating effect, encouraging much more redrafting and rewriting than would otherwise be the case.

One very powerful motivation is for the writers to prepare their books to read to much younger children and class books may also be compiled. Gardner (1990) showed how able children's creative abilities could be developed and extended by a mixture of study skills and language experience approaches.

References

Arends, R. and Ford, P. M. (1964) Acceleration and Enrichment in the Junior High School. A Follow up Study. Research Report 03-05 (Olympia, WA: State Superintendent of Public Instruction).

Bennett, N. (1986) 'Co-operative learning. Children do it in groups or do they? Paper presented at the DECP Conference London, April.

Birenbaum, M. (1994) Towards an adaptive assessment – the students' angle. Studies in Educational Evaluation, 20, 239–55.

Bloom, B.S. (1956) Taxonomy of Educational Objectives, Vol 1 (London: Longman).

Bowers, S. and Wells, L. (1985) Ways and Means: A problem solving approach (Kingston: Kingston Friends Workshop Group, Eden St).

Brand, C. (1996) The g Factor: general intelligence and its implications (Chichester: Wiley).

Butler-Por, N. (1987) Underachievers in School (Chichester: Wiley).

Callow, R.W. (1983) Editorial. PACE Newsletter, 1 May.

Covington, M.V., and Crutchfield, R.S., Olton, R. and Davies, L. (1972) The Productive Thinking Program (Columbus, OH: Merrill).

Cox, C.M. (1926) Genetic studies of genius, Vol. 2. The early mental traits of 300 geniuses (Stanford, CA: Stanford University Press).

Cropley, A.J. (1994) Creative intelligence. A concept of true giftedness. European Journal of High Ability, 5, 16–23.

Dearing, R. (1994) National Curriculum Revised (York: National Curriculum Council).

de Bono, E. (1970) Lateral Thinking (Harmondsworth: Penguin).

de Bono, E. (1976) Thinking action (Blandford Forum: Direct Educational Services).

Denton, C. and Postlethwaite, K. (1985) Able Children: Identifying them in the classroom (Windsor: NFER-Nelson).

de Haan, R.F. and Havighurst, R.J. (1957) Educating Gifted Children (Chicago, IL: Chicago University Press).

DES (1974) Gifted Children and Their Education (London: HMSO).

Ediger, M (1994) Measurement and evaluation. Studies in Educational Evaluation, 20(2), 169–74.

Elshout, J. (1990) Expertise and giftedness. European Journal of High Ability, 1, 197–203.

Feldhusen, J.F. (1990) Conceptions of creative thinking and creativity training. Presentation at the 1990 International and Research Networking Conference, Buffalo, New York.

Feldhusen, J.F. (1992) Talent Identification and Development in Education (Sarasota, FL: Center for Creative Learning).

Feller, M. (1994) Open book testing and education for the future. Studies in Educational Evaluation, 20(2), 235–8.

Feuerstein, R. (1980) Instrumental Enrichment (Baltimore, MD: University Park Press).

Feuerstein, R. (1993) Mediated learning experience. Keynote presentation MLE Conference February, Regents College, London.

Feuerstein, R. (1995) Mediated learning experience, Keynote presentation and training day, MLE Conference, August, Regents College London.

Flavell, J.H. (1979) Metacognition and cognitive monitoring. American Psychologist, 34, 906–11.

Freeman, J. (1991) Gifted Children Growing Up (London: Cassell).

Galton, F (1869) Hereditary Genius (London: Collins).

Galton, M. Simon, R. and Croll, P. (1985) Inside the Primary Classroom (London: Routledge and Kegan Paul).

Gardner, H. (1983) Frames of Mind (New York: Basic Books)

Gardner, H. (1993) Creative Mind (London: Basic Books).

Gardner, H. (1990) Frames of Mind. The theory of multiple intelligences, 2nd edn (New York: Basic Books).

Getzels, J.W. and Jackson, P.W. (1962) Creativity and Intelligence Explorations with Gifted Students (Chichester: Wiley).

Glaser, R. (1985) Thoughts on Expertise Report No 9 (Pittsburgh, PA: University of Pittsburgh).

Gowan, J.C. and Demos, G.D. (1964) The Education and Guidance of the Ablest (Springfield, IL: Charles C. Thomas).

Guilford, J.P. (1959) The three faces of intellect. American Psychologist, 14, 469–79.

HMI (1992) Provision for Very Highly Able Pupils in Maintained Schools (London: HMSO).

Hollingworth, L. (1926) Gifted Children (New York: World Books).

Kelly, G.A. (1955) The Psychology of Personal Constructs (New York: Norton).

Kerry, T. (1983) Finding and Helping the Able Child (London: Croom Helm).

Kolb, D.A. (1984) Experiential learning. experience as a source of learning and development (New York: Prentice Hall).
Maidenhead Group (1987) The Motorway Project. Townscapes (Wisbech: Learning development aids).
Mönks, F.J. and Mason, E. J. (1993) Development theories and giftedness, in Heller, A., Mönks, F.J. and Passow, A. H. (Eds.) International handbook of research and development of giftedness and talent (Oxford: Pergamon), pp 89–101.
Montgomery, D. (1985) The special needs of able pupils in the ordinary classroom (Maldon: Learning Difficulties Research Project).
Montgomery, D. (1991) The special needs of able pupils in the ordinary classroom, revised edn (Maldon: Learning Difficulties Research Project).
Montgomery, D. (1993) Learner managed learning in teacher education, in Graves, N. (Ed.), Learner Managed Learning: Policy, theory and practice (Leeds: HEC/World Education Fellowship), Ch 7, pp. 59–70
Montgomery, D. (1995) Education for renewal: changing teaching for learning worldwide. New Era in Education, 76(3), 69–77.
Montgomery, D. (1996) Educating the Able (London: Cassell).
Montgomery, D. (1997) Spelling: Remedial Strategies (London: Cassell).
Nickerson, R.S., Perkins, D.N. and Smith, E.E. (1985) The Teaching of Thinking (Hillsdale,NJ: Lawrence Erlbaum).
Noller, R.B., Parnes, S.J. and Bondi, A.M. (1976) Creative Action Book (New York: Scribner).
Ogilvie, E. (1973) Gifted Children in Primary School (London: Macmillan).
Painter, F. (1982) Gifted secondary pupils in England. School Psychology International, 3(4), 237–44.
Passow, A.H. (1982) Differentiated curriculum for the gifted/talented. A point of view, in Kaplan, S.N. and Passow, A.H. (Eds.) Curricula For The Gifted (Ventura County, CA: Ventura County Superintendent of Schools Office).
Passow, A.H. (1990) Needed research and development in teaching high ability children. European Journal of High Ability, 1, 15–24.
Paul, R. (1990) Critical Thinking Theory (Sonoma, CA: Sonoma State University, Centre for Critical Thinking and Moral Critique).
Peters, M.L. and Smith, B. (1986) The productive process. An approach to literacy for children with difficulties, in Root, B. (Ed.) Resources for Reading: does quality count? (London: UKRA/Macmillan), Ch. 13, pp. 161–71
Poorthuis, E., Kok, L. and Van Dijk, J. (1990) A curriculum assessment tool. Paper presented at the 2nd Biennial European Conference of the European Council for High Ability (ECHA) Budapest, October.
Renzulli, J.S. (1977) The Enrichment Triad. A model for developing defensible programs for the gifted and talented (Mansfield Center, CT: Creative Learning Press).
Renzulli, J.S. (1995) New directions in the schoolwide enrichment model, in Katzko, M.W. and Mönks, F.J. (Eds.) Nurturing Talent. (Assen, The Netherlands: Van Gorzum).
Resnick, L.B. (1989) Knowing, learning and instruction. Essays in Honour of Robert Glaser (Hillsdale, NJ: Laurence Erlbaum), pp. 1–24.
Shore, B.M. (1991) How do gifted children think differently? Journal of the Gifted and Talented Education Council of the Alberta Teacher's Association, 5(2), 19–23.
Shore, B.M. and Tsiamis, A. (1986) Identification by provision. In Heller, K.A. and Feldhusen, J.F. (Eds.) Identifying and Nurturing The Gifted (Bern: Huber).
Simonton, D.K. (1988) Scientific Genius. A psychology of science (Cambridge: Cambridge University Press).

Span, P. (1993) Self regulated learning in highly able children, in Freeman, J. Span, P. and Wagner, H. (Eds.) Actualising Talent: A life-long challenge (Gottingen: Hogrese).

Sternberg, R.J. (1986) Beyond IQ. A triarchic theory of intelligence (New York: Cambridge University Press).

Tannenbaum, A.J. (1993) History of giftedness and gifted education in world perspective. In Heller, K.A., Mönks, F.J. and Passow, A.H. (Eds.) International Handbook of Research and Development of Giftedness and Talent (Oxford: Pergamon), pp. 3–27.

Terman, L.M. (1925) Genetic Studies of Genius. The mental and physical traits of a thousand gifted children, Vol. 1 (Stanford, CA: Stanford University Press).

Terman, L.M. (1937) Genetic Studies of Genius. Twenty five years follow up of a superior group, Vol. 3 (Stanford, CA: Stanford University Press).

Torrance, E.P. (1966) Torrance Tests of Creative Thinking (Princeton, NJ: Personnel Press).

Urban, K.K. and Jellen, H.G. (1986) Assessing creative potential via drawing production. The test for creative thinking and drawing productivity, in Cropley, A.J., Urban, K.K., Wagner, H. and Wievezerkowski W. (Eds.) Giftedness. A continuing world wide challenge (New York, Trillium Press).

Wallace, B. (1983) Teaching the Very Able Child (London: Ward Lock).

Yewchuk, C. and Lupart, J. (1993) Gifted handicapped: a desultory duality, in Heller, K.A., Mönks, F. and Passow, A.H. (Eds.) International Handbook of Research and Development of Giftedness and Talent (Oxford: Pergamon).

Ziehl, D.C. (1962) An evaluation of an elementary school enriched instruction program (Ann Arbor, MI: University of Michigan Microfilms N 62 - 4644)

Chapter 14
Parent–professional partnerships in provision for children with special educational needs

SALLY BEVERIDGE

This chapter explores the role of parent–professional partnerships in provision for children with special educational needs. Its primary emphasis is on the significance of the home–school relationship for children's development and learning, but it goes beyond this to embrace aspects of wider professional and community links. Home–school relationships are regarded as central in special educational provision, and the discussion begins with a consideration of why this should be. Changing patterns of parental involvement are then reviewed in order to highlight some future directions for the extension of professional practice.

The development of a close relationship between home and school has long been acknowledged as important for the education of all children. Most writers date official recognition of its significance from the publication of the Plowden Report (CACE, 1967), in which partnership between parents and teachers is described as 'one of the essentials' for promoting children's educational achievements. Almost all government reports since then have endorsed the general principle of increased communication and consultation between home and school. It is important to acknowledge that there are both political and educational reasons for this emphasis. Prevalent political themes of consumerism and the accountability of services have found expression within the educational legislation of the 1980s and 1990s in a continual strengthening of parents' rights in relation to their children's schooling. These have been summarised in the updated Parent's Charter (DfE, 1994a). At the same time as these changes have been introduced, there has also been a growing body of research evidence which demonstrates the benefits that children experience when their parents and teachers work together, for example in the teaching of reading and literacy skills (Wolfendale and Topping, 1996). This research has been underpinned by considerations which are quite different from those governing current political ideology. A guiding principle has been the explicit acceptance that home is a primary context for children's learning and that schools must seek to build upon and extend the learning experiences of home if they are to be fully effective. Furthermore, to do this, they need to value the powerful educational resource which parents can represent.

Where children experience special educational needs, it can be argued that it is even more important that their parents and teachers collaborate with each other. The impact of learning difficulties on children's attainments and behaviour is influenced by the nature and extent of the support they experience, and they are likely to make best progress when their parents and teachers share a positive commitment to meeting their needs. This argument was put forward very strongly in the Warnock Report (DES, 1978), where partnership with parents is described as vital for the successful education of children with special educational needs. There is no doubt that acceptance of the Warnock Committee's views has required a fundamental shift in attitudes in many cases for, as Croll and Moses (1985) have demonstrated, teachers can more readily see parents as the cause of their children's difficulties, rather than as partners with a valuable contribution to make to their education.

Some have suggested that the Warnock Committee's arguments were based on consultation with an unrepresentative sample of parents, and it is notable that Warnock herself has publicly questioned whether the Committee went too far in its advocacy of parents as equal partners in the educational process (1985). Nevertheless, the principles that were embodied in the Warnock Report have continued to be strongly influential. Most recently they have been reiterated and reinforced in the Code of Practice on the identification and assessment of special educational needs (DfE, 1994b), which was drawn up by the government following the Education Act of 1993. The Code of Practice identifies partnership with parents as one of the 'fundamental principles' which should govern special educational provision and, again in line with the Warnock Report, it sets this within a context of wider professional relationships:

> the knowledge, views and experience of parents are vital. Effective assessment and provision will be secured when there is the greatest possible degree of partnership between parents and their children and schools, LEAs and other agencies (para 1:2).

Parental partnership and interdisciplinary involvement are thus both predominant themes in the development of special educational provision. Two others which have also gained particular significance since the publication of the Warnock Report are early intervention and the integration of specialist and community services. A unifying framework for considering these themes which has had long-lasting influence in special education is that which has been derived from Bronfenbrenner's (1977) ecological approach to intervention.

The ecological framework

Bronfenbrenner's framework has been particularly associated with approaches to early intervention. Early intervention which takes place in the preschool years is generally provided for those children who have developmental delays and impairments and also for those who for other reasons are judged to be at risk of later educational failure. LEAs have a responsibility to make provision for children from the age of two years if they have identified special educational needs, but there is a great deal of variation among them with respect to their preschool policies and practices. A number of voluntary agencies are also involved in service provision during the preschool years, but this is similarly variable from authority to authority. As a result, for some parents there is little provision to choose from outside the special school sector, whereas for others there may be a range of both home-based and community-based services. Home-based services are often based upon the Portage model (White and Cameron, 1987), which relies on parents as the primary educators of their own children. Community-based services may include specially resourced community nurseries and mainstream nursery schools and classes, as well as more specialist provision.

Among those who are involved in the field of early intervention there is a working assumption that it may alleviate the effects of disabilities and other disadvantages. Mitchell and Brown (1991) have described common aims as: to provide early stimulation as a basis for subsequent learning; to minimise existing difficulties; and to try to prevent later difficulties from arising. In an influential review of early intervention schemes, Bronfenbrenner (1976) identified the active participation of parents as one of the necessary conditions for their effectiveness. Accordingly, parental involvement is now regarded as a key component, and most services include among their aims some which are specific to parents and the family as a whole, such as: 'to support families in achieving their own goals' (Bailey and Wolery, 1992). Both teachers and parents who are involved in early intervention tend to see it as not only crucial for children with special educational needs, but also as bringing benefits for their families (Beveridge, 1996a).

However, an ecological approach goes beyond a consideration of parental and family involvement to an acknowledgement of the wider influences upon them. Two key features of Bronfenbrenner's (1977) model highlight:

- the influences on children's development of their reciprocal interactions with significant learning contexts;

- the role of both immediate and wider environments and of the inter-relationships between these.

The first of these fits very well with current understandings of the interactive nature of special educational needs. Children are active participants in their environments, both influencing and being influenced by the interactions which take place. Special educational needs can be characterised as resulting from a mismatch between the demands made by a child's learning environment and his or her personal resources to meet these. It follows from this that any assessment of needs must take account of the settings in which they arise.

For most children, home and school are the immediate environments which represent their most significant learning contexts, and it is parents and teachers who usually play a key role in the identification of any difficulties that they experience. When special educational needs are identified, other significant settings for children can include both community and home-based services, in which they may be involved with a wide range of different professionals such as health visitors and paediatricians, physio- and speech therapists, specialists in hearing and vision, and so on. Bronfenbrenner's model emphasises that it is not only these immediate environments in themselves which influence children's development, but also the relationships and interactions between them.

Home, school and other services are themselves embedded in the wider environment of the local community. Parents often express a strong desire that any specialist services their children require should not result in their being isolated from that community. They want their children to have local friends and belong and to 'feel a part of the whole', as one mother put it (Beveridge, 1996a). This is one of the primary reasons given by parents in support of the trend towards greater integration or inclusiveness in education, summed up by another mother as follows:

> The children would feel part of the real world, their parents would feel that they weren't being shut away and treated as different and it would do the mainstream children good (ibid. p26).

Local policies and practices regarding the integration of special and mainstream services reflect the prevailing ideology of the time. The ecological model highlights the way in which these 'influence, delimit or even determine' (Bronfenbrenner, 1977) the relationships between home, school and community and, through this, have an impact on children's learning and development.

This brief overview of Bronfenbrenner's ecological perspective demonstrates that its applicability goes beyond early intervention. It provides both a rationale and a framework for bringing together the themes of parental, interdisciplinary and community involvement in educational provision for children with special educational needs.

Concepts of partnership

Both the Warnock Report (DES, 1978) and the Code of Practice (DfE, 1994b) use the term 'partnership' to describe the nature of the relationship that professionals should seek to develop with parents of children with special educational needs. Professionals use the term frequently, and they use it to describe a range of different forms of collaboration. It is important to recognise, however, that what characterises partnership is neither the frequency of contact nor any particular format for this, but rather the quality of the interaction which takes place. The concept is based on the recognition that parents and professionals have complementary contributions to make to children's development and learning and that they have what Wolfendale (1988) refers to as 'equivalent expertise'. It follows, therefore, that professionals must seek out, listen to and value parental perspectives, and demonstrate that they treat what parents have to say as important. It can take time to build up the positive relationships which facilitate this, and while many teachers and other professionals aim to develop communication with parents which is based on mutual trust and respect, it must be acknowledged that parental experiences of contacts with professionals can be far removed from the partnership ideal. As Sandow, Stafford and Stafford (1987) have noted, partnership is a term which is far more readily used by professionals than by parents.

If partnerships between parents and professionals are difficult to achieve, partnerships between all those professionals involved with the family of a child with special educational needs can be more so. Essentially similar conditions are required for effective interdisciplinary working as are needed for individual professional partnership with parents. These include, for example:

- an explicit acknowledgement of what each has to offer
- a sense of shared purpose and common goals
- clarity about respective roles and responsibilities
- flexible two-way channels of communication
- reciprocal respect, trust and support.

Davie (1993) and Dessent (1996) have explored the nature of the current obstacles to interdisciplinary partnerships. These lie, for example, within separate professional development and administrative systems and in discrete legal frameworks. However, both authors see some grounds for optimism in Russell's (1992) argument that:

Perhaps the greatest potential for change in resolving inter-professional boundary issues has come through the changing role of parents (p. 179).

Russell is referring here to the unique role of parents and the way in which their perspectives on their own children, embracing as they must the whole child in both formal and informal learning contexts, could serve to integrate the individual concerns of all the professionals who are involved. Davie (1993) makes a similar point about the integrative function which might be played by the children themselves, whose right to be involved in decisions affecting their provision has been endorsed in the Children Act, 1989 as well as in the Code of Practice. While both parents and children have rights concerning the way in which needs are characterised and the form of provision which is made to meet these, however, there is ample evidence that professionals do not give up their decision-making power readily (Galloway, Armstrong and Tomlinson, 1994). Parents and their children may, therefore, need support if they are to exercise their rights.

The current context for developing partnership

The current context for developing parent–professional partnerships for children with special educational needs has been established by the Code of Practice (DfE 1994b). This sets out a five-stage framework for identification, assessment and intervention which gives explicit recognition to the full continuum of special educational needs. The five stages represent increasing levels and complexities of need, and are characterised by increasingly systematic and formalised procedures for assessment, planned intervention and review, and by the involvement of a wider range of school staff and other professionals. Throughout, constructive communication with parents is identified as central to the effectiveness of the special educational provision which is made. Accordingly, there is an explicit expectation that schools must give detailed consideration to the information they provide for parents, their accessibility and the arrangements which they make in order to promote partnership.

The information that schools provide for parents should include clear and accurate details of the SEN policy, and of the sort of support that staff will give to their children. Parents should also be informed of the ways in which they can expect to be involved by school in the assessment, decision-making and review process. Schools have an important role to play in providing information about the possible involvement of support from the LEA or other outside agencies. In addition, the Code of Practice suggests that they need to be familiar with voluntary organisations in the community that parents might find helpful as further sources of information, advice and support.

As far as their accessibility is concerned, schools need to give attention both to the ways in which they communicate information and also to their general approachability for parents. That is, information should be monitored to ensure that it is easily accessed and readily understandable, and physical arrangements should be reviewed to check that they are perceived as welcoming and comfortable and do not pose any unnecessary barriers which deter parents from coming into school.

In order to promote working partnerships with parents, the Code of Practice emphasises that schools need to develop procedures for encouraging, recording and responding to parental views and concerns, with the intention of making sure that the provision they make for children with special educational needs is as fully informed as possible by ongoing dialogue with their parents.

It is important to highlight the additional demands for consultation with parents that the Code of Practice places on schools. In the past, practice has varied a great deal between schools, but there have been three main elements to the ways in which they have sought parental participation when children have special educational needs. Initially, teachers have tended to consult parents if they feel concerned that a child is experiencing difficulties. Then, when difficulties persist, they have often asked parents to support programmes initiated at school, for example by working on literacy or numeracy or behaviour management programmes at home. The subsequent involvement of parents in the review of progress has typically taken place through parent–teacher consultation evenings and annual written reports, although depending on the child's needs, there might be more frequent informal communication. For the parents of children with statements of special educational need, there should also be the opportunity to participate in annual reviews.

The Code of Practice envisages a far more active partnership role for parents than this. It emphasises that parents, through their daily family interactions, are often the first to notice any aspects of their children's development which give cause for concern, and that schools should capitalise on this potential contribution to their early identification procedures. Parents and teachers also have much to learn from one another when it comes to continuing assessment of children's needs. Parents have in-depth knowledge, information and experiences of their own children which can add greatly to a teacher's understanding of those children's individual educational needs. At the same time, if they are fully involved by teachers at all stages of the assessment process, then parents are themselves likely to gain increased insights into the sorts of strategies which might best help their child.

In addition to the unique perspectives that they can bring to assessment, parents are also likely to have their own priorities for their children, and preferences for the forms of provision which might best meet their needs. Schools need to ensure, therefore, that decision-making is properly informed by parental perspectives and that:

> school-based action should take account of the wishes, feelings and knowledge of parents at all stages (DfE, 1994b, para 2:28).

In recognition of the importance of the contribution that parents can make to the educational process, the Code of Practice puts forward an approach to parent–teacher partnership that involves a two-way process of shared understandings and insights throughout a continuing cycle of assessment, decision-making and review.

Such an ongoing partnership process makes demands of schools which are of three main kinds. First, schools need to introduce systematic procedures for all parents of children with special educational needs, not only those whose children have statements. Further, they should consult with parents not only during the preliminary stages of identification and assessment, but also throughout a regular ongoing cycle of assessment, decision-making and review. Finally, if they are to engage in genuine two-way communication with parents, then this requires that they actively elicit parental perspectives and provide support for their contributions to the educational process. It might also be noted that, while the Code of Practice places primary emphasis on the importance of parent–teacher relationships, schools can also have a role to play in coordinating parental consultation with the wider range of professionals who may be involved.

Changing patterns of practice

The Code of Practice has, in theory, provided an impetus for schools to take a fresh look at their approach to the involvement of parents of children with special educational needs. In practice, the priority for many schools has been to develop their within-school systems for assessment, decision-making and review. Some have hardly begun to explore the ways in which they might involve parents in these; others, particularly those with well-established procedures for home–school liaison, have found that the main impact of the Code so far has been to make their communications with parents more systematic and focused (Beveridge, 1997).

In order to highlight some of the issues which schools need to consider, it is helpful to draw upon the experiences of those parents whose children have statements. These parents have been legally entitled to participate in formal assessment and annual reviews ever since the implementation of the 1981 Education Act. Their perspectives on involvement with professionals provide significant insights into the ways in which schools might seek to develop and extend their partnership policies.

The intention of the 1981 Education Act, reinforced by the 1993 Education Act which has largely replaced it, is that parents and professionals should come to an 'agreed understanding' of the nature of children's special educational needs and the provision which is required to meet these. However, special educational needs are complex, and their assessment must take account of the interactive learning contexts in which they arise. As a result of this complexity, there is considerable scope for misunderstandings and discrepancies between parental and professional perspectives (see, for example, Galloway et al., 1994). Parents may feel that professionals are not looking at their child as a whole person and are therefore not seeing the child that they know. They may think professionals have too narrow a focus, leading to an underestimation of the difficulties experienced in home and community contexts. Conversely, they can be distressed by what they see as an undue emphasis on their child's weaknesses (Russell, 1991) or, in some cases, on their own parenting skills (Galloway, Armstrong and Tomlinson, 1994).

Professionals vary in the extent to which they recognise the validity of differing perspectives, or what Dale (1996) has referred to as the 'legitimacy of dissent'. They also vary in their skills in reconciling differing viewpoints where these exist. It is clear from parental experience of involvement in the statementing process that professionals must continue to develop their skills of listening to what parents have to say. They need to recognise and respect parental contributions, avoid making assumptions about the home learning environment and seek to establish a comprehensive and balanced picture of their children's strengths as well as their weaknesses. They need to be sensitive too to the personal and emotional investment that parents feel, and the stressful experience that formal assessment procedures so often represent.

Although parents have both rights and also a potentially very important role to play in assessment and review, there is strong evidence that they need clear and accurate information to enable them to exercise their rights. They may also require structure and support to help them prepare their contributions (e.g. Wolfendale, 1988; Hughes and Carpenter, 1991). In the absence of appropriate assistance, it is rare for parents to feel that their views have been taken fully into account. Armstrong (1995) has argued that even those professionals who are committed to the ideal of working in partnership with parents can sometimes inadvertently raise barriers to their full participation. For example, they may be so familiar themselves with the formal assessment and review procedures that they misjudge parental understanding of these. As a result, parents may not appreciate the relevance or significance of the information the professionals provide, and this puts them at a marked disadvantage in any subsequent 'joint' decision-making. The feelings of powerlessness that parents can experience in this situation are not always recognised, because parents and professionals can come away from a meeting with very different perceptions of what has gone on. Whereas a professional may believe that the meeting has involved parents as full participants, parents may have seen its purpose as being to gain their agreement to a professional decision.

The Audit Commission/HMI (1992) carried out an interview survey of parents of children with statements which confirms that they are often strongly influenced by professional judgements when it comes to decisions about school placements, even though professionals may have perceived it differently. In this survey, a significant minority of the parents whose children were placed in special schools wished to move them to mainstream settings. Although some of them expected to raise this as an issue at an annual review, the Audit Commission/HMI argued from what they had learned of the review process that there was little likelihood that these parental preferences would be acted upon. It was one of their recommendations, therefore, that annual reviews were strengthened to reflect greater accountability to parents.

Since the publication of that report, the Code of Practice has made explicit the need for annual reviews to take account of both parents' views and also those of the children themselves. In addition, it emphasises that schools may need to seek contributions from other professionals. Dessent (1996) has summarised some of the difficulties that parents can experience when there is poor coordination between the different professionals who are concerned with their child. These essentially involve a lack of clarity about roles and responsibilities, with too many professionals asking the same questions and ambiguities arising about who should be responsible for ensuring that specified services are received. Other problems result from a breakdown of communication between the different professionals, when relevant information is not shared between them, and conflicting advice and guidance may be given to parents. In its attempt to promote a better coordinated approach, the Code of Practice acknowledges that it is unlikely that all relevant professionals will be able to attend all annual review meetings. However, it envisages that schools will take a significant liaison role in ensuring that their perspectives are taken into account.

It would appear from this overview of the experiences of parents of children with statements that, if schools are to aim for genuine partnership in assessment, decision-making and review, then they need to:

- show sensitivity to parental perspectives and acknowledge their validity
- demonstrate the way in which assessment of the whole child in his or her family and wider learning contexts informs the decision-making process

- seek, support and respond to parental contributions as intrinsically important
- be prepared to negotiate, reconcile perspectives and share decision-making
- ensure that where other professionals are involved, roles, responsibilities and what each expects of the other, are clear to all concerned.

There is no doubt that professionals who are knowledgeable and informed about the nature of special educational needs and about the sorts of intervention which may help children overcome their difficulties, are likely to communicate a more positive approach both to children and their parents as well as a greater confidence about working in partnership. It is vital therefore that whole school policies and staff development practices are designed to promote the attitudes, knowledge, skills and understanding that will best support good relationships with parents. Parents respond most readily to those professionals who show genuine care about their children, who express concerns about their development and learning in constructive ways, and who view the identification of difficulty as a positive first step towards meeting individual needs. They appreciate the 'approachability' of those staff who demonstrate commitment to openness and a full sharing of information, as well as genuine respect for the distinctive contribution which they have to make as parents (Beveridge, 1997).

Future directions

When looking at current patterns of practice it is possible to identify a number of areas of parent–professional partnership where there is scope for future development. Perhaps the most significant of these concerns parental participation in the decision-making process. Two further associated issues relate to parental involvement in the implementation of programmes at home, and the role of the children themselves in any educational partnership.

If professionals are to involve parents as fully as possible in decision-making, then this requires an extension of their skills. That is, they not only need the sorts of positive attitudes, confidence and commitment to partnership that have already been discussed above. In addition, they must also feel ready to acknowledge that parental viewpoints may necessarily be different from their own, and that this does not make them in any sense less valid. Further, they must be willing to seek ways to reconcile varying perspectives and negotiate shared understandings.

Professionals also need to give more thought to the sorts of information, preparation and support that parents may require to enable them to participate in decision-making. There is evidence that parents do not always remember or understand information which has been offered (e.g. Armstrong, 1995; Dale, 1996), and there is scope for work on the clarity and vocabulary of professional communication. While parents may welcome the opportunity for face to face communication with relevant professionals, this needs to be complemented by more extensive use of written information which they might refer back to and reflect upon at greater length.

Professionals themselves plan, sometimes in considerable detail, for meetings with parents when decisions are to be made. However, it is still relatively rare for them to give parents the opportunity to contribute to the agenda for discussion, or to provide further information and support of the kind which would allow parents to be similarly well-prepared when meetings take place. This does not lead to equal participation in decision-making, for as one mother has described it: 'unprepared, you're just on the defensive the whole time' (Beveridge, 1997).

Some parents are likely to require more support than others, both in order to recognise what it is that they have to contribute and also to put forward their perspectives as effectively as possible. As a number of authors have noted, unless parents are sufficiently informed and knowledgeable about decision-making systems and confident of the role they have to play, then the extent to which they can exercise their rights is limited (e.g. Wragg, 1989; Armstrong, 1995). Accordingly, some have argued that a greater degree of involvement in decision-making requires that partnerships are developed within the context of community education and the 'empowerment' of children and their families (e.g. Watt, 1989).

Irrespective of the level of information, preparation and support that parents have, few feel confident in their knowledge of the formal academic curriculum or of specific therapeutic programmes, and they may well expect professionals to take the lead in decisions about appropriate interventions for their children. Nevertheless, they have perspectives, aspirations and priorities which need to be addressed. This becomes particularly important when, as is often the case, parents are asked to support professional intervention by working with their child at home.

The emphasis which is currently given by many professionals to involving parents in learning, behaviour and therapy programmes at home is a sign of a high level of acknowledgement that parents represent a potentially powerful teaching resource. The challenge now is to develop this sort of work with parents in ways which are in line with partnership. This requires professionals to find a balance in which they encourage parents to feel confident that they can contribute in significant ways, but do not place them under undue pressure or lead them to believe that they have sole responsibility for their children's progress. An important shift in professional thinking is to recognise what parents have to offer in their own right as parents, rather than simply as teacher or therapist aides.

Parents hold varied views both about what it is that constitutes teaching and also about how far this is an integral part of their parental role. From their research, Atkin and Bastiani (1986) have described a number of dimensions of individual diversity in how parents perceive teaching. They vary, for example, in the extent to which they believe that teaching:

- is primarily concerned with systematically planned and adult directed activity or also incorporates more incidental and child-initiated interaction;
- involves the use of tasks and methods with a specifically educational focus or also embraces improvised approaches and materials;
- requires a formal learning context or can take place anywhere within the context of daily routines.

Atkin and Bastiani's study was concerned with parents whose children do not have identified special educational needs, but it seems reasonable to suppose that there may be similar dimensions of difference among all parents. Diversity in such parental beliefs, as well as the variation families typically show in their roles, routines and interactive styles, must all have an effect on the teaching which takes place at home. One significant difference which can arise for many parents when their children have special educational needs, though, is a greater level of professional expectation that they should see explicit teaching as part of their role.

There is little evidence about the basis for this expectation as far as the majority of parents of children with special educational needs are concerned. Among parents of young children who have significant developmental delays and impairments, it is clear that many do want to know what they can do to best facilitate their children's development and learning (e.g. Mittler and Mittler, 1982). However, there is also evidence (e.g. Dale, 1996) that parents can feel that too much responsibility is placed on them to carry out programmes at home. It should be noted too that the close emotional bonds between parents and their children can sometimes make it stressful for them to work together on formal teaching activities or behaviour management programmes, and some parents feel unable to be directly involved in these ways. Furthermore, it is not uncommon for parents to feel that with increasing age, their children's independence and identification with their peer group gain in priority, and therefore direct work together on specific programmes at home should have a lower profile.

There is a need then for professionals to explore the extent to which they can negotiate shared responsibilities with parents, and develop joint interventions which do not add to family stress, but which take account of individual diversity and parental priorities and concerns for their children. They must also take account of the perspectives of the children themselves. In recent years, there has been a growing acknowledgement of the need to listen to and respect the views of children and young people concerning decisions which affect them. As discussed earlier, this principle is endorsed in both the Children Act, 1989 and the Code of Practice:

> children have a right to be heard. They should be encouraged to participate in decision-making about provision to meet their special educational needs. (DfE, 1994b, para 2:35).

The Code of Practice is explicit that children and young people with special educational needs not only have a right to be involved, but also have an important contribution to make to the process of assessment, decision-making and review.

It is notable that researchers have now begun to focus more directly on pupils' perspectives, for example on integration and other aspects of special educational provision (e.g. Cooper, 1993; Wade and Moore, 1993; Lewis, 1995; Lloyd-Smith and Dwyfor Davies, 1995; Beveridge, 1996b). However, children need help from both parents and professionals if they are to exercise their rights to participate as fully and effectively as possible. The fundamental aim underpinning parent–professional partnerships must be to enhance the development and learning of the children concerned. It is a continuing challenge for professionals, therefore, to develop forms of support which will enable the children to become active participants in those partnerships themselves.

References

Armstrong, D. (1995) Power and Partnership in Education (London: Routledge).
Atkin, J. and Bastiani, J. (1986) 'Are they teaching?': an alternative perspective on parents as educators. Education 3(13,14), 18–22.
Audit Commission/HMI (1992) Getting in on the Act (London: HMSO).
Bailey, D.B. and Wolery, M. (1992) Teaching Infants and Preschoolers with Disabilities. 2nd edn (New York: Macmillan).
Beveridge, S. (1996a) Dimensions of preschool provision for children with special educational needs, in Broadhead, P. (Ed.) Researching the Early Years Continuum. BERA Dialogues, 12 (Clevedon: Multilingual Matters).
Beveridge, S (1996b) Experiences of an integration link scheme: the perspectives of pupils with severe learning difficulties and their mainstream peers. British Journal of Learning Disabilities, 24, 9–19.
Beveridge, S. (1997) Implementing partnership with parents in schools. In S. Wolfendale (ed.) Working with Parents of SEN Children after the Code of Practice (London: David Fulton).
Bronfenbrenner, U. (1976) Is early intervention effective? Facts and principles of early intervention: a summary. In Clarke, A.M. and Clarke, A.D.B. (Eds.) Early Experience: Myth and Evidence (London: Open Books).

Bronfenbrenner, U. (1977) Towards an ecology of human development. American Psychologist, 32, 513–31.
Central Advisory Committee for Education (1967) Children and their Primary Schools (The Plowden Report) (London: HMSO).
Cooper, P. (1993) Learning from pupil perspectives. British Journal of Special Education, 20, 129–33.
Croll, P. and Moses, D. (1985) One in Five: The assessment and incidence of special educational needs (London: Routledge and Kegan Paul).
Dale, N. (1996) Working with Families of Children with Special Needs (London: Routledge).
Davie, R. (1993) Interdisciplinary perspectives on assessment, in Wolfendale, S. (Ed.). Assessing Special Educational Needs (London: Cassell).
DES (1978) Special Educational Needs (The Warnock Report) (London: HMSO).
Dessent, T. (1996) Options for partnership between health, education and social services. Policy Options for Special Educational Needs in the 1990s, Seminar Paper 6 (Tamworth: NASEN).
DfE (1994a) Our Children's Education: The updated parent's charter (London: HMSO).
DfE (1994b) Code of Practice on the Identification and Assessment of Special Educational Needs (London: HMSO).
Galloway, D., Armstrong, D. and Tomlinson, S. (1994) The Assessment of Special Educational Needs: Whose problem? (London: Longman).
Hughes, N. and Carpenter, B. (1991) Annual reviews: an active partnership, in Ashdown, R. Carpenter, B. and Bovair, K. (Eds.) The Curriculum Challenge (London: Falmer Press).
Lewis, A. (1995) Children's Understanding of Disability (London: Routledge).
Lloyd-Smith, M. and Dwyfor Davies, J. (Eds.) (1995) On The Margins: The educational experience of 'problem' pupils (Stoke-on-Trent: Trentham Books).
Mitchell, D. and Brown, R.I. (Eds.) (1991) Early Intervention Studies for Young Children with Special Needs (London: Chapman & Hall).
Mittler, P. and Mittler, H. (1982) Partnership with Parents (Stratford-upon-Avon: NCSE).
Russell, P. (1991) Access to the National Curriculum for parents, in Ashdown, R., Carpenter, B. and Bovair, K. (Eds.) The Curriculum Challenge (London: Falmer Press).
Russell, P. (1992) Boundary issues: multidisciplinary working in new contexts - implications for educational psychology practice, in Wolfendale, S., Bryans, T., Fox, M., Labram, A. and Sigston, A. (Eds.). The Profession and Practice of Educational Psychology (London: Cassell).
Sandow, S., Stafford, D. and Stafford, P. (1987) An Agreed Understanding? (Windsor: NFER-Nelson).
Wade, B. and Moore, M. (1993) Experiencing Special Education: What young people with special educational needs can tell us (Buckingham: Open University Press).
Warnock, M. (1985) Teacher teach thyself. The 1985 Richard Dimbleby Lecture. The Listener, 28 March, 10–14.
Watt, J. (1989) Community education and parental involvement: a partnership in need of a theory. In Macleod, F. (Ed.) Parents and Schools: The contemporary challenge. (Basingstoke: Falmer).
White, M. and Cameron, S. (1987) The Portage Early Education Programme (Windsor: NFER-Nelson).

Wolfendale, S. (1988) The Parental Contribution to Assessment (Stratford-upon-Avon: NCSE).

Wolfendale, S. and Topping, K.J. (Eds.) (1996) Family Involvement in Literacy (London: Cassell).

Wragg, T. (1989) Parent power, in Macleod, F. (Ed.) Parents and Schools: The contemporary challenge (Basingstoke: Falmer).

Chapter 15
The No Blame Approach to bullying

BARBARA MAINES AND GEORGE ROBINSON

> The literature on bullying is beginning to proliferate. The trouble is that most of it offers data on percentages of bullies and victims or elegant conceptual analyses of what might be the root causes in psychological, sociological or pedagogical terms. What few publications yet do, is to offer individual teachers, pupils or schools practical advice on how to deal with this many-headed hydra.
>
> Bob Burden, *Special Children*, September 1991.

Thirty ago when we began our careers in education, the job of the educational psychologist was largely restricted to the assessment of young people who were struggling in the school system and for whom an IQ test was deemed a helpful intervention. The resulting report often led to a special school placement, a decision jointly made by the psychologist and the school medical officer. Teachers were not viewed as colleague professionals but as clients for whom a diagnostic service was offered. Psychologists were rarely invited to participate in planning helpful interventions for young people and the usefulness of their reports, peppered with jargon and statistics, was not evaluated. In the 1970s an influential publication introduced educationalists to the process of consultation and offered an opportunity for change in work practice – the chance to negotiate alternatives to pupil assessments and to collaborate with teacher colleagues (Caplan, 1970). In the 1980s, psychologists were being trained in systems approaches and the introduction of complex legislation gave them an opportunity to offer inservice training and consultation to support the implementation of the 1981 Education Act. Increasing demands upon teachers to comply with constantly changing curriculum and assessment demands has kept that door open; stressed and sometimes desperate teachers have continued to express some dissatisfactions with the service offered to them by their educational psychologists but in spite of the complaints they almost universally want more of the psychologist's time in schools. The emergence of psychologists from behind the IQ test forced them to risk their credibility in systems and curricular areas such as bullying. In November 1990 a pupil in a Bristol comprehensive school attempted suicide. The distress and confusion amongst students, teachers and parents offered an opportunity for new and exciting work.

What is bullying?

Not every act of aggression or nastiness is bullying, and it is important to define the particular behaviours and processes before planning helpful interventions. Bullying is a relationship between individuals or groups over a period of time during which one party behaves in a way that might meet needs for excitement, status, material gain or group process without recognizing or meeting the needs and rights of other people who are harmed by the behaviour. The person or group that is harmed does not have the resources, status, skill or ability to counteract or stop the harmful behaviour.

Occasional acts of aggression would not be described as bullying unless there is a continuing fear or torment for the victims. It is also important to differentiate bullying from 'war-like' behaviours where opposing groups confront each other because they have different belief systems or territorial claims. These values may be strongly held through generations and are very resistant to change.

We do not differentiate between 'bullying – by an individual' and 'mobbing – by a group' as discussed by Anatol Pikas (1989). This is because we are describing situations in which, even if the bully is operating solo, his or her behaviour is usually witnessed in some way by others. If the witness supports the bully, however passive that support might be, then the behaviour is in some way owned by the whole group and the strengths of the group can be enabled in order to confront the behaviour. Where the bullying occurs in true secrecy, unknown to any witness other than the victim, then interventions are unlikely unless the behaviour is reported by the victim.

We have been to several workshops and heard accounts of incidents which have served to confirm our worry about the scale and seriousness of bullying at a group and institutional level. This chapter sets a challenge to its readers. We believe that the interventions which are likely to combat bullying in schools demand much more from us than the impeccable intention to convey to bullies that their behaviour is unacceptable.

Defining the terms

Our definitions are as follows.

> **Bully**: a person or group behaving in a way which might meet needs for excitement, status, material gain or group process and does not recognize or meet the needs and rights of other people who are harmed by the behaviour.
> **Victim**: a person or group that is harmed by the behaviour of others and who does not have the resources, status, skill or ability, to counteract or stop the harmful behaviour.
> **Bullying**: a 'relationship' between those involved which takes place over time and within which a persistent fear or anxiety is experienced by the victim. It differs from random acts of aggression in that it is predictable.

Bullying is 'normal'

Many of those reading this chapter will have had some close relationship with a very young baby at some time in their lives and they will remember the self-centered and relentlessly demanding behaviour exhibited by a tiny, dependent human being. If babies were big and parents small then parents would undoubtedly be bullied! You may also remember, if you are a parent or have had close relationships with young children, the first time that the child was upset or cried, not because some need or demand of their own was unmet, but because of a sadness or hurt felt on behalf of another person or creature. This emergence of 'empathy' is a complex step in social and emotional development and it is upon these feelings that kind and unselfish behaviours are based.

We believe that it is not helpful to regard bullying as abnormal or evil. Many of us will remember standing back and at least colluding with, if not participating in, some hurtful behaviour towards another person because it increased our own sense of belonging or identity that we were not the one being rejected. Parents and teachers will often observe very nice kids behaving in a very nasty way when the need to belong to a group of peers is an over-riding factor. Today's young people living in affluent countries are subjected to strong pressure by the manufacturers of trendy clothes and toys. Wearing the right trainers is all important but they are only the right trainers if someone else isn't wearing them!

A willingness to step outside a peer group and stand alongside someone who is rejected and harmed takes strength and courage. It also puts the 'rescuer' at risk of rejection, and the success of this stand is likely to depend upon the social or physical status of the rescuer. We are likely then to take this risk only when we identify with the distress of the victim and when we feel that our intervention is likely to bring about some change; when we feel involved and powerful.

Witnesses of bullying or those who care for the victims might have very strong feelings of anger and a need to punish the perpetrators. If an adult who is in a position of power uses his or her authority to stop the bullying then it may have a short term effect upon that particular situation but it is unlikely to change the status or identity of the bully and victim. There may well be a risk that the victim is further damaged because the bully was thwarted . . . 'I will get you later!'

This chapter will suggest that the primary focus of our plan to reduce bullying should be upon the feelings and status of the bully. By involving the peer group, colluders and bystanders, it is possible to enhance the empathic responses of healthy members of the group. This, in turn, has an effect on the behaviour of the group leader who no longer has the group's consent to behave in a bullying manner.

Data collection and whole school approaches

Bullying in British schools is now recognized as a serious problem and there is evidence from reported work in Sheffield and other LEAs that more and more schools are developing and implementing whole school policies. (Maines and Robinson, 1991; Smith and Sharp, 1994; Sharp and Smith, 1994).

These are generally planned to:

- protect the victims through assertiveness training and open communication
- develop a school ethos which gives clear messages that bullying will not be tolerated, that bullies will be punished and that victims will be protected.

At the same time, schools persist in maintaining structures which might promote bullying. Teams and houses create the identity of groups. The members will belong only because others do not and they will support the identity of the group by strengthening the boundary around it. Are we expecting too much when we ask a young person to discriminate between winning on the sports field through superior strength and using the same strategy to win power or possession in the playground? The very language of success, 'I beat her, thrashed her, wiped the floor with her,' is applauded if it refers to a 'game' and punished if it refers to a 'fight'.

The challenge to school practice

Many of the strategies we use may be ineffective in changing the behaviour of the bully. We approach the situation with strong feelings of anger and frustration towards the bully and sympathy for the victim. We have a responsibility to the students and their parents to respond effectively and the measure of the success of our intervention has to be the degree to which it stops the bullying. Some of the responses often made by teachers are not successful in achieving this and we discuss them below. Please try and set aside any feelings of retribution towards the bully – your aim is not justice or morality; it is to change behaviour and thus achieve the best outcome for the victim.

Dangers of labelling

Although we use the terms 'bully' and 'victim' in this and other publications we do not think it is helpful to use them as labels in school. We know that to call a young person by any name must affect that person's self-image and must be difficult for parents to accept when we want to work co-operatively with them. We have heard of one London school where bullies are required to wear a badge saying, 'I am a bully!' Is such a label likely to decrease or increase the bullying behaviour?

Getting to the bottom of it

It seems like common sense to question students when bad behaviour is brought to our attention. Teachers suggest that before they can take effective action they need to gather the evidence and establish the facts. Interviews are arranged and written accounts prepared, and the result is a collection of subjective and very varying recollections. If young people are interrogated about an event they will give their own perspective and these are often contradictory, especially when a bully is trying to extract him or herself from blame. Young people often report that they give teachers the answers that will appease – the answers that will get them out of trouble and out of the room as quickly as possible. The quest for the truth may become a distraction and achieve nothing to encourage improved behaviour in the future.

Even less helpful is to ask students to explain why they behave in a certain way. It is very hard to explain our actions, maybe impossible in a way which will satisfy a teacher. We were recently told about a small pupil who undid the safety bolts on a climbing frame and his teacher asked him why he had done it. His predictable reply was, 'Don't know, Miss.' The teacher became frustrated and we asked her why she thought he had done it. 'Because he is disturbed and attention seeking,' she replied. Was the teacher really expecting the boy to reply, 'Well, Miss, It is because I am disturbed... ?'

Changing the victim

'You have to learn how to stand up for yourself,' says my mother.

'Don't let them push you around. Don't be spineless. You have to have more backbone.'

I think of sardines and their backbones. You can eat their backbones. The bones crumble between your teeth in one touch and they fall apart. This must be what my own backbone is like; hardly there at all. What is happening to me is my own fault, for not having more backbone. (Margaret Attwood, 1990).

Over and over again we hear from victims that they are advised and urged to change their behaviour in some way, either by parents, teachers or through group work. They try to 'stand up for themselves', 'hit back', 'walk away', 'pretend you don't care', and each time their failure to act in a way which ends their misery just makes it worse. They feel it is their own fault that this is happening to them. It is not. Whatever their own inadequacy or difficulty, it is not their fault and it is not their responsibility to stop it. It is our responsibility and we must give them that message loud and clear if we are not to compound their unhappiness.

There is nothing wrong with assertiveness training for everyone. There is plenty of benefit to be gained from social skills programmes for lots of students who are having difficulties in making relationships. However, these interventions should not be linked directly with the victim's plight but with more general developmental work.

Punishment

Maybe the biggest challenge to existing school practice is the advice to abandon punishment as a response to the bullies, for two different reasons.

- There is no evidence that punishment taught a bully how to behave in a different way or that it has encouraged more positive relationships within school. These desirable goals are better achieved by processes such as Circle Time and mediation where empathic, altruistic and problem-solving behaviours are taught and where staff are models of these activities in daily school life. Circle Time is a recent and very popular innovation in British schools. It offers, through regular meetings and by a very structured set of rules, games and processes, a way of teaching social, moral and spiritual development (Bliss and Tetley, 1994; Bliss, Robinson and Maines, 1995).
- There are several accounts of increased suffering by victims when bullies take revenge after having received punitive actions:
'If we'd been punished, if we'd been shouted at or told off we wouldn't have wanted to help, to be her friend because she'd got us into trouble.' *That's Life*, interview, February 1993.

If you want to encourage disclosure and you want to work positively with bullies, then everyone in school must know that effective action will be taken, but that it will not lead to punishment. For this reason, we cannot agree with the following views. In *Bullying – a Practical Guide to Coping for Schools* (Elliott, 1991), Eric Jones writes,

> Punish bullies. Record punishment and the reasons for it. Show him what you are putting on file and make him pay with whatever time it cost you to sort it out (p. 23).

In another chapter from the same book, John Pearce advises that when a bully is caught in the act we should respond by

> Telling a bully that he or she will be dealt with later, without specifying how or when, can be very effective. The bully is likely to worry about what may happen...'(p. 84).

Bullying is an antisocial behaviour resorted to by young people with inadequate or inappropriate social skills and we must respond in a way which will be helpful to their learning of improved behaviour. Increasing their anxiety and alienation from us is not likely to work!

The United Nations Convention on the Rights of the Child (1989) gives schools the responsibility to ensure that 'in all actions concerning children...the best interests of the child shall be a primary consideration' (Article 3)

Responses by schools to bullying behaviours must be in the best interests of the bully, the victim and the community.

The use of power

Bullying seems to be a clash between the powerful and the powerless, but power is seen in many aspects of human behaviour. Bullying can be viewed as part of a normal process of socialization in which the group establishes its identity which is reinforced by the exclusion of others. The strength of the group lies in its sense of cohesion and without somebody out-grouped – that is visibly outside the group, the boundaries are hard to define.

Jack Straw highlights this in a newspaper article:

> It wasn't classic bullying. There was no single lad beating up a smaller one. Indeed, very little of the bullying was physical at all.
>
> It was verbal, psychological, insidious and, in many ways, the worse for that. Paul had been 'chosen' as the odd one out. I have no idea how the rest of us made that choice. Certainly, it was never a conscious decision. But the rest of us – each of whom, I guess, also found the frugal atmosphere of a fifties boarding school quite hard to bear – picked on Paul. He smelt – but didn't

we all with only one bath and one shirt a week, who wouldn't? He was stupid – though his academic results were the same as the rest of us. He didn't join in – we made sure of that. Above all, he was different. I cannot for the life of me remember why, or how, except that we had to make him different. And we did. So a low level campaign was undertaken against him. In a crowd, he'd find that he was always more likely to slip on muddy surfaces than the rest of us. None of us – though standing next to him – could ever explain why. His games kit hung up neatly in the changing room before he went to bed at night, somehow ended up on the floor in the morning. And beside all this, he had to put up with the sense of isolation – that he was, literally not, 'one of us'.

For, as I now understand, we had defined our group by reference to him. (Jack Straw, *Daily Mirror*, January 1995.)

The use of power by the bully can be seen in the way the bully dominates and the reasons put forward, be they generic, family background, low self-esteem, poor social skills, gender differences, are not discussed in this chapter. Whatever the reason, we take the view that we have bullies and victims in school, and that this is not a healthy situation. We need to provide a safe environment for all, and we need to question our solutions to the problem. The use of power to stop the bully may confirm to the bully how power can be used to intimidate the weak, and to suggest to the victims that they need to be more powerful, may leave them feeling even more powerless. The crucial element that is overlooked in much of the research is the potentially proactive role of those who observe or collude.

The observer

Though a sizable minority of pupils may be victims or bullies, the majority will not be involved other than as observers. There is a need to make these pupils aware of the important role of a witness and to allow them to devise and practice safe interventions they might make.

A whole school approach

Besag (1989) writes, 'The whole school system should be organized to support all children and staff so that no one child or teacher is left alone to try to resolve a bullying problem'. There are two distinct approaches which must be integrated in order to ensure that bullying is reduced:

- Prevention: a school environment where bullying is seen by all to be inappropriate
- Dealing with incidents: help for victims and bullies when it happens.

All staff need to know how to respond to a bullying incident. Some staff, such as form tutors or class teachers, can be ideally placed to help with these procedures. Direct action against bullying should occur within a context which reminds all pupils that bullying behaviour is unacceptable to the school and will not be tolerated. Department for Education (1994), p.17.

The reader of books and articles on bullying will find a host of strategies and interventions planned to enhance the environment, develop the social and friendship setting of the school and supervise young people at play. These strategies will reduce the frequency of bullying but as young people feel safer they may report bullying incidents more frequently, hoping for effective interventions. This is where the inquiring teacher will be surprised to find that there is little advice available.

Our approach to bullying behaviour in school

Taking the view that bullying is an interaction which establishes group identity, dominance and status at the expense of another, then it is only by the development of 'higher values' such as empathy, consideration, unselfishness, that the bully is likely to relinquish her or his behaviour and function differently in a social setting. If the preventive policy depends upon policing the environment, forbidding the behaviour, encouraging the victims and punishing the perpetrators then no lasting change can be expected.

The No Blame Approach

When bullying has been observed or reported then the following steps can be taken.

> **Step 1: listen to the victim.** When the teacher finds out that bullying has happened, she starts by talking to the victim about his or her feelings. She does not question the victim about the incidents but she does need to know who was involved.
> **Step 2: convene a meeting with the people involved.** The teacher arranges to meet with the group of pupils who have been involved. This will include some bystanders or colluders who joined in but did not initiate any bullying. We find that a group of 6–8 young people works well.
> **Step 3: explain the problem.** The teacher tells the group about the way the victim is feeling and might use a poem, a piece of writing or a drawing to emphasize his distress. At no time does she discuss the details of the incidents or allocate blame to the group.

Step 4: share responsibility. The teacher does not attribute blame but states that she knows that the group is responsible and can do something about it.

Step 5: ask the group for their ideas. Each member of the group is encouraged to suggest a way in which the victim could be helped to feel happier. The teacher gives some positive responses but she does not go on to extract a promise of improved behaviour.

Step 6: leave it up to them. The teacher ends the meeting by passing over the responsibility to the group to solve the problem. She arranges to meet with them again to see how things are going.

Step 7: meet them again. About a week later the teacher discusses with each student, including the victim, how things have been going. This allows the teacher to monitor the bullying and keeps the young people involved in the process.

The results so far

Since we began training teachers in this approach in November 1991, we have undertaken evaluations of the usefulness of the programme from two perspectives. Studies one and two are based on questionnaire data. Alongside these we record accounts of the impact that the work has had on users of the programme. The important points to consider are:

- Does the distress of the victim reduce after the intervention?
- Do the users, mainly teachers, find the programme easy to use?

Study one

The initial evaluation was a questionnaire by interview in June 1992 of teachers trained in December 1991 and January 1992.
    The results reported were as follows:

Primary success rate	8/8
Secondary success rate	47/49
Further Education success rate	2/2

Success is defined as the teacher, having discussed the outcome with the victim, reports that the intervention was helpful or very helpful.

Study two

The No Blame Approach is supported by a training video and workbooks (Maines and Robinson, 1992). A questionnaire was sent to 100 schools which had bought the materials. In order to collect useful data the paperwork was quite substantial, which might explain the poor returns –

only 13, of which 2 were eliminated. One stated that the LEA did not participate in any data collection and the other returned an incomplete questionnaire. Reports came from 2 middle, 1 junior and 8 secondary schools reporting on 46 separate incidents.

In all instances the approach was rated as successful; in one case the sequence was repeated as the effect was not immediate.

Of the 11 schools all described the approach positively; very good [3], positive [4], incredibly successful [1], very effective [1], very useful [2].

Ten schools reported an increase in willingness on the part of staff to tackle the problem with confidence.

Five schools involved parents in 16 of the interventions.

Consideration of these evaluations

There has been no attempt to compare the data with that which might be obtained from a control group for whom another intervention was used. The authors did not wish to encourage the use of interventions which might be less helpful or even harmful, so a control group for which (1) there was no intervention and (2) aggressors were punished could not be justified for ethical reasons.

It is important to record the impact made by the many users of the approach, some of whom began the work with a degree of scepticism, but later contacted us with detailed accounts of the success of the intervention and the positive results for all involved.

> The No Blame Approach is a neat, concise, effective system that deals both with the short-term and longer-term responses to bullying, providing opportunities for learning that lead to personal and social growth. In this respect I see the No Blame Approach as a 'giant above the rest' among packs to deal with bullying. (Advisory teacher, 1995)
> Both teachers and psychologists find its uncomplicated process and philosophy appealing and its effectiveness can be demonstrated in all but the most complex of bullying situations. (Educational psychologist, 1995)
> Dealing with bullying is no longer a stressful and long-drawn out process but a quick and positive way of resolving bullying behaviour. (Primary school deputy head, 1995)
> Our student population is diverse and each classroom will have the full breadth of New Zealand's economic, social and racial landscape. Our community has few shared values and the success of the No Blame Approach in this mix is a testimony to the robust nature of the programme. If for nothing else, the experience of discussing the complex relationships that take place in adolescent groups in a group of involved teenagers and being amazed at

their mature, sensitive approach is worth it. (New Zealand high school deputy principal, 1995)

At the start of the training I was not convinced that the No Blame Approach would be effective or that it would be appropriate in our school. I was wrong. The best way forward for someone who is unconvinced, as I was, is to give it a go. I used to feel as though I spent a good portion of my time chasing my tail, punishing, and making little progress. I now feel that I am resolving problems effectively. The evidence is in some of the faces of the pupils I see at school every day. (Comprehensive school year head, 1995)

Evaluating anti-bullying interventions in schools

Any 'hard' research is difficult to undertake when the experimental method might put at risk the well-being of the young people involved. A non-intervention control group cannot be used to establish a baseline for spontaneous remission. Although it is true that the victim is likely to disclose distress at a time of crisis and there may be an improvement in time irrespective of any intervention, the idea that an adult might respond to the disclosure with just the assurance that 'it will probably get better soon' would be unacceptable to most teachers and parents.

Reliable evaluations of punitive responses, bully courts, exclusion, etc. are not available and would not be considered by the authors.

The only other intervention which might provide a satisfactory comparative group might be the group using the common concern method (Pikas, 1989). The success of this method has been evaluated in the Sheffield Project (Smith and Sharp, 1994) and a 70 per cent success rate is described. The two approaches have some similarities but the No Blame Approach does not require such an intense training programme and is much less time-consuming to implement.

It is important to see this intervention as part of a whole programme which includes strategies that will reduce the frequency of bullying and which makes a clear statement to staff, students and the community that bullying is taken seriously and is not acceptable. The school community will not allow young people to suffer because of the unkind behaviour of others. Whenever it is reported then the group will accept the responsibility to put it right.

This method of working with young people is not universally accepted by other professionals in the field who favour a punitive response to the bullies.

> It seems to me that the No Blame Approach will only reinforce the attitudes of joy-riders, lager louts, muggers and others like them, who ultimately take no blame...for the consequences of their

actions. (Dr Michele Elliott, Director of Kidscape, *Sunday Times* letters, 14 November 1993)

The No Blame Approach is sometimes misunderstood as a 'soft' option. This could not be further from the truth. To ask young people to take this responsibility is a tough and very grown-up demand. The imposition of punitive interventions is the soft option, leaving the young person in a position of childish dependence upon adult methods of control.

Responding to the 'Yes, but... !'

You are not seen to be taking strong action – what will parents, pupils, colleagues, think?

A school which has a clear, written policy on its anti-bullying procedures is not likely to incur disapproval from the community. In our experience most dissatisfaction arises when teachers do not take parental complaints seriously or when they respond by blaming the victim: 'It's six of one and half a dozen...', 'She doesn't do much to help herself.'

We have attended many parents meetings and explained the No Blame Approach and the reaction has been very positive. Parents of victims may have feelings of revenge and anger, but when we reassure them that something will be done, we find they agree that the most important thing is to stop the bullying.

What do you do if there is a serious incident of violence?

When a pupil is seriously assaulted by another then the usual sanctions must be applied, even calling the police if appropriate. This does not mean that the No Blame Approach cannot be tried as well, since the particular incident of violence would not be discussed. The issue addressed is the misery of the victim and how that might be alleviated.

Surely you need to know exactly what went on?

It is only necessary to know that bullying is happening and to have the names of the young people involved. Any attempts to take accurate accounts about the events are likely to stir up further disputes, to increase hostility towards the victims and to waste a lot of time because the 'truth' may be hard to find and may vary from one person's perspective to another. Bullying is a complex process and you are not likely to discover all its ramifications and certainly not all its causes by questioning the participants.

What if only one bully is involved?

We believe that it is very rare that bullying takes place in real isolation – there is nearly always some knowledge and even consent from a group, even if they disapprove and refuse to join in. Secret bullying of one person by another is rare and hard to discover but if it is revealed then the No Blame Approach might still be tried. A peer group could be given the opportunity to help put things right, even if they have not been involved in the unhappiness.

What if the bully is seriously disturbed?

Pupils with seriously maladaptive behaviours should be helped in the usual way. The no blame approach is planned to stop bullying, not to treat for pathological conditions. Any individual who is involved in this process may be offered other additional interventions or referred for specialist advice as necessary.

What about victims that provoke bullying? Why can't we help the victim directly?

Some victims may display behaviours which appear to encourage bullying from their peers. Any young person who has poor social and friendship skills or who is very unassertive should be offered help and support in order to learn appropriate social interaction. This should not be implied as a responsibility to stop the bullying for themselves.

When the group convenes to discuss the plight of the victim, someone may suggest that he or she is encouraged to behave in a different way: 'we could ask her to stop...' That is fine, as long as the group take the responsibility to help her and the changes are within her ability.

Conclusion

Bullying is a serious problem which spoils the lives and learning of a significant number of young people in schools. It is time to stop collecting the data on frequency. Bullying does occur in all schools. Preventive approaches will reduce it, but it will still happen and teachers need to know how to deal with it when it does.

The No Blame Approach seems almost too simple and it is hard for teachers to let go of the traditional ways of dealing with the behaviour – interrogation and punishment. However, the students and parents tell us that all they care about is that the behaviour stops and this intervention achieves just that.

The No Blame Approach was devised in 1991 as a crisis response to the extreme distress of a young person in school, suffering great torment and at breaking point. It met the needs of that young person who stayed on happily in school and went on to university. Subsequent users have discovered that the success of the work has achieved more than the crisis intervention required at the time. It has provided an opportunity to encourage empathy and altruism, the essential building blocks of a humanistic society. Education has now left the world of work behind, where management and unions are continuing to look for adversarial methods to combat bullying in the workplace. It is time that adults left behind these conflict strategies and took a mature, no blame, approach to bullying in the workplace, the neighbourhood and in all institutions where people live, work and play alongside each other. What have we got to lose?

References

Attwood, M. (1990) Cats Eyes (London:Virago).
Besag, V.E. (1989) Bullies and Victims in Schools (Milton Keynes: Open University Press).
Bliss, T. and Tetley, J. (1994) Circle Time (Bristol: Lame Duck Publishing).
Bliss, T., Robinson, G. and Maines, B. (1995) Developing Circle Time (Bristol: Lame Duck Publishing).
Caplan, G. (1970) The Theory and Practice of Mental Health Consultation (London: Tavistock).
Department for Education (1994) Bullying, Don't Suffer In Silence (London: HMSO).
Elliott, M. (Ed.) (1991) Bullying – A practical guide to coping for schools (London: Longman in association with Kidscape).
Jones, E. (1991) Practical considerations in dealing with bullying in secondary schools, in Elliott, M. (Ed.) Bullying – A practical guide to coping for schools (London: Longman in association with Kidscape).
Maines, B. and Robinson, G. (1991) Stamp Out Bullying (Bristol: Lame Duck Publishing).
Maines, B. and Robinson, G. (1992) The No Blame Approach (Bristol: Lame Duck Publishing).
Pearce, J. (1991) What can be done about the bully? In Elliott, M. (Ed.) Bullying – A practical guide to coping for schools (London: Longman in association with Kidscape).
Pikas, A.(1989) The common concern method for the treatment of mobbing, in Roland, E. and Munthe, E. (Eds.) Bullying, An International Perspective (London: David Fulton).
Sharp, S. and Smith, P.K. (Eds.) (1994) Tackling Bullying In Your School (London: Routledge).
Smith, P.K. and Sharp, S. (Eds.) (1994) School Bullying, Insights and Perspectives (London: Routledge).
Straw, J. (1995) Burdened by memories of bullying. Daily Mirror, London, 18 January.
United Nations (1989) The convention on the rights of the child. Adopted by the General Assembly of the United Nations 20 November 1989.

Chapter 16
Some advances in sign language communication with deaf people

STEWART SIMPSON

Dennis Child developed qualifying courses for teachers of deaf children at the University of Newcastle from 1976 and the University of Leeds from 1988. He was Chairman of the Council for the Advancement of Communication with Deaf People (CACDP) from 1989 to 1994 and is Chairman of the Council's Standards and Accreditation Board. CACDP is the national examining board committed to developing all human aids to communication. These include sign language, sign language interpreting, lipspeaking, speech to text reporting, deaf awareness and communication with deafblind people.

This chapter explores some recent advances in communication with deaf people. It focuses on the growing use and acceptance of sign and sign language in the education of deaf children and amongst hearing adults.

Deafness is complex. The term includes those who are hard of hearing as well as those who are totally deaf. Within this gradation the age of onset has a profound influence on methods of communication. It is not a homogenous group. There are, in the UK, some 50 000 users of sign language, an estimated 80 000 deafened people and a further 8.4 million who are hard of hearing (data from the Institute of Hearing Research, Davis, 1995). This chapter focuses on those who are often referred to as 'prelingually profoundly deaf' – in essence those who are born deaf or became deaf in early childhood and whose first or preferred language is sign language. The issues concerning them are different from those who are deafened and those who are hard of hearing.

Education of deaf children

There can be few more challenging tasks than the education of deaf children. To a large extent, this issue has been influenced by the development of educational provision which sought a unified response to a complex problem. Policies were established at a time which predated the impact of technical aids and their capacity to use residual hearing.

Controversy in the education of deaf children has focused on the debate beween oralists and manualists. Educationalists who favour oralism believe that deaf children can, and should, be taught to speak and lipread. The acquisition of speech and lipreading will then, it is claimed, allow the integration of deaf people into wider society. Pure oralists believe that if the child is allowed to sign, the ability to develop speech is inhibited. Those who advocate the manualist approach include signing in their teaching and school environment. In contrast to the oralists, they believe that signing and fingerspelling are natural means of communication for deaf people and are essential tools in the learning process. Further, they believe that lipreading and speech are beyond the capacity of most deaf children.

Such controversy did not always exist. For much of the nineteenth century combined methods – using speech, lipreading, sign language and fingerspelling – were used in large charitable institutions set up to provide protection and training for deaf children, but by the second half of the nineteenth century there was growing support for an oralist approach which was established at the second international congress on the education of deaf children. The Milan Conference of teachers of the deaf took place in 1880 and agreed on 'the superiority of speech over signs for restoring deaf mutes to social life and for giving them greater facility in language'. It further agreed that 'the simultaneous use of signs and speech has the disadvantage of injuring speech, lipreading and the precision of ideas'(Milan, 1880).

By the time of the Milan Conference there was already growing criticism of the charitable institutions which were regarded as oppressive, insular and focused on provision of shelter, physical care and spiritual guidance. Earlier, the Education Act of 1870 had established the principle of 'education for all' and oralism was seen as a means of bringing deaf children into the educational system which the large charitable institutions had, for the most part, denied. The Education Act of 1893 extended provision of the 1870 legislation to include 'deaf, dumb and blind children', consequently the oralist system dominated education of deaf children for almost 100 years. One early effect of change in policy was that deaf teachers employed in the large asylums were no longer required lest their signing undermine the development of speech and lipreading – thus denying an influence of deaf adults in the development of deaf children.

Throughout the nineteenth century and for much of the twentieth century there were children with residual hearing who would have benefited from hearing aids. In recent years earlier diagnosis and rapid technological advances in hearing aids and radio aids have allowed a growing proportion of deaf children to make use of their residual hearing and develop spoken language, thus underpinning an oral/aural approach to educating deaf children.

It was not until the 1960s that the oralist method was effectively challenged. Until that time, communication research had focused almost entirely on the use of residual hearing, on lipreading and on the understanding of speech. Teachers were trained to use the oral/aural method, parents were advised on its importance and schools practised it.

Integration into wider society has been a dominant objective in the education of deaf children. It underpinned the deliberations in the Conference of Milan and was subsequently influential some 80 years later in the movement towards educating a growing number of deaf children in mainstream schools. By the mid 1960s the opening of many new partially hearing units (PHUs) meant that the majority of deaf children were receiving full-time education in ordinary schools, where it was expected they would be able to make continuing progress in speech and language by oral/aural teaching. As a consequence of this trend the special schools focused more on the profoundly deaf and those with other disabilities. Such children required a range of responses which could not be provided through a purely oral method.

In 1968 a committee of enquiry set up by the Department of Education and Science (DES, 1968) endorsed the prevailing use of oral teaching but recommended further study into the use of manual communication and combined methods. This report, the Lewis report, did at least prompt research into the use of combined methods and by the late 1970s a number of schools were using 'total communication' – a combination of signing, speech, lipreading, writing and making use of residual hearing through hearing aids and amplification (Evans, 1982). The signing used in total communication in Britain draws heavily on signs from British sign language (BSL) in sign supported English (SSE) or, with additional signs denoting grammar and punctuation, in signed English. In other English-speaking countries there are alternative sign languages. For example, America has its own American sign language (ASL).

Sign language is the language of deaf people and a binding element of the deaf community. It is a visual gestural language with grammatical rules quite distinct from those of English. Though its use can be traced over many centuries, the term has only gained credence since the mid 1970s. Linguistic research into recognition of sign language owes much to the work of William Stokoe and others in America and, later in the identification of BSL to Woll, Kyle and Decher (1981) and Brennan, Colville and Lawson (1984). Other countries acknowledged the need for legislation and in Sweden in 1981, Swedish sign language (SSL) was legalised as the first language of deaf people. Denmark followed suit. In 1988 the European Parliament recognised the sign language of member states. A further development was publication of the first BSL/English dictionary in 1992.

Bilingual education in which BSL and English are given equal weighting has gained increasing recognition in recent years. It both accepts deaf people's language and culture and provides access to the curriculum. The extent to which bilingual education can be developed may be dependent on the competence of teachers in both languages. Given that 90 per cent of deaf children are born to hearing parents it is unlikely that dual fluency of language can be obtained in the majority of homes.

The move towards mainstream education was further boosted by the Education Act of 1981 which, following recommendations in the Warnock Report (1978), established the principle that children with special educational needs should be educated in ordinary schools. Of particular importance was emphasis placed on the need for early diagnosis. It is estimated that there are almost 35 000 hearing impaired children receiving some form of special education. Of these, 80 per cent are in ordinary classes in mainstream education, 12 per cent are in special units attached to ordinary schools and 8 per cent are in special schools for the deaf and/or partially hearing (Densham, 1995).

An inevitable effect of mainstreaming was a reduction in the number of special schools – from 75 in 1980 to 40 in 1989 (Child, 1991). During this period there has been a significant movement from purely oral teaching methods to total communication. In a further study by Baker and Child (1993) an increasing openness towards the potential value of BSL was found. Amongst teachers of deaf children there was demand for better training opportunities in sign language.

In recent years, despite considerable public expenditure, concern has been expressed regarding the fragmented training of teachers who have special responsibility for children with special educational needs. A working report to the Department for Education and Employment (SENTC, 1996) reviewed current provision and made recommendations for improvement. In its report the working party agreed a statement of principles as a basis for their discussions and recommendations. These principles emphasised the need for effective and appropriately trained qualified teachers.

The report follows a decision in 1984 by the DES to discontinue initial training for specialist teachers of pupils with hearing (and visual) impairment in the belief that post-experience training opportunities would be developed. In the absence of appropriate funding, the recruitment and funding teachers for full-time courses was significantly reduced. At the same time the number of part-time courses increased. One such course was established in the School of Education at Leeds. The number of teachers of the deaf qualifying in 1996 was 23 from full time courses and 60 from part time courses. The figures for 1989 are 130 (full time) and 23 (part time). Whilst there has been a greater diversity of training courses (including distance learning) the total number qualifying has fallen from 153 to 83. In its conclusions, the report calls for

> a more coherent approach...to support teachers in acquiring the confidence and competence to meet their responsibilities in teaching pupils with special educational needs, and it emphasises that special needs issues must inform all aspects of teacher development *since every teacher is a teacher of pupils with special educational needs.*

It also requests that urgent consideration be given to improving the training opportunities for non-teaching staff and those working as pre- and post-school staff. The report lists specific competencies required by teachers of the deaf. It also lists prerequisites for trainee teachers of deaf children and states that a person should be a 'qualified teacher who is effective and competent, and an effective spoken language communicator with clear lip-patterns.' In addition, the report goes on to say a trainee should:

- have met a range of deaf adults and children before training
- have a positive attitude towards deaf people
- have a commitment to acquire basic sign language skills to CACDP Stage 1 or equivalent.

Among the skills listed as competencies required by teachers of the deaf are:

- developing expressive and receptive skills which demonstrate practical knowledge of the structure and function of BSL
- developing expressive and receptive skills of signed English or SSE if appropriate to given educational settings.

In summary, signing and BSL are now an accepted part of the range of skills required of those who become teachers of deaf children.

With 90 per cent of all deaf children integrated into mainstream schools it is not only teachers who are developing skills in signing. In Middlesbrough a project has been initiated to teach sign language to primary school children. The project not only encourages hearing children to learn to communicate with deaf children, it is based on the hypothesis that the learning of BSL can be of real benefit to hearing children. Apart from the benefits of social integration, it would appear that hearing children have gained in their own language development. By learning a second language (BSL) the children appear to be developing their knowledge of English (Williams, 1995).

Provision for adults

Provision for deaf adults was largely initiated by the church and by those associated with schools for the deaf. From the mid-nineteenth century every major town had developed a mission which was a focal point for deaf people. Mutual aid, the practice of religion and social intercourse were the principal activities (Grant, 1990). Heading each institution was a missioner, who identified with the need for deaf people to use their natural language in sign and fingerspelling. The mission provided deaf people with community support, advice and advocacy in a hearing world which was largely indifferent and occasionally hostile to their needs.

The need to ensure competence amongst those who were employed as missioners was developed by the Joint Examination Board (later renamed the Deaf Welfare Examination Board, DWEB), formed in 1927. Its purpose was to train and examine candidates who wished to work as missioners or welfare officers with deaf people. Candidates had to serve a 2 year apprenticeship in one of the main missions before sitting examinations. The examinations included a test of sign language skills. Intense involvement with deaf people during training usually ensured a high level of competence in signing skills. Although residential schools for deaf children attempted to educate by oral methods, beyond formal education, it was the missions who provided a social and spiritual refuge based on signing and fingerspelling.

In the provision of services for deaf adults, two major reports had a profound influence on services for deaf people – the Younghusband Report in 1959 and the Seebohm Report in 1968. The former advocated a new common basic training for all social workers in health and welfare services, and the latter recommended a basic restructuring of personal social services. Subsequent legislation led to generic full-time training to replace the specialist training for a range of workers from child care officers to welfare officers, and generic local authority social services departments to replace the muddle of health and welfare services which had grown rapidly in postwar years. The introduction of full-time generic training also replaced part time training supervised and accredited by the DWEB and, as a consequence, the only specialist training available for those working with deaf adults ceased to exist. Attempts to establish a national college providing full time social work training for those working with deaf people failed, as did DWEB, the only national scheme which included training and accreditation in sign language interpreting skills. DWEB awarded its last certificates and diplomas in 1972.

Introduction of full-time generic social work training not only brought about the cessation of specialist training of social workers with deaf people, it also devalued such work and ended the only national system of training and examinations in sign language.

That apart, there was a deep-seated movement for change. Many of the old missions were in decline and services for deaf people were increasingly being provided by local authorities. Deaf people, so long reliant on the missioner and the mission, were seeking the independence and opportunities long denied them. An increasing number of deaf people regarded social workers as inappropriate for their needs. They argued that their problem was one of communication, not of social inadequacy: their need was for interpreters rather than social work support. This demand followed developments, most notably in USA and Scandinavia, of sign language interpreting services distinct from social work. Such provision, backed by anti-discrimination legislation, stimulated the development of a new profession – that of sign language interpreter.

In 1976 the British Deaf Association made an application to the Department of Health and Social Security, pointing out that communication skills were declining at a time when deaf people were seeking greater opportunities to play a part in the wider society. It went on to say the only way in which the quality of life of the pre-lingual deaf can be improved and their potential realised is by easing and increasing communication between them and the community at large.

The application for a 3 year project to develop basic communication skills and establish a register of competent interpreters was successful. There were some initial problems in bringing national organisations together, even for a common purpose, but by December 1980 the Council for the Advancement of Communication with Deaf People (CACDP) had been formed with representatives from all the major national organisations concerned with deafness, with the purpose of promoting training and conducting examinations in communication skills, and administering a register of interpreters. Some organisations came together more readily than others. Organisations for teachers, social workers, parents of deaf children, profoundly deaf adults and hard of hearing adults had historical perspectives and current policies which were not easily reconciled. Nevertheless the outcome was the establishment of a system of examinations which set standards in signing and interpreting. Despite critical funding problems in the 1980s, CACDP survived to become the national examining board in sign language and other human aids to communication.

A temporary register of qualified interpreters was formed from those who had gained the DWEB qualification which included a test of interpreting skills, and CACDP also established interpreter training and examinations for interpreters of known ability. Those holding DWEB qualifications were required to take CACDP's interpreting examination before 1987. Other organisations, including a number of universities, took over the training of interpreters, but CACDP has remained the examining body.

Development of basic sign communication skills began in 1982 with curriculum and examinations at three levels or stages. Prior to the formation of CACDP, 'sign language' training took place in centres for deaf people. It was usually taught by hearing people and such classes, lacking curriculum and goal, were usually of short duration. At the time, few people had understanding of BSL as a language and the basic curriculum focused on an ability to communicate in sign. Initially, CACDP used hearing examiners – members of the register of sign language interpreters – accompanied by a deaf person. Increasingly, emphasis was placed on the use of deaf people as examiners.

In 1988 a new curriculum in BSL was introduced. DHSS funding was made available to train examiners, and the face to face examinations at Stage 1 level (Basic) were (and are) conducted by a single deaf examiner. Similar movement towards the use of deaf examiners was introduced at Stage 2 (Intermediate) and Stage 3 (Advanced). This process was independently assisted by the British Deaf Association securing European funding to set up the BSL Training Agency (BSLTA) with the task of training deaf people to teach their language. The appearance of sign language interpreters at public meetings, on television and in the theatre, has not only raised the profile of deafness, it has also helped create interest in sign language. This is reflected in the number of candidates taking CACDP's examinations in sign language. (Table 16.1)

Development of training and examinations in BSL has created many challenges, not least of which is the preparation of deaf people for their work as deaf tutors and examiners. The overwhelming majority of deaf tutors and examiners left school at 16, and some of them have limited understanding of their second language, English. Although the BSLTA programme was valuable in introducing basic teacher training for deaf tutors it did not go far beyond that level and the scheme was hard to sustain when initial European funding was discontinued.

Table 16.1. Number of candidates taking CACDP examinations in sign language

Year	Stage 1	Stage 2	Stage 3	Total
1982	188	–	9	197
1983	614	27	25	666
1984	1174	63	22	1259
1985	1506	116	15	1637
1986	1902	218	53	2173
1987	3104	118	46	3268
1988	2404	317	47	2768
1989	2463	488	88	3039
1990	3476	519	164	4159
1991	4803	527	203	5533
1992	8532	796	244	9572
1993	10279	1021	213	11513
1994	10435	1254	353	12042
1995	13468	1661	441	15570
1996	16008	2139	490	18637

CACDP has developed a tutor policy which actively encourages tutors to gain additional qualifications. Many have done so through the traditional Further Education route of City and Guilds 730 and by taking CACDP's Advanced certificate in BSL. Even so, the rapid growth of demand for sign language classes has meant that many deaf people are being recruited to teach sign language without having any preparation or training.

> Nothing, but nothing is more crucial to the development of Human Aids to Communication than an understanding of the educational experience of deaf people. If deaf people are used as tutors and examiners – and it is CACDP's policy they should – then there must be a serious attempt to compensate for further and higher educational opportunities unavailable to deaf people in the past. The financial support needed by CACDP in training examiners and those who train tutors is directly linked to an educational system which failed to prepare deaf people for such tasks. (Simpson, 1993).

Sadly, this basic necessity was largely overlooked by the Commission of Enquiry into Human Aids to Communication. It remains the case that between one third and one half of the 1000 tutors of sign language in the UK have no basic qualifications in teaching.

Although CACDP has no responsibility for the training of tutors, their lack of training and the rapid growth in demand for CACDP's examinations impacts on CACDP's need to recruit qualified and experienced tutors as its examiners. The shortage of deaf examiners, coupled with a continuing and rapid growth for examinations, has created very real problems in meeting the demand for face to face examinations. This is not helped by the fact that 75 per cent of examinations take place in June and July. Attempts to encourage colleges to enter their students at other times of the year have so far failed. Restrictions on the number of examinations offered by CACDP, or differential fees linked to peak periods, have for the time being been rejected as impractical. The introduction of hearing examiners (with high level skills in BSL, and teaching qualifications) remains too sensitive an issue in the deaf community.

CACDP's response has been to train more deaf examiners. This in itself is a major task, for, apart from the restricted training opportunities afforded to deaf people, they often socialise in a community – a deaf community – which brings additional pressure on tutors and examiners in their quest for objectivity. At this stage of development relatively few profoundly deaf people, though with a normal range of intelligence, have had the opportunity to attend full time further or higher education. This lack of experience and training contrasts sharply with, say, the normal requirements for a GCSE examiner in French. Such an examiner would have an appropriate language degree plus a teaching qualification followed by 3 years' full time teaching of the specialist subject area: in total some 7 years' full time further and higher education beyond the age of 16 in preparation for his or her role as a teacher, some 10 years for his or her role as an examiner. This full time period of training is largely paid for by the government. By contrast, CACDP has to prepare its examiners – in days rather than years – from whatever resources are available.

There is of course a more positive side. Today sign language is taught mainly by deaf people, and usually in colleges of further education alongside other languages. It is in popular demand, which continues from Stage 1 (Basic) to Stage 3 (Advanced), and there are some 1000 deaf people teaching sign language. A decade ago only a tiny minority of that number would have had the confidence to enter a college of further education at all, let alone as a lecturer. The identification and popularisation of sign language has been a remarkable achievement. It has brought with it considerable pride; pride in a language which was largely unrecognised, and pride in status – that of lecturer or tutor – which provides opportunity and income. A decade ago such confidence did not exist.

To sign or not to sign – that has been the question. A cartoon published in the *British Deaf Mute* of 1893 depicted a football match between manualists and oralists – with the manualists winning by five goals to one. Entitled 'The War of Methods', it reflected the anger and bitterness amongst many profoundly deaf people whose education denied them their natural language. But the goalposts have shifted since then, particularly over the past 30 years. Hearing aids have made remarkable technical advances in the use of residual hearing. The introduction of technology – textphones, fax, television, video, interactive video telephone – has aided communication in visual form. These aids are used by pre-lingually deaf people, deafened and hard of hearing people. Human aids to communication such as sign language interpreters, lipspeakers, speech to text reporters and note-takers serve the varying needs of all who are deaf in educational, social and work settings. Although such provision falls far short of demand, it is increasingly available and the Disability Discrimination Act of 1996 will hasten the process of meeting that need. No longer is the education of deaf children provided within the confines of dogma. No longer is sign language regarded as an inferior mode of communication. Integration remains the key to deaf people's involvement in society, but it can only be achieved by access to information and, most important, a right to choose the means of access – through both technical and human aids to communication. As Kyle and Woll (1993) points out, there 'must be a sharing and an offering which takes into account the dignity of deaf people'. Amen to that!

References

Baker, R. and Child, D (1993) Communication approaches used in schools for the deaf in the UK – a follow up study. Journal of the British Association of Teachers of the Deaf, 17(2), 36–42

Brennan, M., Colville, M. and Lawson, L. (1984) Words in Hand (Edinburgh: Moray House).

Davis, A. (1995) Hearing in Adults (London: Whurr).

Densham, J. (1995) Deafness, Children and the Family (Aldershot: Arena Ashgate Publishing Ltd.)

Department of Education and Science (1968) The Education of Deaf Children: The possible place of fingerspelling and signing (London: HMSO).

Grant, B. (1990) The Deaf Advance: A history of the British Deaf Association (London: The British Deaf Asscociation).

Milan International Congress on the Education of the Deaf, 1880. Milan, Italy.

Kyle, J.G. and Woll, B. (1993) Sign Language – The study of deaf people and their language (Cambridge: Cambridge University Press).

Evans, L. (1982) Total Communication: structure and strategy (Washington, DC: Gallaudet College Press).

SENTC (1996) Professional development to meet special educational needs. Report to the Department of Education and Employment Special Educational Needs Training Consortium.

Simpson, T.S. (1993) A Stimulus to Learning a Measure of Ability (London: The Alliance of Deaf Service users and Providers).

Warnock, H.M. (1978) Special Education Needs: Report of the Committee of Enquiry (London: HMSO).

Williams, E. (1995) Times Educational Supplement, 24 November.

Woll, B., Kyle, J. and Decher, M. (1981) Perspectives in BSL and Deafness (London: Croom Helm).

PART IV
MOVING INTO THE WORLD OF WORK

Thematic introduction and summary

DIANE SHORROCKS-TAYLOR

The introduction to this book gave the rationale for the decisions about what the various sections should be. The solution was provided by Dennis's work which seemed to have four major aspects to it. It was during the later part of his career that he turned his attention to the application of psychology in occupational settings, broadly, in the use of personality and motivation inventories, and more particularly in the design of an ability measure (the DC test) as an alternative selection device in the context of nurse recruitment. The chapters in this section take up this theme and develop it in various ways, investigating selection, progression and performance through a career and the problems that can arise along the way.

Chapter 17, by Alan Smithers, deals with an aspect of vocational education (NVQs and GNVQs) which he believes have not matched up to expectations by delivering what they were supposed to deliver. He argues that the designers of the qualification system were wrong-footed from the beginning because they started with a competency analysis of what people could already do in their workplace. As he says, the new vocational awards seemed to be qualifying people for the jobs they already had.

He suggests that the proposed new body that will be in charge of the system (the Qualifications and Curriculum Authority – QCA) which combines the functions of two previous organisations (the School Curriculum and Assessment Authority and the National Council for Vocational Qualifications) is a better solution, at least in principle. It should prove more appropriate if it oversees the setting of standards in an effective way (in collaboration with the employers) and designs the qualifications more appropriately. He makes a strong case for introducing two kinds of award, one addressing the issue of selection for work and the other concentrating on improving skills competencies during work, that is, qualifications for progression and performance improvement.

Chapter 18, by Roy Childs, deals broadly with selection and developmental appraisal at work, that is performance and consequent progression, in order to reap the best harvest from the talents of employees. He adopts an approach which outlines the kinds of experiences likely to be encountered by a graduate when first applying for jobs and then, later, when employed by a company. For the more enlightened employers, work competence, behaviour, personality and effective feedback all form part of the developmental appraisal process that should enhance job satisfaction and progress.

Since personality tests now figure extensively as part of the selection and progression process in many companies and organisations, they clearly affect the career and job prospects for employees. In Chapter 19, Dennis Child highlights some of the current technical problems associated with them. To make his main points, he uses recent material from a highly popular personality test, the 'Big Five'. He argues that the use of this test, and others like it, requires an honest appraisal of its shortcomings along with a realistic notion of the predictive powers of any test. In the context of the present bandwagon, with its often oversimplified approach, these may well prove to be timely words.

Cheryl Travers and Cary Cooper are researchers who are well known for their work on occupational stress. In Chapter 20 they apply their ideas to the teaching profession. The chapter sets out a definition of stress and its causes for teachers in schools. These many and varied causes are well summarised here. They go on to show what effects stress has on teacher progress and performance, finally providing an important section of advice on managing it. This is a chapter that has important messages for all of us.

Chapter 17
Improving vocational education: NVQs and GNVQs

ALAN SMITHERS

In late 1993 my Centre, then at Manchester University, produced a report (Smithers, 1993) which dubbed recent attempts to improve vocational education 'a disaster'. In an accompanying television programme (Channel 4, *Dispatches*, 15 December 1993) this was raised to the hyperbole of 'a disaster of epic proportions'. The publicity machine of the National Council for Vocational Qualifications, the body responsible for introducing the new National Vocational Qualifications (NVQs) and General National Vocational Qualifications (GNVQs), rolled into action in an attempt to discredit the report, but did not answer its charges (Hillier, 1994).

The hammer blow was due to be delivered at a conference on GNVQs specially convened by the Confederation of British Industry (CBI, 1994a). A contribution from me was to be tucked away among some heavyweight presentations expressing support for the new awards and demonstrating how irrelevant the criticisms were. A minister was to open the session, and leading for the CBI was Gordon Beaumont, Chairman of its Training Policy Panel. In the written version of his speech (a copy of which subsequently fell into my hands) he opened by strongly associating himself with the minister's remarks dismissing the report.

The Parliamentary Under Secretary of State for Further and Higher Education, Tim Boswell, began and the trap was sprung (DfEE, 1994). But much to the organisers' dismay and consternation, the minister did not weigh in with criticisms. Instead, he used the platform to underline the importance the government attached to high quality vocational qualifications, to express concern that they were not yet right and to announce a six-point plan for improving GNVQs. There was stunned silence. A somewhat bemused Gordon Beaumont took the stage, jettisoned the first part of his speech, and attempted to link in the rest with the tenor of the minister's remarks (Beaumont, 1994).

That for me was the beginning of the long way back. It showed that the government, in spite of all the political capital it had invested in the success of NVQs and GNVQs, and in spite of NCVQ's attempts to steamroller any criticism, was alive to the flaws of the NCVQ approach. It recognised that some major mistakes had been made and it was attempting to get vocational reform back on track. The error was so fundamental, however, that even as I write in 1996 a new £10 million improvement programme has been announced to overhaul GNVQs once more. Where did NCVQ go wrong?

The fatal flaw

NVQs and GNVQs have been fatally flawed from the outset because the council charged with their introduction started in the wrong place. It began by devising a model suitable for accrediting prior learning in the workplace – in effect qualifying people for jobs they already had – and attempting to use this as the basis of all vocational qualifications. Instead, therefore, of there being training programmes with appropriate assessment, qualifying vocationally became evidence-gathering in relation to hundreds of performance criteria.

Nor was this mere oversight. Gilbert Jessup, the chief architect of NVQs and GNVQs, proudly wrote, in Bees and Swords (1990), of doing away with 'the syllabuses, the courses or the training programmes, i.e. the specification of the learning opportunities provided'.

He also had particular views on assessment. In his book, *Outcomes: NVQs and the Emerging Model of Education and Training* (1991), he wrote, 'what I am proposing is that we forget about reliability altogether and concentrate on validity, which is ultimately all that matters', seemingly unaware that assessments which are not reliable cannot be valid. These idiosyncratic ideas were not to be the basis of some experiment however. They were to be a Procrustean bed on which all other awards were going to be forced to lie:

> the Government intends that GNVQs, together with National Vocational Qualifications (NVQs), will replace other vocational qualifications and become the main national provision for vocational education and training.(NCVQ, 1993)

When in 1992 Parry Rogers, the Chairman of the Business and Technology Education Council, in his speech at the launch of BTEC's Annual Report (Rogers, 1992) asked whether BTEC could deliver quality education 'if it is put within the skills-based straight jacket of NCVQ', the Department for Education (as it was then) made it clear both to him personally and to BTEC that it must comply with NCVQ or put itself at risk.

Origins

Britain has always lagged behind its continental neighbours in vocational education. The trouble was not that it was no good, but rather that there was not enough of it. In the 1980s it became increasingly accepted that there was the need for a national vocational qualifications framework to rival the well-established academic ladder of 'O' levels, 'A' levels and degrees. The government established the De Ville Committee (1986) and accepted its recommendations for a National Council for Vocational Qualifications to oversee a national system. This was carried forward in the 1986 White Paper, *Working together – education and training* (an unfortunate title in the light of the consequences). This required NCVQ, among other things, 'to ensure standards of competence are set'.

The emphasis on standards was to underline, quite rightly, that the system was to be employer-led, geared to the nature and levels of performance required by them. A qualification to be a qualification must be *in* and/or *for* something. Since the *raison d'être* of vocational education is to prepare for, or enhance performance in, work it is essential that employers be involved in specifying what a particular qualification is to be about.

NCVQ, however, interpreted 'standards of competence' literally and tried to turn every standard into a statement of competence. What NCVQ inexcusably failed to do was to distinguish between, on the one hand, setting standards and, on the other, designing qualifications to enable those standards to be met. It tried to turn one directly into the other, missing out the vital stages of settling what was to be covered and the tests by which we would know that the standards had been reached. In other words, job analysis became confused with qualification design.

National Vocational Qualifications

NCVQ's misinterpretation led to an orgy of analysis, glorified as the technique of 'functional analysis'. Qualifications were broken down into units and further subdivided into 'elements' which are based on lists of 'performance criteria'. The candidate has to collect 'evidence', usually in the form of a 'portfolio', that the performance criteria have been met over certain 'ranges'. Although superficially plausible, setting out the requirements in this way means that the content of the qualifications is not clearly specified, nor is there any assessment of overall performance. More specifically, as regards content, the approach lacks precision, is fragmentary, does not prioritize and devalues knowledge and understanding. Assessment is atomised, internal and bureaucratic, and is not robust enough to withstand payment by results.

Precision

NCVQ's analytical approach becomes in practice a search for the elusive irreducible building blocks of competence. The NVQ Level 2 Care (Residential/Hospital Support), for example, is set out as 11 units, 39 elements and 338 performance criteria. Although this detail is assumed to give precision, in fact, the performance criteria come out as very generalised. In the unit 'Enable clients to eat and drink' the first element is 'Enable clients to choose appropriate food and drink' of which the first performance criterion is, 'The support required by the client is established with him/her.' Similarly, in the NVQ Level 3 in Engineering Assembly, the unit, 'Produce assembled output by joining and fastening operations' contains the element 'Process materials to produce assembled output', which has as a performance criterion, 'Materials presented to the assembly operation are completely compliant with operational specification.'

Not only are the performance criteria generalised, but they hang in the air and are addressed to no one. If they had been written for candidates they would have said something like. 'In order to get this qualification you will have to show you can...' Or if for employers, 'A person holding this qualification is able to...' But they are written in an odd abstract language which has been shown to break the rules of grammar and therefore be very difficult to read (Channell and St John, 1996).

Fragmentation

The fault is, however, more than technical; it is fundamental. There is no guarantee that numerous individual competencies – even if they could be identified, and simply and unambiguously stated – would amount to skilled overall performance. Being able to dribble and to head the ball does not make a footballer. It is the way these skills fit together that matters.

Prioritization

NCVQ's lists of performance criteria are not only not integrated, they are not prioritized. In the NVQ Level 2 Bus and Coach Driving and Customer Care, for example, the minutiae of customer care are treated on a par with keeping the vehicle safely on the road. NVQs take no account of time, and thus difficult decisions as to what is essential, as opposed to being merely desirable, do not have to be faced. This is claimed as a virtue (Jessup, 1991), moving beyond the time-serving basis of old apprenticeships, but discounting time altogether conveniently sidesteps difficult decisions about what can be fitted in.

Knowledge and understanding

The telephone directory approach also has profound consequences for the way knowledge and understanding (used by NCVQ as a compound noun) is treated. It was first considered to be embedded in the performance criteria and implied by them. But even in the Revised Criteria (NCVQ, 1995), which are intended to lay greater stress on knowledge and understanding, it comes out as itemised and disparate 'knowledge specifications'. This means that NVQs are virtually useless as qualifications for 14–19 year olds, or indeed adults preparing *for* work, since there is no coherent statement of content. Nor is there a reservoir of knowledge and understanding to enable people to cope with a changing working world, however the working world turns out to be, or provide a platform for progression.

Assessment

The unsuitability of NVQs as a qualification *for* work, as opposed to accrediting prior learning *in* work, is underlined by the way they are assessed. NVQs were said to have been devised on the driving test model. That is, it does not matter how you have learned to drive – through a school or from a spouse or friend or in any other way – what is important is that you can do it, and satisfy an independent examiner that you can. However, as they have emerged, NVQs have no equivalent of the driving test, but consist of long lists of performance criteria that have to be signed off. Given that there may be several hundred of them, the only practicable way of achieving this is to leave it to the teachers/trainers whose main task becomes signing their name.

There is some check through external verification but that is based on inspecting portfolios of evidence rather than observing the candidate in action. Moreover, because the requirements are so loose, the external verifiers are to some extent able to invent the qualifications by insisting that in the portfolio the candidate does or does not include this or that, uses 'I' or 'we', and so on. Some private providers are, for the sake of their candidates, having to deploy a member of staff specifically to get to know the foibles of particular verifiers.

NVQ assessment, instead of being based on tests of skilled overall performance, depends on collecting evidence in relation to checklists. It lacks the fairness, reliability and authenticity that would make it believable. If it is not trusted, the qualification cannot act as a passport between training provider and employer. Increasingly, the only training in which an employer can have confidence is that provided in-house. Far from enabling education and training to work together, NVQs have driven a wedge between them.

Output-related funding

The assessment of NVQs is not strong enough to bear the weight of the payment by results that is increasingly being adopted by Training and Enterprise Councils and, to a lesser extent, by the Further Education Funding Council. As the instances of malpractice that surface from time to time in the press illustrate, the assessment arrangements leave a lot to be desired. (See, for example, Colleges in scandal of exam passes, *Observer*, 27 March 1994; Inquiry set up into worthless qualifications, *Observer*, 3 April 1994; Second training scam alleged, *Guardian*, 27 May 1994; Sleaze and loathing in the classes of conflict, *Observer*, 12 March 1995; Fraud squads to root out phantom studies, *Independent on Sunday*, 28 May 1985; Minister acts on exams for cash scandal, *Evening News*, 2 May 1996; Arrests in £1m NVQ 'fraud', *TES*, 18 October 1996.)

There is ample scope to, in effect, sell NVQs (or give them away if the state is paying). What NVQ assessment amounts to, in practice, is a bit like your driving being passed by your trainer with each item – gear changing for example – signed off as you achieve it, and the trainer only being paid if he or she passes you. No wonder most employers do not automatically accept NVQs.

General National Vocational Qualifications

If NVQs work at all, it is in the accreditation of prior learning in the workplace. Whatever their merits for accrediting people for the job they already have, NVQs are not, as we have seen, a good way of preparing people for work. This makes it even more bizarre that, in 1991, the Government should give NCVQ the job of developing applied education in schools and colleges. The White Paper (1991) introducing the new qualifications reads as if the original intention was to build on the success of qualifications like those of the Business and Technology Education Council, but what emerged, in response to the NCVQ credo, was something quite different (NCVQ, 1993).

The General National Vocational Qualification in health and social care at intermediate level (said to be equivalent to five GCSEs at grades A–C) came out as four mandatory units, two optional units and three core skill units comprising 31 elements and 129 performance criteria (for example, 'Key social factors which influence well-being are identified and explained'; 'Key lifestyle patterns which affect individuals are identified'). The advanced GNVQ in leisure and tourism (said to be equivalent to two 'A' levels) has eight mandatory units, four optional and three core skill units consisting of 52 elements and 310 performance criteria (for example, unit, 'Providing customer service', element, 'Identify the function of customer service in leisure and tourism facilities', performance criterion 'Situations when customer contact or service is commonly needed are correctly identified').

Originally NCVQ intended GNVQs to be assessed on a pass/fail basis through evidence collection in the way that NVQs are, but the government insisted on external testing and grading of performance. Reluctantly NCVQ introduced one-hour multiple choice tests into the mandatory units, but side-lined them from contributing to the grading which was carried out by inspecting the portfolios against the themes of data handling and evaluation, with quality only becoming a criterion later. It was this hotch-potch that the government's six-point plan, with which we opened, was intended to sort out.

The weaknesses, however, were further brought into focus when NCVQ was obliged to cooperate with the School Curriculum and Assessment Authority in developing GNVQ Part I. These were mooted by Sir Ron Dearing in his review of the national curriculum (Dearing, 1993) to make vocational education available to 14–16 year-olds in the time of two GCSEs. The two halves of the joint SCAA/NCVQ committee found themselves speaking very different languages. At one stage, each pilot GNVQ Part I was drafted with a line down the middle of the page with NCVQ's performance criteria, range statements and evidence indicators on the left, and, on the right, SCAA's amplification which amounted to a syllabus and test arrangements. It was only through SCAA's approach that it was realised that most of the biology was missing from the intermediate GNVQ in health and social care.

Gradually, the SCAA view prevailed and it is beginning to suffuse the whole GNVQ structure, not just Part I. In November 1996 the government announced yet another revamp of GNVQs (DfEE, 1996e). The multiple-choice questions and low-level coursework are to be replaced by externally marked written exams and substantial assignments set by the vocational boards. All the work will now contribute to the grading. The content will be set out more clearly, specifying the knowledge, skills and understanding that the qualification covers. But what a lot of time and money has been wasted by starting in the wrong place.

Take-up

What has really forced a reappraisal of both NVQs and GNVQs has been the growing realisation that the people for whom they are intended are not signing up for them and, even if they do, they drop out in unacceptable numbers. Even the CBI (1994a) published a report in 1994 exposing the low take-up and high cost, and making 68 recommendations for improvement which amounted to a complete re-design.

John Hillier, the Chief Executive of NCVQ, comfortably reassured the Education Committee of the House of Commons in January 1996:

> To refer to the low uptake of a qualification that has only existed since 1990, now has in excess of a million people holding the qualification, and over three million working towards it, and whose uptake has been increasing steadily at the rate of 30 per cent per year and is continuing to do so, does seem to me simply to fly in the face of the facts. (Hillier, 1996a)

Meanwhile Peter Robinson (1996) of the London School of Economics was beavering away checking all the publicly available figures. He found:

- 660 000 *not* 3 million working towards NVQs
- only 2 per cent of the workforce were working towards NVQ Level 3 by Spring 1995 compared to a target of 50 per cent by 1996
- of 794 NVQs on the books, 364 had not been completed by anyone and 43 had been completed by only one person
- the NVQs that are taken tend to be in the internationally sheltered service occupations – clerical, secretarial, personal service and sales
- over two-thirds of vocational qualifications currently awarded are the old-style pre-NVQ awards
- NVQs do not appear to have added to total training but have increased the complexity of provision.

The take-up of GNVQs has also officially been presented as a great success story. In August 1995 the National Vocational Awarding Bodies brought out a confident press release claiming, '100 000 GNVQs successes and still growing' (NVAB, 1995). However, the notice contained figures which showed:

- the 100 000 was based on only 61 604 completions to which 41 378 who had passed some units had been added
- the completions were only about a third of the registrations
- that of the 13 165 advanced passes up to 1995 (compared with 64 000 BTEC National Diplomas in 1995), 6651 were in business and 1669 in art and design (compared with 21 818 and 31 534 at 'A' level respectively); only health and social care (1936) and leisure and tourism (2340) seemed to be breaking new ground.

The Joint Council of National Vocational Awarding Bodies followed up their '100 000 successes' a year later with a press release in August 1996 proclaiming 'record numbers of GNVQ awards' (National Vocational Awarding Bodies, 1996). But this time the registration figures were conspicuously absent. However, comparing the 1996 advanced GNVQ completions with the 1994 registrations (since the courses could be expected to take 2 years) reveals a pass rate of about 40 per cent at most. Over 90 per cent of these awards were in business, leisure and tourism, health and social care, and art and design. Manufacturing, engineering, construction and the built environment, information technology and science contributed only 1749 awards between them.

Response to criticism

The NCVQ's response to criticism has characteristically been to attempt to rubbish or suppress it. The Robinson Report attracted long letters in the press from John Hillier, the Chief Executive, suggesting the statistics are out-of-date, the data are misinterpreted and that 'it is disappointing that a body such as the London School of Economics should produce such an unbalanced piece of work' (Hillier, 1996b; 1996c). Yet the data are just those Hillier would have had at his disposal when apparently providing inflated figures to the House of Commons Education Committee.

The attempt to bully institutions as well as people also emerged earlier in 1996 when Dr Terry Hyland, a lecturer at Warwick University who had written an article suggesting that the new system of NVQs had brought 'precious few benefits for employers, employees and vocational courses', found he was the subject of a letter to his Vice Chancellor. John Hillier had written:

> The University of Warwick's Centre for Education and Industry recently completed a major market review for NCVQ. It was well produced and provided valuable information, but it may be difficult to justify placing further work if Dr Hyland's is the prevailing view of the university. (Authers, 1996)

Neither has NCVQ been slow to use litigation. An article by Caroline Churchill (a pseudonym, I believe) in the *Daily Telegraph* in December 1994 headed 'A vocational charter for cheats' (Churchill, 1994) led to a prolonged bout of legal fisticuffs. An article of mine in *Personnel Today* (Smithers, 1996), headed 'Beaumont's report hides flaws in NVQs', resulted in a submission to the Press Complaints Commission which I am happy to say was thrown out.

Through an almost religious conviction in its own rightness and aggressive public relations, NCVQ managed for a long time to deflect criticism and remain unmoved even in the face of pressure from the Government. Letters from academics like that signed by 14 of us in the *Financial Times* in January 1996 (Senker *et al*. 1996) were brushed aside. It has taken the cumulative effect of four recent government reviews to make a significant impact.

Reviews

Of late the NCVQ system has come under intense scrutiny. Gordon

Beaumont (1996) was asked to review the top 100 NVQs. Dr John Capey (1995), Principal of Exeter Further Education College, was asked to review the GNVQ assessment system. The ubiquitous Sir Ron Dearing (1996), on completing his review of the National Curriculum, was asked to consider and report on qualifications for 16–19 year olds. But, perhaps most important of all for the future of vocational education, NCVQ itself was subject to a quinquennial review (DfEE, 1995).

Beaumont

Beaumont's review of NVQs was originally intended to be an in-house affair, with NCVQ operating under a contract from the then Employment Department, with Beaumont advised by NCVQ's Evaluation and Advisory Group and with his report to go first to NCVQ Council. In the event, Beaumont was encouraged by ministers to become more independent and several new members were added to the committee including myself. His report also went directly to government, with NCVQ Council allowed to comment on it subsequently.

Beaumont produced a potentially hard-hitting report.

- It suggested that setting standards and designing qualifications should be separated. (p. 5: 'It is proposed that standards are written for employers. Qualifications, training and the development of assessment needs should be separately specified.')
- It recognised that NVQs as presently framed are all but incomprehensible. (p. 13: 'Standards are marred by complex jargon ridden language'; p. 28: 'The complex and jargon ridden language used is universally condemned.')
- It identified a number of problems with assessment. (p. 13: 'Assessors and verifiers are unsure of the standards they are judging and their views differ'; p. 19: 'External verifiers suffer from combining incompatible roles.')
- It found that the assessment system is not robust enough to withstand output-related funding. (p. 7: 'Funding programmes and policy should be harmonised with qualification systems'; p. 40: Funding by outputs brings a potential for conflicts of interest.')
- It is recognised that NVQs do not provide a training route for unemployed young people or adults. (p. 26: 'The fact that NVQs are work-based prevents those not in work from obtaining the qualifications.')

But the edge is taken off it by the claim, 'There is widespread support for the NVQ concept.' There is certainly widespread support for introducing good occupational awards but it is not clear that this is for NVQs as they stand. For example, 'competence' is defined in the Consultation Document (1995) as

The ability to apply knowledge and understanding in performing to the standards required in employment, including solving problems and meeting changing demands. ('Skills' was added later).

Most people, myself included, would have no difficulty in signing up to this. But it is different from 'competence' as it is used in devising NVQs where 'functional analysis' seeks to arrive at numerous (often several hundred) 'competencies'. Beaumont himself used competence in this sense on p. 13 where he wrote 'Candidates are unsure of the competencies they are trying to achieve.' So just what is 'the concept' for which there is apparently widespread support – capability or a competence catalogue?

The claim in the report that most employers are in favour of NVQs (the percentage variously put at between 80 and 90 per cent) is based on a very shaky sample. In fact, fewer than one in five of the employers contacted bothered to respond, in spite of boosting the sample and frequent follow ups. Neither do the claims tally with the CBI report (1994b) expressing concern at the low take-up of NVQs. If employers were using them there would be no problem. They are not, so there it is.

It gradually dawned on Beaumont that NVQs were not working, but what he saw as a language problem is, in my view, a concept problem. This will become increasingly apparent as attempts are made to get NVQs into plain English (or indeed plain Welsh, as if there were such a thing, given that Wales was part of Beaumont's remit). So long as NVQs are frozen at the stage of fragmentation into competencies there will be problems.

Capey

Capey had a specific remit: 'to review GNVQ assessment and grading'. The findings of the report, as encapsulated on p. 22 of Capey (1995), are that 'the evidence presented to the review group was unequivocal in identifying the need for a further simplification of the GNVQ assessment and recording requirements'.

But the recommendations are disappointing in that the review group seems to have got bogged down in NCVQ-speak rather than going to the heart of the matter.

Capey recognises (p. 23): 'The GNVQ differs significantly from the NVQ in its broader purpose and range...this in itself is sufficient to justify a different approach to the assessment of outcomes.

But this is not followed through by asking what good applied education should consist of, and how should it be assessed. NCVQ's idiosyncratic language tends to cause people, including Capey, to take their eye off the ball. Essentially with applied education it matters *what* is being learned not *how*. Curiously, this was one of the early tenets of NCVQ which seems to have got lost in its keenness to prescribe particular styles of learning.

Capey becomes enmeshed in learning styles and goes beyond his remit when in the executive summary he contends, 'Many students are being motivated by the independent approach to learning that GNVQ offers.' (p. 7)

This does not square with the failure of two-thirds of registered students to complete. Moreover, the style of learning is largely irrelevant if the focus is on outcomes. Crucial here is the credibility of the assessment process. This should involve some external practical and written tests. This is just what Capey was set up to advise on, in fact, and where notably he fails to give a clear lead. Even so, the government has now taken action.

NCVQ attempted to put a gloss on both Capey and Beaumont. In the NCVQ's foreword to the Capey report it claims to have support for 'the characteristics of GNVQ' and 'the philosophy and structure' when neither was part of the remit. Nor are these claims sustainable when so many of those attempting to deliver GNVQs are gagged from commenting on them. (See, for example, Lecturers loathe to report on GNVQs (letter), *Times Higher Education Supplement*, 11 November 1994; Colleges impose sound of silence, *Guardian*, 15 November 1994; Quango blunders (letter) *Guardian*, 29 November 1994).

Dearing

Dearing asked Capey to consider:

- modifying the tests so that they contribute to grading
- introducing standard assignments
- the use of end-of-course externally set examinations or projects through which students could show they had integrated the knowledge and skills from the course.

Dearing's own remit was far wider: to consider the whole range of qualifications for 16–19 year olds. In doing so he addressed the thorny question of the respective roles of 'A' levels, GNVQs and NVQs. The existence of advanced GNVQs alongside 'A' levels in business studies, art and design, the sciences and technology does raise the question of why a student should take one type of qualification rather than the other in, say, science. Is it a case of those who can, do 'A' levels, those who can't, do GNVQs? And what about the advanced GNVQ in hospitality and catering and the nine Level 3 NVQs in catering and hospitality. Do the awards serve different purposes? If so, what are the differences?

Dearing recommended that:

- A-levels and GCSE should be pursued 'where the primary purpose is to develop knowledge, understanding and skills associated with a subject or discipline'
- GNVQs should be for applied education 'where the primary purpose is to develop and apply knowledge, understanding and skills relevant to broad areas of employment'
- NVQs should be for vocational training 'where the primary purpose is to develop and recognise mastery of a trade or profession at the relevant level'.

To underline the importance of the applied pathway he recommended renaming advanced GNVQs as Applied 'A' levels, and transferring 'A' levels such as business studies to become flagships of the new route. But this was seen by some as threatening the gold standard of 'A' levels, and has been rejected by the government.

Quinquennial review

The largely unsung and unheralded review of NCVQ itself, conducted by the Department for Education and Employment, has thrown the future of the body into the melting pot. Although it came about as a regular five-yearly monitoring exercise 'a prior options review' was added to determine 'whether the functions delegated to NCVQ remain essential to Government and Department objectives' and, if so, 'whether there is scope for merger with or transferring some or all of the functions to another body.' In other words, the future of NCVQ was up for grabs.

The review reported in two parts, in November 1995 and February 1996, with an executive summary added later (DfEE, May 1996c). It concluded that NCVQ has not been able to establish a national framework for all, or even a majority, of vocational awards and despite all its achievements, there remains a negative perception of the organisation from some quarters. The executive summary notes that The Review Team thought that NCVQ's marketing function might lend itself to separate contracting out. This would provide the solution to what some saw as a fundamental problem, that of the incompatibility of NCVQ's regulatory and promotional roles.'

Qualifications and National Curriculum Authority

Sir Ron Dearing in his review of qualifications for 16–19 year olds gave a lot of thought to how they might be regulated (the rough equivalent of Ofwat or Ofgas, Ofqual perhaps) and put forward two options:

- setting up two new bodies, one responsible for qualifications from 14+, the other responsible for the curriculum and for statutory assessment by national tests
- replacing SCAA and NCVQ with one body to oversee qualifications, the curriculum and statutory assessment.

The Government consulted (DfEE, 1996a) on the two options in May 1996, expressing a preference for a single body. This led, not unexpectedly, on the basis of about 75 votes for and 25 against, to a proposal (DfEE, 1996b) to establish, after a little difficulty with the acronym (QUACC was, I believe, the first thought), a Qualifications and Curriculum Authority (QCA) to bring together the work of SCAA and NCVQ. A clause to that effect was included in the Education Bill laid before parliament in Autumn 1996, and the post of Chairman (£55 000 for a three-day week) was advertised.

At best, the new authority could be just the shake-up vocational education needs. With NCVQ gone there would be room for fresh thinking. At worst, however, it could mean the take-over of SCAA by true adherents of the NCVQ faith and an undermining of academic qualifications through competence-speak.

What next?

QCA's immediate task will be to drive forward the recommendations of the Dearing, Beaumont and Capey reports. This is an enormous undertaking. It will have to come up with a qualifications framework for young people and adults (with higher education no longer excluded) which embraces the three types of learning identified by Dearing – subjects and disciplines, applied learning, occupational training – and the interrelationships between them.

It will have to clear up the mess created by NCVQ. A decade after it was established, with over £107 million of public money spent, we not only have the confusion that vocational reform was intended to sort out, but adding to it we have NVQs and GNVQs.

NVQs were supposed to be National Vocational Qualifications but have become Niche Vocational Qualifications suitable, if anything, for assessing prior learning in the workplace. GNVQs emerged as an odd variant of them for colleges and schools. Over two-thirds of vocational qualifications currently conferred are old-style awards.

A truly national system of vocational awards, which can accommodate the qualifications that employers value whether old or new, will, I hope, be at the top of QCA's agenda. The key is probably the distinction Beaumont makes between setting standards – the responsibility of employers – and designing qualifications – the province of the awarding bodies. The role of the authority then becomes checking that the award meets the standards through appropriate content and assessment. It is likely, as Beaumont and Capey suggested, that there will have to be different qualification modes for preparing *for* work and upskilling *in* work.

GNVQs will need to be properly designed as applied education. They are, if anything, further back than NVQs. At least with NVQs employers were given the chance to say what they should be about, even if they did not always recognise what the consultants wrote for them. But with GNVQs too little thought has gone into the defining cores. Do leisure and tourism – swimming pool supervision and selling holidays – really belong together, for example?

There is also work to be done on GCSEs and 'A' levels, and the overall framework. But the severe criticisms of both school and further education inspectors (FEFC, 1994a; 1994b) of GNVQs and NVQs underline just how big the task is.

Conclusion

Just over 10 years ago the government took some bold decisions. It recognised that a crucial problem was how Britain was going to pay its way in the world and it has come to see an improved system of vocational education as making a major contribution towards increased competitiveness. It has also accepted that in countries such as Germany, Switzerland and Hungary, many young people are able to reach levels of attainment in maths and their mother tongue through applied learning and vocational training well above what their counterparts in this country are able to achieve through concentrating on the subjects themselves.

Educating everyone and economic competitiveness are still urgent issues. The fact that NCVQ went down the wrong path has set us back, but QCA gives us a chance to put things right. Let us hope the chance is taken and we at last get in place a national system of awards that mean something and lead somewhere.

References

Authers, J. (1996) Lecturers in row over academic freedom. Financial Times (London) 19 April 1996.
Beaumont, G. (1994) CBI Perspective, 1 March.
Beaumont, G. (1996) Review of 100 NVQs and SVQs Consulation document, October .
Bees, M. and Swords, M. (1990) National Vocational Qualifications and Further Education (London: Kogan Page/NCVQ).
Capey, J. (1995) GNVQ Assessment Review (London: NCVQ).
CBI (1994a) GNVQs: Policy and Practice. Conference, Centre Point, London, 1 March.
CBI (1994b) Quality Assessed: The CBI Review of NVQs and SVQs (London: Confederation for British Industry).
Channell, J. and St John, M.J. (1996) The language of standards. Competence and

Assessment, Issue 31, February.

Churchill, C. (1994) A vocational charter for cheats. Daily Telegraph (London), 14 December.

Dearing, R. (1993) The National Curriculum and Its Assessment: final report (London: SCAA).

Dearing, R. (1996) Review of qualifications for 16–19 year olds (London: SCAA).

De Ville, H.G. (1986) Review of Vocational Qualifications in England and Wales: A report by the working group (London: HMSO).

DfEE (1994) Government policy, report by Timothy Boswell, 1 March.

DfEE (1995) NCVQ 1995 quinquennial review. Stage One Report, November.

DfEE (1996a) NCVQ 1995–96 quinquennial review. Stage Two Report, February.

DfEE (1996b) NCVQ 1996 quinquennial review. Executive Summary, May.

DfEE (1996c) Building the framework: a consultation paper on bringing together the work of NCVQ and SCAA. May.

DfEE (1996d) Top advisers join forces to raise standards. DfEE News 281/96, September.

DfEE (1996e) GNVQ goes from strength to strength – Henley. DfEE News 369/96, 4 November.

FEFC (1994a) NVQs in the further education sector in England – national survey: report from the inspectorate. September.

FEFC (1994b) GNVQs in the further education sector in England – national survey: report from the inspectorate. November.

Her Majesty's Chief Inspector (1996) Annual Report, June 1996.

Hillier, J. (1994) A statement by the National Council for Vocational Qualifications on All Our Futures – Britain's Education Revolution (Channel 4, Dispatches, 15 December 1993) and associated report by the Centre for Education and Employment Research, University of Manchester; letter to David Lloyd, Senior Commissioning Editor, News and Current Affairs, Channel 4 Television, dated 10 February 1994.

Hillier, J. (1996a) Oral evidence to the Education Committee of the House of Commons, 17 January.

Hillier, J. (1996b) Misleading view of NVQ progress (letter). Financial Times (London), 9 October.

Hillier, J. (1996c) Developing a framework for vocational qualifications is always going to be expensive (letter) Times Educational Supplement, 18 October.

Jessup, G. (1991) Outcomes: NVQs and the emerging model of education and training. (London: Falmer Press).

NCVQ (1993) GNVQ Information Note (London: NCVQ).

NCVQ (1995) NVQ Criteria and Guidance (London: NCVQ).

National Vocational Awarding Bodies (1995) 100,000 GNVQ successes and growing. Press Release, 21 August.

National Vocational Awarding Bodies (1996) Record number of GNVQ awards in 1995/96. Press Release, 28 August.

OFSTED (1996a) GNVQs in schools: quality and standards of General National Vocational Qualifications, 1993–94. November.

OFSTED (1996b) Assessment of General National Vocational Qualifications. June

Robinson, P. (1996) Rhetoric and reality: Britain's new vocational qualifications (London: Centre for Economic Performance, LSE).

Rogers, P. (1992) Chairman's speech. Launch of BTEC Annual Report, 27 May.

Senker, P. and 13 others (1996) Vocational training needs serious evaluation (letter).

Financial Times (London), 17 January.
Smithers, A. (1993) All Our Futures: Britain's Education Revolution (London: Channel Four Television).
Smithers, A. (1996) Beaumont's report hides flaws in NVQs. Personnel Today, 30 January.
White Paper (1986) Working Together – Education and Training. Cmnd. 9823 (London: HMSO).
White Paper (1991) Education and Training for the 21st Century. Cm 1536. Volume 1 (London: HMSO).

Chapter 18
Assessment in the world of work: 'the life of Brian'

ROY CHILDS

For many pupils and students the move into the world of work means leaving behind the formal assessments, tests and exams that form a consistent theme throughout our educational lives. The National Curriculum, SATs and records of achievement, GCSEs, degrees and PhDs – whatever the point at which you left full time education, you will have had the experience of being assessed. So what happens next? Is that the end of formal assessment? Is assessment now a question of being judged by practical achievements? Depending on the emotions that tests and exams stir up in you, it is either fortunate or unfortunate that the world of work is taking the process of assessment ever more seriously. I remember finishing my own final exams and thinking 'never again'. A friend of mine, in fact, made a bonfire with all his notes and danced around it shouting 'I'm free, I'm free'. This chapter introduces you to the range of tests and assessments you are likely to encounter once you enter the world of work. I shall use the career path of a graduate called Brian tracing his path from graduation through to his current position as managing director. In this way, I hope you can appreciate not only the range of assessments in the world of work, but also how work assessment has something to teach education and education has something to teach people at work.

Getting a job

What happens?

Before Brian graduated he had felt confident about his abilities. He believed he had what it takes to succeed – and he was clearly an ambitious sort. He had applied for three jobs and had already decided which one he was going to accept. It was to be with HBJ Ltd, a fast growing electronics company which desperately needed his kind of

Assessment in the world of work: 'the life of Brian'

technical knowledge. When Brian had not heard from HBJ after 2 weeks, he phoned to see if his application had been lost in the post.

'I'm sorry sir', said the personnel assistant, 'you haven't been short-listed, but thank you for your interest in HBJ'. Brian did not even ask why. He was so surprised and hurt. He had received his first lesson that continuing success at school and university and the expectation of a good degree were not a guarantee of success in the world of work. Educationally, he had been able to choose what he wanted – where to study, what to study, when to study. Clearly, different criteria were being applied now. What were they?

What Brian did not know was that his application form had not even been read! Imagine HBJ wanting to appoint to one technical post and receiving 200 application forms. The first sift through the applications can often be rather arbitrary. Perhaps those short-listed are those whose application forms are typed; perhaps only applicants from universities X, Y and Z are considered; perhaps other criteria such as interest in sport or computers is desired. In fact, I know of one company that had so many applicants that it sorted them into two piles – the brown and the white envelopes. Only the white envelopes were processed!

Assessment methods

Although such practices are clearly unfair, the practical issue of making judgements based on little information confronts companies all the time. The applicants need to get past the first criterion, which means paying attention to the practical difficulties and presenting themselves in a way that is both acceptable and likely to 'stand out'. To overcome such unreliable and potentially unfair processes the better companies may take a number of steps:

- Creating a more specific application form which ensures that relevant information is collected which can serve as an initial screen. Carrying this to an extreme, some companies have developed application forms where the answers given have been 'validated', that is certain answers correlate with successful performance later at work. Such forms, properly researched, are called Biodata and are certainly better than choosing the colour of an envelope!
- Replacing simple criteria such as five GCSEs or a BSc. Honours (first class or upper second) and requiring all applicants to attend a short screening interview or to take some psychometric tests.
- Introducing self assessment questionnaires which encourage applicants to judge their own skills in relation to the job requirements.

Whatever method is used for the first sift, it is the next stage where the really important assessments and judgements are made. It is true that the most popular method for making the judgements is still the interview. However, the dominance of the interview has declined, or it may be more accurate to say that the use of other methods has increased. The reasons for this are various, but they are all influenced by the need of companies to make better judgements.

When companies bother to calculate the cost of re-advertising, of manager's time spent interviewing, of paying the cost of assessment materials and, most expensive of all, when they calculate the cost of reduced output from lower performers together with possible dismissal costs, the argument for improving selection decisions becomes overwhelming.

At this stage it is worth looking at the effectiveness of different assessment methods. To do this it is necessary to review the literature and to see how different research studies have validated interviews, tests, etc. A useful way to summarise the effectiveness of the various methods is by using the correlation coefficient. In effect, the question we are asking is whether someone who is highly rated by an interviewer, a test or an observer of a simulation, subsequently performs better than someone who was not so highly rated. The more clearly the answer is 'yes', the closer our correlation coefficient gets towards a value of 1. The more unclear the answer (i.e. the more random the relationship between ratings and subsequent job performance) the correlation coefficient approaches zero. Sometimes, it has been known for people with higher test scores to become the lower job performers! In such cases the correlation coefficient is negative. In my own experience, I know of one company that was selecting candidates with high test scores but they later discovered that the correlation with subsequent performance was negative. They had therefore been selecting candidates who had less of a chance of becoming good performers than the candidates they rejected!

It should now be obvious that we can represent the average effectiveness of different assessment methods using the correlation coefficient as an index. Table 18.1 presents the results of a search through the published literature. Relevant data is then subjected to a statistical technique called meta-analysis which, in effect, calculates a weighted grand average based on the studies involved. The results in Table 18.1 come from one of the most quoted meta-analyses (Hunter and Hunter, 1984).

Description of the various assessment methods

Interviews

There is an increasing range of techniques used at interviews. The job applicant should no longer expect a meander through his or her application form. Good practice involves a much tighter defined purpose with a lot more structure which research shows to be far more predictive.

Table 18.1. Meta-analysis of some predictors with supervisor ratings.

Predictor	Mean validity	Number of correlations	Number of subjects
Ability test (composite) [a]	0.53	425	32 124
Biodata[a]	0.37	12	4 429
Reference check[a]	0.26	10	5 389
Academic achievement[a]	0.11	11	1 089
Interest inventory[a]	0.10	3	1 789
Interviews[a]	0.14	10	2 694
Assessment centres[b]	0.41	21	15 345
Peer ratings[a]	0.49	31	8 202

[a]Extracts from Hunter and Hunter (1984).
[b]Extract from Schmitt et al.(1984).

Figures such as these do vary depending on the studies which are considered by the analyst to be worthy of inclusion. This table tries to give a picture of the more commonly found results.

However, there are still wide differences in philosophy. Some interviews are clearly focused on obtaining real behavioural evidence of past behaviour, on the premise that past behaviour is the best predictor of future behaviour. These are usually called targeted or behavioural interviews. A quite different approach is the situational interview where applicants are required to describe what they would do given a particular scenario. Traditionally such 'hypothetical' questions have been frowned upon. However, evidence is accumulating which shows that such an approach can be very effective as long as the situations are properly selected and the answers are carefully evaluated according to strict rules.

Ability tests

There has been a dramatic increase in the use of pencil and paper tests requiring applicants to reason using words, passages, numbers and abstract shapes. Usually timed, such tests can be considered as a kind of simulation of the thinking skills a person will need for certain aspects of a job. Although ability tests do not always have high face validity, they obviously require a person to extract the right information, to see patterns and logical sequences and to draw appropriate conclusions. Such thinking appears to have a wide applicability for many jobs. Ability tests can present unfamiliar material (or familiar material but in a new way) which means that the reasoning involved does test skills which relate to dealing with new situations rather than applying accumulated knowledge. As such, they contribute information which is not necessarily measured by a person's track record and

Table 18.1 illustrates how they can sometimes be amongst the best predictors of job success.

Personality questionnaires:

Unlike ability tests, which look at how well a person can reason, personality tests look at how a person behaves. They rely on a person saying how they might typically respond. Such self report is obviously dependent on honesty and self awareness, and personality questionnaires vary widely in the manner and style of their questions. Some are very direct and obvious, which can help to avoid accusations of discrimination. Others are more obscure, relying on research to explain and justify the interpretation of the results. There is also an extremely wide range of ideas, constructs and models of personality which different questionnaires attempt to measure.

It is not the case, therefore, that one questionnaire is generally applicable across most situations. Careful selection is required and, even more important, careful integration of personality questionnaire data with other evidence is essential. The biggest misuse of personality questionnaires is by those who believe that they measure more than the actually do – often inferring competence of performance rather than style.

Assessment centres

To the uninitiated, assessment centres may sound like buildings for carrying out assessments. However, the term is used to describe a combination of assessment techniques which usually involve simulations such as group discussions, in-tray exercises and presentations as well as psychometric tests and interviews. Where such exercises take place is not the point.

The exercises in an assessment centre usually take place over 1–3 days and involve a high ratio of observers (i.e. people trained to record and score the various exercises) to participants. A feature of assessment centres is that any judgements made by observers will be challenged by others to ensure that clear behavioural evidence is available to justify any ratings made. Such observational assessments are therefore seen as reducing subjectivity and personal bias; Table 18.1 illustrates how they can therefore become one of the more predictive forms of assessment.

Biodata

As mentioned above, this is a method of collecting information about a candidate without the need for personal contact. As such it can often form a first stage screen process, although some companies place much higher value on it. The method is essentially an extended application form. However, the reason for its increasing use is that, when carefully constructed, it becomes much more predictive than a traditional application form.

Biodata forms are usually constructed by writing lots of questions. These questions have been suggested from a job analysis or by the examination of critical events which successful employees manage. The questions are then trialled and analysed statistically. Only those which have a correlation with job success are used. Such forms can then be scored.

Other

There are other forms of assessment in use for selection. There is evidence that reference checks can be predictive (see Table 18.1 – value 0.26) as can academic achievement, interest inventories (see Table 18.1, values 0.11 and 0.10) and interviews (Hunter and Hunter 1984; Schmitt *et al*. 1984; value 0.14). Certain methods, such as graphology and astrology, have yet to show any consistent pattern of validity. They are currently seen as being little better than chance except by certain practitioners and devotees.

Whereas the figures in Table 18.1 are much quoted, it must be remembered that they represent only an average based on a particular set of research studies. The figures could, therefore, change if a different set of studies was selected. The conclusion from the figures in Table 18.1 might be to encourage employers to use ability tests and to stop using the interview. In fact, there are a number of reasons for not using the results too strictly. This is because more recent evidence suggests that the figure for tests is an overestimate, especially when research published after 1975 is considered. The evidence also suggests the figure for interviews and personality tests is an underestimate, especially when they are implemented properly. To draw appropriate conclusions from such data, it is clearly necessary to understand the figures and their limitations. However, an important message does appear to come through consistently – employers do allow the interview to be over-dominant in selection decision and, generally, they would benefit from collecting information about candidates from a wider range of assessment methods.

Good practice in occupational selection

Over the past 20 years, assessment for selection has become increasingly sophisticated and professional. Clearly this is driven by greater knowledge, the costs of poor selection and the requirements of fairness legislation. Companies aspiring to best practice need to address three clear stages of the selection and assessment process represented in Figure 18.1.

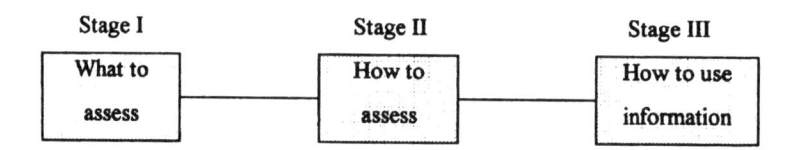

```
Stage I              Stage II             Stage III
┌──────────┐        ┌──────────┐         ┌──────────┐
│ What to  │────────│  How to  │─────────│ How to use│
│  assess  │        │  assess  │         │information│
└──────────┘        └──────────┘         └──────────┘
```

Figure 18.1. Selection and assessment process

What to assess

Knowing what to assess requires not only a good knowledge of the job (and companies are getting much better at job analysis) but also an identification of the critical personal attribute (often called competencies) which differentiate top performers from the rest. This has been a boom area in the past few years and, when done well, involves extensive observation, interviews and use of other techniques which are analysed to uncover the real behaviours and characteristics which differentiate excellent performers from average performers.

How to assess

Knowing how to assess enables one to design an assessment procedure and requires a good knowledge of which characteristics are best measured by which methods. Thus it has become reasonably well established that assessing intellectual capacity is not done well by interview, which is why practitioners are strongly advised to use a carefully selected ability test instead or as well. However, best practice also requires that the assessment of any characteristic should involve more than one method. This is because every method has its own strengths and biases. Using several methods makes it more likely that these biases are evened out. This kind of principle should be emphasised on training courses for selection and recruiting skills.

An important aspect of how to assess people is that the judgements are informed. Knowledge of the value and predictive power of different assessment methods is therefore highly recommended. An example of training which helps people to become more informed are those which qualify people to use psychometric tests. Many of these courses are run to fulfil guidelines laid down by the British Psychological Society. In fact people can now obtain a nationally recognised certificate issued by the British Psychological Society through 'verified' assessors. This qualification may become recognised internationally, and one of the benefits of this kind of training, apart from the better understanding of how to carry out assessments, is that it is linked to a professional body which adheres to some kind of best practice model and code of ethics and guidelines. This helps to ensure that professional rather than commercial interests guide the learning process and people are therefore trained to understand when not to use tests as well as to understand when they may be usefully used.

How to use the information

Much time can be spent deciding what to assess and how to assess, and then the whole process may be trivialised by the poor use of the information collected. It is important, therefore, that there is some discipline in using the information and we can refer to this as 'creating a decision model'. This is not necessarily for selection, but all assessment should have a purpose and this is to clarify how the information will be used to aid that purpose.

To create a decision model for, say, a selection decision there is a need to carefully evaluate the importance of the attributes required and the quality of the data collected by the various methods. These then have to be combined. This process is obviously done in any selection process but it is rarely made explicit. In fact, many apparently sophisticated selection processes fall over because the final stage is left to 'intuition' or 'gut feel'. Whilst the subtlety of human judgement can be a tremendously effective and powerful thing, unfortunately it is often a smokescreen for ill-thought-through issues and personal biases. This stage in selection is, nowadays, probably the weakest link in the chain.

To return to our life of Brian, after he obtained his degree, he went through various selection procedures. He failed to be selected after attending a two day assessment centre where he thought that he had performed extremely well, but eventually he got a job as a graduate trainee after only a short interview! Such are the vagaries of life. The next section looks at what assessments Brian could experience in the early years of his new job.

Assessment early in your career

When Brian finally got his first job he felt that he had experienced the full range of assessments. He had finished his educational assessments, he had experienced a variety of interviews of variable challenge and rigour, he'd been through simulations and psychometric tests and he even suspected one company of using graphology. And after all that, the company who finally offered him a job had based their decision on a very short informal interview and his degree result! However, he was now ready to put his energies into the challenge of a new job with a dynamic company.

Unfortunately for Brian, he was not aware of the politics within his new company until some time after he joined. The advert had made the job sound exciting and challenging. It is not unusual for companies to over-sell themselves in an attempt to attract a good field of applicants. It is always worth remembering that selection is a two-way process and it is not only employers who should be improving their assessment and selection techniques!

The reality for Brian was that his appointment was the result of the chief executive believing in the need for 'new blood'. The majority of senior managers, however, were extremely dubious – partly because they felt threatened and partly because experience was valued far more than an academic track record. As a result, Brian was taken on expecting to be welcomed and given exciting and challenging projects. The reality was that his appointment was resented and he was given small projects involving a lot of tedious administration. He could not help wondering why they had valued his degree. He then faced the next form of assessment – the performance appraisal.

Performance appraisal

Most companies have a form of appraisal which is designed to review an employee's progress or contribution and level of performance. Methods and systems vary widely, as do the skills of the managers who carry them out. At their best, appraisal processes are opportunities for open and honest feedback in such a way that the employee feels supported and the process increases motivation. Unfortunately, surveys of employee attitudes to appraisal suggest that this is not the norm. Too often the process is seen either as a waste of time, or worse, as a negative and unpleasant exercise.

It is still the case, in my experience, that many employees claim never to have had a 'proper appraisal'. Now, clearly, using appraisal in the general sense of the word (meaning some kind of performance evaluation) this cannot be true. Being promoted, or passed over for promotion, means that some form of evaluation has taken place. What such people mean by 'no proper appraisal' is that they have never had quality time with their manager or that they have never been given honest feedback concerning their style and perceived value to the company. In fact, it is not uncommon for people to say that the only feedback they receive is when things go wrong. Things have begun to change in the last 10–15 years and more and more companies recognise the value not just of performance evaluation, but also of feedback concerning an employee's whole style and approach. Below I will try to trace the changes that have (and still are) taking place concerning assessment in the workplace.

Management by objectives

All employees deserve greater clarity concerning the elements of which they are to be appraised. Many appraisal schemes use an overall 'MERIT

RATING' which results in a global classification from, say, A to E. Such ratings are notoriously unreliable and subjective. In many cases they simply do not provide any indication of difference in performance. I remember examining the appraisal ratings in a large insurance company where 95 per cent of the people were graded B although it was clear that performance standards varied widely. Sometimes managers were 'guided' to make such merit ratings, using concepts as integrity, enthusiasm, maturity, etc. Assessment of such concepts is very hard, given the woolliness and personal interpretation which people will make. It can also be argued that managers have no right to evaluate on such general and non-job related concepts.

The emergence of management by objectives (MBO) was partly a reaction to such subjective assessments. A key element of MBO is that people should be assessed on their behaviour and achievements rather than on vague and ill-defined personality characteristics. Another element of MBO, however, is the belief that people deserve to know what they are supposed to achieve. Without this their efforts are in danger of being misdirected. If people are clear about what they are supposed to be doing, at least they can have the opportunity to self correct. As Drucker (1968) said :

> Effective management must direct the vision and efforts of all managers towards a common goal.

It is interesting that the concept of MBO can be seen as providing clarity of direction and purpose. The process involves specifying the key objectives for the company, the team and then the employee. Unfortunately, this was often done badly and became a way of detailing key tasks. This can lead to a culture which focuses on activity rather than achievement. However, done well, it provided clear, tangible objectives which were observable and measurable. This allowed employees to self monitor and to take responsibility for their own achievements. It can therefore be seen as part of the process toward 'empowerment' which is the currently fashionable term for devolving responsibility downwards – for increasing the autonomy and responsibility of all employees at all levels in the organisation. However, MBO fell into disrepute because it was often seen to achieve the opposite! In some organisations, it became a bureaucratic process for detailing tasks and of increasing manager's control and the employees' accountability. It also tended to focus on the more easily quantifiable aspects of the job.

MBO did not need to become such a control process, but in practice it often did. Since this coincided with the adoption of a new philosophy which rejected the 'command and control' approach to management, it meant that more progressive companies adopted other approaches.

Making appraisal developmental

It was not just the tendency for MBO to become a bureaucratic control system that made it lose favour. It was also the fact that clarity of purpose and measurable objectives are only one aspect of improving perform-ance. What happens when an individual fails to achieve? A poor manager can dwell on the evidence and admonish or blame in an attempt to create more effort next time – a strategy which is not particularly effective. A good manager will try to use the failure to pick out the learning points, but quickly move on to the future. However, an approach which some companies have found particularly useful to help managers to look forward and develop employees is one that uses competencies.

The first thing to clarify is that the term competencies is used in two quite different ways. The most commonly understood is the way competencies are used in the National Vocational Qualifications (NVQ) system (see also Chapter 17) and such bodies as the Management Charter Initiative (MCI). They define a competency as an activity, behaviour or piece of knowledge together with a standard of performance. It is therefore the output – what a person can do or has achieved – and the perform-ance standard sets a level of competence. The other use of the term competency is quite different. Rather than defining the output, it defines the input. It is not what a person achieves it is what they contribute. An input competency is a characteristic of the person; it is what they bring to an area of activity which helps them to be successful, rather than being a measure of the success of that activity.

Let me illustrate with a topical area of activity: recruiting high quality staff. The output might be to fill 20 posts within 6 months. The perform-ance standard might be that 15 are still in post performing satisfactorily 6 months later. The input competencies might be organisation and judgement of people. In other words, a person will need to have good organising skills and to be a good judge of people to produce the result. Input competencies therefore focus on the qualities an individual needs to develop in order to produce the desired outcomes. A definition of competencies offered by Klemp (1980) is 'an underlying characteristic of a person which results in effective and/or superior performance'.

The effect of using competency frameworks can be to reduce the retrospective and evaluative aspect of appraisal and to concentrate on those qualities a person will need to perform better in the future. To achieve this, managers require many skills which they may not have used as much in the past such as coaching, counselling and feedback.

Although these skills are not dependent on the use of competencies, the whole developmental process is enhanced because:

- Carefully developed competency frameworks identify those characteristics which truly differentiate high quality performers. The

Assessment in the world of work: 'the life of Brian' 339

competencies are not derived logically, but by careful observation, examination or critical incidents and other techniques.
- Competencies, can describe a whole range of personal attributes, traits, motives, skills and elements of the self image. They are usually presented with a succinct definition to reduce misinterpretation and with specific behavioural examples so that they can be recognised across a variety of situations. This means that the competency is more easily recognised. Better assessment can mean better quality feedback which is a pre-requisite for development. It also provides a focus for what is most important to develop;
- Having identified those areas which require development, competencies provide a more tangible framework with which to work. The behavioural examples provide suggestions for the individual to practise.

In one company, an employee had become classified as a 'no-hoper'. All efforts to improve his output had failed. He was close to dismissal. The introduction of a competency framework which became the focus for his next appraisal lead to a dramatic improvement. Previously he had been told to improve and so he had tried harder, but at the wrong things. The competencies gave him a much better idea of what he needed to do to improve. The result was that a poor performer became a star – so much so that he was pinched by the competition! However, it is bad practice to restrict the development of staff simply because they may then become attractive to others!

The appraisal experience

We can now return to Brian facing his first appraisal. He had been called into his manager's office at 4.30 pm on Friday and, without warning, asked to comment on his own progress to date. He had then been told that his progress was satisfactory but not exciting and that, if he wanted to get on, he would have to try harder. Brian was left with the weekend to contemplate his failings and had to imagine what he should try to do harder. He made the right decision – he tried harder to find another job and the company lost not only an employee with considerable potential, but also nearly a year of their own and Brian's time. This is a story of shameful waste and bad management. However, Brian's next company was different.

Assessment later in your career

In Brian's next company his initial 6 months involved a careful induction process. During this he was welcomed into various parts of the business, given responsibility for small but meaningful projects and allocated a mentor who provided information and advice, who could play devil's advocate, who opened doors to senior people that Brian would not have thought to approach and who generally kept an eye on him.

Brian proved himself in a number of ways, mostly because of his sharp intellect, and he was promoted to leader of a small team after 2 years. He now experienced a different kind of assessment – assessment by complaint. Apparently Brian did not delegate enough; he did not listen; he failed to communicate, etc. Clearly managing others required more than just intellect. He was now moving into a form of assessment he had not previously encountered except, perhaps, informally in the pub. This was an assessment of his personality. Fortunately for Brian, help was close at hand.

Team development

The company, well aware of how critical it was for the work teams to be effective, had set up a series of team building courses. It was not long before Brian found himself being lowered down a cliff face on a stretcher by the rest of his team – this was a trust-building exercise, not because he had suffered an injury! Now, not all team building courses use the great outdoors but it is often this image which is aroused when people talk about it. In practice, there are many different approaches to team building. Many are still locked into the idea of 'an event' where team members share thoughts, feelings and issues. To facilitate this process there is usually some element of invoking principles of openness and trust (and exercises designed to encourage it), some element of activity for people to experience working together, some element of debriefing and feedback and some element of self analysis – often using questionnaires to provide information and a framework. This clearly involves assessment in its loosest sense since any kind of feedback involves a judgement and inferred 'level' of the characteristic being discussed. However, team building events can involve much more formal assessment such as 'observer ratings' about performance or style.

The result for Brian of the 4 day 'event', which involved activities, discussion, feedback and psychometric testing, was a much more open environment with closer personal relationships which certainly survived the transition back to work. However, as some members of Brian's team moved on and new members joined, some of the old problems began to re-emerge. Improvement to Brian's style was going to take more than a team building event. It is for this reason that team building is beginning to be seen as a much more continuous process. The best processes now involve a careful diagnosis of the issues and the desired outcomes followed by an integrated approach to managing performance of which a team building event is a clear part of a much bigger process. One way of building such an integrated approach is to use an appropriate competency framework to provide the structure for managing performance, for selecting and developing staff, for facilitating feedback in the

Assessment in the world of work: 'the life of Brian' 341

workplace and on team build events. We shall now look at how Brian was launched into such a process.

360 degree feedback

The concept of 360 degree feedback is essentially simple. You don't only ask your boss to tell you how you are getting on; '360 degree' means that you could invite feedback from any one around you – peers, subordinates, customers, etc. Since feedback can be blunt and unhelpful sometimes, it is usual for the process to be managed around a competency framework. This is what happened to Brian.

Using the company's competency framework for the specific aspect of a manager's job (the performance management competencies), a questionnaire was developed and Brian was invited to complete it in order to give him a self assessment. His manager and six of his staff also completed the questionnaire and the results are displayed graphically in Figure 18.2. The process was very powerful. Certain beliefs that Brian held concerning his strengths and weaknesses were severely challenged. Both he and his manager had viewed Brian as quite democratic, but the figure shows how his staff had a very different perception.

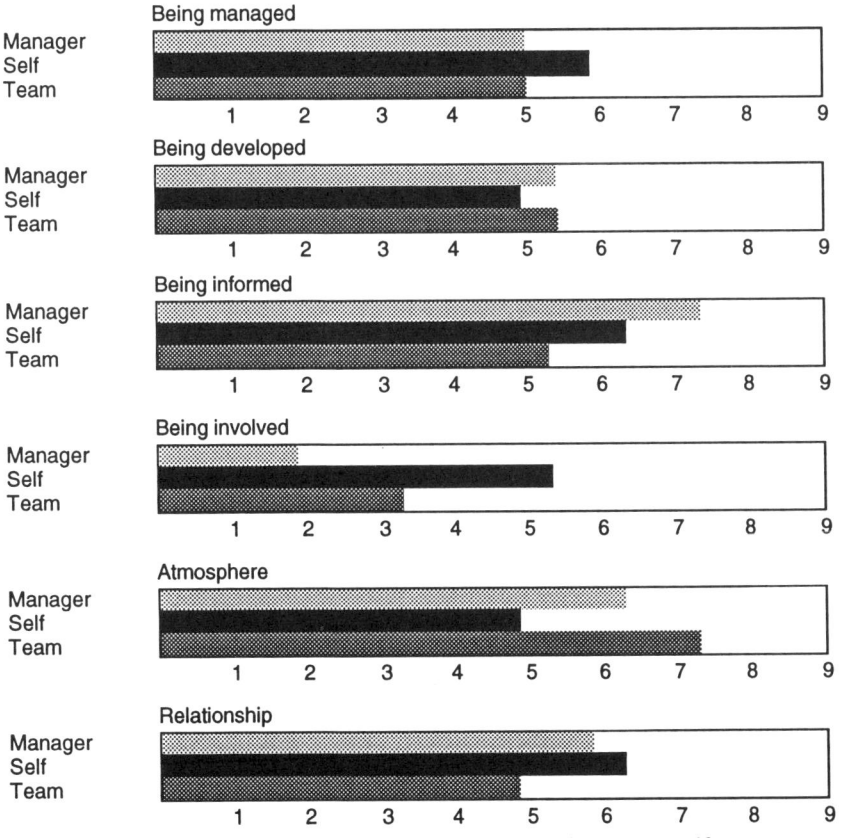

Figure 18.2. Manager, self and team assessments of Brian's (self) management competencies

It is interesting when conducting 360 degree feedback to note the agreements and disagreements. The example given for Brian and his manager is not unusual. There appears to be a tendency for a person and his or her manager to have a much closer agreement than the person with his or her team or staff. Such information often challenges people about the way they make judgements of others – another essential form of feedback which should, eventually, help to develop this much neglected managerial skill.

Figure 18.2 illustrates only one of the displays that are possible with 360 degree feedback. Numerous further analyses can be carried out. For example, there are numerous gap analyses that could be explored such as the gap between Brian's view and his team's view which might look like Figure 18.3.

The whole process could have been very demoralising for Brian. He was fortunate, however, that his manager was a very open and positive person who was a natural coach. Brian found that, with this kind of support, he began to develop a style which was not only more effective but it was vastly more satisfying. The morale of his team began to climb. This gave him the confidence to put himself forward to trial a new 360 degree feedback process which included customer perceptions as well.

The discerning reader will have noticed that although we talked about 360 degree feedback, Figure 18.3 refers to a process called 400 degree feedback. This is because 360 degree refers to the data collec-

400° Feedback

Model: Performance managment A   **Person Assessed:** Brian
Gap Analysis   *Sorted by gap between Self and Team*

COMPETENCIES	Data Sources
INFORMATION SHARING	Self / Team
OPENNESS	Self / Team
DEVELOPING OTHERS	Self / Team
VISION	Self / Team
CO-OPERATION	Self / Team
COACHING ORIENTATION	Self / Team
MOTIVATING OTHERS	Self / Team
TEAM MANAGEMENT	Self / Team
MONITORING PERFORMANCE	Self / Team
POSITIVE REGARD	Self / Team

Figure 18.3. The gaps between Brian and his team in selected management competencies

tion, reporting and feedback process. The trouble is that it often stops there. The 400 degree process is a reminder that, after the reporting and feedback, there is an ongoing process of development which should be encouraged. 400 degree feedback is a proprietary process which builds it into the performance management process.

In Brian's case, he received his development report which gave him practical suggestions for developing his weaker competencies and his manager helped him to build in long term development goals together with the support and monitoring which eventually enabled him to reach a very senior level.

A model for managing performance

The previous sections introduced or described a variety of different assessments that people experience at work. There are many different assessment methods and there are considerable differences concerning what characteristics are to be assessed. The best companies will integrate all of these into a process which truly manages and enhances performance. My own definition of performance management is as follows:

> The process which motivates an employee to give his or her best in a focused way.

All other processes are subservient to this one. Thus MBO may help, but the barometer is the way it motivates people. The various methods of assessment are useful, but only if they are used in a way which enhances performance. A schematic model for managing performance which I use is shown in Figure 18.4.

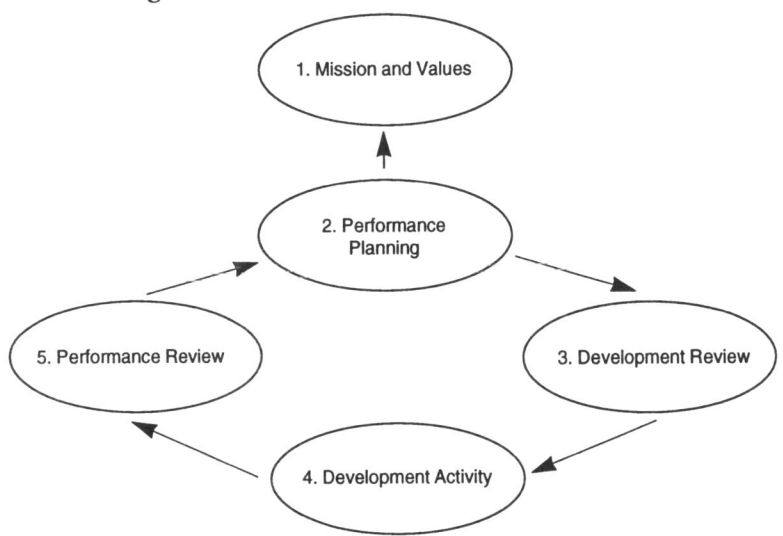

Figure 18.4. Managing performance

Much of the assessment in the world of work is or should be in some way related to this process. In overview terms, the process can be described as follows :

- Most companies now recognise the need for a clear vision of where their company wants to be as well as a distinctive character or climate by which it intends to operate – this is what is usually meant by *mission and values*.
- *Performance planning* requires the alignment of company, department, team and individual effort and a definition of the outputs or effects to be achieved.
- *Development review* requires that a person can obtain quality feedback on his or her current skill levels and future potential. To make this a valuable process it is desirable that the reviewer helps the person to use their strengths and develop their weaknesses. The reviewer therefore needs the skills of a counsellor, of a coach, of a challenger and motivator. These skills are beginning to redefine the qualities required of tomorrow's managers.
- *Development activities* require that the performance management process is supported by ideas, time and resources.
- *Performance review* requires that the accountability issues are not forgotten.

Clearly, development effort does need to produce results. Where an individual's performance is below standard there is a need to have a process which will help to highlight the reasons and to refocus the review on to what can be done to prevent reoccurrence. Using clear outputs and targets to give direction and using competencies to provide the mechanism for identifying what is needed, the performance review can quickly be refocused to look forward to the next development review. Thus it builds a cycle of performance and development and makes it much easier to overcome the traditional difficulty for the appraisal process – that of being too negative and backwards looking. Managers must also remember, when reviewing performance, how important it is to celebrate success as well as to address underperformance issues!

Summary and conclusions

This chapter has tried to describe some of the assessment methods and processes which are used in the world of work. Hopefully it is now clear that assessment can be expected at all stages and at all levels. It may be useful, now, to summarise by contrasting assessment as carried out in the educational and occupational worlds.

Perhaps the emphasis in the educational world is for assessment to focus around attainments and abilities. Tests and exams are used to measure mental development, knowledge and competence. Personal style is assessed much more informally – perhaps as subjective judgements on end of year reports and eventually as references.

In the world of work similar assessments are certainly found – especially for selection. However, the majority of assessments are carried out within the company and have an increasingly developmental purpose. Certainly the more enlightened companies use assessment to develop the personality and behaviour of their staff as well as their knowledge and task performance.

It is, perhaps, strangely ironic that the educational world makes a greater verbal commitment to developing their pupils' and students' character and yet it is in the world of work that assessment is being used to achieve this kind of development. The use of behavioural assessment, of personality assessment, of 360 degree or even 400 degree feedback could all be used very powerfully by teachers, lecturers, pupils and students to deal with the biggest challenge for the new millennium – the mission, values and character of our citizens all of whom go through the educational system and yet, sadly, not all of whom go through the world of work.

References

Drucker, P.F. (1968) The practice of management (McGraw-Hill, New York).

Hunter, J.E. and Hunter, R.F. (1984) Validity and utility of alternative predictors of job performance. Psychological Bulletin, 96, 72–98.

Klemp (1989) Fairness in employment testing (National Research Council).

Schmitt, N., Gouding, R.Z., Noe, R.A. and Mirsch, M. (1984) Meta analyses of validity studies. Personnel Psychology, 37, 407–15.

Chapter 19
Some technical problems in the use of personality measures in occupational settings illustrated using the 'Big Five'

DENNIS CHILD

No one need be surprised at the popularity of personality measures in occupational selection. Most of the terms used by trait theorists have a superficial ring of relevance about them when applied to work-related phenomena. For example, a glance down a list of facets in the NEO (Neuroticism, Extraversion, Openness) personality inventory or the primary factors of the 16PF (e.g. emotional stability, trust, gregariousness, openness, dutifulness, self-reliance) soon reveals many useful concepts. What I hope to show in this chapter is that while there is a case for believing in more than a skin-deep relevance of personality measures in selection, the topic is riddled with technical problems. There is a long way to go before we can use personality test results with confidence.

Demand and supply

Before embarking on an exploration of some of the problems, it might interest readers to get some idea of the extent of test use in occupational settings.

The growth of psychological testing for occupational selection, promotion and counselling in British organisations has been almost exponential in the past 30 years. This is especially true of the business sector, although local government has been a regular user. Many companies have their own psychologists, but for the purposes of specialist training in the use of test materials or providing a testing service for those companies without psychologists there are now quite a large number of companies offering consultancies.

In two surveys by Mabey (1989, 1992), he approached about 1000 large businesses in 1989 and a further 1000 in 1992. The response rate was approximately a third in each case. Of these, roughly half use personality tests and two-thirds use cognitive tests for selection or development. Slightly fewer are reported for local government users (Williams, 1991). However approximate these figures might be, they represent a considerable number of organisations when applied to the population of large organisations. There are likely to be proportionally fewer small companies using tests, but there is little evidence on this point. These same reports show an increase in usage over the years and leave us in no doubt about the extensive demand from industry.

Williams (1994) wrote a useful summary of recent British practice in occupational testing up to 1993. He listed several reasons why companies use personality tests. In descending order of importance for businesses, the key reasons were

- predicting work group compatibility
- filtering out unsuitable candidates at selection
- predicting subsequent job performance
- providing objective and unbiased information
- cost-effectiveness
- speed and ease of use
- tradition (have always used them).

A similar list was obtained from a local government study but with the 'objective and unbiased' reason coming higher up the order. Most companies use the tests for recruitment and selection, about half (in the sample quoted by Williams) use them for training and development and about a third use them for career counselling. These figures apply mainly to professional, managerial, scientific, technical and marketing personnel. The tests are not used quite so often with those in clerical or manual occupations.

In hard times when work is scarce and there are many applicants for each job, it is not surprising to see industry looking for objective ways of pruning the list of applicants. Also, 'efficiency' in some industries has come to mean not only fewer people doing more work, but each person doing a wider range of work, often outside or tangential to their qualifications or experience. So industry has to look for people whose profiles give promise of being able to tolerate this sort of burden. Promotion, to create efficient line management and keep good people, is another critical selection problem in which personality testing has played a part.

It is important to point out that very few companies, if any these days, use only personality tests. Most use a range of criteria which include biodata, cognitive tests, work-sample tests, references and the interview. The later is particularly interesting because it is the most universally adopted procedure and held by some to be a reliable method for assessing personality. Most psychologists now accept that general, unstructured ('let's have a chat') interviews, which are neither fact-finding nor job-related, are not reliable in the process of predicting performance. Volumes have been written about the effectiveness of interviews in the selection process (for summaries see Herriot, 1989; Cook, 1993). At best, it is a naïve method of personality assessment relying on superficial observations of external criteria (e.g. appearance, response patterns) for evidence of complex human traits. There has been much more success in structured interviewing especially when this involves questions derived from detailed job analysis.

In research (Child *et al.*, 1988a) for the UKCC (the body responsible for selection, assessment and training standards for nurses), we found that one of the best adjuncts to selection was detailed information about the job. A job information checklist (JICs), which consisted of many questions about the role of the nurse, was prepared for potential recruits to nurse training. The inaccuracy of applicants' answers was alarming. Correct answers were provided after the completion of the questionnaire serving to show applicants what the job entailed and to help them in the decision as to whether the job was for them. Here, the emphasis in the interview, which followed the completion of the JICs, was shifted from a crude method of assessing personality to an information exchange about the work involved. One benefit of the method was that applicants were better able to make a reasoned judgement as to whether *they* wanted to become nurses – in effect, a self-selection device.

On the demand side, then, the evidence presented by Williams (1994) speaks for itself; there seems little doubt that psychological tests are in great demand by industry and this is on the increase, with personality tests taking a substantial place alongside other selection devices.

If people are still not convinced, they should look at the supply side. If there was no demand, the suppliers would disappear. However, hundreds of supply companies have sprung into being recently. I gather through the consultancy grapevine that at the last count (1994) there were upwards of 500 companies purporting to design, administer, advise on, sell and train in the use of psychological tests suitable for selection, recruitment, training, development and career counselling. Many of these companies are prepared to run the selection process, including assessment centres.

But supply companies are faced with a serious dilemma, a dilemma which brings into conflict all the scientific language of caution and probability expected of the trained psychologist with the optimism and hard-sell techniques necessary in a highly competitive market place. Unfortunately, the product is far from perfect. It's not even like a new car which should start every time you turn the key. With, for example, predictive validities of personality tests on the low side, one could not expect certainty in the outcomes. Tests are fallible and supply companies have the awkward task of letting customers know what the shortcomings are without putting them off the product. It reminds me of the hard-sell investment mail which floods through my letter-box containing pages of goodies one could not possibly be without. Right at the end is a sentence in small print something like this – 'the value of your investment may go down as well as up and you may not get back the original amount invested'.

Some key problems in personality test design

Much has been written about the pros and cons of personality tests designed using psychometric methods (Kline, 1993). But those questions of particular interest to industrial users are likely to concentrate on how well-founded are trait descriptions for application in industrial settings, how much detailed information can be gleaned from the traits and what is their predictive validity in occupational competence? These questions are recycled under three headings of 'how is the personality sphere to be delineated?', 'nomenclature' and 'predictive validity'. There are several other technical issues which would require a book, but these three are at the core of industrial concerns about testing.

Exploration of these problems is largely a technical matter, but I hope to make the presentation readable for those with a passing knowledge of psychometrics. As the vast majority of personality inventories are based on factor analysis, readers should not be surprised to discover that some of the following debate hinges on this technique (Child, 1990d).

There are many personality inventories in use today. However, to give focus to the problems, most of my illustrations will be taken from the manual of the revised version of the NEO Personality Inventory (Costa and McCrae, 1992).

How is the personality sphere to be delineated?

Some of the most popular inventories are based on what is referred to as the 'lexical hypothesis' which runs something like this: over the centuries, we have elaborated in the language all the important ways of describing personality. By analysing the language and detecting the groupings of similar words and concepts, we should thereby capture the essence of personality. If the language contains the universe or sphere of personality traits, then the task of psychometricians is to find the most valid, robust and useful of them. Most, but not all, inventory designers have cross-validated the lexical findings with data derived from other sources such as real life data and objective tests (e.g. Cattell, 1946, 1979).

How to cut the sphere into traits has been a bone of contention for many years. The arguments are technical and largely to do with particular preferred methods which reflect the function and purpose of factor analysis. Three will be briefly outlined here and relate to how many traits (factors) are needed to give the fullest account of the correlations (common variance available), what kind of relationship should exist between the traits (uncorrelated or correlated) and what level are the traits being used (surface or source traits or a mixture of both).

Number of traits

The number of traits used to define the sphere is as much a philosophical as a statistical question. Using the principle of parsimony, typical of scientific laws, one would use as few as possible, and as independent as possible consistent with accounting for the relationships between the variables.

Eysenck, for example, uses three large *uncorrelated* dimensions (Extraversion (E), Neuroticism (N) and Psychoticism). Costa and McCrae (1992) in the recent version of the NEO-PI-R use five ('the Big Five') large, *uncorrelated* dimensions (Extraversion, Neuroticism, Openness, Agreeableness and Conscientiousness) and Cattell in the 16PF uses 16 *correlated* primary traits. Eysenck and Costa *et al.*, by adopting orthogonal rotation techniques, rely on their traits being described in terms of a framework where the reference axes are at right angles, i.e. uncorrelated dimensions (like locating the position of a town using the lines of latitude and longitude on the surface of the earth).

Cattell uses oblique rotation (machine programmed followed by hand/eye and rotoplot methods; see Child, 1990d). This means that the descriptive framework allows some (but not a lot of) correlation between the resulting traits. His argument is that few, if any, human characteristics are totally uncorrelated and one should account for whatever correlation there is.

As these researchers are all fishing in the same pond, one would expect a relationship between the dimensions, and there is. If the correlations between the 16 Cattellian primary factors are then factored, eight second-order factors are derived of which two are like Eysenck's Extraversion and Neuroticism and five bear a resemblance to the Big Five.

At first glance this looks like good news for test users in industry, with what appears to be five substantiated dimensions. But I have been careful to use cautious language in the last paragraph – 'are like Eysenck's' and 'bear a resemblance to'. Unfortunately, despite similar names (and we shall look at the question of nomenclature later), the Big Five domains are not identical to Cattell's second-order (or global) factors, nor are Eysenck's E and N identical to the E and N of Costa and McCrae (for more detail and further research references see Kline, 1993). For example, Eysenck's N is much broader then Cattell's equivalent second-order trait of Anxiety, which Cattell regards as one of several characteristics of Neuroticism. For him, Neuroticism is a syndrome or collection of many traits at different levels of complexity.

For practical purposes, it has to be said that users like a reasonable number of reliable, discrete descriptors (Buss, 1989). Practising psychologists find 2–3 descriptors insufficient for distinctions to be drawn between, say, candidates for a job or for promotion. On the other hand, 30 is regarded by some as unwieldy and too many to handle. At 5, the NEO PI-R offers a useful number of factors to interpret, but loses out on descriptive power. Indeed, Costa and McCrae realised this and declared that 'there is also, however, a growing recognition that assessment at the level of the five factors themselves is inadequate to a full and detailed understanding of an individual's personality' (Costa and McCrae, 1992, p.39).

Hence they introduced 6 facets for each of the 5 domains, giving 30 facets in all. The facets within any one domain are moderately correlated and, because of this overlap, interpretation at this level might present problems. The average correlations between the facets within each of the five domains are

Neuroticism	0.48	(range 0.31–0.63)
Extraversion	0.35	(range 0.16–0.52)
Openness	0.28	(range 0.13–0.46)
Agreeableness	0.33	(range 0.14–0.47)
Conscientiousness	0.45	(range 0.25–0.61).

As I have shown elsewhere (Child, 1994 a), low correlations between items or parcels (facets in the NEO) in the same factor need not be regarded as a problem because combinatorial factors are more substantial than tautological ones (i.e. asking the same question in different ways). However, with orthogonal solutions it might become a problem if the variance has to be shared with other domains. One is trying all the time in both oblique and orthogonal solutions to obtain the cleanest possible outcome. With simple structure, more items or parcels get pulled into the hyperplanes. Take, for instance, the lowest value of 0.16 quoted above in the Extraversion domain between facets E1 and E5 (see Table 19.3 for a complete naming of the facets); E1 correlates with O3 to give $r = 0.34$ and E5 with O3 to give $r = 0.22$. Several such cross-correlations give rise to an overall value between the E and O domains of $r = 0.40$, which is not a clean solution. When facets tend to 'stray' into other domains, we have problems when it comes to interpretation, as we shall see presently.

With 8 items in each facet and 6 facets in a domain, there are 48 items defining a domain and adding reliability. This is a healthy sign, provided the domains are validly measuring the concepts intended. As a general rule, as one gains reliability by compounding the smaller facets into larger domains one loses in the detail made available for descriptive purposes in occupational personality. It is analogous to thinking of the personality sphere as a cake. Five large slices are robust, but somewhat indigestible. The same slices cut into 30 pieces would be fragile (less reliable and more difficult to replicate), but provide more variety.

As an aside, it does seem miraculous that the personality domains divide exactly into 6 facets. Of course, as the NEO PI-R is a top-down theory, the researchers can choose whatever number they wish before tying up the parcel. The snag with this procedure is its arbitrary nature and proneness to creating factors or traits to fit a theory (like confirmatory factor analysis), but with the risk of too many or too few being created than is necessary. With a bottom-up theory, such as that used in Cattell's 16PF (Cattell *et al*, 1970), one would have to ensure that absolutely all the necessary ingredients were there before using exploratory analysis. If this is the case, the number of traits found should be the number in existence in the personality sphere.

Correlation of traits

Another decision relating to the 'how many factors' issue is whether to conduct an orthogonal or oblique factor solution. As the personality characteristics are most likely to be related in any case, the question is whether to locate and define them as they are (correlated) or whether to use Occam's razor and define the same characteristics as if they were unrelated. You may ask, what difference does it make?

An illustration showing the difference will be developed. If you take three clusters of variables whose resultants, a_1, b_1 and c_1, all intercorrelate by 0.5 (60 degrees between the vectors), the visual arrangement would look like Figure 19.1a. I have chosen a configuration which enables me to use a two-dimensional arrangement. A popular rule of thumb for how large the angle (the correlation) between factors should be for them to be regarded as independent is about 60 degrees, that is a correlation of 0.5. Smaller angles (larger correlations) would cause the two to collapse to become one factor. For an oblique solution the three variables in the figure would give three factors A, B and C in the same position as a_1, b_1 and c_1 and having separations of 60 degrees.

Whatever the position of the orthogonal vectors for the same three clusters, there can only be two because it is a two-dimensional arrangement. For this reason, oblique solutions remove the restriction and increase the possibility of locating the actual positions of the factor vectors, which would be three in the arrangement in Figure 19.1. Incidentally, the particular arrangement in Figure 19.1 could give a computer apoplexy when trying to find the unrotated position of the orthogonal factors. There are three possible positions for the reference

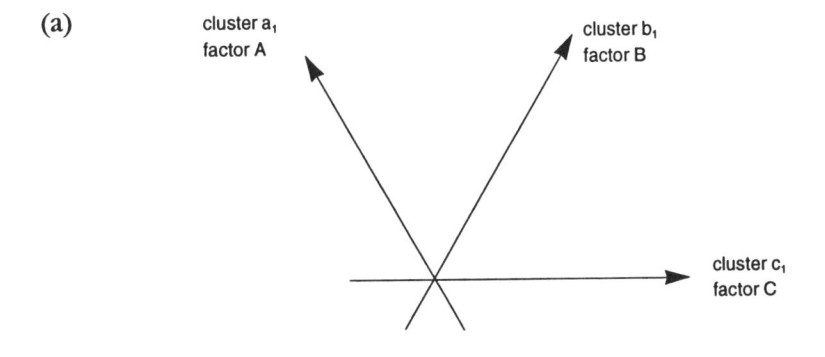

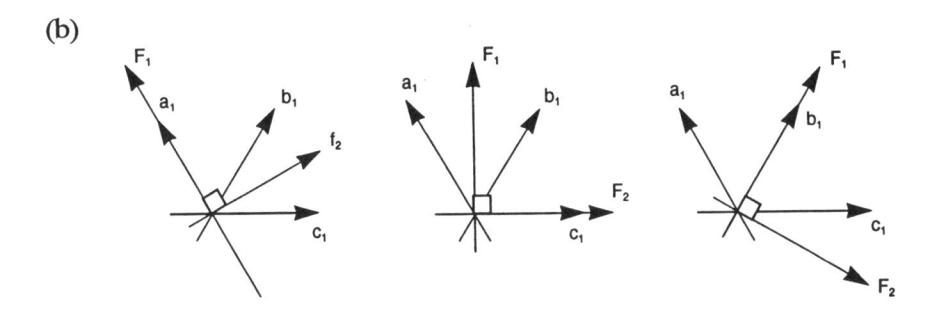

Some technical problems in the use of personality measures 353

Figure 19.1. Orthogonal and oblique solutions: (a) a cluster pattern; (b) possible orthogonal solutions

axes (F_1 and F_2 at right angles to each other) where one variable has a large loading in one factor and the other two have large loadings in the second (a_1 in the first with b_1 and c_1 in the second, b_1 in the first with a_1 and c_1 in the second, etc) as in Figure 19.1b.

Fortunately, this precise arrangement is highly improbable, but it highlights the fact that there is the potential for a greater number of factors possessing common variance in oblique than orthogonal solutions. The former can spread the common variance between and within factors; the latter can only spread variance between factors. That is why it is so important to carry out an oblique solution, even if exploratory, to allow no escape of important common factor variance. The NEO designers use only orthogonal solutions rotated to an orthogonal Varimax solution.

Test users may be forgiven for thinking that factors derived from orthogonal solutions must be unrelated. This is not necessarily true, especially if the underlying structure is oblique. Appendix F on p.100 of the NEO PI-R manual contains a correlation matrix between the domains and some are quite substantially correlated. For example, N (Neuroticism) and C (Conscientiousness) are significantly related, giving $r = -0.53$ (a value which some programmes would collapse into one factor); E (Extraversion) with O (Openness) also gives a large correlation of $r = 0.40$ and part of the reason is given above in our discussions of facet correlations. Other high values are E with N = 0.27 and A with N = -0.25. Unfortunately, the orthogonal compromise disguises both the relationship between domains and the number of factors which could possibly be present in hyperspace.

In the absence of the full factor analysis, which I cannot find in the recommended reading (McCrae and Costa, 1983; Costa *et al.*, 1991), it is not possible to check the number of interpretable factors which might have been present in an oblique analysis of the basic data bank from the NEO PI-R. However, we can check that an oblique solution would result from the data given in Table 5 (p. 44) of the NEO PI-R test manual. Values were taken from this table to show what would happen to the reference vector structure values if the axes of N and C were rotated to an oblique position. Table 19.1 contains the original loadings for the domain factors of Neuroticism (N) and Conscientiousness (C) given in the NEO PI-R Table 5 which is derived from an orthogonally rotated Varimax solution. A second set of loadings was obtained by hand rotating this solution to give the oblique reference vector structure for the N and C facets. This did not include the small loadings from the other three domains and I might be accused of 'cluster chasing'. But to give a general idea of what might happen, I have assumed that most loadings contributed by facets from other domains are sufficiently small to discount their influence in locating the N and C factor vectors (not strictly true).

Table 19.1. The N and C domains before and after oblique rotation

	Before		After	
	F1	F2	F1	F2
N1	0.81	−0.10	0.74	0.14
N2	0.63	−0.08	0.58	0.11
N3	0.80	−0.26	0.68	−0.01
N4	0.73	−0.16	0.64	0.06
N5	0.49	−0.32	0.37	−0.16
N6	0.70	−0.38	0.55	−0.15
C1	−0.41	0.64	−0.20	0.50
C2	−0.04	0.70	0.17	0.66
C3	−0.20	0.68	0.01	0.59
C4	−0.09	0.74	0.14	0.68
C5	−0.33	0.75	−0.09	0.63
C6	−0.23	0.57	−0.05	0.48

The angle between the N and C vectors was 123 degrees or a correlation of –0.54, which cross-checks well with the correlation of –0.53 given in Appendix F of the manual. One immediate outcome is the increased clarity of the N and C domains and the knowledge that Neuroticism and low Conscientiousness are appreciably related. Another is the N5 (Impulsiveness) which is rotated out of N. This problem of domain overlap will be mentioned again later. It provides a reason for the unstable nature of the five factor structure. Work by Parker, Bagby and Summerfeldt. (1993) using LISREL in a confirmatory factor analysis of the information given in the manual confirms the instability of the structure.

For the test interpreter, overlapping factors can be a nightmare if their nature and extent are hidden behind the assumption of uncorrelated dimensions. Compounding primary factors to give secondaries (the equivalent of global factors) and accounting for the degree to which each primary makes its contribution, as in the specification equations of Cattell, seems a more manageable and direct way of allowing for correlation between dimensions.

Surface and source traits

In using personality inventories for selection, promotion, group compatibility, etc., one of the most important aspects for the analyst is to have a thorough knowledge of the complexity of the factors in the inventory. Without this, the subtle interdependence of personality traits is lost and the descriptions become superficial. In this respect, the stratum theory and concepts of surface and source trait (Cattell, 1946) are useful. A digression to describe these concepts will help in later discussion.

A crude analogy for the strata is to imagine a pyramid in which the broad base consists of basic variables (they could be items of an inventory) forming the units of measurement. Ideally, if every human trait is represented adequately by the variables, oblique factor analyses will lead progressively up the pyramid through the first, second and subsequent strata.

The first stratum, that is the outcome of a first-order factor analysis, contains the primary source traits. Further up the pyramid, following second- or third-order analyses, one would obtain more complex source traits such as Extraversion and Anxiety (second stratum) or Extra-personal and Intra-personal response patterns (third stratum).

On the other hand, a surface trait is a cluster of closely associated, superficially observable behaviours or characteristics occurring together and which may, and most do, have many underlying influences. Medically defined illnesses or pathological syndromes (schizophrenia or neurosis) afford examples of clusters of basic symptoms which when they come together give broad behaviour patterns. The surface traits in medicine might be influenza or appendicitis. The source traits might be any combination of pain in a specific place in the body, temperature variation, sweating, headache, sickness, lethargy, etc. Symptoms (sources traits) are common to a number of illnesses (surface traits). High temperature, for instance, accompanies a number of illnesses. In a similar way, Cattell distinguishes between surface and source traits in personality. In his theory, 16 personality factors form the most robust, but not the only, source traits. Various combinations of these source traits give rise to higher order source traits which, as indicated above, have been compared to the five NEO PI-R domains.

Nomenclature (to be mentioned later) is crucial in distinguishing surface and source traits. For example, someone described as 'cooperative' may be using a surface concept. There are so many contextual ways in which individuals can display cooperativeness – by being outgoing and participating (A+), adaptable (E–), non-competitive (L–), group oriented (Q2). These are, in fact, dependent on different Cattellian source traits (see Tyler, 1996 for addition examples).

Are the NEO facets source traits? The design of the NEO was for each domain to have its own specific six facets. But on inspecting either the correlation table in Appendix F, p. 100–1, or the Varimax rotation on p.44, (Costa and McCrae, 1992) there are many significant links between facets outside their own domains. In the correlation table where a sample of 1000 was used, any $r > 0.08$ would be significant at the 1% level. Even using a much more stringent criterion of facet correlations greater than 0.2 (highly significant), there are 122 cases (about 37%) outside a facet's domain, so the objective of specificity of facets to domains was not achieved. This confusion of facets is not surprising. The NEO is atheoretical and based on a top-down approach where the facets, the end of the line in a sense, are arbitrary.

This dispersion of facet common variance into other domains is exemplified in two other ways. Table 5 in the manual (Costa and McCrae, 1992) shows in the extraversion domain, for example, a spread of significant loadings reproduced here in Table 19.2. This same dispersion is verified in two other researches by Church and Burke (1994) and the 16PF5 manual (Conn and Rieke, 1994), also shown in Table 19.2.

Secondly, the manual for the 16PF5 p. 117 (Conn and Rieke, 1994) gives a Promax solution for the globals (16PF5) and the facets (NEO), shown in Table 19.3. The extraversion facets E3 (Assertiveness) and E4 (Activity) are rotated out of extraversion and into the Agreeableness domain. Also notice the number of facets outside the Extraversion and Agreeableness domains which have been included in those factors.

The instability of the factor structure of the Big Five is quite worrying. Test users have to know that the domains and their contributory facets are replicable and do not shift in content from sample to sample. In addition to the replications by McCrae and Costa (1983, referenced in the manual for the NEO) there is work by Gerbing and Tuley (1991),

Some technical problems in the use of personality measures 357

Table 19.2. Extracts from three researches showing Varimax factor loadings for the extraversion domain and over 0.30 absolute for other domains

Facets	Costa et al. (1991) N E O A C	Church and Burke (1994) N E O A C	Conn and Rieke (1994) N E O A C
E1	74 30	37 65	81
E2	72	60	74
E3	–31 48 –33 40	–35 61	–38 35 –56
E4	51 48	53	37 –45
E5	57 –34	56	64
E6	73	35 59	75

nb. Decimal place omitted

Church and Burke (1994), and H.E.P. Cattell (1996) all showing disturbing discrepancies in the factor structure.

From the evidence so far (see also Conn and Rieke, 1994, p. 125, and Cattell, 1996, p. 7), my guess is that the questions used for the facets create three possibilities:

- specifics, e.g. O5 – Ideas, (low correlation with other facets in the same domain and next to none with facets outside)
- mixtures of primaries and secondaries, e.g. the E domain as shown above straddles other domains, also correlations between domains such as N and C (-0.53) or E and O (0.40)
- secondaries roughly equivalent to Cattell's globals, e.g. conscientiousness equivalent to self-control (but missing items from the F primary). There seems little evidence of a facet mapping onto a Cattell primary.

If a test user wanted to compare the results from the NEO PI-R and the 16PF, there would be grave difficulties. Like would not be compared with like at either facet or domain level. In the absence of a thoroughgoing research comparing oblique solutions, it is not possible to answer the question so frequently put by test users – at what level of complexity am I operating when using either facets or domains?

Nomenclature

The problem is compounded by another feature, that of nomenclature. Finding the words to describe personality in a simple, understandable, widely acceptable way is difficult. That is why several psychologists have started their hunt for factors by using the lexical hypothesis – human personality dimensions are captured in our language (Block, 1995). There are thousands of words in use with varying degrees of overlap in

Table 19.3. Rotated (Promax) principal component loadings for the 16PF Fifth Edition Global scales and NEO Personality Inventory-Revised (NEO PI-R) facets

Scale		I	II	III	IV	V
16 PF Global						
Extraversion		68				
Anxiety				89		
Tough-mindedness						−74
Independence					−73	
Self-control			74			
NEO facet						
N1	Anxiety			82		
N2	Angry hostility			72	−44	
N3	Depression			77		
N4	Self-consciousness			70		
N5	Impulsiveness	36		47		
N6	Vulnerability			60		
E1	Warmth	85				
E2	Gregariousness	81				
E3	Assertiveness				−54	
E4	Activity				−45	
E5	Excitement Seeking	71				
E6	Positive emotions	76				
O1	Fantasy					40
O2	Aesthetics					76
O3	Feelings	38				44
O4	Actions					64
O5	Ideas					71
O6	Values					47
A1	Trust	42		−38	39	
A2	Straightforwardness				65	
A3	Altruism	68				
A4	Compliance				74	
A5	Modesty				56	
A6	Tender-mindedness	53			36	
C1	Competence		76			
C2	Order		69			
C3	Dutifulness		74			
C4	Achievement striving		77			
C5	Self-discipline		77			
C6	Deliberation		70			

nb. Decimal place omitted. Factor loadings less than 0.35 absolute are omitted. Reproduced from the 16PF Fifth Edition, *Technical Manual*, by S.R. Conn and M.K. Rieke (1994) with the kind permission of the Institute for Personality and Ability Testing Inc., Champaign, IL, USA.

meaning. Anyone who has tried to elaborate a personality profile from a standardised inventory knows how difficult it is to find not just the 'right' words, but ones which neither confuse nor give the wrong impression to a client. Single words in the language rarely capture entirely the essence of what is there. Consequently, test users are greatly dependent on the designers giving the clearest definitions to the factors.

Unfortunately, it is not uncommon to find the same descriptive terms used in what is presented as different traits. Referring to the NEO PI-R again, although other inventories display similar problems, there are several examples where confusion could arise between facets from different domains. Take the items in N6 (Vulnerability) and C1 (Competence). One thread common to some items in both is capability in problem solving. Also, the idea of competence in C1 applies to people and situations. It is therefore not surprising to see the following correlations (decimals omitted) between the relevant facets:

	N3	N4	N6
C1	−51	−40	−58
C5	−47	−37	−53

As stated before, the correlation between the C and N domains is −0.53. Further examples of verbal confusions at domain and facet level are given in Cattell (1996), p. 11.

Using the Adjective Check List (ACL compiled by Gough and Heilburn, 1983) from Table 7 in the NEO manual, a marked 'verbal' overlap is apparent – given by words in bold in the following list:

C1 Competence: **Efficient, Self-confident, thorough**, resourceful, **confident, clearminded**, intelligent
C5 Self-discipline: organised, −lazy, **efficient, −absent-minded**, energetic, **thorough**, industrious
N3 Depression: −worrying, contented, **confident, self-confident**, −pessimistic,−moody,−anxious
N4 Self-conscious: −shy, **self-confident**, −timid, **confident**, −defensive, −inhibited, −anxious
N6 Vulnerable: **clear-thinking, self-confident, confident**, −anxious, **efficient**, alert, **−careless**.

Minus signs mean negative correlation with the facet scale. The order of words is in descending value of the correlation with the facet.

The identical nature of some terms used or their opposites is striking and provides a sound reason for this high correlation. Similar effects occur across other domains, e.g., E3 (Assertiveness): N4 (Self-consciousness): N6 (Vulnerable). Block (1995) gives many examples of verbal confusions from the NEO.

Predictive validity

One acid test of concern to users is the extent to which personality tests can be used to predict job performance. Research into this issue is a sad story (Herriot, 1989; Kline, 1992; Cook, 1993). A running battle between occupational psychologists as to job performance and test validities, shows only too well the state of things (Blinkhorn and Johnson, 1990; six articles in the journal *Personnel Management*, 1991; Jackson and Rothstein, 1993; Robertson and Kinder, 1993; Handyside, 1994; Johnson and Blinkhorn, 1994). The conclusions give low validity measures ranging up to, and rarely exceeding, 0.30.

In the absence of any data in the NEO manual regarding predictive validity, I have had to rely on other recent research. Three meta-analyses using the NEO scales (Barrick and Mount, 1991; Tett, Jackson and Rothstein, 1991; Hough, 1992) looked at job proficiency as the criterion. The results shown in Table 19.4 are very disappointing.

An impressive research by Mershon and Gorsuch (1988) explores the amount of common variance extracted in the five second-order (global) factors of the 16PF, believed to be related to the NEO domains, plus factor B (intelligence), compared with the full 16 primary factors. It also compared the usefulness of 6 and 16 factors when predicting external real-life criteria. In effect, they wanted to know if 16 was better than the 6 derived from the 16.

Table 19.4. Three meta-analyses of correlations between personality and job proficiency

	Barrick and Mount (1991)[a]	Tett *et al.* (1991)[b]	Hough (1992)[c]
Extraversion	10	16	
Ascendancy			10
Sociability			00
Neuroticism	07	22	09
Agreeableness	06	33	05
Conscientiousness	23	18	08
Openness	−03	27	01

NB. Decimal places omitted.
[a]Based on 82–124 correlations and pooled samples between 14 236 and 19 511. Correlations corrected for restricted range, criterion reliability and test reliability.
[b]Based on 4–15 correlations. Correlations corrected for criterion reliability and test reliability.
[c]Based on 15–274 correlations and samples of 2811 and 65 876. No corrections applied.

A search was made of the literature to find all the 16PF studies used to predict real-life criteria. Various criteria were applied, such as good sample size, measurable real-life criteria, using only Form A of the 16PF and a study not using a pre-selected sample. They finished with 17 studies which met their criteria.

Multiple regression equations were developed with the real-life criterion as the dependent variable and either the 6 or 16 as independent variables. Corrections were applied to allow for sample size and number of predictors giving shrunken multiple correlations. The conclusion from comparing the shrunken multiple correlations for 6 and 16 factors was that the latter was 'considerably more productive' than the former. The median increase in variance accounted for was 110 per cent, and 15 of the 17 studies showed a significant increase in the variance accounted for.

Though the findings are impressive, this ought not to be taken as a direct comparison between the 16PF globals and the five NEO domains. As we have shown above, there is overlap, but it is far from complete. It should also be noted that in deriving the second-order factors from the 16 primaries, some primary factors are used more than once. For example, in the fifth and latest edition of the 16PF, factor H appears in both Extraversion and Anxiety, factors A and F appear in both Extraversion and Tough Poise. This means that the 6 second orders are not independent variables in the regression equation.

For test users, the important question is will more factors give me more information which I can use with confidence? A full-scale research is needed making a direct comparison of several well-established inventories (having different numbers of factors) against work-related criteria.

Concluding comments

It seems as though I have been picking on the NEO PI-R. This was not the intention. The main purpose of the chapter was to raise some general issues about personality inventories and some of the implications when they are used in occupational situations. As a means of illustrating these wide-ranging issues, I though it more efficient to use one test, especially one which has risen to some prominence in the past 10 or so years. A considerable amount of work by Costa, McCrae and colleagues has gone into the development of the NEO and it seems appropriate to follow the progress of this increasingly popular test.

Industry is making increasing use of personality inventories by which to make decisions which affect the job prospects of employees. Other criteria are used alongside personality scores, including more information about the nature of the job, but we have to find effective and reliable ways of combining this information to give trustworthy profiles of potential employees.

For this purpose, a high degree of certainty about the number, nature and extent of personality traits is crucial to users. For obvious reasons, occupational users have a preference for detail. As Buss (1989) points out, 'narrowly defined traits have the advantage of being relatively homogeneous...as such, they tend to be better predictors of a particular behavior, just as tennis performance is better predicted by tennis ability than general athletic ability.' The disadvantage is that the behaviour which defines the narrow trait may only appear infrequently. The trade-off is – narrow traits predict better but may be missed; broad traits are not as useful at predicting but are inclusive.

At whichever stratum the trait is defined, it has to be clear and its relationship to other traits known and accounted for in building up profiles of testees. Also, test designers must not yield to the temptation of giving the impression that their inventories are all-inclusive. The 'Big Five' concept, for instance, has undergone years of refinement based on a wide foundation laid by Cattell. By prophesying five major factors, seeking items which define them and rotating out any factors which conflict with the prophecy, nobody should doubt that an orthogonal (or even an oblique) rotation will reproduce the five factors. The designers of the Big Five have indeed managed to fit the original quart into a pint pot, but where has the other pint gone?

The lexical hypothesis on which the NEO is based starts with many words and ends with a few. The few are intended to summarise, crisply, the many. This is patently not the case. The literature abounds with verbal confusions in the interpretation of the NEO. H.E.P. Cattell (1996), for example, gives several examples.

> Extraversion is conceptualized as Surgency by some; Openness is interpreted as Culture by some and Intellect by yet others; Agreeableness has been conceptualized as Friendly Compliance; Conscientiousness is found by some to denote Dependability, while others see it as Will to Achieve.

Other examples are given at facet level. Such ambiguities are not helpful for the user. There has to be a high degree of universality in the meanings attaching to any technical terminology, especially if the terms are also used in everyday language.

We have to find ways of improving the predictive validity of personality inventories. This is one of their commonest applications and users set great store by the concurrent and predictive powers of the results of testing.

Trait theory has a substantial contribution to make in providing tools for industrial settings. We have to be absolutely sure that design faults are recognised and minimised so that the tools can do the jobs for which they were intended.

References

Barrick, M.R. and Mount, M.K. (1991) The Big Five personality dimensions and job performance: A meta-analysis. Personnel Psychology, 44, 1–26.

Blinkhorn, S.F. and Johnson, C.E. (1990) The insignificance of personality testing. Nature, 348, 671–2.

Block, J. (1995) A contrarian view of the five-factor approach to personality description. Psychological Bulletin, 117(2), 187–215.

Buss, A.H. (1989) Personality as traits. American Psychologist, 44, 1378–88.

Cattell, H.E.P. (1996) The original big five: A historical perspective. European Review of Applied Psychology, 46(1), 5–14.

Cattell, R.B. (1946) The Description and Measurement of Personality (New York: World Book).

Cattell, R.B. (1979) Personality and Learning Theory, Vol 1: The Structure of Personality in its Environment (New York: Springer-Verlag).

Church, A.T. and Burke, P.J. (1994) Exploratory and confirmatory tests of the Big Five and Tellegen's three- and four-dimensional models. Journal of Personality and Social Psychology, 66(1), 93–114.

Conn, S.R. and Rieke, M.L. (1994) The 16PF Technical Manual. Fifth edition (Champaign, IL: Institute for Personality and Ability Testing).

Cook, M. (1993) Personnel Selection and Productivity, 2nd edn (Chichester: Wiley).

Costa, P.T.,Jr. and McCrae, R.R. (1992) NEO PI-R Professional Manual (Odessa, FL: Psychological Assessment Resources).

Costa, P.T.,Jr., McCrae, R.R. and Dye, D.A. (1991) Facet scales for Agreeableness and Conscientiousness: A revision of the NEO personality inventory. Personality and Individual Differences, 12(9), 887–98.

Gerbing, D.W. and Tuley M.R. (1991) The 16PF related to the five-factor model of personality: multiple-indicator measurement versus the *a priori* scales. Multivariate Behavioral Research, 26(2), 271–89.

Gough, H.G. and Heilburn, A.B.Jr. (1983) Adjective Check List Manual (Palo Alto, CA: Consulting Psychologists Press).

Handyside, J. (1994) An insignificant slip-up? Psychologist, 7(7), 344–5.

Herriot, P. (1989) (Ed.) Selection and Assessment in Organisations (Chichester: Wiley).

Hough, L.M. (1992) The 'Big Five' personality variables – construct confusion: description versus prediction. Human Performance, 5, 139–55.

Jackson, D.N. and Rothstein, M. (1993) Evaluating personality testing in personnel selection. Psychologist, 6, 8–11.

Johnson, C. and Blinkhorn, S. (1994) Job performance and personality test validities: desperate measures. Psychologist, 7(4), 167–70.

Kline, P. (1992) Psychometric Testing in Personnel Selection and Appraisal (Kingston: Kroner).

Kline, P. (1993) Personality: a psychometric view (London: Routledge).

Mabey, B. (1989) The majority of large companies use psychology tests. Guidance and Assessment Review, 5(3), 1–4.

Mabey, B. (1992) The growth of test use. Selection and Development Review, 8(3), 6–8.

McCrae, R.R. and Costa, P.T.Jr. (1983) Joint factors in self-reports and ratings: neuroticism, extraversion and openness to experience. Personality and Individual Differences, 4(3), 245–55.

Mershon, B. and Gorsuch, R.L. (1988) Number of factors in the personality sphere: does increase in factors increase predictability of real-life criteria? Journal of Personality and Social Psychology, 55(4), 675–80.

Parker, J.D.A., Bagby, R.M. and Summerfeldt, L.J. (1993) Confirmatory factor analysis of the revised NEO Personality Inventory. Personality and Individual Differences, 15, 463–6.

Personnel Management (1991) Sept, pp. 38–42.

Robertson, I.T. and Kinder, A. (1993) Personality and job competences: the criterion-related validity of some personality variables. Journal of Occupational and Organizational Psychology, 66, 225–44.

Tett, R.P., Jackson, D.N. and Rothstein, M. (1991) Personality measures as predictors of job performance: a meta-analytic review. Personnel Psychology, 44, 703–42.

Tyler, B. (1996) Source and surface traits: structure and interpretation. European Review of Applied Psychology, 46(1), 57–63.

Williams, R.S. (1991) Psychological Testing and Management Selection Practices in Local government: Results of a survey (Luton: Local Government Management Board).

Williams, R.S. (1994) Occupational testing: contemporary British practice. Psychologist, 7(1), 11–13.

Chapter 20
Stress in teaching

CHERYL TRAVERS AND CARY COOPER

The nature of stress: what is it?

The word 'stress' has become largely a buzz word that is used in a variety of settings, often with little understanding of what the term actually means.

Defining stress

When attempting to define stress, researchers have distinguished between the terms 'stressor' and 'strain' (Beehr and Franz, 1986). A 'stressor' is something in the environment that acts as a stimulus and is either physical, psychological or behavioural in nature. A 'strain' response is used as an indicator of ill-health and/or well-being of the individual.

Stress can have both positive and negative consequences for the individual. It can, to some extent, be a stimulant, as when a new coping skill or resource is developed (Hoover-Dempsey and Kendall, 1982). But it is important that individuals find their optimal stress level because an event will not have the same stressful implications for all individuals. Certain characteristics of the individual (e.g. age, sex, education, personality characteristics, social situations, past experiences) can all lead to variations in stressful experiences.

Ways of conceptualising stress

In studying occupational stress, researchers have focused on one of three approaches (Travers and Cooper, 1996). Stress can be treated as:

- a *response*, where stress is the dependent variable. Here, stress is considered to be a response by the individual to stimuli in a disturbing

situation or environment, e.g. classes of low ability and motivation
- a *stimulus*, where stress is the independent variable. Stress is outside the individual, taking no account of that individual's perceptions and experience
- an *interaction*, where stress is the intervening variable between stimulus and response. The degree of stress depends on the amount of fit between the person and the environment.

Of these, the interactive model has grown in prominence and there are major aspects of the interactive model that need to be considered in any study of stress (Travers and Cooper, 1996).

- *Cognitive appraisal*: this is the subjective perception of the situation leading to the experience.
- *Experience*: the perception of the situation or event will depend on the individual's experience, i.e. familiarity with the situation, previous exposure, learning training (i.e. actual ability). This also is determined by past success or failure (i.e. reinforcement of past response).
- *Demand*: this comprises actual demand and perceived demand in addition to perceived ability and actual ability. Their perception of the demand is further influenced by the individual's needs, desires and immediate arousal level.
- *Interpersonal influence*: the way a potential source of stress is perceived will largely depend upon the presence or absence of others which will influence the subjective experience of stress, response and coping behaviours and can be both detrimental and beneficial.
- A *state of imbalance*: when a stage of imbalance occurs between perceived demand and perceived ability to meet that demand, coping strategies are derived, with feedback of the consequences of these actions, (i.e. positive restores balance, negative exacerbates the situation).

The ideas behind the above model originate from the concept of 'person–environment fit' (Edwards and Cooper, 1990).

A definition of teacher stress

Many definitions of teacher stress exist. The one favoured by the authors is that of Kyriacou and Sutcliffe (1979a) who, in a revised version of their definition, describe teacher stress as:

> a response syndrome of negative affect (such as anger and depression), usually accompanied by potentially pathogenic

physiological changes (such as increased heart rate) resulting from aspects of the teacher's job and mediated by the perception that the demands made upon the teacher constitutes a threat to his (or her) self-esteem or well-being and by coping mechanisms activated to reduce threat.

They explain that the extent and type of stress experienced by teachers will largely depend upon whether or not teachers feel threatened by particular demands facing them, and whether or not the individual teacher may, after facing an initial threat, be able to modify or ameliorate the threat by particular actions.

What causes stress in teachers?

What actually causes stress in teachers? The following sections will outline the causes using the six-factor theory outlined in the work of Cooper (1986).

In general terms the model suggests the following causes of stress for individuals at work.

- *Stressors intrinsic to the actual job*, i.e. physical working conditions, level of participation and decision-making latitude and workload.
- *Role in the organisation*, i.e. role ambiguity and role conflict, levels and types of responsibility.
- *Relationships at work*, i.e. superiors, colleagues and subordinates and the demands made interpersonally.
- *Career development*, i.e. the presence of over or under promotion, possible lack of job security.
- *Organizational structure and climate* – stressors which may be those that restrict behaviours, i.e. the politics and culture of the organizations and how individuals interact with these. Specific features include level of participation and involvement in decision making.
- *Home and work interface* – the stressors resulting from a mismatch in the relationship between work demands and family or social demands. This may be viewed as 'overspill' of one life into the other.

The six categories overlap. For example, a teacher may find that the roles expected of her at school are varied and conflict with her role as a mother. Also, individuals are dynamic in their behaviour and the whole process must be seen as an interactive one (i.e. *lack of job security*, included in the category of *career development* could be included in *organizational structure and climate*).

The following sections will outline each of these in more detail using research into teacher stress.

Stressors resulting from the job of teaching: intrinsic factors

Every job has its own unique set of factors leading to pressure which results in negative stress. Typical aspects which have been identified over the years are physical working conditions, shift working, work overload or underload, occupational level, repetition and boredom and the 'person–environment' fit (Edwards and Cooper, 1990).

Physical working conditions

A large number of teachers believe their circumstances, such as poor physical working conditions (e.g. Wanberg, 1984), cause them to do their jobs badly (Esteve, 1989). These poor conditions are largely reinforced by a lack of resources. Esteve refers to these as 'primary factors', because they directly affect teaching, create limitations or produce tension in the teacher's day-to-day practice. Other factors are class size, unsuitable buildings, noise level and inadequate resources (e.g. Connors, 1983; Kyriacou and Sutcliffe, 1978b). The significance of each of these factors does vary in importance depending on the specific circumstances of schools in terms of parental support, inner city schools, local industry support, etc.

The lack of materials, or the means by which to obtain them, can be a great source of frustration or disillusionment for a teacher. The general feeling among many teachers is that there is a contradiction imposed upon them by outside bodies (i.e. the demand for modern methods, but without the adequate equipment to do the job). This situation is exacerbated by reduced expenditure on equipment due to a worsening financial situation in a number of schools (Fimian and Santoro, 1983). An ILO report (1981) and the Breuse report (1984), have revealed that 'lack of resources' in teaching means more than a lack of teaching materials. Problems of space, poorly preserved and dilapidated buildings, poor quality furniture, inadequate heating and lack of suitable premises are also relevant. Poor staffroom facilities and the contemporary problem of teaching at a split-site school are other reasons given for both dissatisfaction and stress at work (e.g. Dewe, 1986). With reorganisation in education and the resulting school closures, a large number of schools are experiencing the 'split-site' phenomenon.

Limitations in teachers' working environments are not just physical ones. Often institutional limitations are imposed. For example, Goble and Porter (1980) and Bayer and Chauvet (1980) emphasise that the institutional framework within which they work often dictates what teachers can do (e.g. timetable problems, internal rules, standards that have been laid down by the Inspectorate). They are also often required to set time aside for staff meetings, students, governing bodies, examination meetings, parents evenings, etc.

Work Overload and underload, long hours and the school day

Many studies (Cooper and Payne, 1988), in a variety of research settings and in various occupations, have consistently concluded that work overload and underload can lead to stress (e.g. Shaw and Riskind, 1983). A curvilinear relationship exists between stress and performance, known as the Yerkes–Dodson law (Yerkes and Dodson, 1908). This suggests that both low and high levels of workload are related to stress and that we need to find an optimum level of workload to enable us to be healthy, in a psychological sense, to achieve the most effective performance.

Many studies have investigated the role of workload in teacher stress and the types of overload and underload that can occur are widespread, e.g. job overload may result from a poor teacher–pupil ratio (e.g. Kalker, 1984; Russell, Altmaier and Van Valzen, 1987). Another aspect of the teaching profession, which can be seen to be directly related to work overload, is the problem of having a wide mixed-ability class. This may require more lesson planning and more detailed and lengthy assessment (e.g. Dunham, 1980; Fimian and Santoro, 1983; Hawkes and Dedrick, 1983). Work overload is also linked to pressures from the amount of work teachers have to fit in during the day and take home at night, thus intruding into their personal lives (e.g. Smith and Cline, 1980; Austin, 1981; ILO, 1981; Fimian and Santoro, 1983).

Researchers have discussed the actual stress of the school day in terms of the constant workload that it imposes upon the teacher. Tension and stress among teachers arises partly from their having timetables that permit few or no breaks. In addition, Kyriacou (1987) has suggested that a main source of stress for teachers may be the 'general level of alertness and vigilance required' of them.

Teachers' role in the school a source of stress

Research evidence suggests that structural factors such as *role conflict* (conflicting demands) and *role ambiguity* (lack of clarity about the task) can be potential causes of stress (Kahn *et al.*, 1964). On a more general point, change may lead to stress, as it can introduce conflict or ambiguity into what was originally a stable teaching role (Kelly, 1974). However, Dunham (1984) has pointed out that change might equally be welcomed as an alleviation of stress, depending upon circumstances and participants. He studied the stress imposed by the demands of specific managerial roles in teaching and found that tension was created by role conflict and role ambiguity. Blackie (1977) discusses the effect of role conflict on teachers as predictive of stress. Also, change in the teacher's role is a source of ambiguity and stress (Travers and Cooper, 1993c).

Role underload is portraying a situation where too little time is available to devote to teaching (Needle, Griffin and Svendsen, 1981). This may be a concern of many teachers as more and more time is required on administrative and pastoral tasks and responsibilities. Problems connected with role overload may include constant interaction with pupils which allows little time for relaxation, lunch, etc. (Weiskopf, 1980), constant interaction with others (Schwab, 1983), too many roles (Austin, 1981), and the problem of being physically and emotionally drained (Sparks, 1979).

When examining one's role in an organisation it is important to consider levels of responsibility. Research has discovered the necessity to distinguish between responsibility for people and for things, as the former is significantly more likely to lead to cardiovascular disease (French and Caplan, 1970). However, it is also the case that a lack of responsibility can result in stress outcomes, if, for instance, it is perceived as being due to work and role underload.

One of the most potentially exhausting aspects of teaching must surely be that teachers are, in most cases, constantly responsible for others (Weiskopf, 1980; Brenner, Sorbom and Wallius, 1985). Dealing with pupils is their major task, and many problems and potential sources of stress can result from this as they can be disruptive and undisciplined in their behaviour. This means that, depending on the nature of the pupils, teachers can spend vast amounts of time controlling this poor behaviour (e.g. Mykeltun, 1984; Wanberg, 1984; Russell, Altmaier and Van Velzen, 1987).

Role preparedness is being inadequately prepared for the role of 'teacher', i.e. by inadequate training (Fimian and Santoro, 1983). This is also an example of 'role shock', explained by Minkler and Biller (1979) as the stresses encountered when moving from familiar to unfamiliar roles. With the rapid changes that have taken place within teaching in the last decade, it is very possible that a teacher's training may well be out of date by the time he or she starts to teach. Also the 'teacher of today' probably has a very different role to that of a teacher starting 10 years ago, and many teachers may find that it is not the job they expected.

More recently, studies have addressed in more detail the effects on the head teachers, who are finding themselves in the dual position of being both managers of people and financial managers. A study by Cooper and Kelly (1993) assessed occupational stress amongst 2638 head teachers of primary and secondary schools, together with principals or directors of further and higher education establishments, throughout the United Kingdom. Data were collected on personal/job demographics, sources of job stress, mental health, job satisfaction and coping strategies.

It was found that the levels of job dissatisfaction and mental ill-health were higher in secondary and primary school head teachers than in the further/higher education sector. In addition, it was found that, with the exception of primary schools, female head teachers in secondary and further/higher education seem to be suffering significantly greater job dissatisfaction than their male counterparts, although this does not translate itself into mental ill-health. Male head teachers, on the other hand, seem to suffer more mental ill-health than their female counterparts. And finally, the two main sources of occupational stress which are predictors (in the statistical sense) of job dissatisfaction and mental ill-health are 'work overload' and 'handling relationships with staff'.

Relationships at work as a source of teacher stress

Much research has also revealed that teachers are experiencing stress from their relationships with

- *teaching colleagues* (Wanberg, 1984; Brenner et al., 1985)
- *headteachers* (Clark, 1980; Needle et al., 1980; Tellenbeck, Brenner and Lofgren, 1983)
- *administrators/education authorities* (Hawkes and Dedrick, 1983 Kalker, 1984; Wanberg, 1984; Russell et al., 1987)
- *parents* (Kalker, 1984; Mykeltun, 1984; Wanberg, 1984)
- *the community* (Cox, 1985; Needle et al., 1980)
- *pupils* (Tellenbeck et al., 1983; Brenner et al., 1985).

Dunham (1977) found that working relationships with *colleagues* were reported as a source of stress for teachers. It has been argued that the dominant source of stress is the quality of these interpersonal relationships, and that good social relationships are of great value when providing support which may alleviate stress (Brenner et al., 1985).

Kyriacou (1981) has suggested that schools should attempt to improve the social support received by staff, the responsibility lying largely with the head teacher. However, good working relationships may only flourish if the organisational structure is designed in such a way that it facilitates good working relationships between individuals. If a formal structure exists (i.e. with regard to responsibility and communication), then this can reduce the opportunities for these relationships. Teachers may also fear protesting about their problems, when they are overburdened, because they do not want to let fellow teachers down. For example, although the only way to cope with stress might be absenteeism, they fear the resulting overload this may impose on other teachers in the school (Kyriacou, 1987).

One of the potential stressors facing teachers is that of the *pupils'* attitudes and behaviour. Although this has been borne out in some of the literature, there are contradictions. A study by Litt and Turk (1985) concluded that pupil misbehaviour and discipline problems were not major sources of teacher stress, whereas a study by Cichon and Koff (1978) had suggested that the threat of personal injury and verbal abuse from problem children was a major source of stress, greater than other aspects of the teacher's experience, such as management and teaching methods. There are various possible explanations for these contradictions. Teachers may actually differ in their willingness to admit to experiencing problems with pupils, as this is seen by many to be a major feature of the teacher's job. In addition, there are many different types and levels of misbehaviour, from minor examples of restlessness to serious physical attacks. When pupil misbehaviour has been examined in relation to stress, some studies have made no distinction between different types of behaviour problem, while others have concentrated solely on major stressful events (e.g. Comber and Whitfield, 1979). Whatever the findings, it has been suggested that single, serious disruptive incidents may be a lesser cause of stress than the cumulative effect of constant or repeated 'low level' disruption (Kyriacou, 1987). In addition, teachers have differing perspectives as to what constitutes a discipline problem. Freeman (1987) has observed that expectations may differ according to the particular nature of a situation, and the level of stress associated with a disruptive incident may also vary.

Several aspects of pupil attitudes and behaviour have been identified as causing teacher stress. Those mentioned frequently include reference to a lack of motivation, and Kyriacou and Roe (1988) found that 'underachieving' was rated as the most serious source of behaviour problems among first year pupils, and the fifth most serious among fifth year pupils.

Teachers' concern with pupils' behaviour may also be seen to contribute towards job dissatisfaction. Freeman (1987) has argued that for most teachers, job satisfaction lies in the experience of teaching itself and in the 'positive feedback' that comes from successful lessons. Therefore, events interfering with this feedback (e.g. poor attitudes and behaviour of pupils), could be a cause of job dissatisfaction. In addition, Mancini *et al.* (1982, 1984) have suggested that 'burnout' may be associated with the breakdown in teacher–pupil relationships, as they found that 'burned out' teachers gave significantly less praise and information and showed less acceptance of their students.

A further problem leading to undesirable stress outcomes in teachers is the threat of actual violence. By examining medical records of teachers in the United States who had been subjected to physical or threatened assault, Bloch (1978) found that they had suffered symptoms similar to 'post-traumatic combat neurosis'. Much research has documented violence as a source of stress in school settings (e.g. ILO, 1981; Hammond, 1983; Wanberg, 1984). But violence is not the only problem facing teachers in schools. They also have to deal with disinterest in education, apathy and the problems which children may have due to their home backgrounds. Teachers also find themselves in the added role of social worker, for instance in carefully observing any evidence of home-related problems experienced by children (e.g. child sexual abuse).

The type of school as an influence on teacher stress

Does the type of school have an effect on the nature and levels of stress experienced by teachers? A number of differing characteristics exist (i.e. the size of the school, the pupil–teacher ratio, pupil age and academic pressures) between school types (e.g. primary and secondary schools), which may create problems for teachers. However, information regarding the type of school and its relationship to the level of stress experienced is very limited. Due to unequal distribution of the sexes (i.e. predominantly female teachers in primary schools and males in secondary schools), a real comparison is difficult (Rudd and Wiseman, 1962). There is an assumption that certain types of school (e.g. inner city, special education) create stress. The majority of studies have considered the effects of teaching in special education (e.g. Pratt, 1978), and the problems of dealing with pupils having learning difficulties. The limitations mean that no reliable conclusions may be drawn concerning differences between primary and secondary school teachers. This is largely because studies have failed to utilise standard measurements and large cross-sectional samples.

Relationships with management (largely head teachers)

A great deal of overlap exists between the stress related to relationships with management in schools and the organisational structure and climate of the school itself. A number of features will be discussed in a later section (i.e. involvement in decision-making and level of participation), but this section will address issues that are more related to the personal characteristics of the manager (in this case the head teacher), that may create stress for their subordinates.

Research has shown that particular individuals in a working environment may cause undue stress to others because they do not recognise the interpersonal feelings and sensibilities in social interaction (Sutherland and Cooper, 1991). Levinson (1978) has devised the label 'abrasive personalities' to describe them. They are usually achievement-orientated, intelligent, hard driving, though less efficient with regard to emotional situations. For example, if the head teacher of a primary school has the above characteristics, is a perfectionist and is self-centred, then this might create feelings of inadequacy and conflict between staff.

Career development

Potential stressors in career development have been identified as two major clusters (Marshall, 1977). These are *lack of job security* (i.e. the fear of redundancy, obsolescence, forced early retirement, and the fear of being banned from practice) and *status incongruency* (i.e. under- or over-promotion and frustration at having ambitions thwarted or reaching a 'career ceiling').

An added dimension in job insecurity is the threat of re-deployment, school closure with potential job change or loss of job. Teaching used to be a secure job. Increasingly, this is not necessarily the case. The insecurity of teachers' jobs is well documented (e.g. Needle *et al.*, 1981; Wanberg, 1984). Individuals having to relocate are particularly vulnerable to stress as actual job change is a potential source of high stress (Lazarus, 1981). In addition, the rapid pace of change within teaching, both in terms of the nature and requirements of the job, and the technologies and materials that they have to deal with, means that teachers need to consider retraining and possible career change.

Status incongruence is a feature that is also relevant to the section concerning relationships at work, and refers to the situation where the actual status bestowed on an individual does not match their status expectations and beliefs. This is of particular relevance to teachers at the moment, as they complain they are suffering from a poor public image in terms of prestige, salary and respect for their professional status as teachers (e.g. Laughlin, 1984; Wanberg, 1984).

Slow promotion has also been related to stress in teachers (e.g. Fimian, 1983; Wanberg, 1984). Thwarted ambitions are a cause of job insecurity. Criteria for promotion are unpredictable and uncertain, and this reinforces an external locus of control in the individual (Kyriacou and Sutcliffe, 1979b). Other problems may result from discrimination resulting in, for example, restricted job mobility for women (Wanberg, 1984). Further related to this is the lack of advancement opportunities (Eskridge, 1984; Mykletun, 1984).

Organisational structure and climate

Another important feature in determining the levels of stress a teacher experiences is the structure and climate of his or her school. It is possible that organisations have a corporate 'personality' determining the way it treats the members within it. The important element is not just how the organisation treats its workers, but how the individual perceives the actual culture, climate and customs that exist, and how they react to this in terms of their job satisfaction, commitment to the organisation and other behavioural outcomes, e.g. absenteeism. Travers and Cooper (1993a) found that pressure from the structure and culture of the school was the major statistically significant predictor of job dissatisfaction in their sample of 1790 teachers. Structural stressors also include the effects of highly interdependent departments and a high degree of departmental specialisation and formalisation, with little opportunity for individual advancement.

Other stressors include poor communication, an inadequate amount of feedback about performance, inaccurate or ambiguous measurement criteria for performance and unfair control systems (Brief, Schuler and Van Sell, 1981). Other features that may be relevant to teachers at present are those concerning participation in decision making, lack of effective consultation and communication, and restrictions on behaviour (e.g. lack of sanctions to deal with unruly pupils). Of these, participation in decision-making, performance appraisal and organisational culture are central.

Participation in decision-making refers to the involvement of subordinates with their superiors in the managerial decision-making process (Tannenbaum and Masserik, 1989; Miller and Monge, 1986). Teachers have recently been expressing resentment at the lack of involvement in many of the changes that have taken place within education and, consequently, their schools. Traditionally the job of the teacher has been one that involved a great deal of autonomy. In the light of recent changes taking place within education, we may suggest that this is yet another source of pressure for teachers.

The process of being evaluated by others, *performance appraisal*, can be a very stressful experience for some people, especially when evaluation has an effect on job prospects and career progression (Baron, 1986). In addition to this formal appraisal, the very job of teachers necessitates that they are on show all day, in front of the pupils. Their actual performance is evaluated every time a pupil takes an examination, or parents visit for a 'parents' evening'.

Organisational culture is generally believed to be concerned with shared values and norms and is a major force for organisational change. More overt and crucial aspects of culture are the norms and behaviours, dominant values, rules and regulations, and overall ethos that makes up the organisation. Many changes are taking place affecting the ethos, i.e., a move toward an emphasis on financial and curriculum modification management or toward pastoral aspects of the job. Many teachers complain that teaching is not what it used to be. Teachers new to the job will, after all of these changes, have a different expectation of what the job entails compared with experienced teachers. This may create a conflicting culture within some schools.

Additional social pressures facing teachers are legislation which limits responses to social situations (Needle *et al.*, 1981), the financial and social deprivation of children (Pratt, 1978; Tellenbeck *et al.*, 1983), parent–pupil relationships (Wilson, 1980), the macro-environment (Pettigrew and Wolf, 1981), and public pressures (Instructor, 1979). This suggests that teachers' problems do not just result from limitations within their own organisation but also the structure and climate of society.

The home–work interface

So far this chapter has concentrated on the sources of pressure in the teacher's working environment. There are, however, potential stressors that exist in the individual teacher's life outside work, affecting work and requiring consideration when assessing the sources and impact of work stress. Potential stressors include stressful life events, pressure resulting from conflict between organizational and family demands, financial difficulties, and conflicts between organizational and personal beliefs. Events occurring in the home may be both a source of stress and a source of support, just like relationships at work, and may also mitigate or exacerbate the effects of stressors experienced at work.

How are teachers responding to stress?

The extent of the problem

Having outlined the nature and the causes of teacher stress, we shall now examine the extent of the problem and show how teachers are reacting to stress, explaining the role the individual teacher plays in this reaction.

In the last few years, the incidence of stress among teachers has received considerable attention, particularly by the press, teacher unions and academics (e.g. Kyriacou and Sutcliffe, 1979a; Phillips and Lee, 1980; Travers and Cooper, 1991, 1993a, 1994, 1996). Those involved in education are now recognising that attention needs to be paid to its alleviation. In an international review of teacher stress and burnout, Kyriacou (1987) refers to the occurrence and consequences of stress in the teaching profession in countries as widespread as Great Britain, the USA, Israel, France, Canada and New Zealand. Due to the findings from these studies and the public display by teachers and their unions, teaching has become high ranking in the league table of high-stress occupations (e.g. Milstein and Golaszewski, 1985).

Comparing French and English teachers, Travers (1997) found higher levels of job-related pressure, lower levels of job satisfaction and poorer levels of mental ill-health among English teachers. This was revealed by greater intention to leave the profession (55 per cent English, 20 per cent French). English teachers, though taking similar days off sick to their French counterparts, believe that 21.6 per cent of these are due to stress-related causes compared with only 1 per cent of French teachers. Of major concern for English-based teachers is pressure from home–work interface problems, though they actually report a lower average number of hours spent taking work home than the French. French teachers are more concerned with pupil welfare issues, the value placed on education and teaching their subject and lack of opportunities for promotion. These findings are based on a study of 480 teachers

Stress in teaching

based in the south of England and 385 from the north of France, using the same questionnaire for both samples.

Estimates of the percentage of teachers actually experiencing high levels of perceived stress have varied considerably, from 30 per cent to 90 per cent (e.g. Hawkes and Dedrick, 1983; Laughlin, 1984). British research has reported between one-fifth and one-third of teachers experiencing a great deal of stress (Pratt, 1978) with 'more teachers than ever before experiencing severe stress' (Dunham, 1983). The most effective way to measure the impact of teacher stress is to compare teachers with other highly stressed occupational groups. It seems that UK teachers are suffering from poorer mental health and lower job satisfaction than doctors, tax officers, and nurses (Travers and Cooper, 1991, 1993a, 1994, 1996).

Teachers reacting to stress

At a general level, occupational stress has been found to result in a variety of manifestations – psychological, physiological and behavioural. The long term effects of these stressors have also been well documented (Cooper and Payne, 1988). Individuals who are unable to cope effectively with environmental demands which they perceive to be threatening, soon begin to show distress by:

- *Emotional manifestations*: feelings of undefined anxiety, dissatisfaction, depression, fear, frustration and low self-esteem sometimes culminating in burnout
- *Behavioural manifestations*: behavioural problems such as appetite disorders, excessive smoking and alcohol or drug abuse, violence or inability to sleep and withdrawal (i.e. absence and resignations from the profession)
- *Physiological manifestations*: heart disease, psychosomatic illness, fatigue and depleted energy reserves (Milstein and Golaszewski, 1985). Fimian and Santoro (1981) claim that emotional manifestations are often precursors for behavioural and physiological manifestations of stress in teachers, and so these should never be seen as discrete in nature.

The following sections present research evidence, where available, relating specifically to teachers though in some cases, where teacher research is not available, evidence relating to other occupational groups will be presented.

Mental ill-health and teachers

Tinning and Spry (1981) suggest that in excess of 40 million days are lost per year due to psychological disorder (poor mental well-being, nervous debility, tension, headaches, etc.) in the general population of workers.

There have been a number of studies highlighting a positive relationship between self-reported teacher stress and overall measures of mental ill-health (e.g. Pratt, 1978; Galloway *et al.*, 1982 ; Tellenbeck *et al.*, 1983). Kyriacou and Pratt (1985) emphasise, however, that it may be more beneficial to examine more specific mental symptoms in order to arrive at more appropriate coping strategies, as purely 'overall' indicators may not be precise enough (e.g. Beech, Burns and Sheffield, 1982; Fletcher and Payne, 1982). Emotional reactions may take the form of depression, anxiety, helplessness, insecurity, vulnerability and inadequacy, general uneasiness, irritability, emotional fatigue, resentment towards administration, negative self-concept and low self-esteem. Travers and Cooper (1993a), in a study of UK teachers, found that almost a quarter were suffering from levels of free floating anxiety, somatic anxiety and depression comparable with those seen in psychoneurotic outpatients.

Dunham (1976) has identified the two most common types of reactions to teacher stress, namely, frustration and anxiety. Frustration can be seen to be associated with the physiological symptoms of headaches, sleep disturbances, stomach upsets, hypertension and body rashes and in severe cases, depressive illness, whereas anxiety can be linked to loss of confidence, feelings of inadequacy, confusion in thinking and sometimes panic. In severe cases, anxiety can lead to the physiological psychosomatic symptoms of a nervous rash, twitchy eye, loss of voice and weight loss. In prolonged cases, a nervous breakdown may result.

Burnout in teachers: an extreme reaction to stress

A more extreme result of long-term effects of teacher stress is total emotional exhaustion, known as *burnout* (Hargreaves, 1978). Burnout may lead to out-of-school apathy, alienation from work and withdrawal into a number of defensive strategies. Burnout may be identified as a type of chronic response to the cumulative, long-term, negative impact of work stress (Blase, 1982). It varies with the intensity and duration of the stress, but usually results in workers becoming emotionally detached from their jobs (Daley, 1979). This is different from short-term acute stress; it is far more intense, and refers to the negative working conditions, when job stress seems unavoidable to an individual, and sources of satisfaction or relief appear unavailable (Moss, 1981). Since it was first identified by Freudenberger in 1974, it has been identified as a separate phenomenon to stress, though research into the two have inevitably overlapped, achieving an increasing amount of attention since the mid 1970s (Gillespie, 1983).

Certain studies have identified the conditions that precipitate burnout. It appears that it is frequently experienced by those professionals who deal with other people (e.g. lawyers, accountants, managers, nurses, police officers, social workers and, in particular, teachers). Another view expressed by Harvey and Brown (1988) is that those who experience job burnout as a result of job-related stress are those who are professionals and/or self-motivating achievers seeking unrealistic or unattainable goals. As a consequence of this, they cannot cope with the demands of their job and their willingness to try drops dramatically.

Perhaps of greatest concern with the burnout phenomenon is the actual symptoms that result. Pines (1982) has identified high emotional exhaustion, high depersonalisation and low personal accomplishment. Burnout can detract from the quality of teaching. Mancini *et al.*, (1982, 1984) have shown that burned-out teachers give significantly less information and less praise, show less acceptance of their pupils' ideas and interact less frequently with them.

What causes teachers to burn out?

Studies of burnout in teachers have shown that it is largely a result of excessive work stress over extended periods of time (Blase, 1982), and relentless work demands (Begley, 1982). A study of 33 teachers of emotionally disturbed children by Lawrenson and McKinnon (1982) revealed that a way of preventing burnout was to be aware of the stressful nature of the job. Nagy (1982) found that Type A personality, workaholism and perceptions of working environment were individual factors that contributed to burnout. However, none of these was a good independent predictor of its occurrence.

Westerhouse (1979) and Schwab (1981) have shown that role conflict and role ambiguity were significantly related to teacher burnout. A study of 40 American teachers by Cooley and Laviki (1981) concluded that individual, social-psychological and organisational factors were all strongly associated with the burnout response, therefore it was important to study all of these factors together to be able to understand the relative importance of each.

Lowenstein (1991) found that burnout was also a product of a lack of social recognition, large class sizes, lack of resources, isolation, fear of violence, classroom control, role ambiguity, limited professional opportunities and lack of support. These are all factors which British teachers are reporting as causes of stress (Travers and Cooper, 1996).

Job dissatisfaction

One of the most significant manifestations of stress at work is low job satisfaction. A study of 148 UK teachers by Fletcher and Payne (1982) found that the majority of the sample actually liked their job, but at the same time felt a considerable amount of pressure. However, a comparison of teachers' experience compared with participants in the University of Michigan's (Institute for Social Research) 1977 Quality of Employment Survey revealed that teachers were less satisfied with their jobs (Cooke and Kornbluh, 1980) than other professionals. This study did show that levels of job satisfaction varied from school to school.

More detailed analysis of the issues relating to job dissatisfaction reveals that factors such as salary, career structure, promotion opportunities and occupational status are involved (Tellenbeck et al., 1983). Kyriacou and Sutcliffe (1979a), in a study of 218 teachers from mixed comprehensive schools in England, found that self-reported teacher stress was negatively correlated with job satisfaction. However, there was no significant difference in terms of age, length of experience and position held in school. Moreover, job satisfaction was significantly negatively correlated with job stressors such as poor career structure, noisy or individually misbehaving pupils, inadequate salary and disciplinary policy of school, difficult classes, trying to uphold or maintain standards and having too much work to do.

Travers and Cooper (1993a) found that teachers' job satisfaction was significantly lower than other comparable occupational groups (i.e. doctors, nurses, tax officers) and that the major predictor of this was the pressure they experience from the management and structure of the schools in which they teach. Also, the lack of recognition currently perceived by teachers plays a part in what is acknowledged as an alarmingly low level of job satisfaction.

Behavioural responses to stress

Many changes in behaviour may result from stress, such as impulsive behaviour, excitability, restlessness, emotional outburst, excessive eating or loss of appetite, drug taking, including excessive drinking and smoking, absence from work and unstable employment history (Cox, 1985). Many of these have direct and indirect consequences for the health and well-being of the individual.

Though there is little evidence on the teaching population with regard to stress related smoking and drinking, we may suppose that teachers will be as vulnerable to these responses to stress as has been shown with other occupational groups. What little evidence we have relates to alcohol consumption. The authors, in a study of UK teachers (1993a), found that a large proportion of the sample were drinking above the recommended weekly average, and in a longitudinal study of teachers in London (Travers and Cooper, 1994) it was found that the presence of alcohol indicators in their blood increased as the term progressed.

Withdrawal from teaching as a response to stress

Recent years have witnessed increasing problems associating teacher stress with turnover, early retirement, absenteeism and intention to leave – all forms of withdrawal. These are the 'escape' options teachers take when they find themselves in intolerably stressful situations.

Turnover in teaching

A turnover rate in any profession of 7–8 per cent may be seen as healthy, but in teaching the rate has been far greater. The *Independent* newspaper (18 September 1990) reported a survey of 8500 schools in England and Wales showing that the resignation rate went from 9.4 per cent in 1987 to 13 per cent in 1989.

The resignations would appear to be affected by both the subject area in which teachers teach, the type of school and the sector. In the study by local authority employers and teacher unions (*Independent*, 18 September 1990), it was revealed that higher rates were found in foreign language, business, commercial and music teachers. Other findings suggest that Greater London has been worst hit, and evidence reveals that teachers within the primary sector may be the most likely to 'escape' from the profession:

> Greater London has a higher regional rate of resignations (in primary 17.1% in 1985 compared to 23.5% in 1989) and other regions show a dramatic increase (in primary in the West Midlands 6.7% in 1985 compared with 12.1% in 1989) (*Independent*, 18 September 1990).

This results in an unexpectedly older workforce in primary schools. The same survey discovered that half of all primary teachers were over 40 and very few are under 30.

Early retirement and teachers

> The number of retirements due to ill health increased from 1,617 in 1979/80 to 4,123 in 1989/90, with a large jump in 1988 when the Education Reform Act brought in the National Curriculum (*Independent*, 25 January 1991).

In addition to the problems of absenteeism and turnover, a large number of teachers are looking for early retirement as a way out of teaching. This is not to say that for the vast majority this is not legitimate on the grounds of ill-health, but for many this is the only way they see to get away from the job that is causing them excessive pressure. This means the education system and society as a whole are losing a large proportion of their experienced workforce.

Sickness absence in teachers

Simpson (1976) has suggested that sickness absence enables teachers to withdraw temporarily from stress at work, without having to make a definite break. It might enable teachers to readjust to stressful work situations and, at the same time, develop skills necessary to deal with the sources of stress that they face. A problem with this interpretation, however, lies with the fact that it is difficult to distinguish between somewhat 'voluntary' absenteeism related to psychological causes (e.g. depression) and stress-related physical illness.

Kyriacou and Sutcliffe (1979a), investigating an association between self-reported teacher stress, job satisfaction, absenteeism and intention to leave the teaching profession, found small but significant associations existed between stress and satisfaction, total days absent and intention to leave teaching.

The authors' own research (1993a) revealed that most days off sick were due to stress related causes, e.g. persistent virus, anxiety and depression, bowel and stomach disorders.

Intention to leave the profession

The same study by the authors found that 66 per cent of teachers had actively considered leaving the profession in the five years prior to the survey. This is an alarming rate, and one which merits further examination to attempt to determine how many of these teachers will actually leave, and what factors will help them make this decision.

It is not always possible to make turnover predictions unless factors from both inside and outside the immediate work environment are considered, because negative reactions do not always result in leaving. Other factors (e.g. education, availability of alternative employment) can also affect intention to leave (e.g. Martin, Jr, 1979), or actual leaving itself (Spencer, Steers and Mowday, 1983). Other factors affecting the decision will be those associated with the immediate job context or organisation (e.g. valuable investment outcomes or accumulated gains). This means that even if teachers are very job dissatisfied, they might still endure their jobs, if they weigh up the 'pros and cons' and believe that they have too much to lose. It is not always possible to transfer such accumulated gains from one organisation to another (e.g. Steers and Mowday, 1981).

Managing teacher stress

This final section attempts to present some ideas about how the problem of teacher stress can be dealt with based upon the research findings outlined above.

How can teachers help themselves?

There is usually a barrier erected when individuals are encouraged to manage their own stress. Many individuals feel that to attempt to manage stress is in some way admitting liability for it in the first place. This is not the case. If teachers are sensible, they will make attempts to change the stress within their environments in the long term, but in the short term they must do something constructive for themselves before it is too late.

Williams (1995) presents a helpful model for dealing with stress. He suggests that there are four main stages to the process:

- awareness
- responsibility
- action
- feedback.

This model is quite useful for looking at how individual teachers and schools can deal with this increasing problem.

Awareness is the first stage. Teachers need to become aware of what causes their stress. They also need to recognise the typical symptoms accompanying negative or extreme pressure. These will vary from individual to individual; for one teacher it may be a patch of eczema, a stye on the eye, slight palpitations in the chest or heartburn, or it could be 'negative self-talk' and irrational fears.

Once the teacher has done this initial diagnosis, it is time to take *responsibility* for things that they can change. This means assessing what is within and outside their control. Many teachers are getting frustrated and anxious about aspects of teaching over which they have little or no control in the short term. Also, it is important not to attempt to take responsibility for everything, there needs to be one step at a time. It is important that teachers see that taking responsibility is not a sign of failure, but a very valuable attempt to sort out their lives so that they have a better quality of working life, greater satisfaction, lower anxiety and make for better teachers. At this stage, goals need to be set for change.

Having decided on which aspects of the stress situation they are going to take responsibility for teachers need to take *action*. In the long term they may well get involved with making greater organisational changes, but in the short term they must take actions for themselves. Examples of possible actions are:

- relaxation
- cognitive techniques

- time management
- goal setting
- planning ahead.

Relaxation is essential to prevent excessive levels of anxiety building up over periods of time and consequent stress. There are two main ways in which we can learn to relax – by mind and body relaxation using learnt techniques such as yoga, meditation, listening to a tape, or by some kind of physical activity, e.g. aerobics, running, going to the gym.

Relaxation training involves a number of methods that teachers could apply both during the school day and at home – breathing exercises, muscle relaxation, meditation, autogenic training (muscle relaxation and meditation), and mental relaxation strategies. The benefits would seem to be reduced levels of anxiety, alcohol consumption and perceived stress, which are all problems experienced by teachers.

The aim of *cognitive techniques* is to allow and encourage individuals to reappraise or restructure the stressful situations so they are no longer stressful – by removing cognitive distortion such as over-generalisation, magnifying and personalisation, and introducing assertiveness training. The benefits are that ultimate control may be handed over to individuals to enable them to control their reactions to stressors.

When carrying out their own research, the authors found that one of the most overwhelming characteristics of their sample of teachers was the level of 'time conscious-impatient behaviour' and its impact on mental ill-health (Travers and Cooper, 1993b). It is probably beneficial therefore to encourage teachers to improve their *time management skills* both inside and outside of work. This is not necessarily managing time to be able to get more work done, but rather to give teachers more time for themselves.

Goal setting and planning ahead are important. Often when work takes over people's lives they forget to pay attention to what they really want out of work and life. Teachers need to stop and think about what they want to get out of teaching – to visualise a working life that is free of excessive stress, then make plans to create that future. For teachers to manage stress and become motivated they need to inject back into their working lives some aspects that are pleasurable for themselves. A lot of this involves getting back in touch with the values that teachers have and desire as part of their lives.

The final stage in this model of managing stress is to utilise regular *feedback*. This means looking for signals that stress is being managed more effectively, or seeing if some strategies are not working. This is about making sure that dealing with stress is part of our everyday lives, and is recognised as a skill just like any other. Teachers need to monitor what does and does not work for them. Of course one of the best ways to obtain feedback on how one is managing stress is to look at the ways others begin to react to us.

Stress management at the level of the school and society

The last section suggested some ways in which teachers might attempt to manage stress in the short term, but they cannot manage alone indefinitely.

Managers in schools and decision-makers in education must also become aware, accept responsibility and then take action to make schools less stressful places. They can do this by employing a number of strategies:

- providing counselling services and helplines for teachers to use in confidence
- improving organisational support in the form of resources and investment for better working conditions
- giving better support in the classroom and across break times
- rethinking sanctions for behavioural problems and unruly pupils
- improving management training for managers within schools
- giving opportunities for more retraining and sabbaticals for teachers
- improving training before and during teaching to come up to date with the changing role of the teacher and to help clarify roles within teaching
- improving public and professional image by better advertising and PR.

After initiatives have taken place, they should seek feedback in terms of measurables (e.g. sickness absence) and the attitudes of the teachers to any changes that have taken place.

Whatever happens, it is very important that teaching becomes a more attractive profession so that recruits can be targeted to make up for the vast number who are leaving or who intend to leave.

Conclusions

We have defined stress and outlined its nature, causes and management. Currently there is a crisis in Britain's schools that needs to be dealt with urgently so that the working lives of a great number of people are not destroyed along with the educational experience of the young. Responsibility for dealing with stress needs to be accepted by all of those in the education sphere, and should be treated as a problem for all, not just teachers themselves. Although teachers would be well advised to do something about their own stress levels before it is too late, they should not be relied on to take all the responsibility. All is not well in the teaching profession and management must recognise that stress is not an indication of weakness or incompetence.

If this approach is taken and the methods for alleviating stress utilised, then it might well be possible to witness an improvement in the experience of teachers at work.

References

Austin, D.A. (1981) The teacher burnout issue. Journal of Physical Education, Recreation and Dance, 52, 9, 35–56.

Baron, R.A. (1986) Behaviour in Organisations, 2nd edn (Newton, MA: Allyn & Bacon).

Bayer, E. and Chauvet, N. (1980) Libertés et constraintes de l'exercise pedagogique. Faculté de Psychologie et Sciences de l'Education, Géneve.

Beech, H.R., Burns, L.E. and Sheffield, B.F. (1982) A Behavioural Approach to the Management of Stress (New York: Wiley).

Beehr, T.A. and Franz, T.M. (1986) The current debate about the meaning of job stress. Journal of Organizational Behaviour Management, 8 (2), 5–18.

Begley, D. (1982) Burnout among special education administrators. Paper presented at the Summer Convention of the Council for Exceptional Children, Houston, Texas.

Blackie, P. (1977) Not quite proper. Times Educational Supplement, No. 3259.

Blase, J.J. (1982) A social-psychological grounded theory of teacher stress and burnout. Educational Administration Quarterly, 18(4), 93–113.

Bloch, A. (1978) Combat neurosis in inter-city schools. American Journal of Psychiatry, 135, 1189–92.

Brenner, S.D., Sorbom, D. and Wallius, E. (1985) The stress chain: a longitudinal study of teacher stress, coping and social support. Journal of Occupational Psychology, 58, 1–14.

Breuse, E. (1984) Identificación de las fuentes de tensión en el trabajo professional del enseñiante, in Esteve, J.M. (Ed.) Profesores en Conflicto (Madrid: Narcea).

Brief, A.P., Schuler, R.S. and Van Sell. M. (1981) Managing Job Stress (Boston, MA:Little Brown).

Cichon, D.J. and Koff, R.H. (1978) The teaching events stress inventory. Paper presented to the American Educational Research Association annual meeting, Educational Research Information Centre, No 160–162

Clark, E.H. (1980) An analysis of occupational stress factors as perceived by public school teachers. Unpublished doctoral dissertation, Auburn University.

Comber, L. and Whitfield, R. (1979) Action on Indiscipline: A practical guide for teachers (NAS/UWT).

Connors, S.A. (1983) The school environment: a link to understanding stress. Theory in Practice, 22(1), 15–20.

Cooke, R. and Kornbluh, H. (1980) The general quality of teacher worklife. Paper presented at the Quality of Teacher Worklife Conference, University of Michigan, Ann Arbor.

Cooley, E. and Lavicki, V. (1981) Preliminary investigations of environmental and individual aspects of burnout in teachers. Paper presented at Oregon Education Association, Otter Rock, Oregon.

Cooper, C.L. (Ed.) (1986) Stress Research: Issues for the eighties (Chichester: Wiley).

Cooper, C.L. and Kelly, M. (1993) Occupational stress in head teachers. British Journal of Educational Psychology, 63, 130–43.

Cooper, C.L. and Payne, R. (Eds.) (1988) Causes, Coping and Consequences of Stress at Work. (Chichester: Wiley).

Cox, T. (1985) The nature and management of stress. Ergonomics, 23, 1155–63.
Daley, M.R. (1979) Burnout: smouldering problem in protective services. Social Work, 24(5), 375–9.
Dewe, P.J. (1986) An investigation into the causes and consequences of teacher stress. New Zealand Journal of Educational Studies, 21(2), 145–57.
Dunham, J. (1976) Stress situations and responses, in Stress in schools (Hemel Hempstead, NAS/UWT).
Dunham, J. (1977) The signs, causes and reduction of stress in teachers, in The Management of Stress in Schools (Clwyd County Council).
Dunham, J. (1980) An exploratory comparative study of staff stress in English and German comprehensive schools. Educational Review, 32, 11–20.
Dunham, J. (1984) Stress in Teaching (Beckenham: Croom Helm).
Edwards, J.R. and Cooper, C.L. (1990) The person-environment fit approaches to stress: recurring problems and some suggested solutions. Journal of Organistaional Behaviour, 11, 293–307.
Eskridge, D.H. (1984) Variables of teacher stress, symptoms, causes and stress management techniques. Unpublished research study, Texarkaua, TX: East Texas State University.
Esteve, J. (1989) Teacher burnout and teacher stress, in Cole, M. and Walker, S. (Eds.), Teaching and Stress (Milton Keynes: Open University Press).
Fimian, M.J. (1982) What is teacher stress? Clearing House, 56(3), 101–5.
Fimian, M.J. (1983) A comparison of occupational stress correlates as reported by teachers of mentally retarded and non-mentally retarded handicapped students. Education and Training of the Mentally Retarded, 18(1), 62–8.
Fimian, M.J. and Santoro, T.M. (1981) Correlates of occupational stress as reported by full-time special education teachers. I. Sources of stress. II. Manifestations of stress. Educational Information Research Centre, No. 219–543.
Fimian, M.J. and Santoro, T.M. (1983) Sources and manifestations of occupational stress as reported by full-time special education teachers. Exceptional Children, 49(6), 540–3.
Fletcher, B. and Payne, R.L. (1982) Levels of reported stressors and strains among school teachers: some UK data. Educational Review, 34(3), 267–78.
Freeman, A. (1987) Pastoral care and teacher stress. Pastoral Care in Education, 5(1), 22–8.
Freudenberger, H.J. (1974) Staff-burnout. Journal of Social Issues, 30, 159–65.
French, J.R.P. and Caplan, R.D. (1970) Psychosocial factors in coronary heart disease. Industrial Medicine, 39, 383–97.
Gillespie, D.F. (1983) Understanding and Combatting Burnout (Monticello, IL: Vance Bibliographies).
Goble, N.M. and Porter, J.F. (1980) La Cambiante Functión de Profesor (Madrid: Narcea).
Hammond, J.M. (1983) School improvement using a trainer of trainers approach: reducing teacher stress. Journal of Staff Development, 4(1), 95–100.
Hargreaves, D. (1978) What teaching does to teachers. New Society, 9(43), 540–3.
Harvey, D.F. and Brown, D.R. (1988) OD interpersonal interventions, in Harvey, D.F. and Brown, D.R. (Eds.), An Experiential Approach to Organizational Development, 3rd edn (Englewood Cliffs, NJ: Prentice Hall).
Hawkes, R.R. and Dedrick, C.V. (1983) Teacher stress: phase II of a descriptive study. National Association of Secondary School Principals Bulletin, 67(461), 78–83.
Hoover-Dempsey, K.V. and Kendall, E.D. (1982) Stress and coping among teachers: experience in search of theory and science. Educational Information Research Service, No 241503.

ILO (1981) Employment and Conditions of Work of Teachers (Geneva: International Labour Organisation).

Instructor, (1979) Teacher burnout: how to cope when the world goes black. Inspector, 88(6), 56–62.

Kahn, R.L., Wolfe, D.M., Quinn, R.P., Snoek, J.D. and Rosenthal, R.A. (1964) Organisational Stress: Studies in role conflict and ambiguity (Chichester: Wiley).

Kalker, P. (1984) Teacher stress and burnout: causes and coping strategies. Contemporary Education, 56(1), 16–19.

Kelly, A.V. (1974) Teaching Mixed Ability Classes (London: Harper and Row).

Kyriacou, C. (1981) Social support and occupational stress among schoolteachers. Educational Studies, 7(1), 55–60.

Kyriacou, C. (1987) Teacher stress and burnout: an international review. Educational Research, 29(2), 146–52.

Kyriacou, C. and Pratt, J. (1985) Teacher stress and psychoneurotic symptoms. British Journal of Educational Psychology, 55, 61–4.

Kyriacou, C. and Roe, H. (1988) Teachers' perceptions of pupils' behaviour problems at a comprehensive school. British Educational Research Journal, 14(2), 167–73.

Kyriacou, C. and Sutcliffe, J. (1978a) Teacher stress: prevalence, sources and symptoms. British Journal of Educational Psychology, 48, 159–67.

Kyriacou, C. and Sutcliffe, J. (1978b) A model of teacher stress. Educational Studies, 4, 1–6.

Kyriacou, C. and Sutcliffe, J. (1979a) Teacher stress and satisfaction. Educational Research, 21(2), 89–96.

Kyriacou, C. and Sutcliffe, J. (1979b) A note on teacher stress and locus of control. Journal of Occupational Psychology, 52, 227–8.

Laughlin, A. (1984) Teacher stress in an Australian setting: the role of biographical mediators. Educational Studies, 10(1), 7–22.

Lawrenson, G.M. and McKinnon, A.J. (1982) A survey of classroom teachers of the emotionally disturbed: attrition and burnout factors. Behavioural Disorders, 8, 41–8.

Lazarus, R.S. (1981) Little hassles can be hazardous to health. Psychology Today, July, 58–62.

Levinson, H. (1978) The abrasive personality. Harvard Business Review, 56, May–June, 86–94

Litt, M.D. and Turk, D.C. (1985) Sources of stress and dissatisfaction in experienced high school teachers. Journal of Educational Research, 78(3), 178–85.

Lowenstein, L.F (1991) Teacher stress leading to burnout: its prevention and cure. Education Today, 41(2), 12–16.

Mancini, V., Wuest, D., Clark, E. and Ridosh, N. (1982) A comparison of the interaction patterns and academic learning time of low-burnout and high-burnout physical educators. Paper presented at Big Ten Symposium on Research on Teaching, Lafayette, Indiana.

Mancini, V., Wuest, D., Vantine, K. and Clark, E. (1984) Use of instruction and supervision in interaction analysis on burned out teachers: its effects on teaching behaviours, level of burnout and academic learning time. Journal of Teachers in Physical Education, 3(2), 29–46.

Marshall, J. (1977) Job pressures and satisfactions at managerial levels. PhD Thesis, UMIST, Manchester.

Martin, T.N. Jr (1979) A contextual model of employee turnover intention. Academy of Management Journal, 22, 313–24.

Miller, K.I. and Monge, P.R. (1986) Participation, satisfaction and productivity: a meta-analytic review. Academy of Management Journal, 29(4), 727–53.
Milstein, M.M. and Golaszewski, T.J. (1985) effects of organisationally-based and individually-based stress management efforts in elementary school settings. Urban Education, 19(4).
Moss, L. (1981) Management Stress (Reading, MA: Addison-Wesley).
Mykletun, R.J. (1984) Teacher stress: perceived and objective sources and quality of life. Scandinavian Journal of Educational Research, 28(1), 17–45.
Nagy, S. (1982) The relationship of Type A personalities, workaholism, perception of the school climate and years of teaching experience to burnout of elementary and junior high school teachers in Northwest Oregon school district. Unpublished Doctoral Dissertation, University of Oregon, Eugene, Oregon.
Needle, R.H., Griffin, T. and Svendsen, R. (1981) occupational stress: coping and health problems of teachers. Journal of Health, 51(3), 175–81.
Pettigrew, L.S. and Wolf, G.E. (1981) Validating Measures of Teacher Stress (Chicago, IL: Spencer Foundation).
Phillips, B.L. and Lee, M. (1980) The changing role of the American teacher: current and future sources of stress, in Cooper, C.L. and Marshall, J. (Eds.), White Collar and Professional Stress (Chichester: Wiley).
Pines, A. (1982) Helpers motivation and the burnout syndrome, in Wills, T.A. (Ed.) Basic Processes in Helping Relationships (London: Academic Press).
Pratt, J. (1978) Perceived stress among teachers: the effects of age and background of children taught. Educational Review, 30, 3–14.
Rudd, W.D. and Wiseman, S. (1962) Sources of dissatisfaction among a group of teachers. British Journal of Educational Psychology, 32(3), 275–91.
Russell, D.W., Altmaier, E. and Van Velzen, D. (1987) Job-related stress, social support and burnout among classroom teachers. Journal of Applied Psychology, 72(2), 269–74.
Schwab, R.L. (1981) The relationship of role conflict, role ambiguity, teacher background variables and perceived burnout among teachers. Doctoral Dissertation, Storrs, CT:University of Connecticut; Dissertation Abstracts International, 41 (09-A), (2), 3823-a.
Schwab, R.L. (1983) Teacher burnout: moving beyond psychobabble. Theory into Practice, 22, 21–5.
Shaw, J.B. and Riskind, J.H. (1983) Predicting job stress using data from the position analysis questionnaire. Journal of Applied Psychology, 68, 253–61.
Simpson, J. (1976) Stress: sickness absence in teachers, in Stress in Schools (NAS/UWT).
Smith, J. and Cline, D. (1980) Quality programs. Pointer, 24(2), 80–7.
Sparks, D.C. (1979) A biased look at teacher job satisfaction. Clearing House, 52(9), 447–9.
Spencer, D., Steers, R. and Mowday, R. (1983) An empirical test of the inclusions of job search linkages in Mobley's turnover decision model. Journal of Occupational Psychology, 56, 603–9.
Steers, R. and Mowday, R. (1981) Employee turnover and post decision accommodation process, in Staw, B. and Cummings, I. (Eds.), Research in Organizational Behaviour, (Greenwich, CT: JAI Press).
Sutherland, V.J. and Cooper, C.L. (1991) Understanding Stress: A psychological perspective for health professionals (London: Chapman & Hall).
Tannenbaum, R. and Massarik, F. (1989) Participation by subordinates in the managerial decision-making process, in Matteson, M.T. and Ivancevich, J.M.(Eds.),

Management and Organizational Behaviour Characteristics (Homewood, IL: Irwin).

Tellenbeck, S., Brenner, S.D. and Lofgren, H. (1983) Teacher stress: exploratory model building. Journal of Occupational Psychology, 56, 19–33.

Tinning, R.J. and Spry, W.B. (1981) The extent and significance of stress symptoms in industry – with examples from the steel industry, in Corlett, E.N. and Richardson, J. (Eds.), Stress, Work Design and Productivity (Chichester: Wiley).

Travers, C.J. (1997) Vive la difference: the experience of stress in teachers on both sides of the Channel. British Psychological Society, Occupational Psychology Conference Proceedings, 7–9 January 1997, pp. 185–98.

Travers, C.J. and Cooper, C.L. (1991) Stress and status in teaching: An investigation of potential gender-related relationships. Women in Management Review and Abstracts, 6(4), 16–23.

Travers, C.J. and Cooper, C.L. (1993a) Mental ill health, job satisfaction, alcohol consumption and intention to leave in the teaching profession. Work and Stress, 7(3), 203–20.

Travers, C.J. and Cooper, C.L. (1993b) Can teachers' Type A behaviour seriously ruin their health? Paper presented to the Annual Conference of the British Psychological Society Occupational Psychology Conference, Brighton.

Travers, C.J. and Cooper, C.L. (1994) Psychophysiological responses to teacher stress: A move towards more objective methodologies. European Review of Applied Psychology, 44(2) 137–46.

Travers, C.J. and Cooper, C.L. (1996) Teachers Under Pressure: Stress in the teaching profession (London: Routledge).

Wanberg, E.G. (1984) The complex issue of teacher stress and job dissatisfaction. Contemporary Education, 56(1), 11–15.

Weiskopf, P.E. (1980) Burnout among teachers of exceptional children. Exceptional Children, 47, 18–23.

Westerhouse, M.A (1979) The effects of tenure, role conflict and role conflict resolution on the work orientation and burnout of teachers. Doctoral dissertation, University of California at Berkeley. Dissertation abstracts international, 41 (01A), 8014928, 174.

Williams, S. (1995) Managing Pressure for Peak Performance (London: Kogan Page).

Wilson, C.F. (1980) Stress profiles for teachers: test manual and preliminary data, Department of Education, San Diego County, San Diego.

Yerkes, R.M. and Dodson, J.D. (1908) The relation to the strength of the stimulus to the rapidity of habit formation. Journal of Comparative Neurology and Psychology, 18, 459–82.

Bibliography for Dennis Child

Entries in date order

The relationship between introversion, extraversion, neuroticism in school examinations, British Journal of Education Psychology 34, 187–196 (1964).
The sixth form myth, Education, 3rd December 1965.
Admission qualifications for the BEd degree, Education for Teaching, 22–27 (1966a).
Personality and social status, British Journal of Social and Clinical Psychology, 5, 196–199 (1966b).
Reminiscence and personality – a note on the effect of different test instructions, British Journal of Social and Clinical Psychology, 5, 92–94, (1966c).
Convergent and divergent thinking and Arts/science choice, Bulletin, British Psychology Society, (1968a).
A study of divergent thinking, subject specialisation and threshold of intelligence theory using Secondary school children. Bradford University, (1968b).
Staff-student relations in Colleges of Education, report to Bradford University, (1968c).
Initiating Research in Colleges of Education (joint author with Collier, G.), Association of Teachers in Colleges and Departments of Education, (1969a).
Some sociological and psychological factors in university failure, Durham Research Review, 22, 265–272, (joint author with Cohen, L.), (1969b).
A comparative study of personality, intelligence and social class in a technological university, British Journal of Educational Psychology, 39, 40–46 (1969c).
Career orientations of some university freshmen, Educational Review, 21, 209–217, (joint author with Musgrove, F.), (1969d).
The Essentials of Factor Analysis, Holt, Rinehart and Winston, 1970.
Predicting the performance of undergraduate chemists, Education in Chemistry, 7, 156–158, (joint author with Sherwin, E.), (1970).
Some reference groups of university students, Educational Research, 13, 145–149, (1970).
Some aspects of study habits in higher education, International Journal of Educational Sciences, 4, 11–20, (1970).
Social attitudes of university students, Durham Research Review, 25, 471–476, (1970).
A comparison of self and friends' ratings using the EPI, (joint author with Stefanuti M.) Bradford University, (1970).
Parents' expectations of a university, Universities Quarterly, 26 484–490, (joint author with Cooper, H.J., Hussell, C.G.I., Webb, P.), (1971a).
The development of local-cosmopolitan attitudes amongst undergraduates and sixth

formers, Sociological Review, 19, 325–341, (joint author with Toomey, D.), (1971b).

A chapter entitled 'Extraversion, neuroticism and attainment in school children', in Readings in Extraversion-Introversion: Vol. 2, edited by Eysenck, H.J., Staples Press, (1971c).

Some cognitive and affective factors in subject choice, Research in Education, 5, 1–9, (joint author with Smithers, A.), (1971d).

Self-estimates of convergent and divergent thinking styles, University of Bradford (1972).

Psychology and the Teacher, Holt, Rinehart and Winston, (1973a).

An attempted validation of the Joyce-Hudson scale of convergence and divergence, British Journal of Educational Psychology, 43, 57–62, (joint author with Smithers, A.G.), (1973b).

The Physiotherapist – is there an occupational stereotype? Physiotherapy, 60, 302–305, (1974a).

Convergers and divergers – different forms of neuroticism? British Journal of Educational Psychology, 44, 304–306, (joint author with Smithers, A.G.), (1974b).

Motivation and Dynamic Structure, (with Cattell, R.B.), Holt, Rinehart and Winston, 1975.

Sibling Association and Occupational Interests, British Journal of Guidance and Counselling, 4, 74–78 (1976), (joint author with Bowen, J.).

Changing attitudes to the subject, and the teaching of mathematics amongst student teachers. Educational Studies, 2, 1–10 (1976). (joint author with Lumb, D.).

Readings in Psychology for the Teacher, Holt Rinehart and Winston, (1977a) Edited by Child, D. Chapters by him not appearing elsewhere were, 'Motivation and dynamic structure – Cattell's theory of motivation and its application in education', pp.44–56, and 'Psychometric measures of personality and achievement', pp.301–320.

Divergent thinking and ability: is there a threshold? Education Studies, 3, 2, 101–110, (1977b), (joint author with Croucher, A.).

Personality profiles and divergent thinkers. Durham and Newcastle Research Review, 8, 1–8 (1977c) (joint author with A. Croucher).

A chapter entitled, 'Intelligence and Creativity' in Education of the Young Child, (Ed.) Fontana, D. Open Books (1978a).

Affective Influences on Academic Achievement. Inaugural Lecture. Published for School of Education, Newcastle upon Tyne (1978b).

Occupational interests and cognitive style in relation to subject choice and university attainment. Vocational Aspect, 31, 22–30 (1979). (a joint author with Smithers, A.).

Cyril Burt: Psychologist (review of), L.S. Hearnshaw, Stodder and Stoughton, London. Durham and Newcastle Research Review, 51–52, (1979).

*Report to the British Council: University of Yucatan Comision de Planeacion y formento de Actividades Academicas. 32pp. (1979).

A chapter entitled 'The Educational Context', in The Teaching of Psychology, (Eds) Radford, J. and Rose, D.Wiley, (1980).

*Report to the British Council following a visit to Botswana and Malawi, 20pp. (1980).

Study and the Student, University of Newcastle upon Tyne, (1980).

Home, School and Peer Group Sentiments and their Relationship to Study Habits and School Achievement. The Irish Journal of Psychology, 5, 30–39 (1981). (joint author with Dobson, C.B.).

*Second Report to the British Council and the University of Yucatan Comision de Planeacion y formento de Actividades Academicas. 30pp. (1981).

*Third Report to the British Council and the University of Yucatan Comision de Planeacion y formento de Actividades Academicas. 27pp. (1982).

*Fourth Report to the University of Yucatan Centro de Desarrollo and British Council. 27pp. (1983).

*Fifth Report to the University of Yucatan Centro de Desarrollo and British Council. 53pp. (1984).

Revision of chapter entitled 'The growth of intelligence and creativity in young children' in The Education of the Young Child, 2nd Edition, edited by Fontana, D. Blackwell (1984).

*Report to the DES Science in Schools, Age 15 report No. 2, from the APU team at Leeds University, 230pp. (1984). (Joint author).

Psychology in the Service of Education published in The University of Leeds Review, Vol. 27, 23–38 (1984) Inaugural Lecture delivered 1983.

Biggs' SPQ: a British study of its internal structure, British Journal of Educational Psychology, 54, 228–234 (1984) (joint author with O'Neil, M.).

Motivation and dynamic calculus: A teacher's view. Multivariate Behavioural Research, 19, 288–298 (1984).

Perspectives in Postgraduate Initial Training: The CNAA validated PGCE. Report of a working party of the Committee for Education. CNAA, London, (1984).

*The DC tests 1, 2 and 3. Answer Keys and Manual, HMSO, (1985a). (Closed test.)

*Sixth Report to the University of Yucatan Department of Education and British Council. 20pp. (1985a).

'Educational Psychology: past, present and future', in Entwistle, N.J. (Ed.) New Directions in Educational Psychology 1. Learning and Teaching, Lewes, Falmer Press, (1985b).

'Cognitive styles: some recent ideas of relevance to teachers' in Bagley,C. and Verma, G. (Eds.), Personality, Cognition and Values, Macmillan, London (1985c).

Applications of Psychology for the Teacher, Holt Rinehart and Winston, (1986).

A-levels as a predictor, Leeds University Reporter, 255, (1986). Summary from a report to the University of Leeds.

*Seventh Report to the University of Yucatan and British Council, 20pp, (1986).

*University links – British Council publication from the Committee for International Co-operation on Higher Education, 31pp, (1987).

*Academic links with China Scheme. Report of a visit to East China Normal University,(1987).

*The Nurse Selection Project: Phase II – Assessing Professional Potential. (joint author with Borrill,C.). A research report submitted to the DHSS, 240pp. (1987).

Selection for Nurse Training: Making Decisions (with Borrill,C. Jagger, J.B. and Bygrave,D.), University of Leeds Press (1988a).

After the DC test.Conference paper at Robinson College, Cambridge and subsequent published material, (1988b).

'Recent Developments of the MAT and SMAT', in The Analysis of Personality in Research and Assessment: A Tribute to Raymond B. Cattell pp. 81–92, Independent Assessment and Research Centre: London, (1988c).

The Nurse Selection Project. Interchange, School of Education, University of Leeds, pp16–20, Autumn (1988d).

*Report to the British Council Following a visit to Beijing Foreign Studies University, 10pp, (1988e).

*Practice and Coaching for the DC tests, Submitted to UKCC 25pp, (1988f).

*Report and proposal 'Higher degree and professional courses in Education at the University of Chihauhau, Mexico', for the British Council, 21pp, (1989a).

*Notes of Guidance for Markers, UKCC publication for DC markers, 22pp, (1989b).

*Age and Performance Trends on the DC1 test, submitted to UKCC, 6pp, (1989c).
*The DC Pass Mark for the 15+ Age Group, Submitted to UKCC, 13pp, (1989d).
*Is the Timing Procedure for the DC Tests a Disadvantage to Older Candidates?, Submitted to the UKCC 12pp, (1989e).
*Validation Study of the DC tests – Final Report to UKCC, 21pp, (1990a).
Taking the DC Test – a Guide for Candidates, (joint author with Borrill,C.), University of Leeds Press, (1990b).
*Report of a visit to Chihuahua, Mexico, for the British Council, 43pp, (1990c).
The Essentials of Factor Analysis (2nd Ed. major revision), Cassell, London, (1990d).
*Age Trends in DC Scores using a 72 000 Sample, submitted to UKCC, 13pp, (1990e).
A Survey of Communication Approaches used in schools for the Deaf in the UK. Journal of the British Association of Teachers of the Deaf, 15, 20–24, (1991).
Communication approaches used in schools for the Deaf in the UK – a follow-up study. Journal of the British Association of Teachers of the Deaf, 17,2, 36–47, (1993). (Joint author with R. Baker).
Psychology and the Teacher, 5th Ed., London, Cassell, 1993.
Personality: The Psychometric View by Paul Kline. (review of) British Journal of Education Psycology. June (1994a).
Painters in the Northern Counties of England and Wales, University of Leeds (1994b).
Psychology and the Teacher, (6th Ed. major revision), Cassell, London, 1997.
Some Technical Problems in the use of Personality Measures in Occupational Settings Illustrated Using the 'Big Five', in Shorrocks-Taylor,D. Directions in Educational Psychology, Whurr publishers, London, 1998.

* Entries preceded with an asterisk are unpublished reports submitted to Government Departments or for Government funded research most of which are confidential.

Index

Page numbers in *italics* refer to illustrations or tables

ability training and learning difficulty, 217–19
advice to victims of bullies, 286
affective outcomes of education, *192*, 199–200
aggregation of scores in testing, 176–8
   minimal assignable grades, 176
   partial tolerance methods, 176, 177
   test scores and teacher assessment, 177
   thresholds and cut scores, 178, 184
ALIS ('A' Level Information System), 190, 191, *192*, 198
alternative psychologies of skill, 93–101
   commonsense behaviourism, 95–7
   commonsense nativism, 97
   commonsense rationalism, 98–9
   formal behaviourism, 94–5
Angoff procedures, 178
Artificial Intelligence (AI), 21
APU (Assessment of Performance Unit), 170, 172
authentic examinations, 192

basic learning processes, 6–8, 20
   schema, 6
   accretion, 7
   tuning, 7
   restructuring, 7
behavioural and life–chance outcomes of education, *192*
big five facets, 351, *358*
   complexity of, 356–7
   nomenclature and, 359
big five factors (or domains), *351*
   complexity of, 356–7
   oblique solution of, *354*, 354–5
   stability of, 356–7, *357, 358*
bilingual education, 299
biodata, 329, 332–3
British Sign Language (BSL), 298
   examinations in, 303–4
   teaching, 303–5
bullies
   evaluating intervention methods against, 292–4
   and power, 287–8
   and punishment, 286–7
   and victims, 285
bullying
   definition of, 282–3
   and labelling, 285
   and the No Blame Approach, 289–90
   as normal behaviour, 283–4
   and whole school approaches, 284, 288–9
burnout, 378–9

classroom management, 232–3
classroom work cycle, *10*
Code of Practice (DfE, 1994), 214, 266, 269, 272–4, 278
cognitive outcomes of education, 191, *192*, 192–199
cognitive process teaching methods, 258–61
   cognitive study skills, 259
   collaborative learning, 260–61
   experiential learning, 260
   games and simulations, 258
   language experience methods, 261
   problem-solving and investigative learning, 259

collaborative learning and computers, 33–5
constructive learners in the classroom, 11–12
control of the curriculum, 171
competency
    as input, 338–9
    as output, 338
    and performance management, *341*, 341–3, *342*
Computer Assisted Learning (CAL), 19
computer networking and learning, 25–6
computers and IT in educational research, 135
council for the Advancement of Communication with Deaf People (CACDP), 296, 302–5
criterion-referenced assessment, 172, 173–8
    domain definition and mastery, 173, 175, 178
    aggregating scores in, 176–8
culture of classrooms, 9–11
culture of measurement and credentialism, 159
curriculum-embedded examinations, 191, 192

deaf
    children's education, 298
    oralism and the, 297–8
    prelingually profoundly, 296
    provision for adults who are, 300–305
discipline in classrooms, 230–31
disruptive behaviour in classrooms
    and bullying, 239
    frequency of, 236
    gender differences in, 235–6
    physical and verbal abuse and, 239–40
    prevalence of, 233–5
    severity of, 238
    types of, 236–41
distal variables, 193
dyslexia, 214

Education Reform Act (1988), 156, 157, 215

educational provision for able pupils, 253–8
    integral differentiation in, *254*, 255–8
    structural differentiation in, 254–5, *254*
educational research, 106–110, 135–6
    conceptual basis, 106
    data collection and analysis, 135
    definition, 106
    ecological validity, 109–110
    experimental tradition, 108
    identification of variables and criteria, 136
    individual differences, 108
    processing data, 143
    qualitative and quantitative methods, 122–3, 143
    role of psychology, 106
    selection of attributes to study, 136
effects of testing
    narrowing of the curriculum, 159
    teaching to the test, 158
effectiveness of job selection methods, 330–3, *331*
    ability tests, 331–2
    assessment centres, 332
    interest inventories, 333
    interviews, 330–1, 347–8
    personality questionnaires, 332
    reference checks, 333
enrichment teaching programmes, 257
    and developmental differentiation, 257–8
equating scores from tests, 178
expectations and pupil achievement, 53–5, 67–70
    communicating expectations, 54
    dimensions of expectations, 73–5
    functions of expectations, 71–3
    general high expectations, 53–4, 68–9
    individual and shared expectations, 70–1
    low expectations and achievement, 76–7
    normative basis of expectations, 75–6
    prescriptive and probabilistic expectations, 70
    providing intellectual challenge, 54–5

Index

external examination system, 191
  and instructional effects, 193

factor analysis, 149, 350, 352–5, 356–7
feedback
  360 degree, 341–3
  400 degree, 342–3
FEFC (Further Education Funding Council), 209
formative assessment, 158, 181–3

General National Vocational Qualifications (GNVQs), 316–19
giftedness
  biographical data and, 247
  checklists and trait ratings for, 251–3
  creativity and, 248, 250
  curriculum-based assessment of, 253
  defined, 244–5, 249
  IQ and, 245–6, 247
  measurement and assessment of, 245–6
  and process analysis, 253
Grade Point Average (GPA), 191, 193
  at GCSE as predictor of 'A' level, 193, *194*, 195
graphical user interfaces and learning, 21–3
  the process of measuring, *22*

high stakes examination, 192

implications of conceptualising teaching as skill, 101–102
inclusive education, 214
  and deaf children, 298–9
Individual Educational Plans (IEP), 216–17
internet and learning, 31–3
IT tools for exploratory learning, 26–30
  LOGO, 26–8
  VARILAB, 28–9
interviews for work, 330

job performance appraisal, 336–9
  developmental, 338–9
  merit ratings in, 336–7
  predictive validity and , 360–1
job satisfaction, 379–80
knowledge use and application in classrooms, 12–14

learning and 'connectedness', 119
learning difficulty
  defined, 213–15
  identification and assessment of, 216–17
learning how to teach, 15–16
learning outcomes and characteristics of students, 116
learning strategies, 118
  holist, 118
  serialist, 118
lexical hypothesis, 349
linking teaching and learning, 56–9
  knowledge and skills of teaching, 57
  features of effective teaching, *58*, 58–9

management by objectives (MBO), 336–7
managing teacher stress, 382–5
  self-help in, 383–4
  by the school, 385
  by society, 385
marketing of schools, 159, 166
measurement in education
  characterising measurement, 141
  classical measurement approaches, 138–9
    attitude models, 138
    Rasch analysis, 138–9
  measuring change, 140
    generisability theory, 140
    Bayesian methods, 140
  measuring trends, 139
  naturalistic viewpoints, 141
  measurement in context, 142
    sensitivity to context, 142
  meta-analysis, 143
  qualitative methodologies, 143
  processing data, 143
  reliability/dependability of outcomes, 180–1, *180*
  validity of outcomes, 179–80, *180*
mental ill-health and teachers, 377–8
methodology in educational research, 137
  factor analysis, 149
  group differentiation, 149
  inter-relatedness of variables, 144
  LISREL and structural equation modelling, 144–5

multi-dimensional scaling, 148
multilevel modelling, 145–6
multiple regression, 146
'real-world' research, 137
styles and typologies, 147
value-added analyses, 146
models of ability and motivation, 77–81
  self-perception, 77–8
  teacher beliefs, 78–9
  attributions, 79
  goals and beliefs, 79–80
motivation and academic performance, 196–7
multi-level modelling, 145, 196
multimedia systems and learning, 23–5
  simulation scenarios, 24
multiple intelligences, 250–51
multivariate analysis of academic performance, 111–14
  typologies and clusters, 111–13

National Council for Vocational Qualifications (NCVQ)
  Beaumont review of (1996), 320–1
  Capey review of (1995), 321–2
  Dearing review of (1996), 322–3
  quinquennial review of (Nov. 1995, Feb. 1996), 323
  response to criticism, 319–20
National Curriculum Authority (NCA), 232–4
national curriculum testing
  aggregating scores, 176–9
  Dearing review of National Curriculum, 178, 185
  dependability of scores, 180–1
  Key Stage 1 tests, 173, 182, 183, 185, 186
  Key Stage 2 tests, 178, 195
  Key Stage 3 tests, 178, 182, 183
  origins, 171–2
  performance analysis of results of tests, 183
  principles of the tests (TGAT), 170, 172
    criterion-referencing, 172, 173–8
    formative assessment, 181–3
    moderated grades, 183–4
    progression, 184–5
  structure (curriculum and testing), 136, 173, 174

national curriculum testing (cont.)
  Attainment Targets, 173, 174
  Level descriptions, 175, 178
  Statements of Attainment, 174–5
  10-level scale, 184
  validity of scores, 179–80
National Vocational Qualifications (NVQs), 311–25, 338
  assessment methods for, 315
  competence precision, 314
  design faults, 312
  fragmentation and, 314
  and knowledge and understanding, 315
  origins of, 313
  output-related funding for, 316
  and prioritisation of performance criteria, 314
No Blame Approach to bullying, 289–90
  and its success, 290–92
nomenclature in personality, 357–9, 358

occupational selection and good practice, 333–5
OFSTED, 202

parent – school partnerships in special needs, 266, 269–272
  and clear communication, 276–7
  and the Code of Practice, 272–4
parental choice, 159, 164
Parents' Charter (DfE, 1994), 265
Partially Hearing Units (PHUs), 298
performance management at work, 343–4, *344*
personality test design
  and correlation of traits, 352–5, *353*
  and delineation of personality sphere, 349–56
  key problems in, 349
  and number of traits, 350–2
  surface and source traits and, 355–7
predictive validity, 360–1
  personality, job proficiency and, 360, *361*
  and real-life criteria, 360
proximal variables, 193
prediction of academic performance, 111–14

Index 399

in relation to previous attainment, 111
motivation, 111
personality, 111
study methods, 111
pupil attitudes, *200*
  to extra-curricular activities, 200
  to school, *200*
  to subject, *200*
pupil outcomes and school effectiveness, 42
purposeful teaching and effective schools, 50-3
  efficient organisation, 51
  clarity of purpose, 51
  structured lessons, 51
  adaptive practice, 53

records of achievement, 165-166
  and pupil motivation, 165
  National Record of Achievement (NRA), 166
  negotiation, 165
  partnership, 165
  pupil involvement, 165
  Records of Achievement National Steering Committee (RANSC), 166
reflective practitioner, 60-1
regression analysis of school examinations, 193, *194-5*, 196-8, 203
Renzulli's three ring concept of giftedness, 248-9, *249*
responsive learning environments, 20-6

school assessment
  expert inspectors for, 201-2
  market forces and , 202
  mutual inspection for, 201
  quantitative, 200
school effects, 193
school effectiveness, 39-40, 185
  key characteristics, 44-7, *46*
school performance tables ('league tables'), 41-2, 157, 198
schools as complex systems, 191-2
selection assessment, *334*
  growth in, 346-9
  how to assess, 334-5
  how to use assessment information, 335
  personality tests in, 347-9

what to assess, 334
sign language interpreters
  a register of , 302
Sign Supported English (SSE), 298
social outcomes of education, *192*, 199-200
special needs
  ability training and learning difficulty in, 217-19
  community-based intervention and, 267
  and early childhood, 266
  ecological approach to intervention in, 267-9
  and Education Acts, 215-6
  home-based intervention and, 267
  teaching children with, 217-26
'Standards' debate, 171
  Callaghan's speech, 171
  'Black papers', 171
Standard Assessment Tasks (SATs), 161, 176-9, 181, 183-4, 186
statistical process control graphs, 196-7
statutory assessment in special education, 216, 274
stress
  behavioural changes and, 380
  causes of
    career development problems, 373-4
    organisational structure and climate, 374-5
    physical work conditions, 369
    relationships at work, 371-2, 373
    teacher's role in school, 369-71
    type of school, 373
    work load, 369
  definition of, 365
  extent among teachers, 376-7
  and home – work interface, 376
  occupational, 365-6
  stress symposium, 1995, 150-1
  in teachers, 369-71
studaxology, 122
student understanding, 118-121
study strategies and student learning, 114-15
  learning environment, 116
  student perception of courses, 115
  study orientations, 114-15
summative assessment, 160, 182

supporting student learning, 123–5
  ASSIST (Approaches to Study Skills Inventory for Students), 124
  games on academic achievement, 123–4
  PASS (Personalised Advice on Study Skills), 124

take up of NVQs and GNVQs, 317–9
talent, 249, 250
Talking Out Of Turn (TOOT), 237–9, 236–40
TGAT (Task Group on Assessment and Testing), 161, 172, 181
teacher appraisal, 158
teacher Assessment, 160, 161, 162, 163, 177, 182
  and record keeping, 177, 182
  role of, 181–183
teacher boycott of testing, 161
teacher professionalism and testing, 160
teachers of the deaf, 299–300
teachers' response to stress, 376–7
teaching as skill, 85–92
  acquisition of skill, 91
  complex, open skills, 87
  characteristics of skill, 89–91
  open and closed skills, 89
  phases of skill learning, 92
  the need for conceptual clarity, 86–7
  understanding the meaning of skill, 88
teaching children with learning difficulties
  behavioural approach to, 219–21
  class versus individual instruction and, 224–6, 227–8
  cognitive approach to, 221–2
  information processing and, 223–4
  practical programmes and, 224
teaching and learning in effective schools, 47–50
  maximisation of learning time, 47–8
  academic emphasis, 48–9
  focus on achievement, 49–50
teaching and learning in higher education, *117*
teaching knowledge use in classrooms, 14–15
  active knowledge base, 114
  strategies of application, 114
  capacity to deal with problems, 114
  positive 'can-do' attitude, 114
teaching learning community, 29–30
teaching styles and school effectiveness, 55–6
team development, 340–1
testing and accountability, 156
  comparison of pupil attainments, 157, 164
  high stakes testing, 160
  theory and practice, 151–2
theories of learning, 8–9
total communication, 298, 299

value added, 40–1, 146, 185, 198–9
  national project on, 202–3
  and type of school, 198–9

withdrawal from teaching, 381–2
work
  application forms and, 329
  applying for, 328–9
  assessment for, 329–30

YELLIS (Year Eleven Information System), 190, 191, *192*, 198